CRIMINAL LAW

CRIMINAL LAW
FOURTH EDITION

Amanda Powell

This edition published 2024 by
The University of Law
2 Bunhill Row
London EC1Y 8HQ

© The University of Law 2024

All rights reserved. No part of this publication may be reproduced, stored in a retrieval system, or transmitted, in any form or by any means, without the prior written permission of the copyright holder, application for which should be addressed to the publisher.

Contains public sector information licensed under the Open Government Licence v3.0

British Library Cataloguing in Publication Data

A catalogue record for this book is available from the British Library.

ISBN 978 1 80502 130 8

Preface

This book is part of a series of Study Manuals that have been specially designed to support the reader to achieve the SQE1 Assessment Specification in relation to Functioning Legal Knowledge. Each Study Manual aims to provide the reader with a solid knowledge and understanding of fundamental legal principles and rules, including how those principles and rules might be applied in practice.

This Study Manual covers the Solicitors Regulation Authority's syllabus for the SQE1 assessment for Criminal Law in a concise and tightly focused manner. The Manual provides a clear statement of relevant legal rules and a well-defined road map through examinable law and practice. The Manual aims to bring the law and practice to life through the use of example scenarios based on realistic client-based problems and allows the reader to test their knowledge and understanding through single best answer questions that have been modelled on the SRA's sample assessment questions.

For those readers who are students at the University of Law, the Study Manual is used alongside other learning resources and the University's assessment bank to best prepare students not only for the SQE1 assessments, but also for a future life in professional legal practice.

We hope that you find the Study Manual supportive of your preparation for SQE1 and we wish you every success.

The legal principles and rules contained within this Manual are stated as at 1 May 2024.

Author acknowledgements

Amanda would like to thank David Green and Sean Hutton for reviewing and commenting on the content of chapters and sample questions: their input was invaluable.

Contents

Preface		v
Table of Cases		xix
Table of Statutes		xxiii

Chapter 1	**Actus Reus**			1
	SQE1 syllabus			1
	Learning outcomes			1
	1.1	Introduction		2
	1.2	The burden and standard of proof		2
	1.3	General principles of actus reus		3
	1.4	Types of crimes		3
		1.4.1	Conduct crimes	4
		1.4.2	Result crimes	4
		1.4.3	State of affairs crimes	5
	1.5	Omissions		5
		1.5.1	General rule	5
		1.5.2	Statutory offences	6
		1.5.3	Common law offences	6
			1.5.3.1 Duty arising out of contract	6
			1.5.3.2 Special relationship	7
			1.5.3.3 Creation of a dangerous situation	7
		1.5.4	Summary of omissions	8
	1.6	Causation		8
		1.6.1	Factual causation	9
		1.6.2	Legal causation	10
			1.6.2.1 The consequence must be attributable to a culpable act or omission	11
			1.6.2.2 The culpable act must be a more than minimal cause of the consequence	11
			1.6.2.3 The culpable act need not be the sole cause	12
			1.6.2.4 The accused must take their victim as they find them	12
			1.6.2.5 The chain of causation must not be broken	13
		1.6.3	Intervening acts or events	13
			1.6.3.1 Victim's acts	13
			1.6.3.2 Third party intervention	14
			1.6.3.3 Medical negligence	14
			1.6.3.4 Intervening events	16
		1.6.4	Summary of legal causation	16

		Summary		17
		Sample questions		17
Chapter 2		**Mens Rea**		**21**
	SQE1 syllabus			21
	Learning outcomes			21
	2.1	Introduction		22
	2.2	Intention		22
		2.2.1	Direct intention	22
		2.2.2	Indirect intention	23
			2.2.2.1 The legal test for indirect intention	23
		2.2.3	Summary of intent	25
	2.3	Recklessness		26
		2.3.1	Justification of the risk	27
		2.3.2	Subjective recklessness	27
		2.3.3	Summary of recklessness	28
	2.4	Negligence		29
		2.4.1	Comparison of recklessness and negligence	29
		2.4.2	Negligence and common law offences	29
		2.4.3	Negligence and statutory offences	30
		2.4.4	Summary of negligence	30
	2.5	Strict liability offences		31
		2.5.1	Type of offences	31
		2.5.2	Identifying a strict liability offence	32
			2.5.2.1 Statute	32
			2.5.2.2 Case law	32
		2.5.3	Summary of strict liability	33
	2.6	Transferred malice		34
		2.6.1	The doctrine of transferred malice	34
		2.6.2	Limits to the application of transferred malice	35
		2.6.3	When transferred malice may be unnecessary	36
		2.6.4	Summary of transferred malice	36
	2.7	Coincidence of actus reus and mens rea		37
		2.7.1	The general principle	37
		2.7.2	Continuing act	37
		2.7.3	Single transaction	38
		2.7.4	Summary of coincidence of actus reus and mens rea	39
	2.8	Classification of offences		39
		2.8.1	Offences of basic intent	39
		2.8.2	Offences of specific intent	39
		2.8.3	Offences of ulterior intent	39
		2.8.4	Summary of classification of offences	40

		Summary	40
		Sample questions	41
Chapter 3		**Assaults**	**45**
		SQE1 syllabus	45
		Learning outcomes	45
	3.1	Introduction	46
	3.2	Hierarchy of assaults	46
	3.3	Common law assaults	47
	3.4	Simple assault	47
		3.4.1 Actus reus	48
		3.4.1.1 Unlawful	48
		3.4.1.2 Apprehension	48
		3.4.1.3 Assault by words or silence	48
		3.4.1.4 Immediacy	49
		3.4.1.5 Conditional threats	49
		3.4.2 Mens rea	49
		3.4.3 Summary of assault	50
	3.5	Battery	50
		3.5.1 Actus reus	51
		3.5.2 Mens rea	51
		3.5.3 Practical application of assault and battery	51
	3.6	Statutory assaults	52
	3.7	Assault occasioning actual bodily harm (OAPA 1861, s 47)	52
		3.7.1 Actus reus	52
		3.7.1.1 Assault or battery	52
		3.7.1.2 Occasioning	52
		3.7.1.3 Actual bodily harm	52
		3.7.1.4 Mental harm	53
		3.7.2 Mens rea	53
		3.7.3 Summary of s 47 assault	54
	3.8	Wounding or inflicting grievous bodily harm (OAPA 1861, s 20)	55
		3.8.1 Actus reus	55
		3.8.1.1 Grievous bodily harm	55
		3.8.1.2 Wounding	55
		3.8.2 Mens rea	56
		3.8.2.1 What must the defendant intend or foresee?	56
		3.8.3 Summary of s 20 assault	56
		3.8.4 Practical application of s 20 assault	57
	3.9	Wounding or causing grievous bodily harm with intent (OAPA 1861, s 18)	58
		3.9.1 Actus reus	58

		3.9.2	Mens rea	59
			3.9.2.1 Intention to cause grievous bodily harm	59
			3.9.2.2 Intention to resist or prevent arrest	59
		3.9.3	The four ways of committing a s 18 assault	59
		3.9.4	Summary of s 18 assaults	60
	3.10	Overview of the non-fatal offences against the person	61
	3.11	Consent as a defence	62
		3.11.1	Simple assault and battery	62
		3.11.2	The statutory assaults	62
			3.11.2.1 The general rule	62
			3.11.2.2 Exceptions to the general rule	63
			3.11.2.3 Limits to the exceptions	63
		3.11.3	Valid consent	63
		3.11.4	Summary of consent	64
	Summary			64
	Sample questions		65
Chapter 4	**Homicide I: Murder and the Partial Defences**		**69**
	SQE1 syllabus		69
	Learning outcomes		69
	4.1	Introduction	70
	4.2	Homicide	70
		4.2.1	Actus reus of homicide	70
			4.2.1.1 Unlawful	70
			4.2.1.2 Victim	70
			4.2.1.3 Causes death	71
	4.3	Murder	71
		4.3.1	Definition	71
		4.3.2	Actus reus	71
		4.3.3	Mens rea	71
		4.3.4	Summary of murder	72
	4.4	Manslaughter	73
	4.5	Voluntary manslaughter	73
		4.5.1	Actus reus and mens rea	74
	4.6	Diminished responsibility	74
		4.6.1	Evidential issues	75
		4.6.2	Abnormality of mental functioning	75
		4.6.3	Recognised medical condition	75
			4.6.3.1 Diminished responsibility and intoxication	76
		4.6.4	Substantial impairment of the defendant's ability	76
			4.6.4.1 'Substantial'	77
			4.6.4.2 Impairment of the defendant's ability	77

		4.6.5	Provides an explanation for the defendant's acts or omissions in killing	77
		4.6.6	Summary flowchart of diminished responsibility	78
	4.7	Loss of control		78
		4.7.1	Evidential issues	79
		4.7.2	Loss of control	79
			4.7.2.1 No need to be sudden	79
			4.7.2.2 Considered desire for revenge	80
			4.7.2.3 Practical application	80
			4.7.2.4 Summary diagram of loss of control	81
		4.7.3	The qualifying trigger	82
			4.7.3.1 The fear trigger	82
			4.7.3.2 The anger trigger	82
			4.7.3.3 Sexual infidelity	83
			4.7.3.4 Summary flowchart of qualifying triggers	84
		4.7.4	Similar reaction of a person of the same age and sex	85
			4.7.4.1 A person of the defendant's age and sex	85
			4.7.4.2 The defendant's circumstances	85
			4.7.4.3 Practical application of same reaction	85
			4.7.4.4 Summary flowchart of similar reaction	86
		4.7.5	Summary of the partial defence of loss of control	87
		4.7.6	Sufficiency of evidence	87
	Summary			87
	Sample questions			88
Chapter 5	**Homicide II: Involuntary Manslaughter**			**93**
	SQE1 syllabus			93
	Learning outcomes			93
	5.1	Introduction		94
	5.2	Murder, voluntary and involuntary manslaughter		94
	5.3	Unlawful act manslaughter		95
		5.3.1	Unlawful act	95
		5.3.2	Dangerous act	96
			5.3.2.1 Test for dangerousness	96
			5.3.2.2 Knowledge required	96
			5.3.2.3 Summary of 'dangerous'	97
		5.3.3	Causes death	97
		5.3.4	Mens rea	97
		5.3.5	Practical application of unlawful act manslaughter	98
		5.3.6	Summary of unlawful act manslaughter	99
	5.4	Gross negligence manslaughter		99
		5.4.1	Duty of care	100
			5.4.1.1 Approach taken by the courts	100
			5.4.1.2 Omissions	101

		5.4.2	Breach of duty	101
		5.4.3	Causes death	101
		5.4.4	Gross negligence	101
			5.4.4.1 Risk of death	102
			5.4.4.2 How does the jury approach the meaning of 'gross'?	102
		5.4.5	Practical application of gross negligence manslaughter	103
		5.4.6	Summary of gross negligence manslaughter	103
	Summary			104
	Sample questions			105
Chapter 6	**The Property Offences**			**109**
	SQE1 syllabus			109
	Learning outcomes			109
	6.1	Introduction		110
	6.2	Theft		110
		6.2.1	Definition	110
		6.2.2	Actus reus	110
		6.2.3	Appropriation	110
			6.2.3.1 Later assumption of the rights of an owner	111
			6.2.3.2 Can property be stolen more than once?	111
		6.2.4	Property	112
			6.2.4.1 When can land be stolen?	112
			6.2.4.2 What cannot be stolen?	113
		6.2.5	Belonging to another	113
			6.2.5.1 Theft of own property	114
			6.2.5.2 When does ownership in property pass?	114
			6.2.5.3 Obligation to deal with property in a particular way	115
			6.2.5.4 Abandoned property	115
		6.2.6	Summary of actus reus	116
		6.2.7	Mens rea	116
		6.2.8	Dishonesty	116
			6.2.8.1 Summary flowchart of dishonesty	119
		6.2.9	Intention to permanently deprive	119
			6.2.9.1 Treating the property as the defendant's own	120
			6.2.9.2 Borrowing in circumstances making it equivalent to an outright taking	120
			6.2.9.3 Parting with the property under a condition as to its return	121
		6.2.10	Summary of theft	121
	6.3	Robbery		122
		6.3.1	Introduction	122
		6.3.2	Theft	122
		6.3.3	Force used or threatened	122

		6.3.3.1	The meaning of the word 'force'	122
		6.3.3.2	Against whom must force be used or threatened?	123
	6.3.4	Timing of the force being used or threatened		124
	6.3.5	The force must be in order to steal		124
	6.3.6	Summary of robbery		124
6.4	Burglary			125
	6.4.1	Introduction		125
	6.4.2	Actus reus		126
		6.4.2.1	Entry	126
		6.4.2.2	Building	127
		6.4.2.3	Part of a building	128
		6.4.2.4	Trespasser in fact	129
		6.4.2.5	Additional actus reus requirements for s 9(1)(b) burglary	130
		6.4.2.6	Summary of actus reus of burglary	130
	6.4.3	Mens rea		130
		6.4.3.1	Knowledge or recklessness as to being a trespasser	130
		6.4.3.2	Additional mens rea requirements for s 9(1)(a) burglary	130
		6.4.3.3	Additional mens rea requirements for s 9(1)(b) burglary	131
	6.4.4	Comparison between the two types of burglary		131
	6.4.5	Summary of burglary		131
6.5	Aggravated burglary			133
	6.5.1	Introduction		133
	6.5.2	Weapons		133
	6.5.3	'At the time'		133
	6.5.4	Summary of aggravated burglary		133
	6.5.5	Summary of the property offences		134
Sample questions				134

Chapter 7 Fraud — 137

SQE1 syllabus				137
Learning outcomes				137
7.1	Introduction			138
7.2	Fraud			138
7.3	Definition			138
7.4	Fraud by false representation			138
	7.4.1	False representation		139
		7.4.1.1	What is a representation?	139
		7.4.1.2	When is a representation false?	140
		7.4.1.3	Effect of a representation	141

		7.4.2	Mens rea		142
			7.4.2.1	Dishonesty	142
			7.4.2.2	Intention to make a gain or cause loss	142
		7.4.3	Summary of fraud by false representation		143
	7.5	Fraud by failing to disclose information			143
		7.5.1	Failing to disclose information		144
		7.5.2	Mens rea		145
	7.6	Fraud by abuse of position			145
		7.6.1	Actus reus		146
			7.6.1.1	Occupation of a relevant position	146
			7.6.1.2	Abuse of position	147
		7.6.2	Mens rea		147
	7.7	Overlap between the fraud offences			147
	Summary				148
	Sample questions				149

Chapter 8 Criminal Damage — 151

SQE1 syllabus					151
Learning outcomes					151
8.1	Introduction				152
8.2	Simple criminal damage				152
	8.2.1	Actus reus			152
		8.2.1.1	Destruction or damage		152
		8.2.1.2	Property		153
		8.2.1.3	Belonging to another		153
	8.2.2	Mens rea			154
	8.2.3	Lawful excuse			155
		8.2.3.1	Belief in consent		155
		8.2.3.2	Need of protection		156
8.3	Arson				158
8.4	Aggravated criminal damage				158
8.5	Aggravated arson				160
Summary					161
Sample questions					162

Chapter 9 Defences — 165

SQE1 syllabus			165
Learning outcomes			165
9.1	Introduction		166
9.2	Intoxication as a defence?		166

9.3	Type of offence		166
	9.3.1	Offences of specific intent	167
	9.3.2	Offences of basic intent	167
9.4	Voluntary intoxication		168
	9.4.1	Impact on criminal liability	168
		9.4.1.1 Intoxication and offences of basic intent	168
		9.4.1.2 Intoxication and offences of specific intent	168
	9.4.2	Summary of voluntary intoxication	170
9.5	Involuntary intoxication		170
	9.5.1	Meaning of 'involuntary'	171
	9.5.2	Legal effect	171
	9.5.3	Summary of involuntary intoxication	172
9.6	Dutch courage		172
9.7	Intoxication and mistake		172
9.8	Intoxication and lawful excuse		173
	9.8.1	Comparison	173
9.9	Self-defence and prevention of crime		174
	9.9.1	The legal and evidential burden	175
9.10	Section 76 of the Criminal Justice and Immigration Act 2008		175
9.11	Was force necessary?		175
	9.11.1	Mistaken belief	176
	9.11.2	Mistaken belief due to voluntary intoxication	176
9.12	Was the amount of force used reasonable?		177
	9.12.1	On what basis is the defendant judged?	177
	9.12.2	What does 'reasonable' mean?	178
	9.12.3	Who decides reasonableness?	179
	9.12.4	Defendant's characteristics	179
9.13	Householder cases		179
	9.13.1	What is a 'householder'?	179
	9.13.2	When is force 'grossly disproportionate'?	180
	9.13.3	Summary of householder cases	181
9.14	No duty to retreat		181
9.15	The 'heat of the moment'		181
9.16	Pre-emptive strikes		182
9.17	Overview of self-defence		183
9.18	Summary		183
	9.18.1	Intoxication	183
	9.18.2	Self-defence	184
Sample questions			184

Contents

Chapter 10	**Attempts**		**187**
	SQE1 syllabus		187
	Learning outcomes		187
	10.1	Introduction	188
	10.2	Attempts	188
	10.3	Definition	188
	10.4	Actus reus of attempt	188
		10.4.1 Liability for actions	188
		10.4.2 'More than merely preparatory'	189
	10.5	Mens rea	190
		10.5.1 Offences with an ulterior mens rea	191
	10.6	Attempts and impossibility	191
		10.6.1 Actus reus and impossibility	192
		10.6.2 Mens rea and impossibility	192
	Summary		193
	Sample questions		194
Chapter 11	**Parties to a Crime**		**197**
	SQE1 syllabus		197
	Learning outcomes		197
	11.1	Introduction	198
	11.2	Terminology	198
	11.3	Definition of accomplice liability	199
	11.4	Actus reus	200
		11.4.1 Aiding	200
		11.4.2 Abetting	200
		11.4.3 Counselling	201
		11.4.4 Procuring	201
		11.4.5 Mere presence at the scene	201
		11.4.5.1 Overview of presence at the scene	202
		11.4.6 Summary of actus reus components	203
	11.5	Links between the principal and the accomplice	203
		11.5.1 Mental link	203
		11.5.2 Causal link	204
		11.5.3 Summary of mental and causal link	205
	11.6	Practical application of actus reus of accomplice liability	205
	11.7	The relationship between the principal and the accomplice	207
		11.7.1 Principal has a defence	207
		11.7.2 Principal cannot be found	207

11.8	Innocent agency	207
11.9	Summary of the actus reus of accomplice liability	208
11.10	Mens rea	208
	11.10.1 Joint venture	208
11.11	Intention to do the act or say the words	208
11.12	Knowledge of the circumstances	209
	11.12.1 Accomplice has full knowledge	209
	11.12.2 Accomplice has knowledge of an offence	210
11.13	Accomplice's liability for a different offence to the principal offender	211
11.14	Liability of the accomplice where the principal goes beyond the plan	213
11.15	Practical application of accomplice liability mens rea	215
11.16	Summary of the mens rea of accomplice liability	216
11.17	Withdrawing participation	217
	11.17.1 Withdrawal before the offence	217
	11.17.2 Withdrawal during the offence	217
	11.17.3 Summary of withdrawal	218
Summary		219
Sample questions		219
Index		223

Table of Cases

A
A (a juvenile) v R [1978] Crim LR 689	152
Adomako [1995] 1 AC 171	102
Ahluwalia (1993) 96 Cr App R 133	73, 80
Allan [1965] 1 QB 130	202
Atakpu [1994] QB 69	111
Attorney General for Northern Ireland v Gallagher [1963] AC 349	172
Attorney General's Reference (No. 1 of 1975) [1975] QB 773	200, 201, 203
Attorney General's Reference (Nos 1 and 2 of 1979) [1980] QB 180	131
Attorney General's Reference (No. 6 of 1980) [1981] 2 All ER 1057	63
Attorney General's Reference (No. 3 of 1992) [1994] 2 All ER 121	191

B
Bainbridge [1960] 1 QB 129	210
Bateman [1925] All ER 25	101
Becerra (1976) 62 Cr App R 212	217
Beckford v R [1988] AC 130	174, 182
Benge (1865) 4 F & F 504	12
Blackman [2017] EWCA Crim 190	76
Blaue [1975] 1 WLR 1411	12
Brown [1985] Crim LR 212	127

C
Calhaem [1985] 2 WLR 826	205
Chan Man-sin v A-G of Hong Kong [1988] 1 All ER 1	120
Cheshire [1991] 1 WLR 844	15
Church [1966] 1 QB 59	38, 96
Clegg [1995] 1 AC 482	178
Clinton [2012] EWCA Crim 2	83
Cogan and Leak [1976] 1 QB 217	207
Collins [1973] QB 100	126–7
Collins, R (on the application of) v Secretary of State for Justice [2016] EWHC 33 (Admin)	180
Cunningham [1957] 2 QB 396	27

D
Dalloway (1847) 2 Cox CC 273	10
Dawson [1976] 64 Cr App R 170	122
Dawson [1985] 81 Cr App R 150	96
Dica [2004] EWCA Crim 1103	55
DPP v Gomez [1993] AC 442	111
DPP v Majewski [1976] 2 WLR 623	168
DPP v Newbury and Jones [1977] AC 500	95
DPP v Smith [1961] AC 290	55
Dudley [1989] Crim LR 57	159, 160

E
Edwards v Ddin [1976] 1 WLR 942	114

F

Fagan v Metropolitan Police Commissioner [1969] 1 QB 439	37–8
Francis [1982] Crim LR 363	133

G

G [2003] UKHL 50	155
G [2004] 1 AC 1034	28
Gianetto [1997] 1 Cr App R 1	201
Gibbins and Proctor (1918) 13 Cr App R 134	7
Gilmour [2000] 2 Cr App R 407	212–13
Gnango [2011] UKSC 59	207
Golds [2016] UKSC 61	77
Grundy [1977] Crim LR 543	217
Gullefer [1987] Crim LR 195	189

H

Hale (1978) 68 C App R 415	124
Hall [1973] 1 QB 126	115
Hardie [1985] 1 WLR 64	171
Hardman v Chief Constable of Avon and Somerset Constabulary [1986] Crim LR 330	152
Heard [2007] 3 WLR 475	167
Hill and Hall (1989) Crim LR 136	156
Hinks [2000] 3 WLR 1590	111
Howe [1987] AC 417	212

I

Idress v DPP [2011] EWHC 624 (Admin)	141
Ireland; R v Burstow [1998] AC 147	48
Ivey v Genting Casinos (UK) Ltd [2017] UKSC 67	109, 118, 121, 142

J

Jaggard v Dickinson [1980] 3 All ER 716	156, 173, 174
Jewell [2004] EWCA Crim 404	79, 87
Jogee [2016] UKSC 8	208, 215
Johnson v DPP [1994] Crim LR 673	157
Johnson v Youden [1950] 1 KB 544	209
Jones [1990] 3 All ER 886	189–90
Jones and Smith [1976] 1 WLR 672	129
Jordan (1956) 40 Cr App R 152	15

K

Kingston [1995] 2 AC 355	166

L

Lamb [1967] 2 QB 981	96
Latimer (1886) 17 QBD 359	35
Lipman [1970] 1 QB 152	169
Lloyd [1985] QB 829	121

M

Martin (Anthony) [2002] EWCA Crim 2245	73, 179
Maxwell v DPP for Northern Ireland [1978] 1 WLR 1350	210–11
Miller [1954] 2 QB 282	52
Miller [1983] 1 All ER 978	8
Moloney [1985] 1 AC 905	71

	Moriarty v Brookes (1834) 6 C&P 684	55
	Morris [1984] AC 320	111
N	National Coal Board v Gamble [1959] 1 QB 11	209, 210, 213, 215
	Nizzar (unreported, July 2012)	141
O	O'Grady [1987] 3 WLR 321	173, 174, 176
	O'Leary [2013] EWCA Crim 1371	141
	Oxford v Moss [1979] Crim LR 119	113
P	Pagett (1983) 76 Cr App R 279	11, 14
	Palmer v R [1971] AC 814	182
	Pembliton (1874) LR 2 CCR 119	36
	Pittwood (1902) 19 TLR 37	6
	Roberts (1971) 56 Cr App R 95	13
	Rouse [2014] EWCA Crim 1128	146
	Ryan [1996] Crim LR 320	127
S	Savage; R v Parmenter [1991] 4 All ER	53, 56
	Shivpuri [1987] AC 1	192
	Singh [1999] Crim LR 582	102
	Smedleys Ltd v Breed [1974] AC 839	32
	Smith [1959] 2 QB 35	15
	Steer [1987] 2 All ER 833	159
	Stone and Dobinson [1977] QB 354	7
T	Thabo Meli v R [1954] 1 WLR 288	38
	Turner (No2) [1971] 2 All ER 441	114
V	Valujevs [2014] EWCA Crim 2888	146
W	Wain [1995] 2 Cr App R 660	115
	Walkington [1979] 1 WLR 1169	129
	Wallace [2018] EWCA 690	14
	White [1910] 2 KB 124	9
	Whybrow (1951) 35 Cr App R 141	190
	Wilcox v Jeffery [1951] 1 All ER 464	202
	Williams (Gladstone) [1987] 3 All ER 411	176
	Woollin [1999] 1 AC 82	23, 24, 190
Z	Zaman [2017] EWCA Crim 1783	103

Table of Statutes

A	Accessories and Abettors Act 1861	
	s 8	199, 200, 203
C	Children Act 1989	6
	Contempt of Court Act 1981	
	s 1	32
	Coroners and Justice Act 2009	71
	s 52	74
	s 54	78, 79
	s 54(1)(c)	85
	s 54(3)	85
	s 54(4)	80
	s 54(5)	87
	s 55	78
	s 55(3)	82
	s 55(4)	82–3
	s 55(6)(c)	83
	Criminal Attempts Act 1981	195
	s 1	193
	s 1(1)	188, 191
	s 1(2)	192
	s 1(3)	192
	Criminal Damage Act 1971	163
	s 1(1)	152, 155, 158
	s 1(2)	152, 158
	s 1(3)	152, 158
	s 5	155, 159, 160, 161, 162
	s 5(2)	173
	s 5(2)(a)	155, 158, 164
	s 5(2)(b)	156, 157, 158, 164
	s 10(1)	153
	s 10(2)	153
	Criminal Justice Act 1967	
	s 8	25
	Criminal Justice Act 1988	
	s 39	46, 61
	Criminal Justice and Immigration Act 2008	
	s 76	175, 183
	s 76(4)	176, 178
	s 76 (5)	176, 177
	s 76(5A)	179, 186
	s 76(6)	178, 186
	s 76(6A)	181

Table of Statutes

F

s 76(7)(a)	182
s 76(7)(b)	182
Criminal Law Act 1967	
s 3	174
s 3(1)	183

Food and Drugs Act 1955	32
Fraud Act 2006	
s 1	143, 148
s 1(1)	138, 139, 144
s 1(2)	138
s 2	138, 139, 140, 141, 143, 145, 147, 148
s 2(1)	138
s 2(2)	139
s 2(2)(b)	141
s 2(3)	140
s 2(4)	140
s 2(5)	141
s 3	138, 143, 144, 146, 147, 148, 150
s 4	138, 145–7, 148, 150
s 5	142, 148

H

Homicide Act 1957	72
s 2	74, 77
s 2(1A)	76

M

Magistrates' Courts Act 1980	
s 44	199
Medicines Act 1968	
s 58(2)	32

O

Offences Against the Person Act 1861	
s 18	45, 47, 58, 64, 66, 67, 98, 131, 167, 169, 185, 190, 211, 213, 221
s 20	45, 47, 55–8, 60, 61, 63, 64, 66, 67, 98, 131, 136, 167, 169, 190, 211, 213, 221
s 47	45, 47, 52, 57–8, 61–4, 67, 167, 169, 172, 221

R

Road Traffic Act 1988	
s 3	30
s 4(2)	5
s 5	32, 33, 201

T

Theft Act 1968	
s 1	32, 113, 119, 134, 167
s 2	110, 116, 117, 119, 121, 135, 146
s 2(1)	116
s 2(1)(a)	116, 135
s 2(1)(b)	117, 135
s 2(1)(c)	117, 135

Table of Statutes

s 2(2)	117, 135
s 3	110
s 3(1)	111
s 4	110, 112, 146
s 4(1)	112
s 5	110, 114
s 5(1)	113
s 5(3)	115
s 6	110, 120, 121
s 6(1)	120
s 6(2)	121
s 8	122, 123
s 9	125, 128, 129, 133
s 9(1)(a)	40, 125-6, 130, 131, 132, 133, 136
s 9(1)(b)	125-6, 130, 131, 132, 133, 136, 198
s 9(3)	125
s 9(4)	127
s 10(1)	133

XXV

1 Actus Reus

1.1	Introduction	2
1.2	The burden and standard of proof	2
1.3	General principles of actus reus	3
1.4	Types of crimes	3
1.5	Omissions	5
1.6	Causation	8

SQE1 syllabus

By the end of this chapter you will be able to apply relevant core legal principles and rules appropriately and effectively, at the level of a competent newly qualified solicitor in practice, to realistic client-based and ethical problems and situations in the area of **actus reus**.

Note that, as students are not usually required to recall specific case names, or cite statutory or regulatory authorities, these are provided for illustrative purposes only.

Learning outcomes

The learning outcomes for this chapter are:

- to explain and apply the concept of actus reus, including the rules of legal and factual causation; and
- to explain the extent to which an omission rather than an action may constitute the actus reus of an offence.

1.1 Introduction

A fair and robust criminal justice system is a cornerstone of all developed countries and lawyers are an essential aspect of this. To be effective, a criminal lawyer must have a detailed understanding of the substantive law including the definitions of the various offences their clients may face.

When considering a criminal offence, there are usually three components required to establish criminal liability:

(a) guilty conduct by the defendant (actus reus);

(b) guilty state of mind of the defendant (mens rea); and

(c) absence of any valid defence.

Thus, for the crime of murder, the defendant must kill the victim (the actus reus) and do so with an intention to kill or cause grievous bodily harm (the mens rea). However, the accused will not be liable for murder if they have a valid defence, such as self-defence.

The concept of actus reus, or guilty act, is the starting point for considering all crimes; and the ability to analyse the evidence and conclude whether or not the suspect has completed the actus reus of a particular offence is essential.

This chapter will consider the following:

- the components that make up the actus reus;
- when an accused may be criminally liable for their omission; and
- the concept of causation.

1.2 The burden and standard of proof

The defendant's guilt is determined in a court of law by the magistrates or a jury who assess the evidence put before them. Before convicting the accused of an offence, there must be proof that the accused commited the criminal behaviour with the required guilty state of mind; but who needs to prove what?

- The *legal burden* of proof is on the prosecution to prove all the elements of the offence, including (in most cases) disproving the defence.
- The *evidential burden* is also on the prosecution to provide sufficient evidence for each element of the offence. This may take the form of police interviews, witness or expert evidence and forensic evidence such as fingerprints or DNA.
- The *standard of proof*, where the prosecution has the burden, is beyond reasonable doubt. This is a very high standard, so that the jury or magistrates should convict only if they are sure of the defendant's guilt.

However, whilst the burden of proving the *offence* is always on the prosecution, there are some (rare) instances where the defendant has the legal burden of proving their *defence*. One such example is the partial defence to murder of diminished responsibility which is covered in **Chapter 4**. When such a burden does fall on the defendant, the standard of proof is lower than for the prosecution, being only on the balance of probabilities; in other words, it is more likely than not that the defence exists.

There are also occasions when the evidential burden falls on the defence. In such cases the defendant must show sufficient evidence to enable them to rely on a defence, which the prosecution must then disprove. This simply means that the defence must raise some evidence to make the issue 'live' and this will usually be done by the defendant and/or someone else giving evidence in court or by cross-examining a prosecution witness. Defences to which this applies are the partial defence to murder of loss of control and also the full defence of self-defence – both of which are considered later in the manual.

⭐ *Example*

Malcolm is charged with an assault occasioning actual bodily harm after he punches Neville in the face, causing him to suffer a black eye.

The prosecution must prove the following elements beyond reasonable doubt:

(a) That Malcolm hit Neville.

(b) That Neville suffered an injury.

(c) That Malcolm had the necessary state of mind to be guilty of the offence, namely that he intended to hit Neville or was reckless as to doing so.

In the witness box, Malcolm claims that he only punched Neville because Neville threatened him with a knife. Malcolm is raising the issue of self-defence. By stating this in his evidence, Malcolm has satisfied the evidential burden placed upon him so that it is now up to the prosecution to demonstrate, beyond reasonable doubt, that the self-defence argument is not valid.

1.3 General principles of actus reus

The actus reus of every offence is different and may be found either:

- in statute, for example criminal damage and theft; or
- in the common law, with murder being the most serious example.

The actus reus elements of an offence are all those that do not relate to the state of mind of the defendant. Thus, the simplest way to identify the actus reus of a criminal offence is to subtract the mens rea elements from the definition of the offence. Those that remain constitute the actus reus.

⭐ *Example*

The definition of theft is the dishonest appropriation of property belonging to another with an intention to permanently deprive. Removing the mens rea elements of dishonesty and intention to permanently deprive leaves the actus reus elements of appropriation of property belonging to another. Although this is a straightforward example, others are less obvious.

The concept of actus reus is commonly referred to as the 'guilty act' but this is misleading as it may be satisfied in a number of ways.

1.4 Types of crimes

In most instances, the defendant must *do* something before they can be said to have committed a criminal offence. However, although this is usually the case, it is not always so. The actus reus may be established by proving that the defendant failed to take action, or even just by proving that a situation exists. The actus reus may consist of the following components:

- an act (or sometimes a failure to act) by the defendant ('conduct' crimes);
- certain consequences flowing from the defendant's conduct ('result' crimes); and/or
- the existence of certain circumstances at the time of the defendant's conduct ('circumstances / state of affairs' crimes).

Although crimes may be labelled in this way, some may contain just one of these elements whilst others may contain two or even all three. Theft is an example as, although it is a conduct crime requiring the appropriation or taking of property, the offence is only committed if the circumstance exists that the property belongs to another at the relevant time.

Table 1.1 Types of crimes

Type of crime	Definition	Example
Conduct	Usually involves an act but may include an omission to act. 'Doing' offences (usually).	Perjury
Result	A result must have been caused by the conduct of the defendant. Proof of causation is required.	Murder Criminal damage
Circumstances	The existence of a set of circumstances or a 'state of affairs'.	Being in charge of a motor vehicle while unfit due to drink or drugs.

1.4.1 Conduct crimes

For most offences, the actus reus is defined so that it requires conduct on the part of the accused. The definition of the offence requires the defendant to behave in a certain way. An example of such an offence would be perjury – wilfully making a statement under oath that the accused knows to be untrue. Perjury may be regarded as a 'pure' conduct crime because it is the defendant's *conduct* rather than the result itself that is criminalised, so it would make no difference whether the false evidence had any impact on the trial or not.

Although crimes may be labelled specifically, this is not always helpful as there is often an overlap. For example, an assault occasioning actual bodily harm requires conduct (such as a punch) but also a 'result', namely some harm to the victim.

The conduct must be voluntary if it is to be criminal and in most cases it will be.

- To be guilty of what is commonly known as an assault, the defendant must apply unlawful force to the victim. Slapping, punching, stabbing and kicking are all examples of voluntary conduct – the defendant decided to act in this way.

However, there are some (rare) occasions when the accused acts in an involuntary way.

- If a motorist is attacked by a swarm of bees while driving and crashes their car as a result, a charge of, say, careless driving would fail as their actions could not be said to be voluntary.

1.4.2 Result crimes

When an offence is described as a result crime, it is not enough that the defendant acts in a particular way; certain consequences must follow from their actions if the actus reus is to be satisfied. Murder is such an example with the 'result' being the death of a human being.

Another is criminal damage because property must be destroyed or damaged if the accused is to be convicted.

1.4.3 State of affairs crimes

Some offences do not require any conduct at all. They are defined so that the actus reus is simply the existence of a state of affairs, or a particular set of circumstances. The defendant may be liable even though they had no control over the situation.

✪ Example

Darryl is at the pub celebrating a friend's birthday, but he drinks only orange juice as he is driving. However, unknown to him, one of his friends spikes his juice with vodka as a joke. At the end of the evening, Darryl gets into his car, which is parked on the road outside, but is so affected by the alcohol that he cannot even get the key into the ignition. He is approached by a police officer, breathalysed and found to be above the legal limit for driving.

Even though Darryl has not actually done anything other than sit in his car, he is guilty of an offence under s 4(2) of the Road Traffic Act (RTA) 1988, which makes it a crime to be in charge of a motor vehicle on a road or other public place while unfit to drive through drink or drugs. This is because the actus reus is complete as soon as Darryl gets into the car, as s 4(2) is a state of affairs offence.

The justification for such offences is public policy; it is regarded as more important to prevent drunken or drugged motorists from driving than being concerned with unfairness in individual circumstances.

1.5 Omissions

In most cases, a defendant will have taken positive steps in relation to a particular crime so will actually have done something. Thus, in a murder case, the accused will have, for instance, shot, stabbed or beaten the victim to death.

However, although most offences are defined so that the actus reus is an action, there are others where the defendant may be convicted simply by doing nothing. In other words, it is possible to be criminally liable for a failure or omission to act. Even murder, that most serious of offences, can be committed in this way. The reason the defendant is guilty is because they have produced a particular result, in this case the death of a human being.

✪ Example

Abira, a doctor, refuses to give an antidote to a patient who has been poisoned and who then dies. Abira is liable for her failure to act.

1.5.1 General rule

The general rule is that there is no criminal liability for omissions. Thus, a stranger is under no obligation to save a child who is drowning in a puddle.

✪ Example

Beatrice is walking along a pavement one cold, snowy morning when she sees a man, Caleb, slip on some ice and fall into the road, knocking himself unconscious. Beatrice is late for work and decides to do nothing despite realising the danger Caleb is in from any passing traffic. Caleb is hit by a car and dies from his injuries. Although Beatrice is under a moral duty to help Caleb, she is under no duty under the criminal law to do so.

However, there are exceptions to this general rule.

1.5.2 Statutory offences

There are a number of statutory offences where the actus reus is specifically defined as an omission, such as the offence of failing to provide a police officer with a specimen of breath when asked to do so or failing to stop after a road traffic collision. There are other statutes that impose a duty on the defendant; for example parents are under a duty to care for their children under the Children Act 1989. Failing to act when required to do so under a statutory provision will usually lead to prosecution for the omission itself.

1.5.3 Common law offences

Under the common law, the general rule is that a defendant will only be criminally liable for an omission if the law recognises that they were under a duty to act and they failed to do so. Hence, the starting point is to establish whether the defendant was under a positive duty to act and, over time, the law has recognised a number of situations where such a duty arises.

1.5.3.1 Duty arising out of contract

If a person is subject to a contract that specifies certain obligations to act, a failure to comply with these can lead to criminal liability. The duty to act will be owed not just to other parties to the contract but also to anyone whose life is endangered by the failure to act. This has long been established in case law.

 In the case of R v Pittwood (1902) 19 TLR 37, a railway worker who was employed to guard the gate at a level crossing went off for his lunch without putting the gate back down. A train later collided with a horse and cart, killing the driver.

Pittwood was contractually obliged to act to protect members of the public and was therefore liable under the criminal law for his failure to act. He was convicted of manslaughter – of causing the death that followed from his omission.

In modern society, those employed as carers or healthcare professionals would be contractually bound to act and could be liable for a homicide offence if they fail to take steps to prevent those in their care from suffering harm.

 Example

Sandra is a care worker who is employed by Great Care Ltd. She is responsible for visiting a number of elderly patients during the day. However, Sandra is rather lazy and often misses out those who are suffering from dementia as she knows they will not be able to inform on her. Muriel is 86 years of age and is scheduled to receive two visits a day to ensure that she eats and drinks properly. Sandra fails to attend many of these appointments and as a consequence, Muriel dies of dehydration. As Sandra is under a contractual duty to care for Muriel, she is liable under the criminal law for her omission.

Other examples of people who are under a similar duty are:

- doctors and nurses (to care for their patients);
- members of the emergency services (to take all reasonable steps to safeguard the public);
- lifeguards (to act to ensure the safety of people using the swimming pool).

1.5.3.2 Special relationship

Where there is a special relationship between the defendant and the victim, either by reason of family ties or because the defendant has assumed a duty towards the victim, the defendant may incur criminal liability for their omission.

In R v Gibbins and Proctor (1918) 13 Cr App R 134, the defendants were charged with, and convicted of, murdering a seven-year-old girl who died of starvation. The father, as a parent, was under a duty to care for his daughter but failed to do so by not feeding her. His partner was also convicted on the basis of her special relationship with the child. The court held that she had assumed a duty towards the child by living with the father and accepting housekeeping money from him.

Although it is unsurprising that the existence of a close relationship may give rise to a duty to act between parents and children, or between spouses, this principle extends further than might, perhaps, be expected.

One such example are those situations where a person voluntarily undertakes to care for another who cannot care for themselves. This could be due to a number of reasons – infancy, mental illness or general ill-health.

In R v Stone and Dobinson [1977] QB 354, the two defendants took in Stone's sister to live with them. She suffered from anorexia and her physical condition deteriorated so that she became bed-ridden. The two defendants had physical and mental difficulties of their own and did little to help the sister, who eventually died of blood poisoning caused by infected bed sores.

The defendants were convicted of manslaughter. By taking the sister in and making occasional but ineffectual attempts to help her, for example by leaving her food, the court held they were under a duty to act. Their failure to do so meant that, as far as the criminal law is concerned, they caused the victim's death.

It is apparent from this case and others that the role of caring for others should not be undertaken lightly because, if done badly enough, criminal liability may result if death or injury occurs. However, an individual is not required to do a great deal to comply with their duty and thus absolve themselves of such responsibility. All that Stone and Dobinson needed to do in the situation in which they found themselves was to summon help, such as an ambulance or social services.

1.5.3.3 Creation of a dangerous situation

A more recent development is the duty that arises if a person creates a dangerous situation. If the defendant does something that endangers the victim and they are aware of it, they are under a duty to take reasonable steps to prevent the harm from occurring.

Example

Gethan parks his car on a hill but forgets to put on the handbrake. As he walks away, he realises his omission but, as he is in a hurry, he does not return to the car. He walks past two young boys playing outside their house a little further down the hill. A few minutes later, the car rolls down the slope and hits one of the children, killing them.

In this situation, because Gethan has created a dangerous situation by failing to apply the handbrake, the law imposes a duty on him to take steps to remove the danger. However Gethan is only required to return to the vehicle and pull the handbrake on; it is his failure to do this that leads to criminal liability.

Criminal Law

 In R v Miller [1983] 1 All ER 978, the defendant was a squatter in a house. He went to sleep smoking a cigarette and woke up to find his bed mattress smouldering. However, rather than do anything to stop the smouldering, he simply moved to the room next door and went to sleep there! Unsurprisingly, the house caught fire.

The defendant argued that he was not guilty of causing criminal damage because he had not actually done anything. Despite this, Miller was found guilty – not because he caused the fire but because he failed to take any steps to put the fire out when he realised what had happened.

The duty is to take *reasonable* steps to avert the danger and this will depend upon the circumstances. **Table 1.2** contains a summary of whether actions that Miller could have taken or did take would be sufficient to comply with his duty in a situation such as this.

Table 1.2 Actions to comply with duty to take reasonable steps to prevent harm

Yes	No	Maybe
Telephoning the fire service.	Leaving the scene without taking any action. Going for a sleep in another room.	Tackling the blaze; this would depend upon (for example): • the size of the fire; and • the availability of fire-fighting equipment such as a fire extinguisher.

Thus it is clear that criminal liability is imposed only on those who create the danger and, having become aware of it, fail to take reasonable measures to counteract it.

1.5.4 Summary of omissions

- The general rule is that there is no liability for omissions.
- There are exceptions to this rule where the defendant is under a positive duty to act, namely, where there is:
  ○ a statutory duty to act;
  ○ a contractual duty to act;
  ○ a special relationship between the victim and the defendant;
  ○ a duty based on a voluntary assumption of care; and
  ○ a duty that arises because the defendant, having created and become aware of a dangerous situation, fails to take reasonable steps to avert it.

1.6 Causation

This section concerns the second type of crime, described earlier as result crimes. For these offences, as part of establishing the actus reus, the prosecution must also demonstrate that the accused's act or omission actually caused the prohibited consequence. This is known as proving causation.

⭐ *Examples*

(a) *Daria stabbed Vera (conduct) leading to Vera's death (result).*

(b) *Deshi failed to seek medical help for his daughter (omission) so that the child died (result).*

In both these examples, the act or the omission led directly to the victim's death so that, in legal terms, the defendants caused the deaths. It is important to emphasise that causation is an element of the actus reus and should be dealt with as such, rather than as a separate entity or as part of the mens rea.

There are two types of causation – *factual* and *legal* causation. Both must be present in order for causation to be established as part of the actus reus. In this chapter, the issue of causation is discussed in the context of homicide but note that it may arise in any result crime.

The general rule is that a defendant is criminally liable only if they can be shown to have caused, both in fact and law, harm to the victim.

1.6.1 Factual causation

Factual causation is the principle that the defendant cannot be considered to be the cause of an event if the event would have occurred in precisely the same way without the defendant's act or omission.

This test is applied by asking the question: but for the defendant's conduct, would the consequence have occurred? If the result would have occurred irrespective (regardless) of the defendant's conduct, then factual causation is not established.

 In R v White [1910] 2 KB 124, the defendant poisoned his mother's drink intending to kill her. However, before the poison could take effect, his mother suffered a fatal heart attack. Medical evidence confirmed that her death occurred from heart failure unconnected to the poisoned drink. Because the mother would have died even if her son had not put poison in her drink, the defendant (literally) got away with murder – although he was at least found guilty of an attempt.

So the question for the jury is:

- Would the result have occurred *but for* (in the absence of) the defendant's actions? If the answer is yes – then the defendant is not liable.

Clearly, everyone must die at some point; however, for causation to be established, the defendant's act or omission must accelerate the death. In most instances, this will be clear.

⭐ *Example*

Johdi shoots Usain at point blank range and kills him. But for Johdi's actions, Usain would not have died as and when he did; thus, factual causation is established.

However, whilst this test provides some assistance in deciding whether the defendant is guilty, it is of limited value. If all the prosecution have to demonstrate is factual causation, because the test is so wide, it could catch people who in reality have only a very tenuous connection with the victim's fate.

⭐ *Example*

Ahmed invites Bal out on a date. Unfortunately, Bal is knifed by a stranger in a random attack while on her way to meet him at the local park and subsequently dies. Applying the but for test, Ahmed's action has caused Bal's death as, but for the invitation, she would not have been in the park.

Clearly in these circumstances, it would be entirely unjust to hold Ahmed responsible for what is in reality a very unfortunate coincidence – Bal walking through the park just as an attacker was looking for a victim. For this reason, in addition to demonstrating factual causation, it is also necessary to demonstrate legal causation. What this means is that, in the eyes of the law, the defendant's action caused the consequence and therefore it is appropriate to punish them.

Set out below is a summary of the test for factual causation.

Figure 1.1 Factual causation

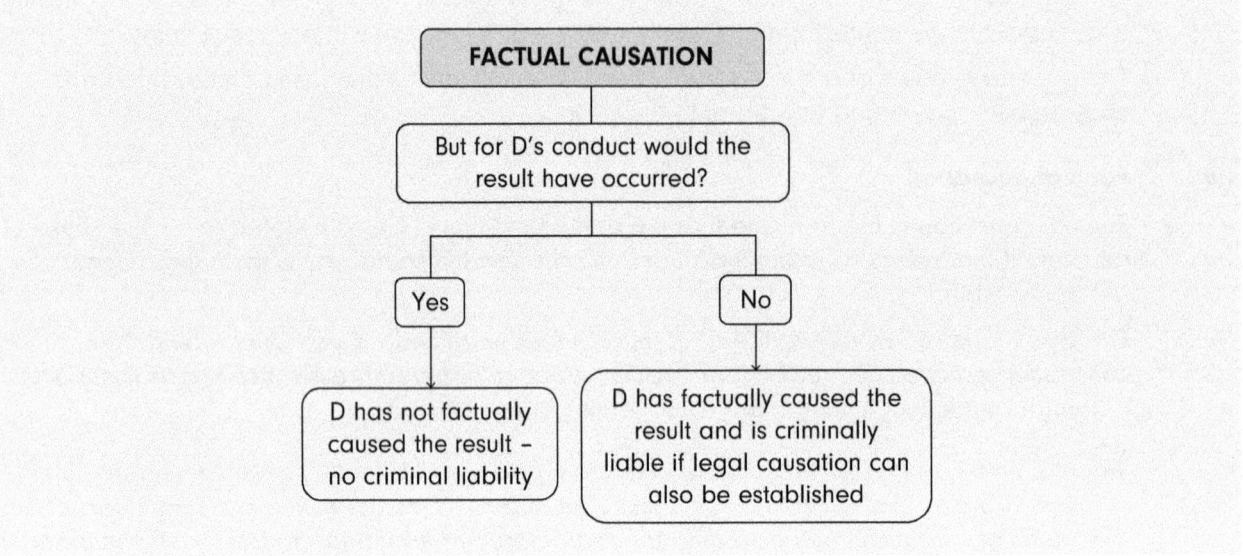

1.6.2 Legal causation

In addition to being the factual cause of the death, the prosecution must also establish that the accused was the legal cause of it. This can be summarised as follows:

- the defendant's conduct must be a substantial and operating cause of the consequence.

Legal causation will only be considered if the prosecution can prove that the defendant was the factual cause of the result, as demonstrated in **Figure 1.2**.

Figure 1.2 Legal causation

```
                            CAUSATION
                                │
                    ┌───────────┴───────────┐
                    │ But for D's conduct,  │
                    │ would the result have │
                    │      occurred?        │
                    └───────────┬───────────┘
           No                   │                   Yes
    ┌──────┴──────┐             │             ┌─────┴──────┐
    │ Causation   │             │             │Causation in│
    │ in fact     │             │             │fact not    │
    │ established │             │             │established │
    └──────┬──────┘             │             │- no actus  │
           │                                  │   reus     │
    ┌──────┴────────────────┐                 └────────────┘
    │ Was D's conduct an    │
    │ operating and         │
    │ substantial cause of  │
    │ the result? Did it    │
    │ contribute            │
    │ significantly?        │
    └──────┬────────────────┘
       Yes │           No
    ┌──────┴──────┐    ┌────────────┐
    │ Legal       │    │Causation in│
    │ causation   │    │law not     │
    │ established │    │established │
    │ unless there│    │- no actus  │
    │ is an       │    │   reus     │
    │ intervening │    └────────────┘
    │ event which │
    │ breaks the  │
    │ chain of    │
    │ causation   │
    └─────────────┘
```

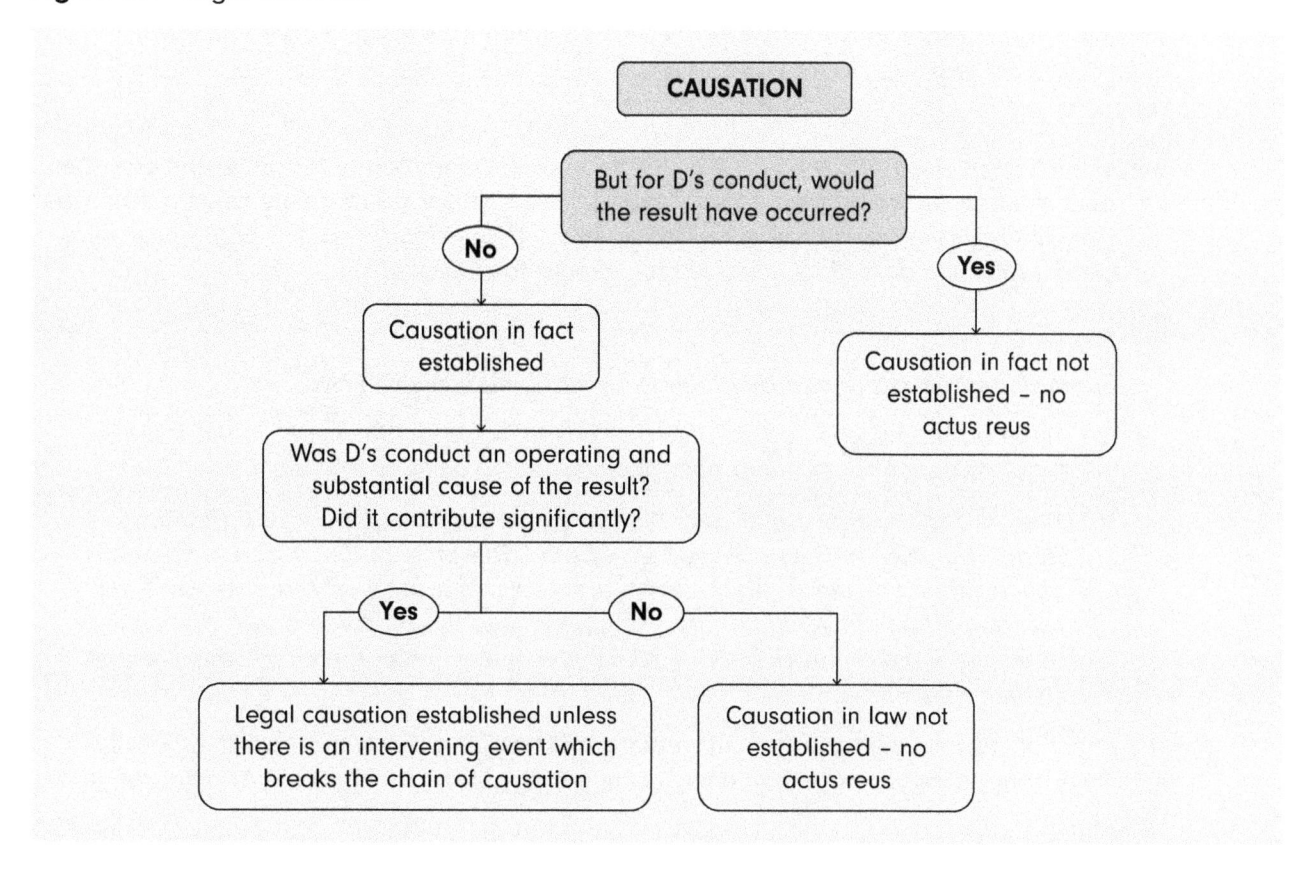

Over time, the principle of legal causation has been developed by the judges in a somewhat piecemeal manner. Hence there are a number of cases that illustrate how legal causation operates in practice, including the effect of events that happen after the defendant's involvement but which have an impact on the final outcome. As such, legal causation is a combination of different rules, not all of which will be relevant to every situation.

1.6.2.1 The consequence must be attributable to a culpable act or omission

The rationale behind this legal principle is that, to attract consequences under the criminal law, someone must be blameworthy in some way. This means that legal causation will only be established if the result was due to the defendant's action.

In the case of R v Dalloway (1847) 2 Cox CC 273, the defendant was negligently driving a horse and cart without holding the reins when a child ran in front of the cart and was killed. The jury was directed to convict for manslaughter only if they were satisfied that holding the reins would have saved the child. The jury acquitted, presumably being of the view that even though there was a culpable act, it did not cause the child's death which could not have been avoided.

1.6.2.2 The culpable act must be a more than minimal cause of the consequence

The prosecution must prove that the accused's contribution to the death of the victim is more than trivial or minimal. For example, a person visiting a dying relative and hastening their death by chatting to them, so exhausting them, would not have caused the death in law.

In the case of R v Pagett (1983) 76 Cr App R 279, the defendant held his girlfriend hostage and then used her as a human shield when the police fired back at him. He was found guilty of manslaughter on the basis that his action 'contributed significantly' to her death.

1.6.2.3 The culpable act need not be the sole cause

There may be multiple causes of the particular result and it does not matter that the defendant's act was just one of these. This is a principle that has long been established in case law.

> In R v Benge (1865) 4 F & F 504, the defendant was a foreman of a track-laying crew and, as a result of misreading the train timetable, the track was up at a time when a train was due. The resulting accident caused death. Although the signalman and train driver were also at fault, the defendant could not rely on this to avoid liability.

Example

Eddie and Hugh attack and kill Maurice, by stabbing him with knives.

(a) The medical evidence establishes that both inflicted fatal wounds. In this instance, legal causation is clear and both defendants are guilty of murder.

(b) The medical evidence indicates that no single stab wound caused Maurice's death. However, it is established that both Eddie and Hugh caused him serious injury and it was the combination of their actions that killed Maurice. Here, the two defendants have contributed significantly to the outcome and it does not matter that their individual act was not the sole or even the main cause of the defendant's death.

The effect of this rule is that, just because there are multiple causes of a particular result, liability is not precluded; more than one person may be liable for homicide or other result crimes.

1.6.2.4 The accused must take their victim as they find them

On occasion, the victim will have an unusual physical or mental condition or belief that contributes to their death. The judges have adopted a robust approach to these cases.

> In R v Blaue [1975] 1 WLR 1411, the defendant stabbed a woman who refused a blood transfusion because of her religious beliefs as a Jehovah's Witness. She died of her injuries although the medical evidence suggested that such treatment would have saved her life. Lawton LJ stated: 'those who use violence on other people must take their victims as they find them. This ... means the whole man, not just the physical man.'

The fact that a victim refuses to take it upon themselves to stop the end result of death is irrelevant – the question for the jury is what caused the victim's death and, in this instance, it was the stab wound. This principle is sometimes referred to as the 'eggshell skull rule' on the basis that if the accused taps the victim on the head with a ruler using force that would normally just lightly bruise, but in this case breaks the victim's skull because it is particularly soft, the defendant should not escape the consequences of their act.

Examples

(a) Debbie slaps Eden around the face. In most people this would cause only a red mark but Eden has a brain tumour and the slap causes a haemorrhage that kills her.

(b) Frank shouts abuse at Geoff, an elderly man who has pushed in front of him in the queue at the cash point machine. Geoff is very frightened by the shouting and suffers a heart attack that kills him.

As a consequence of the thin skull rule, Debbie and Frank would both be liable for their victims' deaths. They must take their victims as they find them and this would include their underlying health conditions (Eden) and particular frailty (Geoff).

1.6.2.5 The chain of causation must not be broken

Defendants have sometimes tried to argue that the link between their act and the result (usually death) has been broken by an intervening act or event. This may be referred to by its Latin name of *novus actus interveniens*, which translates to 'a new and intervening act'.

The effect of an intervening act that breaks the chain of causation is that the defendant will not be the cause of the result and will be absolved of liability for it.

1.6.3 Intervening acts or events

There are three possible ways in which the so-called chain of causation may be broken:

- where the *victim* acts in a particular way;
- where an act by some *other person* intervenes between the defendant's conduct and the result; or
- where some *event* occurs between the defendant's conduct and the end result.

Each of these will be considered in turn.

1.6.3.1 Victim's acts

The general rule is that if the victim does something *after* the initial act or omission of the accused but *before* the consequence occurs, and that intervention is 'free, deliberate and informed' (voluntary), then legal causation will not be established. However, although this principle remains valid, it will rarely apply in practice. For example, if a victim decided not to seek medical help and died of their injuries, the defendant would almost certainly remain liable as their conduct contributed significantly to the victim's demise. Alternatively, the court may find that the victim suffered from a mental condition which influenced their decision, in which case the 'thin skull' rule would apply.

There are two important potential exceptions to the general rule, these being where the victim tries to escape and where they commit suicide.

'Escape' cases

When considering the impact of the victim's escape, the court will consider how foreseeable the victim's response was.

In R v Roberts (1971) 56 Cr App R 95, the victim jumped out of a moving car as a result of the defendant's unwanted sexual advances. The defendant was held liable for an assault occasioning actual bodily harm despite the injuries having been caused in part by the victim's own conduct.

This is an example of what are referred to as 'fright and flight' cases. The chain of causation is not broken here because the victim's act is not free, deliberate and informed; effectively, they have been forced into the situation.

However, a defendant will not always be liable for the consequences of a victim's escape. In the case of *Roberts*, Stephenson LJ stated that if the victim's act was 'so daft as to make it [the victim's] own voluntary act' then the chain of causation would be broken.

Example

Junaid has accepted a lift home from Yonis whom he met at a pub. On the way, Yonis threatens Junaid that if he does not pay £10 towards the petrol, he will slap him. In response, Junaid opens the car door while they are travelling at 50 miles per hour along a busy road and jumps out. Junaid is hit by a vehicle that is following Yonis' car and dies of head injuries which he sustained during the escape. This response would not be regarded as reasonably foreseeable in the circumstances.

In summary, when determining the issue of causation, the court will take into account:

- whether the escape is within the range of reasonable responses to be expected of a victim in that situation;
- whether the victim's response is proportionate to the threat; or
- whether it is so 'daft' as to be a voluntary act; and
- the fact that the victim is acting in 'the agony of the moment' without time for thought or deliberation.

Suicide

In some cases, the impact of the victim's suicide may be covered by the principle that the defendant must take their victim as they find them, as discussed earlier in the chapter. However, this issue was revisited in a recent case.

In R v Wallace [2018] EWCA 690, the defendant threw sulphuric acid upon her partner, Mark van Dongen, while he was asleep. His injuries were horrific including full thickness burns to 25% of his body, amputation of his lower leg and paralysis. After developing further complications, the victim applied for euthanasia, which is legal in Belgium, and his wish was granted.

The Court of Appeal held that voluntary euthanasia does not necessarily break the chain of causation and the question was whether it was reasonably foreseeable that the victim would commit suicide as a result of their injuries. All the circumstances should be taken into account to determine whether voluntary euthanasia fell within the range of reasonable responses that might have been expected from a victim in their situation.

1.6.3.2 Third party intervention

Another way in which the chain of causation may be broken is by a third party. This may cover a variety of situations where someone other than the accused or the victim acts. An example would be an ambulance driver who crashes their vehicle while driving the victim of a stabbing to hospital, resulting in the victim's death.

This is an area where the law has developed over time but the general principle can be summarised thus:

- A defendant will not be liable if a third party's intervening act is either free, deliberate and informed, or is not reasonably foreseeable.

In the case of *Pagett* (see **1.6.2.2**), the victim's death was caused by the action of the police officer in firing at the defendant. Here, the officer's response:

- was *not* free, deliberate and informed – as he was acting instinctively in self-defence; and
- *was* reasonably foreseeable in the circumstances – the defendant was shooting at the officer at the time.

As a consequence, the police officer who shot the victim was absolved of all criminal liability. Furthermore, his action did not break the chain of causation and the defendant, who used his girlfriend as a human shield, was found guilty of her death.

1.6.3.3 Medical negligence

In homicide cases the victim will often receive medical treatment and, if that treatment is negligent, may die as a result. In a number of cases, the defendant has argued that the poor medical treatment was the real cause of the death and, thus, broke the chain of causation.

⭐ Example

Shania attacks Kirit who suffers an injury to his leg as a result of the assault. He is taken to hospital where a junior doctor fails to read Kirit's medical notes. As a consequence, he wrongly gives Kirit a dose of antibiotics to which he is allergic and Kirit dies as a result of a reaction to the medication.

Clearly, Shania satisfies the test for factual causation. But for her actions in attacking Kirit, he would not have been a patient at the hospital and would not have suffered the negligent medical treatment. With regard to legal causation, Shania disputes that the injury she caused to Kirit is the cause of his death, arguing that the medical negligence is not reasonably foreseeable – it is an intervening event that breaks the chain of causation.

If successful, the effect would be to transfer criminal liability from the original defendant to the medical professional. For reasons of public policy, this would not generally be regarded as acceptable and, as a consequence, cases in which the judges have ruled in favour of the accused are rare.

One such example is that of R v Jordan (1956) 40 Cr App R 152. The victim's injuries had mainly healed when he died as a result of medical treatment that was so grossly negligent it was described as 'palpably wrong'. In this case, the cause of death was pneumonia due to the excessive amounts of liquid that were administered to the victim intravenously.

Although the chain of causation was broken, *Jordan* is regarded as an exceptional case based on particular facts. Subsequent cases have developed tests that are more likely to secure the conviction of the defendant who caused the initial injuries.

In R v Smith [1959] 2 QB 35, the victim died at an army medical centre after a fight with another soldier at their barracks. There was evidence that the treatment the victim received was 'thoroughly bad', including him being dropped twice on the way to seek help, inadequately diagnosed and given inappropriate medical treatment. Despite this, the chain of causation was not broken as the original injury was still an 'operating and substantial' cause of death. Lord Parker CJ stated that:

> *only if the second cause is so overwhelming as to make the original wound merely part of the history can it be said that the death does not flow from the wound.*

The effect of this ruling is that, provided the original injury is still operating at the time, the defendant will find it difficult to escape liability for the death. As the injury need not be the sole or indeed the main cause of death, even quite serious medical negligence may not be enough to absolve the defendant. This point was demonstrated in the next case.

In R v Cheshire [1991] 1 WLR 844, the victim was given a tracheotomy as a result of gunshot wounds received. Two months later, he died due to scar tissue at the tracheotomy site that obstructed his breathing. The victim's wounds were no longer life-threatening at this time, yet the original attacker was convicted of murder.

The court held that even if negligent medical treatment is the immediate cause of the victim's death, it should not break the chain of causation unless it is so independent of the defendant's actions and so potent in causing death that it makes the contribution made by the accused's acts insignificant.

As a consequence, the general principle is that only in the most extraordinary and unusual case would medical treatment break the chain of causation.

However, although causation issues can be tricky, in reality, such disputes will rarely arise.

1.6.3.4 Intervening events

A natural event (an 'Act of God') may break the chain of causation with the foreseeability of the subsequent event being the determining factor for liability.

✪ Examples

(a) Charis argues with Bonnie and strikes her, leaving her unconscious by the side of a stream. The injury was not sufficiently serious to cause death. Although it is a sunny afternoon, there is a sudden thunderstorm and the stream becomes swollen with flood water. Bonnie drowns. Charis is not liable for Bonnie's death because the flooding is (objectively) not foreseeable. Consequently, it will break the chain of causation.

(b) Charis argues with Bonnie and strikes her, leaving her unconscious on the beach. The tide comes in and Bonnie drowns. Charis would be liable for Bonnie's death by drowning as the tide coming in is a natural event that is reasonably foreseeable.

The chain of causation may also be broken by events other than natural ones, for example, where the victim is left in a house that is subsequently blown up in a gas explosion.

1.6.4 Summary of legal causation

Figure 1.3 contains a summary of the principles that apply to legal causation and the acts and events that may break the chain of causation so the defendant is no longer criminally liable for the result.

Figure 1.3 Legal causation and intervening acts

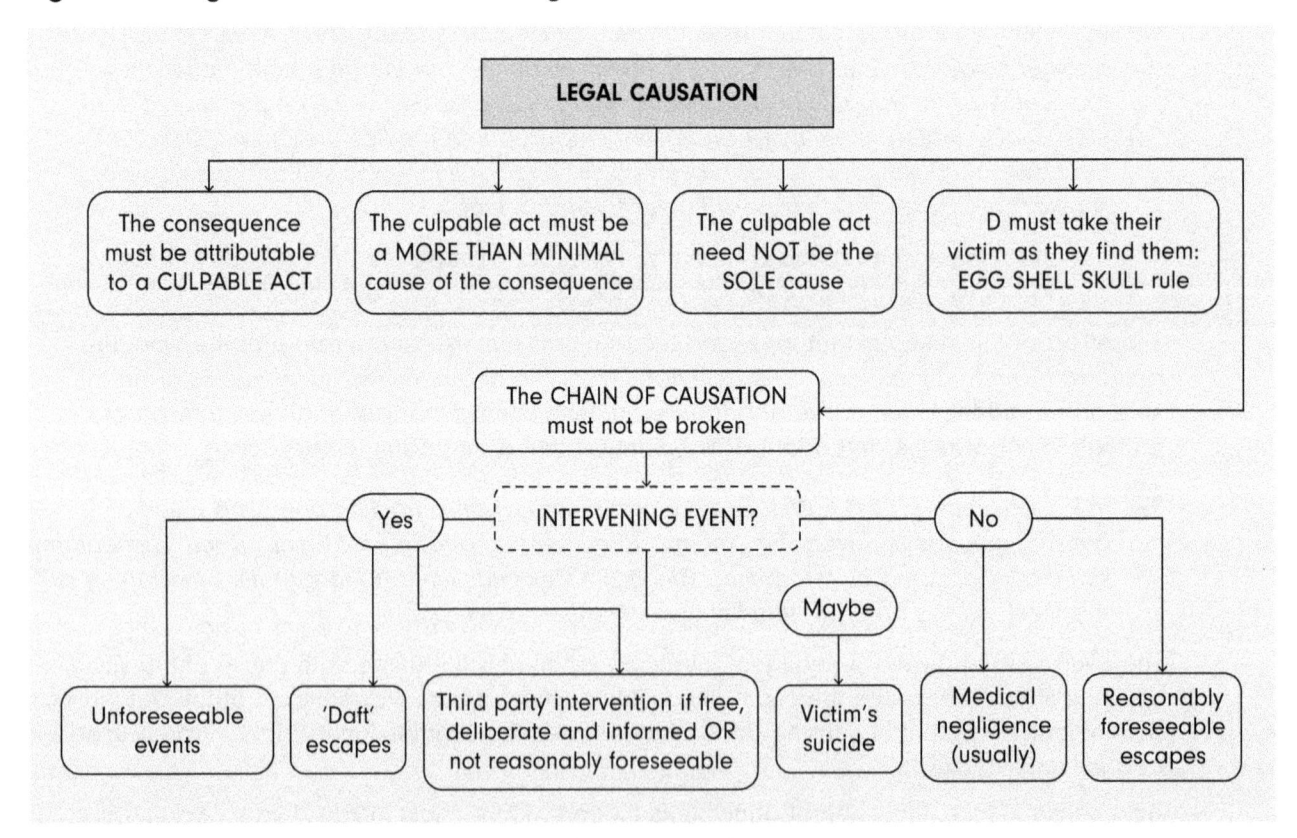

```
                          LEGAL CAUSATION
    ┌──────────────────┬──────────────────┬──────────────────┐
    ▼                  ▼                  ▼                  ▼
The consequence   The culpable act   The culpable act   D must take their
must be attributable   must be a        need NOT be the   victim as they find them:
to a CULPABLE ACT   MORE THAN MINIMAL   SOLE cause        EGG SHELL SKULL rule
                   cause of the consequence

                  The CHAIN OF CAUSATION
                     must not be broken
                              │
              ┌───────────────┼───────────────┐
            Yes         INTERVENING EVENT?     No
              │               │                 │
              │             Maybe               │
    ┌─────────┼────────┐      │         ┌───────┼────────┐
Unforeseeable  'Daft'   Third party intervention if free,   Victim's   Medical      Reasonably
events         escapes  deliberate and informed OR          suicide    negligence   foreseeable
                        not reasonably foreseeable                     (usually)    escapes
```

Summary

- To be criminally liable, the defendant must satisfy all the elements of the actus reus for the particular crime.
- The actus reus of an offence may involve an act or an omission (conduct crimes); certain consequences being caused (result crimes); or the existence of surrounding circumstances (state of affairs crimes).
- The general rule is that there is no liability for an omission to act but there are exceptions, namely statutory duty, contractual duty, special relationship, voluntary assumption of care and duty to avert a danger created.
- Causation must be proved as part of the actus reus for result crimes.
- For factual causation, it must be established that 'but for' the defendant's conduct, the result would not have occurred as and when it did.
- Legal causation requires the defendant's conduct to be a more than minimal cause of the result, so that it is an operating and substantial cause of the outcome.
- If the chain of causation is broken by an intervening event, the actus reus will not be established. Such events include: an unforeseeable escape; a voluntary act by a third party; negligent medical treatment that was 'so independent of the defendant's act' and 'so potent in causing death' that the contribution made by the defendant was rendered insignificant; and events that are not reasonably foreseeable.
- The eggshell or thin skull rule states that the defendant must 'take their victim as they find them'.

Sample questions

Question 1

A defendant is charged with murder after stabbing the victim, her partner, during an argument about money. The defendant was arrested at the scene with the bloodied knife in her hand. The defendant intends to rely upon the partial defence of loss of control.

Which of the following best describes how the legal and evidential burdens would operate in this case, and what standard of proof applies?

A The legal and evidential burden is on the prosecution to prove, beyond reasonable doubt, that the defendant murdered the victim and this is likely to be satisfied by the defendant's arrest at the scene with the knife. There is no burden on the defendant.

B The legal and evidential burden is on the prosecution to prove that the defendant murdered the victim. The jury must be satisfied of this on the balance of probabilities and this is likely due to the defendant's arrest at the scene with the knife.

C The legal burden of proof and the evidential burden is on the prosecution to prove that the defendant murdered the victim. There is also an evidential burden on the defendant in relation to the partial defence of loss of control that may be satisfied by the defendant giving evidence.

D The legal and evidential burden is on the defence to satisfy the jury beyond reasonable doubt that the defendant killed the victim when suffering from a loss of control and the defendant will need to give evidence at the trial to establish this.

E Once the prosecution have provided evidence of the arrest and the bloodied knife, the legal burden of proof moves to the defence to satisfy the jury beyond reasonable doubt that the defendant is not guilty of murder.

Answer

The correct option is C which accurately describes how the legal burden and standard of proof operate on the prosecution and how the evidential burden applies to the prosecution. The answer also correctly states that there is an evidential burden on the defendant in relation to her defence of loss of control.

The legal burden of proof is on the prosecution to prove that the defendant murdered the victim, so both options D and E are wrong. Option A is wrong as the defendant wishes to rely upon the partial defence of loss of control and so she has an evidential burden in this regard, which could be satisfied by her giving evidence in court. Thus, it is not correct to say there is no burden on the defence. Option B is wrong because the jury must be satisfied of the defendant's guilt beyond reasonable doubt and not on the balance of probabilities.

Question 2

A man works as a paramedic for the local health authority. He and a woman are living in the same rented accommodation with shared communal areas. One evening, they are in the kitchen together when they have an argument, during which the man shoves the woman. She stumbles backwards, falls and hits her head on the corner of the kitchen table. The man sees her unconscious on the floor, panics and runs out of the flat.

Shortly afterwards, a total stranger who is delivering leaflets, glances through the window and sees the woman still unconscious on the floor. The stranger does not want to get involved, so he walks away.

Two hours later, the woman regains consciousness and just manages to telephone the emergency services. She is rushed to hospital but dies of her injuries because she did not receive treatment more quickly.

Which of the following best describes the man's liability for the woman's death?

A   The man is not liable for the woman's death because, although his act of shoving her is a substantial cause of the death, it is not the only cause.

B   The man is liable for his failure to get help for the woman because he has a special relationship with her.

C   The man is liable for his failure to summon help because, having created a dangerous situation of which he is aware, he is under a duty to take reasonable steps to mitigate the results of his own actions.

D   The man is liable for his omission to act because he has a contractual duty as a paramedic to assist anyone who has been injured.

E   The man is not liable for his omission because the woman would have lived had she received medical treatment more quickly. The stranger is responsible for her death because he does nothing when he sees the woman on the floor and this breaks the chain of causation.

Answer

Option C is the best answer as it correctly describes the man's liability. Option A is wrong because the man's act of shoving the woman does not need to be the only cause provided it is a substantial and operating cause of her death; it is here as the woman dies of her injuries. The delay in receiving treatment does not break the chain of causation.

Option B is unlikely to be correct and it certainly does not 'best describe' the man's liability because living in a shared arrangement would not count as a special relationship for the purposes of the criminal law. Option D is wrong as, although the man is employed as a paramedic, he is not working at the time of the incident so his contractual duties do not apply. Option E is wrong because the general rule is that there is no liability for omissions unless the defendant falls into one of the exceptions. The stranger is not under a duty to act and is not criminally liable at all.

Question 3

The defendant is angry with the victim as he has just discovered that the victim has been messaging the defendant's girlfriend over social media. They have an argument at college during which the defendant produces a knife and stabs the victim in the stomach. The victim is rushed to hospital by ambulance but subsequently dies and the defendant is charged with his murder. The defendant argues that he is not liable because of an intervening event.

Which of the following events is most likely to break the chain of causation?

- A On the way to the hospital, the car in front of the ambulance stops unexpectedly when it breaks down, causing the ambulance to collide with it. The victim dies while waiting for a second ambulance to attend.
- B The victim is kept waiting for several hours at the Accident and Emergency Department of his local hospital and dies from complications arising from the stab wound.
- C The victim receives prompt medical treatment, but dies a month later after falling into a coma as a result of a carelessly administered anaesthetic during surgery.
- D The victim refuses to accept medical treatment because of his religious beliefs and dies from the stab wound, when he would not have done otherwise.
- E The victim is in hospital recovering from successful surgery for his injuries when a tree falls onto the hospital ward during a violent winter storm and kills him in his bed.

Answer

Option E is the correct answer as the victim dies as a result of an unforeseen and extraordinary natural event. The chain of causation is not broken in option A because the action of the motorist's car breaking down was not free, deliberate and informed (voluntary). Although it may be argued that the event was not reasonably foreseeable, this is unlikely to succeed as road traffic accidents are a common occurrence.

The defendant remains liable for the victim's death in option B as the stab wound is the substantial and operating cause of his demise (he dies from complications arising from the original injury). The negligent medical treatment which the victim receives in option C may not be enough to break the chain of causation as it has to be so independent of the defendant's act and so potent in causing death that the contribution made by the defendant is rendered insignificant. In this instance, the defendant's act of stabbing the victim is not 'insignificant' as without this, he would not have needed an operation at all.

The victim's refusal to accept medical treatment in option D is not an intervening event because the defendant must take his victim as he finds him and this includes the 'whole man' and not just the 'physical man'.

2 Mens Rea

2.1	Introduction	22
2.2	Intention	22
2.3	Recklessness	26
2.4	Negligence	29
2.5	Strict liability offences	31
2.6	Transferred malice	34
2.7	Coincidence of actus reus and mens rea	37
2.8	Classification of offences	39

SQE1 syllabus

By the end of this chapter you will be able to apply relevant core legal principles and rules appropriately and effectively, at the level of a competent newly qualified solicitor in practice, to realistic client-based and ethical problems and situations in the area of **mens rea**.

Note that, as students are not usually required to recall specific case names, or cite statutory or regulatory authorities, these are provided for illustrative purposes only.

Learning outcomes

The learning outcomes for this chapter are:

- to define the different types of mens rea of intention, recklessness, negligence and strict liability;
- to understand how these impact on criminal offences and appreciate the practical implications for clients; and
- to explain the concepts of transferred malice and the coincidence of actus reus and mens rea.

2.1 Introduction

As discussed in **Chapter 1**, three components are required to establish liability for a criminal offence:

(a) guilty conduct by the defendant (actus reus);

(b) guilty state of mind of the defendant (mens rea); and

(c) absence of any valid defence.

In this chapter, the second element will be analysed. Criminal offences usually require the prosecution to prove that the defendant committed the actus reus with the relevant 'guilty mind'. Mens rea is the technical term for the mental state required for a particular offence. If the prosecution cannot achieve this, the accused will not be convicted.

For some crimes such as murder, the mens rea will only be satisfied by intention but, for the vast majority of offences, it is enough that the defendant was reckless as to the consequences. However, for others, mere negligence will be sufficient or even no mens rea at all and these are known as strict liability offences.

The mens rea required for various offences covers an entire range of mental states with intention being at the top of the spectrum. Such a defendant is the most blameworthy as they act deliberately with a criminal aim in mind. At the lower end are strict liability offences where the defendant may not even know they have done anything wrong. In between are recklessness and negligence. All of these will be considered in this chapter.

2.2 Intention

Intention is the most culpable of the types of mens rea because the defendant intends to bring about the actus reus. It should not be confused with motive which may be quite different.

Example

Arthur's wife, Lillian, is terminally ill. The couple have been married for 45 years and are devoted to each other. Arthur is struggling to cope with seeing Lillian in so much pain and distress. One night, he puts a pillow over her face until Lillian stops breathing and dies. Arthur's intention is to kill his wife, but his motive is to end her suffering.

Intention is a subjective concept so the court will consider what this particular defendant saw or perceived as a result of their actions.

2.2.1 Direct intention

Intention is a word that is commonly used and any definition is likely to centre around the person wanting to achieve something or having in mind a specific purpose or outcome. This relatively simple state of affairs is what the law terms direct intention – the situation where the defendant seeks to achieve the consequence of their act.

Example

(a) Jayden is a contract killer. He is hired to kill Marcel and shoots him dead while Marcel is out for a jog in the morning. This is a case of direct intention as Jayden's aim or purpose is to kill Marcel. Thus, he has the required mens rea for murder.

(b) George deliberately fires at Carl from five metres away with his shotgun. Although he does so deliberately and with an intention to kill, George is shocked that he succeeds as he is a terrible shot. However, the fact that George thought he would probably miss is irrelevant as his aim or purpose was to kill Carl and so he has the direct intent for murder.

(c) If George and Carl had simply been fooling around and George did not realise the gun was loaded, the situation would be very different. Here, no such intent to kill exists.

In summary, a defendant has the direct intent to commit an offence if the consequence, whether it be death, criminal damage or an assault, is their aim or purpose.

2.2.2 Indirect intention

Although defining intention should be straightforward, in practice the courts and legislators have sometimes struggled to achieve this. Indeed, case law has broadened the law of intent beyond the everyday meaning so that it also recognises the concept of indirect or oblique intention. This is when the consequences that the defendant achieves by committing the actus reus are a by-product, so not the principal purpose, of what the defendant was aiming to do.

Cases on indirect intent occur most frequently in the context of murder, where the defendant argues that they did not intend to kill the victim and there is an alternative explanation for their actions. It may be easiest to explain this using a scenario.

⭐ Example

Mario and Giuseppe ran a business together leasing out helicopters for private use. Mario wants to take revenge on his partner because he has just discovered that Giuseppe has stolen the company's financial assets, leaving him bankrupt. Mario tampers with the engine management system on the helicopter in which he knows Giuseppe will be flying, knowing also that it will cause the engine to stall mid-flight and crash. Giuseppe and the pilot, Sarah, die immediately on impact with the ground.

Mario's aim or purpose is the death of Giuseppe; thus, he satisfies the mens rea of murder. However, Sarah's death is an undesired consequence of his actions. Given the near certainty of the pilot being killed in a situation such as this, most people would consider that the defendant should also be liable for murder for Sarah's demise. Yet if the ordinary meaning of intention is used, Mario cannot be convicted of this serious offence. However, the criminal law is nothing if not practical and judges have established the concept of indirect or oblique (the terms are interchangeable) intent to deal with this.

2.2.2.1 The legal test for indirect intention

The concept of indirect intent developed to cover those cases where the defendant argued that the outcome was not their main aim but an unfortunate by-product of what they set out to achieve. The question generally arises in the context of murder because this offence cannot be committed recklessly. Whilst this may appear to be a sensible aim, judges struggled for many years over how the courts should approach the issue. Precisely what the accused must foresee, and with what degree of certainty in order to have intended the consequences, arose in a number of cases and was the subject of frequent disagreement between judges. Finally, the law became settled in 1999.

In the case of R v Woollin [1999] 1 AC 82, *the defendant lost his temper with his baby and, in anger and frustration, threw the child across the room. The baby struck a wall, fractured his skull and died. The prosecution accepted that the defendant did not set out with the intention of killing or seriously harming his son but submitted that, in throwing him, there was a very high risk of doing so.*

The House of Lords (now the Supreme Court) stated that the jury should decide the defendant's guilt as follows:

- *A result is intended when it is the accused's purpose to cause it.*

This is uncontroversial and sets out what is meant by direct intent. It was accepted that the defendant in *Woollin* did not have the baby's death or grievous bodily harm as his aim or purpose – he simply wanted to stop the child crying.

If this does not apply, the jury will be told to consider two issues:

(1) Was the consequence virtually certain to occur from the defendant's act (or omission)?

This is an objective test to be decided by the court; but how certain must the consequence be to satisfy this question? The judges did not give a percentage figure; they did not state that the probability needed to be, for example, 75% or even 90%. However, situations that have satisfied this test are:

(a) Two striking miners dropped a concrete block from a bridge onto a taxi that was taking another miner to his employment, killing the driver. The defendants argued that they only intended to block the road and to scare the working miners into stopping work.

(b) Two men were playing 'Russian roulette' – a lethal game of chance. The defendant placed a single bullet in a revolver, spun the cylinder and pulled the trigger. The victim died instantly. The defendant's case was that the game was 'just a lark' and he and his friend were simply fooling around.

In both these scenarios, the reasonable person (those on the jury) would be satisfied that death or really serious injury was virtually certain to occur in these circumstances. It is also likely that the court would have concluded in *Woollin* that the father's actions satisfied this objective test.

Having answered this question in the affirmative, the jury moves on to the next stage.

(2) Did the defendant appreciate the consequences were virtually certain to occur?

This is a subjective test so the court will examine what the defendant themselves foresaw or perceived as a consequence of their actions.

If the answer to both questions is 'yes', the court may find that the defendant did intend the consequence. In other words, despite what the defendant actually says, the jury may infer intent from the circumstances and the evidence. In the case of *Woollin*, the defendant was found not guilty of murder but guilty of manslaughter, presumably on the basis that he did not foresee the consequence as virtually certain – perhaps a rather fortunate outcome for him.

✪ Example

Returning to the case of Mario (above). It was not Mario's purpose to kill or seriously injure Sarah, the pilot of the helicopter; thus, he lacked the direct intent to do so. However:

- *Sarah's death was virtually certain to occur as a result of Mario's actions in sabotaging the helicopter.*

- *Mario himself would have appreciated that the death of the pilot was virtually certain to occur if he were to succeed in his aim of killing Giuseppe. He tampered with the engine management system and the evidence is that he knew this would cause the engine to stall mid-flight and crash.*

- *Mario would be guilty of Sarah's murder on the basis that he indirectly intended her death.*

It is extremely unlikely that if anyone was asked to define intention they would come up with the two-stage test from *Woollin*. Effectively, it is an artificial definition to prevent some (undeserving) defendants literally getting away with murder. The fact that the result must be a virtual certainty is a high degree of probability and will catch only a few defendants who would not otherwise be convicted anyway on the basis of their direct intent.

In cases of indirect intent, the jurors will have to consider what the defendant appreciated at the time of their act (or omission). This may be difficult in the absence of a clear confession, but some assistance is found in s 8 of the Criminal Justice Act (CJA) 1967, which provides that:

(a) although the test is what the defendant *themselves* foresaw, not what a reasonable person would have foreseen;

(b) what a reasonable person would have foreseen is a good indication (which the jury can take into account) in deciding what this defendant *did* foresee.

In other words, the jury does not have to simply accept whatever the defendant says, and the more unlikely their story, the less likely it is that the accused's evidence will be believed. Alternatively, just because the reasonable person would have foreseen the result as virtually certain does not mean this particular defendant actually did.

⭐ Example

Barry, a man of low intelligence, sets fire to his council property to try and force the local authority to rehouse him and his family. The fire quickly takes hold and within minutes the house is burning ferociously, destroying the stairs so that, although Barry and his wife manage to escape, their two young children are trapped in the bedroom. They are overcome by the smoke and die before they can be rescued. Barry is horrified by the deaths as he genuinely loves his children. He is charged with murder.

Direct intent

(a) For murder, the prosecution must prove that the defendant intended to kill or cause grievous bodily harm. Barry is adamant that it was not his intention to do so. Furthermore, killing his children would defeat his aim or purpose as the family would not be rehoused in these circumstances.

Indirect intent

(b) If the jury is not satisfied that Barry had direct intent to kill or cause grievous bodily harm, they will be directed as follows:

    i   Was the consequence – the death of the children – virtually certain to occur as a result of Barry's act? Given that he set fire to a house at night, knowing there were young children asleep upstairs, the jury is likely to conclude that the objective test is satisfied.

    ii Did Barry appreciate that the deaths were virtually certain? This is more problematic and would depend upon his evidence. Barry may have been confident that he and his partner would be able to get the children out of the house before the fire took hold. However, although Barry is of low intelligence, the risks and consequences of a house fire are well known and may be found to be within his contemplation.

(c) To assist, under s 8 of the CJA 1967, the jury may draw such inferences as appear proper from the evidence when deciding what this particular defendant foresaw. Given that Barry loved his children, it is unlikely that the jury would find such intent.

2.2.3 Summary of intent

The law on intent may be summarised as follows:

- Most crimes may be committed either intentionally or recklessly, but there are some (such as murder) where the prosecution must prove the defendant intended the result.

- If the defendant's primary purpose was to bring about a particular consequence, they intended that consequence, however unlikely they were to succeed. This is direct intent.
- In situations where the jury needs more guidance on the issue of intention (in cases of 'indirect intent'), the judge will direct the jury to find intention where it is satisfied:
  - the consequence was virtually certain to occur; and
  - the defendant foresaw that consequence as being virtually certain to occur.
- Where proof of intention is required, the motive of the defendant is usually irrelevant.

The flowchart in **Figure 2.1** summarises the approach the courts will take when deciding whether the defendant has the intention to commit a particular offence.

Figure 2.1 Intent

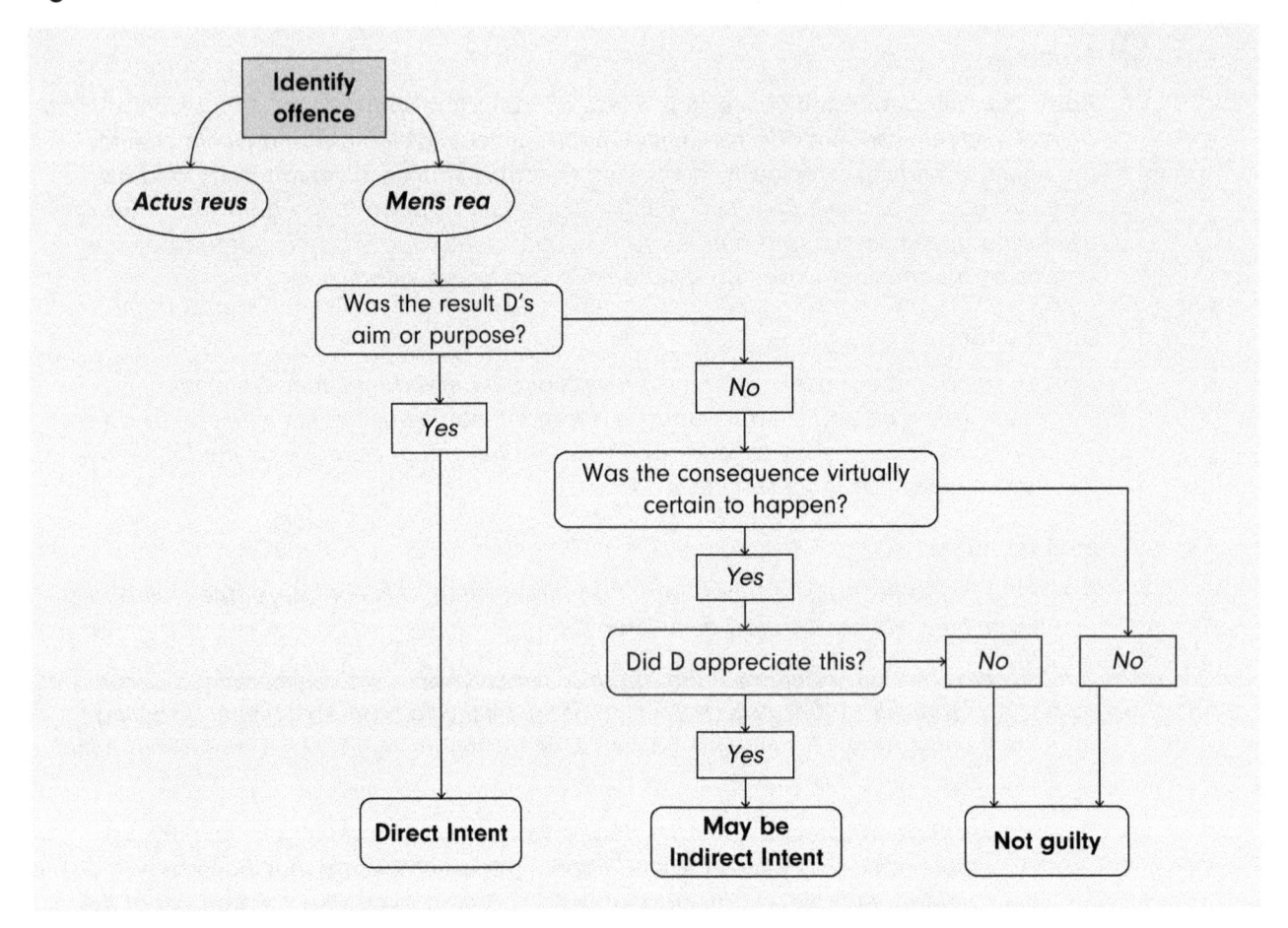

2.3 Recklessness

Although there are crimes that can only be committed intentionally, for the majority of offences, establishing that the defendant intended *or* was reckless as to whether a consequence could occur is sufficient to establish the mens rea.

Recklessness involves the defendant taking an unjustified risk. Although this may sound similar to the test for indirect intent, it is a less culpable form of mens rea than intention as it involves foresight of possible or probable consequences, instead of an appreciation of virtually certain consequences. The difference comes in the level of the risk that the defendant must foresee to be criminally liable.

There are two distinct elements to consider when dealing with recklessness:

(a) The risk must be an unjustified or unreasonable one to take.

(b) The defendant must be aware of the risk and go on to take it.

2.3.1 Justification of the risk

Whether a risk is justified or not will depend upon a number of factors including the reasons why the defendant acted as they did, what the risk was and the likely consequences. The court will balance the social utility or benefit involved in taking the risk against the likelihood or severity of the harm resulting.

The justification of the risk will be assessed according to the standards of reasonable people, with some situations falling clearly at one end of the spectrum, whilst others will require a more detailed discussion. Running into a burning building to save a child is an example of an act that would be both high risk but also of high social utility. In contrast, jumping into a stormy sea to save a dog would be high risk but of low social utility; therefore, an unjustified risk to take.

Fortunately, in the criminal context, this aspect does not tend to take up much of the court's time as in the vast majority of cases the defendant has been involved in an obviously unjustified activity. For example, there is no justification in stabbing or hitting a person, or in throwing bricks near buildings.

2.3.2 Subjective recklessness

Although it is an essential ingredient of recklessness, the taking of an unjustified risk is not enough in itself to establish criminal liability. The prosecution must also establish that the defendant had a particular state of mind when they took that risk. This means that a subjective test is applied. Depending upon the court's conclusions, which will be based upon the evidence heard, the defendant either will or will not be deemed subjectively reckless.

Table 2.1 Subjective recklessness test

The court's findings	Subjective recklessness?
The reasonable person would have foreseen the risk.	No
The defendant should have foreseen the risk.	No
The defendant actually foresaw the risk.	Yes

Only if the court is satisfied that the defendant is subjectively reckless may they be convicted of the offence. As with intention, the mens rea of recklessness has been developed through case law.

> In R v Cunningham [1957] 2 QB 396, the defendant broke a gas meter and cracked a pipe, causing gas to leak into the house next door. His neighbour inhaled the gas and the defendant was found guilty of maliciously administering a noxious thing so as to endanger life. Cunningham's appeal was granted because it was not established that he was aware of the risk of gas escaping and endangering others as a result of his action.

This (subjective) standard was applied to all offences except criminal damage which was, historically, dealt with differently. However, in *R v G* [2004] 1 AC 1034, criminal damage was brought into line with all other offences.

The effect is that there is now one test for recklessness and this is subjective. A defendant is reckless if they foresee a risk that something may happen as a result of their behaviour (or a particular set of circumstances might exist) and, with that foresight, go on without justification to take the risk. An awareness of any level of risk, however small, is sufficient.

✪ Example

Ryan punches Syd once in the face during an argument over money. Syd falls backwards, hits his head on the edge of a nearby table and suffers a fractured skull. Given the circumstances (only one punch and no weapon used), it would be difficult to establish that Ryan intended to cause serious harm.

However, the prosecution are far more likely to be able to prove that Ryan was reckless as to causing such harm and this would satisfy the mens rea for a lesser assault. This is because there is no social utility in punching someone due to a disagreement over money and the risk of causing injury would be considered unjustified by the standards of reasonable people. Furthermore, Ryan is likely to have foreseen there was a risk and yet he went on to take it anyway.

2.3.3 Summary of recklessness

The law relating to recklessness may be summarised as follows:

- The risk that the defendant takes must be an unjustified one (objective).
- The test is whether this defendant foresees that risk (of whatever is required by the specific offence) and goes on to take it (subjective).
- The subjective test for recklessness applies to any criminal offence in which recklessness forms part of the necessary mens rea.

Figure 2.2 Recklessness

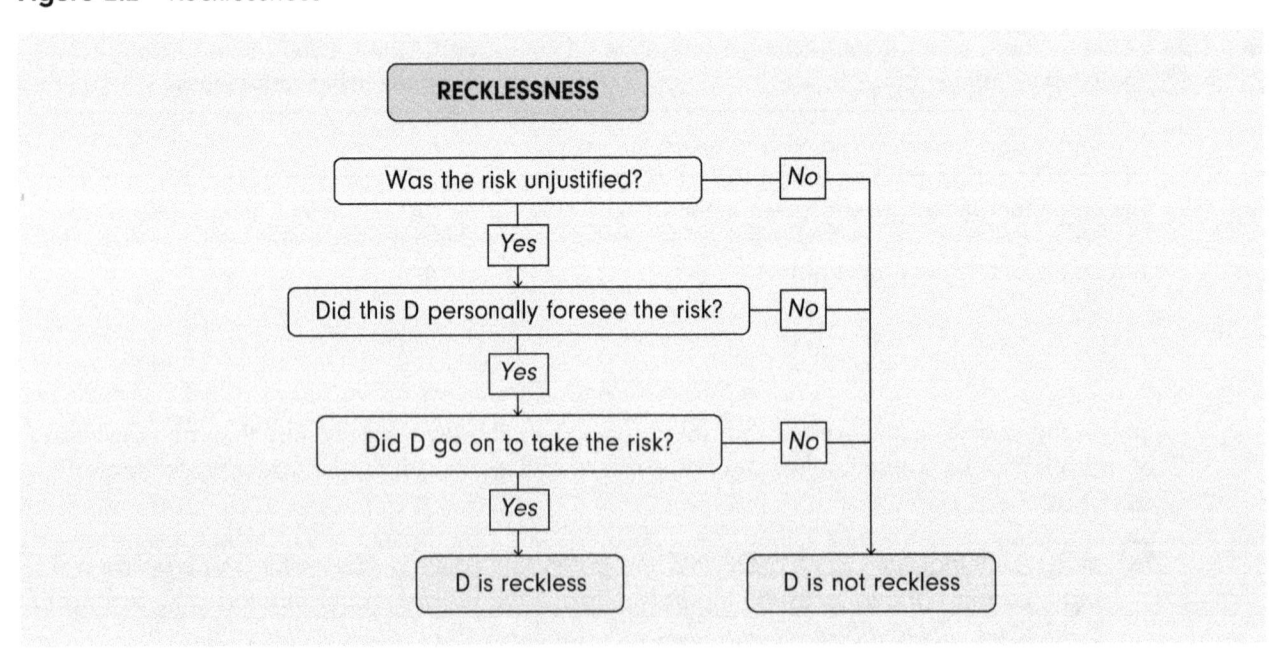

```
                    RECKLESSNESS

            Was the risk unjustified? ───── No ─┐
                        │                       │
                       Yes                      │
                        ▼                       │
        Did this D personally foresee the risk? ── No ─┤
                        │                       │
                       Yes                      │
                        ▼                       │
            Did D go on to take the risk? ───── No ─┤
                        │                       │
                       Yes                      │
                        ▼                       ▼
                 D is reckless           D is not reckless
```

2.4 Negligence

Some offences may be committed without proof of intention or recklessness by the defendant. Where the mens rea only requires negligence, the defendant is judged on an objective standard that can be satisfied even if the defendant is unaware of the risk provided it is an obvious one. Because the defendant is punished for failing to measure up to the standards of the reasonable person, this may operate harshly as the accused may not understand or even be capable of recognising the risk.

The effect of the objective test is as follows:

Table 2.2 Objective negligence test

The court's findings	Negligence?
The defendant failed to foresee a risk that a reasonable person would have foreseen.	Yes
The defendant foresaw the risk but did not take steps to avoid it.	Yes
The defendant foresaw the risk but took inadequate steps to avoid it.	Yes

In all these instances, the defendant fell below the standard to be expected of a reasonable person and thus will be negligent.

2.4.1 Comparison of recklessness and negligence

Both forms of mens rea involve the taking of an unjustifiable risk, but there is a key difference:

- Recklessness is the *conscious* taking of an unjustifiable risk.
- Negligence is the *inadvertent* taking of an unjustifiable risk.

In other words, negligence can be proved simply by showing that the defendant's conduct fell short of an objective standard. It usually involves the defendant being careless in some way.

2.4.2 Negligence and common law offences

Most incidents of negligence give rise to civil rather than criminal liability, but there are situations where, in addition to or instead of any civil claim, the negligent person could be prosecuted for a criminal offence. This occurs only rarely at common law, but one such example of an offence where negligence satisfies the mens rea is gross negligence manslaughter.

⭐ *Example*

Mrs McVey has warned the school attended by her son, Cameron, that Cameron has a severe, life-threatening, allergy to nuts. The information has been passed on to all the catering staff. Despite this, one lunch time, Cameron is given a sandwich by Donna that has traces of nuts in it. This fact is clearly highlighted on the label, which also states that the sandwich should not be eaten by anyone with a nut allergy.

Outcome 1: The error is spotted by Cameron's class teacher before he eats the sandwich and no harm is suffered. There is no criminal liability in these circumstances.

Outcome 2: Cameron takes a bite of the sandwich, suffers an extreme allergic reaction and dies. The catering assistant, Donna, may be liable for the offence of gross negligence manslaughter. This is because her actions may be judged as having fallen so far below the standard of the reasonable employee (the objective standard) as to be criminally liable.

In both scenarios, the action is the same and the differing outcomes were down to chance; nevertheless, because of the harm suffered in the second, Donna's negligence may attract punishment under the criminal law.

Although negligence is sufficient to satisfy the mens rea for the offence of gross negligence manslaughter, this is unusual. Negligence appears far more often in the definitions of statutory offences.

2.4.3 Negligence and statutory offences

Criminal liability can often be established just by the defendant being careless in some way. An example of a criminal offence that requires only negligence as the mens rea is the motoring offence created by s 3 of the RTA 1988 of careless driving. This provides that a person is guilty of an offence if they:

> drive a mechanically propelled vehicle on a road or other public place without due care and attention, or without reasonable consideration for other persons using the road or place.

The test for negligence is an objective one rather than the subjective test that applies to recklessness and, to be guilty of the s 3 offence, the driving must 'fall below what would be expected of a competent and careful driver'. The accused is judged against the reasonable driver and the court is only concerned with the manner of the defendant's driving – not with their state of mind at the time.

Examples of careless driving would be:

(a) Mia, who has just passed her driving test, fails to stop in time at a junction and collides with the vehicle in front.

(b) Akhtar overtakes a van on the brow of a hill as he is in a hurry to get to work.

(c) Jeff drives through a red traffic light on his way to hospital with his pregnant wife who is about to give birth.

(d) Bettina drives at 30 miles per hour in the middle lane of the motorway as she believes it is safer to drive slowly.

All of these drivers fall below the standard of the reasonable motorist and their motive for doing so is irrelevant. This may operate harshly at times, particularly in relation to those such as Jeff who have a good excuse for driving as they did, or Mia who is inexperienced. However, there are public policy factors at play here and the importance of deterring people from driving badly is more important than apparent injustice to some individuals.

For an offence under s 3 of the RTA 1988, the consequences are also irrelevant so it does not matter what happened as a result of the careless driving, whether this be damage to property or personal injury. The manner of the driving is the only factor that the court will consider.

2.4.4 Summary of negligence

For crimes where the mens rea may be satisfied by negligence:

- A person is punished simply for failing to measure up to the standards of the reasonable person.

- Whilst the defendant may have acted intentionally or recklessly, this is not required to establish criminal liability; it is what the defendant *did* that is relevant.
- Because the test is objective, individual considerations such as the defendant's motive for acting as they did, or lack of experience, are not taken into account.

Figure 2.3 Negligence

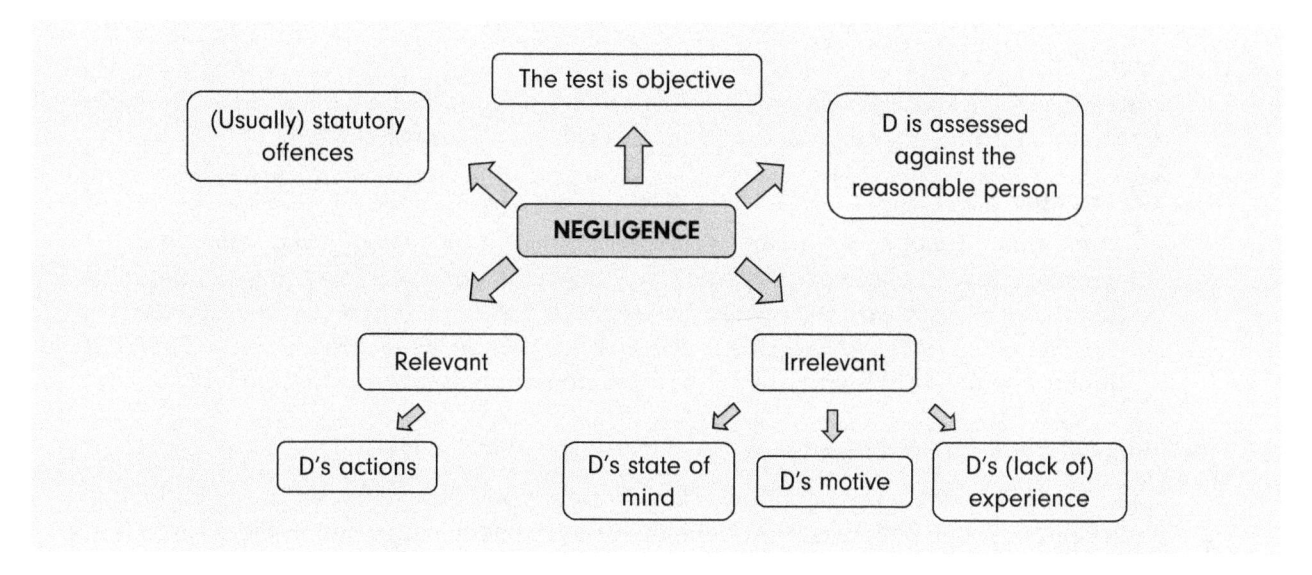

```
                    The test is objective
(Usually) statutory                              D is assessed
    offences          ↖   ↑   ↗                  against the
                        NEGLIGENCE               reasonable person
                      ↙   ↓   ↘
     Relevant                    Irrelevant
        ↙              ↙     ↓      ↘
   D's actions    D's state of   D's motive   D's (lack of)
                     mind                      experience
```

2.5 Strict liability offences

For most crimes, an accused may only be convicted of a criminal offence if they have some sort of 'guilty mind'. However, there are offences where it is not necessary to prove mens rea or negligence in respect of at least one element of the actus reus. This small but important category of criminal offences are called strict liability offences.

2.5.1 Type of offences

As with negligence, most such offences are statutory and they tend to be regulatory in nature. The aim is to discourage incompetence and unsafe actions and to encourage greater vigilance and safety. An example of an offence where an accused may be convicted without proof of fault is driving a motor vehicle in excess of the speed limit on a road. Many others relate to areas such as:

(a) Food safety

(b) Consumer protection

(c) Misuse of drugs

(d) The environment

(e) Road safety

(f) Health and safety.

Strict liability offences do not generally apply to the public at large, but to those people who are engaged in particular forms of conduct. They are designed to regulate certain types of behaviour.

There are a number of public policy reasons as to why these offences are strictly liable. Not having to prove mens rea makes criminal prosecutions much simpler from an evidential point of view and removes a potentially significant line of defence from the accused. Trials tend to be quicker and hence cheaper, as they occupy the court for less time, and the conviction rate is generally higher.

In the case of Smedleys Ltd v Breed *[1974] AC 839, a small caterpillar was found in one of millions of tins of peas sold by the defendant. The company was found guilty under the Food and Drugs Act 1955 despite the difficulties of preventing such an event and the fact they had taken all reasonably practical steps to do so. The justification for the offence being strictly liable was the importance of protecting customers – a matter of social concern.*

However, the strict liability rule may operate harshly and produce injustice in cases where the defendant inadvertently commits the actus reus without any criminal intent.

Example

A pharmacist supplied prescription drugs after being presented with a fraudulent prescription. The pharmacist was not involved in the fraud, had no knowledge that the doctor's signature was forged and believed the prescription was genuine. However, despite being entirely blameless in the situation, because the offence under s 58(2) of the Medicines Act 1968 is one of strict liability, the pharmacist was convicted.

2.5.2 Identifying a strict liability offence

In most instances, the legal definition will state clearly whether mens rea is required for a particular crime but, if there is any doubt, the task of determining whether the offence is one of strict liability will fall upon the court.

2.5.2.1 Statute

If the offence was created by statute, and most now are, this is the first place to look. The legislation may expressly provide that the offence is one of strict liability or not.

- Section 1 of the Contempt of Court Act 1981 states:

    In this Act 'the strict liability rule' means the rule of law whereby conduct may be treated as a contempt of court as tending to interfere with the course of justice in particular legal proceedings *regardless of intent to do so.*

Alternatively:

- the statute may use words in defining the offence that make it clear that mens rea is required, such as intentionally / knowingly / wilfully and so on.

For example, s 1 of the Theft Act (TA) 1968 defines theft as dishonestly appropriating property belonging to another with the *intention* of permanently depriving them of it.

2.5.2.2 Case law

However, not all legislation is as helpful and, on occasion, Parliament has omitted any reference to whether mens rea (or negligence) is required.

Example

Section 5 of the RTA 1988 states:

- *(1) If a person –*

    (a) *drives ... a motor vehicle on a road or other public place ... after consuming so much alcohol that the proportion of it in his breath, blood or urine exceeds the prescribed limit he is guilty of an offence.*

There is nothing in the definition that refers specifically to any mens rea requirements such as 'with intent' or 'recklessly', but neither does the statute make it clear the offence is strictly liable.

In such instances, case law provides some assistance on how to determine if the offence is one of strict liability or not. The starting point is that, if the statute says nothing, there is a presumption in favour of mens rea. However, as with all legal presumptions, it can be rebutted and the factors that the court will take into account in determining this issue are as follows:

(a) The court will look at the statute as a whole. If words suggesting mens rea are used in other sections but not in the section under consideration, the implication is that Parliament left them out for a reason and intended to create a strict liability offence here.

(b) The judges may also look at the social context of a particular offence; the greater the social danger an offence is aimed at preventing, the more likely it will be a strict liability offence.

(c) Where the behaviour is 'truly criminal', the courts are more reluctant to infer strict liability. The presumption in favour of mens rea operates more strongly where conviction of the offence carries a heavy penalty or substantial social stigma, due to the potential injustice caused.

For example, s 5 of the RTA 1988 creates an offence of driving with excess alcohol. The statute is directed towards a particular group of the population (those engaged in driving vehicles) and the aim is to regulate their behaviour, thus preventing accidents being caused by irresponsible drivers (the social context). Given the real danger of injury or death resulting from drivers who are over the legal limit and the impact this may have on people's lives, unsurprisingly, the statute is one of strict liability. As a consequence, a person who drives after consuming excess alcohol is guilty of an offence even if they did not know, nor were they aware of a risk, that the amount of alcohol they had consumed would exceed the prescribed limit.

The effect of the strict liability rule is that even drivers who could not have known they were over the limit, perhaps because their drinks were spiked, are guilty. Although it may seem harsh that a defendant may be convicted despite lacking the mens rea for such a crucial element of the offence – that their alcohol level exceeded the prescribed limit – the injustice caused to those injured by such drivers is far greater.

2.5.3 Summary of strict liability

- Offences of strict liability are exceptions to the general rule that mens rea is required for criminal offences.
- A person may be convicted of an offence even though they lack the mens rea for one or more elements of the actus reus.
- In some instances, the statute expressly states that the offence created is one of strict liability or uses words, such as 'intentionally', that make it clear it is not.
- In the absence of anything express, a rebuttable presumption applies that the offence is not strictly liable.
- Usually, the higher the social stigma and the greater the penalty on conviction, the more likely that mens rea will be required.

Figure 2.4 Strict liability

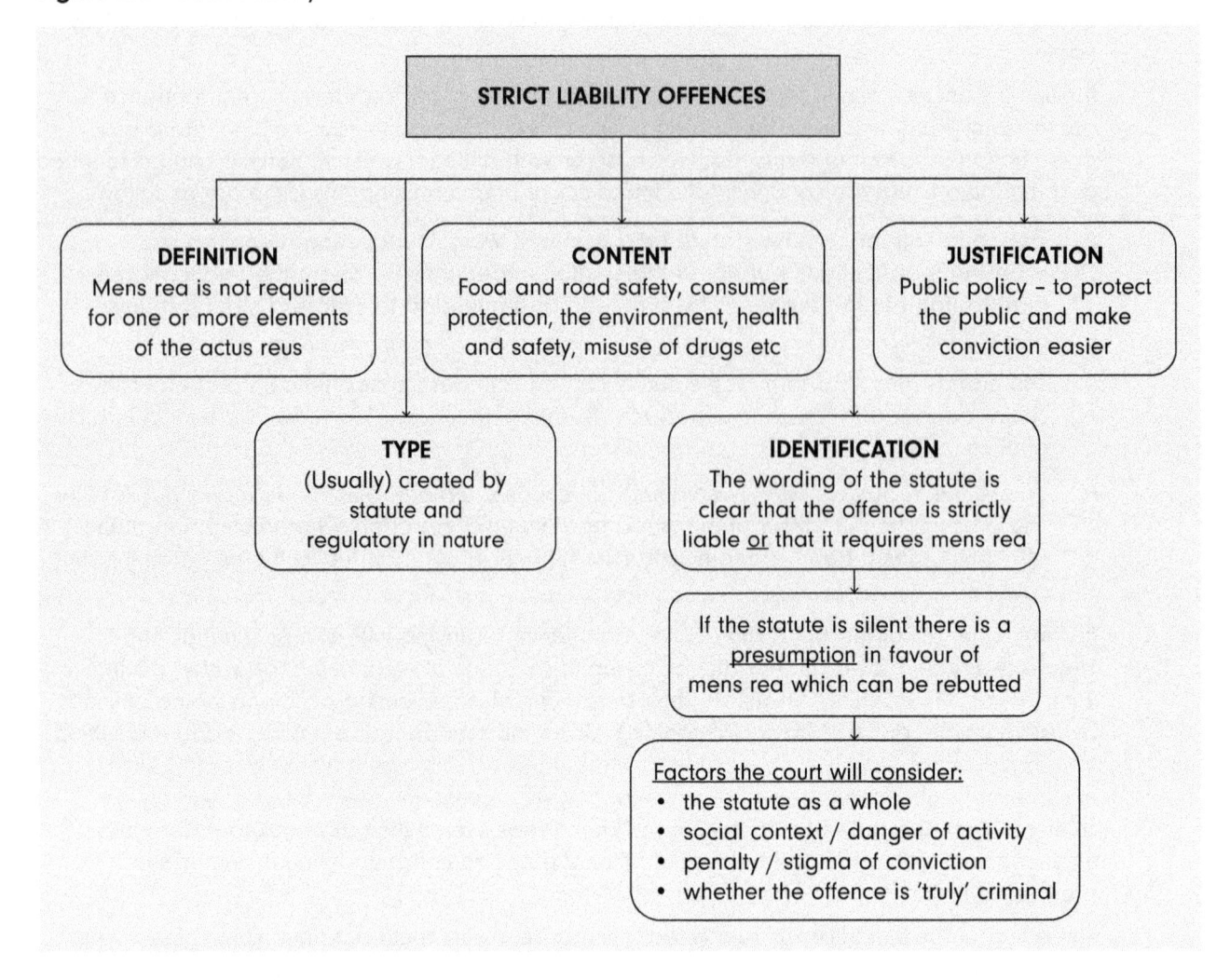

```
                    ┌─────────────────────────────┐
                    │  STRICT LIABILITY OFFENCES  │
                    └─────────────────────────────┘
         ┌──────────────────────┼──────────────────────┐
         ▼                      ▼                      ▼
   ┌───────────┐          ┌───────────┐          ┌───────────────┐
   │ DEFINITION│          │  CONTENT  │          │ JUSTIFICATION │
   │ Mens rea  │          │ Food and  │          │ Public policy │
   │ is not    │          │ road      │          │ – to protect  │
   │ required  │          │ safety,   │          │ the public    │
   │ for one   │          │ consumer  │          │ and make      │
   │ or more   │          │ protection│          │ conviction    │
   │ elements  │          │ the       │          │ easier        │
   │ of the    │          │environment│          └───────────────┘
   │ actus reus│          │ health and│
   └───────────┘          │ safety,   │
                          │ misuse of │
                          │ drugs etc │
                          └───────────┘
```

TYPE: (Usually) created by statute and regulatory in nature

IDENTIFICATION: The wording of the statute is clear that the offence is strictly liable <u>or</u> that it requires mens rea

If the statute is silent there is a <u>presumption</u> in favour of mens rea which can be rebutted

<u>Factors the court will consider:</u>
- the statute as a whole
- social context / danger of activity
- penalty / stigma of conviction
- whether the offence is 'truly' criminal

2.6 Transferred malice

In addition to the general principles of actus reus and mens rea, there are additional issues that arise on occasion and these are discussed in the remainder of this chapter.

2.6.1 The doctrine of transferred malice

What if the defendant attacks the wrong person or damages the wrong property?

⭐ *Example*

Zain intends to shoot Louie. He lies in wait and takes aim as Louie walks into view. Zain does not notice Harry, who is strolling past at the same time, and accidentally kills him instead; does this matter? Instinctively, the answer would be 'no' as Zain should not get away with murder just because he shot a different victim to that intended. The criminal law agrees that if Zain intended to kill Louie but actually killed Harry, he should be punished for the consequence of his actions and the doctrine of transferred malice is the means by which this outcome is achieved.

In a scenario such as this, the defendant has committed the actus reus of murder because they have killed a human being. With regard to the mens rea, the law does not specify which person the defendant intended to kill – just that they did. This is justified in legal terms through the doctrine of transferred malice. In other words, if the defendant has the 'malice' – the intention or recklessness – to commit a crime against one person, this malice is transferred to the *unintended* victim and combines with the actus reus to complete the offence. The outcome makes sense because it would be absurd if the defendant could escape liability for their actions due to incompetence or chance.

> *The authority for the principle of transferred malice is that of* R v Latimer *(1886) 17 QBD 359. The defendant became involved in a fight with a man in a public house. He took off his belt to strike his intended victim but the belt ricocheted off and hit a woman standing nearby, causing a severe wound to her face. Despite having injured the woman accidentally, the defendant was found guilty of an assault.*

Example

In Zain's case (above), as he had the mens rea for murder in respect of Louie, that intention to kill is transferred and coupled with the actus reus of killing Harry to make him guilty of murder.

Figure 2.5 Example of transferred malice

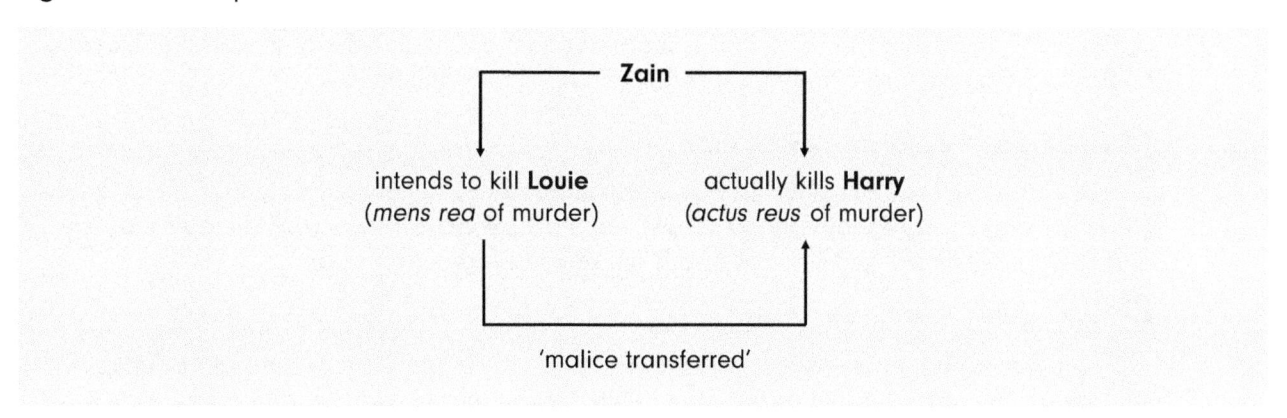

```
                    ┌──────── Zain ────────┐
                    │                      │
                    ▼                      ▼
            intends to kill Louie    actually kills Harry
            (mens rea of murder)     (actus reus of murder)
                    │                      ▲
                    └──────────────────────┘
                         'malice transferred'
```

The principle would also apply if the defendant damaged or stole the 'wrong' property. Thus, a defendant who planned to scratch her ex-husband's car would be liable for criminal damage even if she scratched his work colleague's (very similar) car by mistake. The mens rea she had for damaging her ex-husband's car would be transferred to the colleague's vehicle. This would be combined with the actus reus to make her guilty of the offence.

In both of these examples, the defendant has the mens rea for the type of crime they committed (murder and criminal damage respectively). Logically, they should not evade criminal liability simply because they failed to carry out their plan competently.

2.6.2 Limits to the application of transferred malice

However, the law would be too onerous if a defendant were to be held criminally liable for every unintended consequence and so a limitation is placed on the doctrine of transferred malice.

> In R v Pembliton *(1874) 2 CCR 119*, the defendant threw a stone at a man he was fighting in the street, intending to hurt him, but he missed and smashed a window instead. In this instance, transferred malice did not apply because the defendant committed the actus reus of one offence – criminal damage – but the mens rea of a completely different one, that of assault.

Figure 2.6 Example of malice not transferred

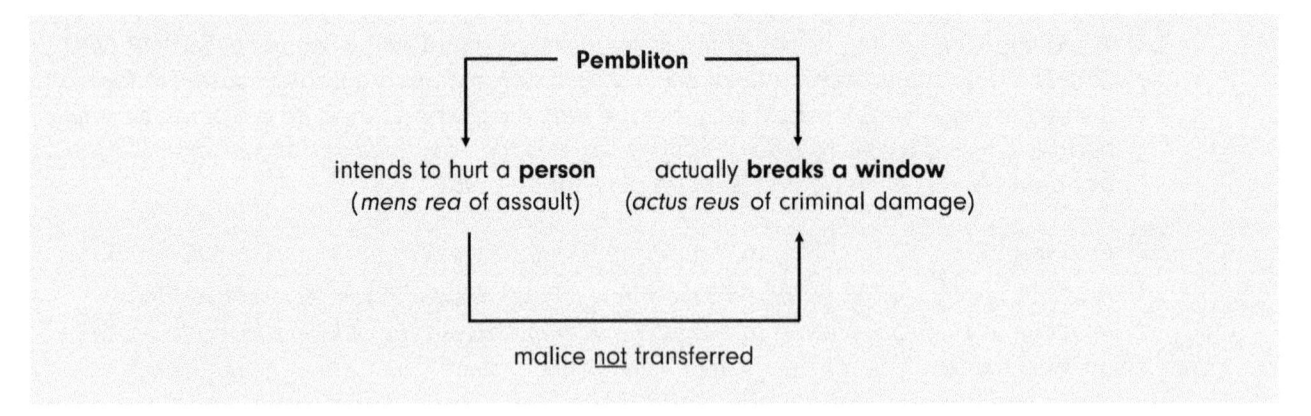

```
                    ┌──── Pembliton ────┐
                    ↓                   ↓
         intends to hurt a person    actually breaks a window
           (mens rea of assault)     (actus reus of criminal damage)
                    └───────────────────┘
                         malice not transferred
```

It is apparent that the doctrine of transferred malice only applies where the actus reus committed is the same type of crime as the defendant originally had in mind. If the intended and actual offences are different, the 'malice' cannot be transferred.

2.6.3 When transferred malice may be unnecessary

Transferred malice is a useful vehicle by which (apparently deserving) defendants can be convicted of the appropriate offence. However, most offences may be committed recklessly and, in such circumstances, the doctrine is unlikely to be required at all.

Example

Isabel throws a vase at William intending to strike him but she misses and hits William's friend, Edward, who is standing next to him. This would be sufficient for the actus reus of the offence of battery. Although the prosecution may rely upon the doctrine of transferred malice, there is another basis upon which Isabel could be convicted.

Most offences (murder being an obvious exception) can be committed recklessly. Although Isabel does not intend to hit Edward, she may be reckless as to doing so. If the prosecution can prove that Isabel foresaw even the smallest risk of hitting Edward, and she went on to take that risk, she is guilty of battery. Given that Edward is standing so close to William, it is likely that the court will find that she satisfies the mens rea of recklessness.

2.6.4 Summary of transferred malice

- Under the doctrine of transferred malice, the defendant's intention towards A may be transferred to B where they commit the actus reus of the same offence in relation to B.
- Malice may be transferred from person to person, or from object to object.
- There is a limit to the scope of this doctrine; where the actus reus and mens rea relate to different types of offences, transferred malice does not operate.
- If the mens rea of the offence includes recklessness, it may not be necessary to consider the doctrine of transferred malice at all.

2.7 Coincidence of actus reus and mens rea

2.7.1 The general principle

Although actus reus and mens rea are discussed in two different chapters, the concepts are inextricably linked. For there to be criminal liability, it is essential that the actus reus and mens rea coincide in time; in other words, the accused must have the required mens rea at the same time they commit the actus reus.

> ⭐ *Example*
>
> *Philip discovers that his partner, Lyra, is having an affair. He is furious and decides that he will kill her. At this point, Philip has the mens rea of murder. However, he does not take any action and so, because there is no actus reus, he is not criminally culpable.*
>
> *After a few minutes, Philip calms down and decides to speak to Lyra instead. While waiting for her return, he climbs up a ladder to repair a broken tile on their roof. When he sees Lyra walking up the drive towards the house, Philip turns and accidentally dislodges a tile which lands on Lyra's head, killing her. At this point, he has committed the actus reus of murder but he no longer has the mens rea; thus, Philip still has no criminal liability.*

For the vast majority of cases, proving the coincidence of the actus reus and the mens rea will not be an issue, but the position becomes more complicated when there is a time lag between the two.

2.7.2 Continuing act

To ensure that the requirement for the coincidence of actus reus and mens rea is satisfied, the courts have been somewhat flexible in interpreting the concept.

> ⭐ *Example*
>
> *Returning to Philip and Lyra, the facts are now somewhat different. Instead of calming down, Philip decides to take his revenge upon his wife for her affair. He is aware that Lyra has invited some friends around on Sunday and so bakes a cake containing poison on Saturday, planning to serve it to her at the gathering. The guests will be given an identical un-poisoned cake to eat. However, when Lyra returns home late from visiting her parents on Saturday evening, she eats the cake containing poison and dies immediately. Philip is charged with murder.*
>
> - *Lyra ate the cake on Saturday – this is when she died (the actus reus of murder).*
> - *Philip intended to kill his partner – the mens rea for murder – on Sunday but Lyra was already dead by then.*
>
> *Murder may seem the most appropriate charge in the circumstances, but Philip submits that the actus reus and the mens rea do not coincide and, on that basis, he is not guilty of murder.*
>
> The answer to the question as to whether he will succeed is found in case law.

> 📖 *In* Fagan v Metropolitan Police Commissioner *[1969] 1 QB 439, the defendant was sitting in his car when he was approached by a police officer who told him to move the vehicle. Fagan accidentally reversed the car onto the officer's foot. At this point, Fagan lacked the mens rea for an offence as his action was inadvertent. However, when he realised what had happened, he refused to move the car and turned the engine off. He was found guilty of assault on the basis that the actus reus was a continuing act that coincided at some point with the required mens rea.*

The outcome of this case is summarised in **Figure 2.7**.

Criminal Law

Figure 2.7 Outcome of *Fagan v Metropolitan Police Commissioner*

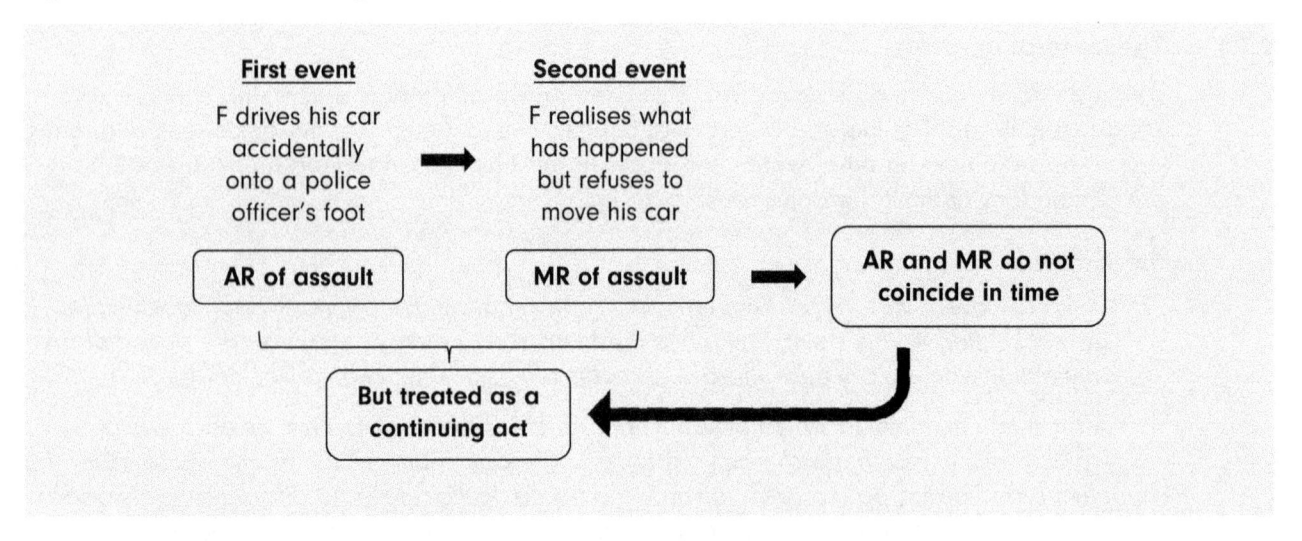

First event: F drives his car accidentally onto a police officer's foot — AR of assault

Second event: F realises what has happened but refuses to move his car — MR of assault

AR and MR do not coincide in time — But treated as a continuing act

In summary, where an actus reus may be brought about by a continuing act, it is sufficient that the defendant had mens rea during its continuance despite not having the mens rea at its commencement.

2.7.3 Single transaction

The examples discussed thus far have involved one act to which the mens rea must be linked. However, the issue has also arisen where a combination of events has led to the unlawful outcome. In such circumstances, the courts have been similarly imaginative in circumventing the principle of coincidence of actus reus and mens rea. They have done this by the interpretation of a number of consecutive events as a 'single transaction'.

Table 2.3 Examples of 'single transaction' from case law

Facts	Outcome	Authority
D struck V on the head intending to kill him. As part of the plan to make the death look like an accident and believing V to be dead, D rolled the body over a cliff. In fact, V died of exposure some hours later.	D was convicted of murder on the basis that it was 'impossible to divide up what was really one series of acts in this way' (Lord Reid).	*Thabo Meli v R* [1954] 1 WLR 288
D fought with V and attempted to strangle her. She fell unconscious and D, believing her to be dead, threw V into a river to dispose of her body. V actually died of drowning.	The Court of Appeal stated that it was sufficient for a conviction if the conduct constituted 'a series of acts which culminated in her death'.	*R v Church* [1966] 1 QB 59

It is apparent from these cases that there are public policy considerations at play. If the event, such as the rolling of the body over the cliff in *Thabo Meli*, is just one of a series of acts, the defendant will be guilty of murder provided they have the mens rea for murder at some point in the transaction. This is logical as a defendant should not avoid liability just because they thought – at the time of death – that their plan had been achieved or that they were either disposing of a body or attempting to cover up a crime.

2.7.4 Summary of coincidence of actus reus and mens rea

- The general rule is that the actus reus and mens rea of an offence must coincide in time in order for the defendant to be guilty of an offence.
- There are two exceptions to this rule:
  - The continuing act principle applies where the defendant's act satisfies the actus reus of an offence and, at some point, they also have the necessary mens rea for that offence.
  - The single transaction principle is relevant where there is a series of events and, from the outset, the defendant is involved in criminal activity. Provided the eventual act that causes death is part of the same sequence of events as the initial act, it does not matter that there is a time lapse between the two.

2.8 Classification of offences

Earlier in this chapter, the mens rea elements of direct and indirect intent were discussed. However, the word 'intent' is also used in a different context in the criminal law, namely to classify offences. An appreciation of what is meant by basic, specific and ulterior intent is vital to understanding, for example, the defence of intoxication.

2.8.1 Offences of basic intent

Crimes of basic intent are those which can be committed either intentionally or recklessly. Simple criminal damage is an offence of basic intent as the actus reus is the destruction or damage of property belonging to another without lawful excuse and the mens rea is that the defendant either intended or was reckless as to that destruction or damage.

The significance of the distinction is that, where the crime alleged is one of basic intent, a defendant cannot rely upon their voluntary intoxication as a defence (see **Chapter 9**).

2.8.2 Offences of specific intent

An offence of specific intent is one that can only be committed intentionally, such as:

- murder – the mens rea is an intention to kill or cause grievous bodily harm; and
- theft – the mens rea requires an intention to permanently deprive.

In contrast to crimes of basic intent, the defendant can successfully plead a defence of intoxication to offences of specific intent in certain circumstances.

2.8.3 Offences of ulterior intent

To complicate matters further, there are offences where the mens rea required goes beyond the actus reus of that offence so the prosecution have to establish an 'extra' element of mens rea against the defendant before they can secure a conviction. **Table 2.4** contains some examples.

Table 2.4 Examples of ulterior mens rea

Offence	Actus reus	Mens rea	Ulterior mens rea
Burglary: TA 1968, s 9(1)(a)	Entering a building (or part) as a trespasser	Knowledge or recklessness as to being a trespasser	Ulterior intent to steal, inflict grievous bodily harm or cause damage inside the building
Aggravated criminal damage	Destroying or damaging property belonging to another	Intention or recklessness as to the damage or destruction	Intention or recklessness as to endangering life by that damage or destruction

In both of these offences, as well as establishing that the defendant committed the required actus reus and mens rea, the prosecution must prove the defendant had an additional mens rea. In other words, that they intended also to bring about some consequence that went beyond the actus reus (for example, a theft for a burglary offence). It is irrelevant whether the defendant actually produces that consequence, thus it does not matter that no-one's life was actually endangered for aggravated criminal damage.

2.8.4 Summary of classification of offences

In conclusion, offences are classified as follows:

- Basic intent – may be committed intentionally or recklessly and cannot rely upon intoxication as a defence.
- Specific intent – may only be committed intentionally and can plead intoxication as a defence.
- Ulterior intent – have a mens rea going beyond the actus reus.

Summary

It is important to understand the concepts of both actus reus and mens rea as these provide the underlying structure to the criminal law. Effectively, they are the 'coat-hanger' upon which hang all the various elements of the different offences that are discussed in later chapters.

Figure 2.8 Actus reus and mens rea

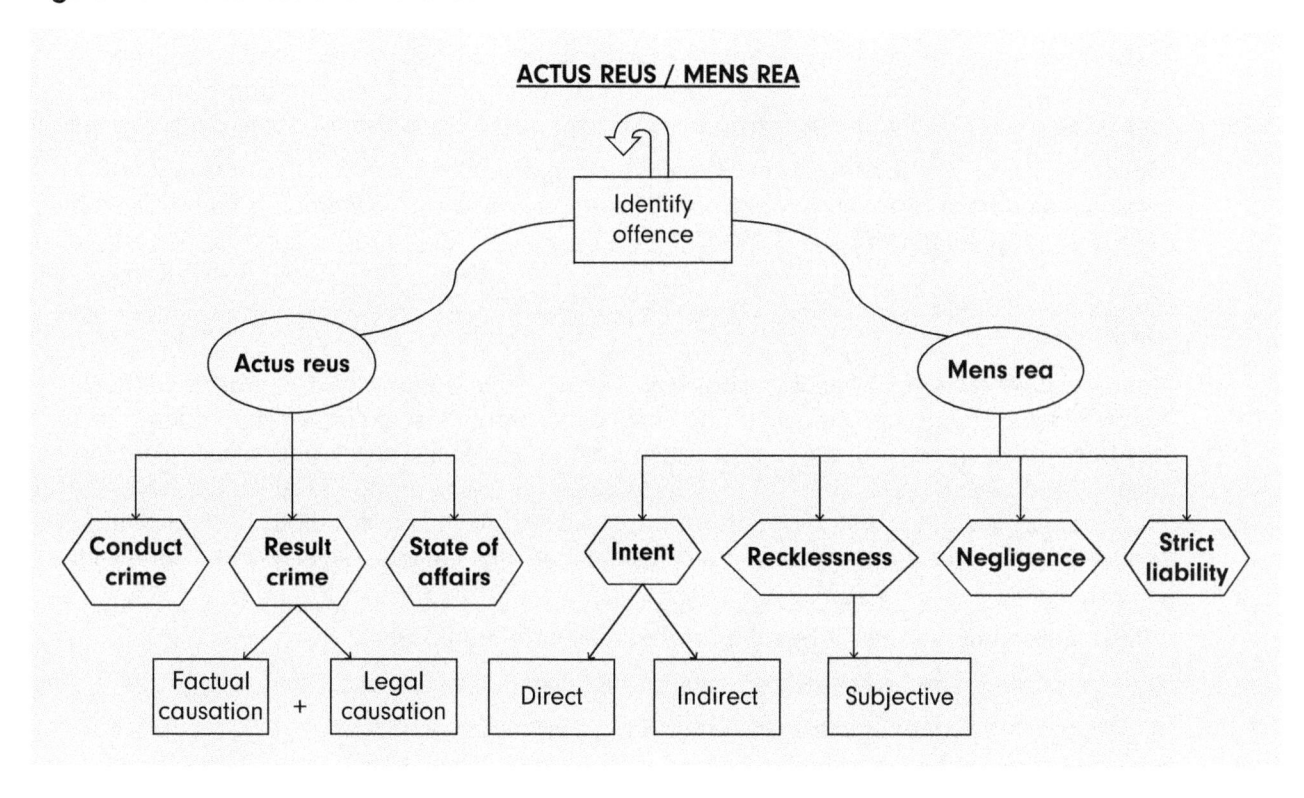

ACTUS REUS / MENS REA

```
                    Identify
                    offence
                   /        \
              Actus reus   Mens rea
```

Actus reus branches: Conduct crime, Result crime, State of affairs
Result crime → Factual causation + Legal causation

Mens rea branches: Intent, Recklessness, Negligence, Strict liability
Intent → Direct, Indirect
Recklessness → Subjective

Sample questions

Question 1

A woman sets fire to her offices in order to claim the insurance money. Unfortunately, one of her employees has stayed late to finish his work and he dies in the fire. The woman is horrified to find that she has killed the employee but accepts that she did not check the building before setting light to it. She also admits she is aware that staff do occasionally stay beyond the official working hours and that she was aware at the time there was a slight risk this may be the case, but the woman cannot recall anyone having been in the offices as late as 11pm before.

Which of the following best describes the woman's mens rea for her employee's death?

A The woman has direct intent to kill her employee.

B The woman indirectly intends to kill her employee.

C The woman is reckless as to causing the death of her employee as she foresaw the risk of death as a consequence of her actions.

D The woman is reckless as to causing the death of her employee as a reasonable person would have foreseen the risk of death due to her actions.

E The woman has no liability for the death of her employee.

Answer

Option C is correct. For recklessness, the risk must be unjustified and it is here, as there is no social utility in setting fire to premises. An awareness of even the smallest risk of causing death would be sufficient to satisfy the mens rea. Although employees rarely stay late, they do on occasion and the defendant did not check the offices were empty.

Option A is wrong as the woman's direct intent – her aim or purpose – was financial and she had no desire to kill her employee. Option B is also wrong. For indirect intent, the consequence (the death) must be virtually certain and this objective test may be satisfied. However, it would be difficult for the prosecution to prove that the woman appreciated this. Her evidence is that she cannot recall anyone having been in the offices at 11pm previously.

Option D is wrong as the test for recklessness is subjective and so what the reasonable person would have foreseen is irrelevant. Option E is wrong as the woman is criminally liable for the employee's death.

Question 2

A man is driving his car when it collides with the vehicle in front which has braked suddenly for no reason. The police are called and carry out a breath test to check whether the man has been drinking. He is shocked to discover that he is over the legal drink driving limit for alcohol and cannot understand why, given that he only drank orange juice at lunchtime. That evening, the man's friend confesses that she added vodka to his drink as she did not realise he had driven to the pub. The man is charged with careless driving and driving with excess alcohol.

Which statement best describes the man's likely criminal liability?

A Not guilty of careless driving, but guilty of driving with excess alcohol.

B Not guilty of either careless driving or driving with excess alcohol.

C Guilty of both careless driving and driving with excess alcohol.

D Guilty of careless driving, but not guilty of driving with excess alcohol.

E Not guilty of careless driving and no charges may be brought for driving with excess alcohol where a drink has been spiked.

Answer

The correct answer is option A. The prosecution are unlikely to prove that the man was guilty of careless driving. To do so, they would need to prove that he was negligent, namely, that his driving fell below what would be expected of a competent and careful driver. This is unlikely because the collision was caused when the vehicle in front braked suddenly without warning. For this reason, options C and D are wrong.

However, the man is likely to be convicted of driving with excess alcohol despite the fact he believed he was drinking orange juice and his drink was spiked because this is an offence of strict liability. Thus, options B and D are wrong. Option E is wrong as there is no rule that states a person may not be charged in circumstances where their drink was spiked.

Question 3

A defendant throws a punch towards a man after they argue outside a pub, but he hits the woman beside the man instead. The impact is such that she is knocked unconscious and slumps back against the garden wall. The defendant picks the woman up but, as he tries to move her back into the pub, she slips from his grasp. She bangs her head on the pavement and dies from a fractured skull.

Which of the following statements correctly describes the defendant's liability for the woman's death?

A   The doctrine of transferred malice does not apply because the defendant's intention to punch the man cannot be transferred to the woman.

B   There is no need to consider transferred malice because the defendant punched the woman and the mens rea of assault includes recklessness.

C   The doctrine of transferred malice would apply if the man had intended to punch the wall rather than hit a person.

D   The man is not liable for the woman's death because the actus reus and mens rea do not coincide in time.

E   The man is not liable for the woman's death because the application of unlawful force and the act causing the woman's death are separate in time.

Answer

B is the correct option. Where the offence may be committed recklessly, there is no need to consider transferred malice as the defendant is only required to foresee the risk of any harm to anyone.

Option A is wrong as the doctrine of transferred malice will apply. The defendant's intention to punch the man may be transferred to the woman as he commits the actus reus of assault against her and this is the same offence which he intends for the man. Option C is also wrong. Malice may be transferred from person to person, or from object to object, but not where the actus reus and mens rea relate to different types of offences. In this example, the man commits assault but intends criminal damage.

Option D does not correctly describe the man's liability. Where a combination of events has led to the unlawful outcome, the courts have interpreted these consecutive events as a 'single transaction'. This is a way of circumventing the requirement for the actus reus and the mens rea to coincide in time. Option E is wrong as the unlawful application of force (hitting the woman) and the eventual act causing death (dropping her) are part of the same sequence of events, so the fact there was a lapse in time between the two does not enable the man to escape liability.

3 Assaults

3.1	Introduction	46
3.2	Hierarchy of assaults	46
3.3	Common law assaults	47
3.4	Simple assault	47
3.5	Battery	50
3.6	Statutory assaults	52
3.7	Assault occasioning actual bodily harm (OAPA 1861, s 47)	52
3.8	Wounding or inflicting grievous bodily harm (OAPA 1861, s 20)	55
3.9	Wounding or causing grievous bodily harm with intent (OAPA 1861, s 18)	58
3.10	Overview of the non-fatal offences against the person	61
3.11	Consent as a defence	62

SQE1 syllabus

By the end of this chapter you will be able to apply relevant core legal principles and rules appropriately and effectively, at the level of a competent newly qualified solicitor in practice, to realistic client-based and ethical problems and situations in the area of **assaults**.

In this chapter, the statutory assaults will also be referenced using the Offences Against the Person Act 1861 as this is how they are referred to in practice. Specifically, assault occasioning actual bodily harm is known as a section 47 assault, wounding or *inflicting* grievous bodily harm is called a section 20 assault and wounding or *causing* grievous bodily harm with intent is a section 18 assault. These terms will be used interchangeably. Otherwise, case names, or statutory or regulatory authorities are provided for illustrative purposes.

Learning outcomes

The learning outcomes for this chapter are:

- to explain the definitions of both common law and statutory assaults and describe how to apply these to factual scenarios; and
- to understand how the defence of consent operates to absolve a defendant from liability for assault in certain situations.

3.1 Introduction

Assault has been on the statute books for over 150 years and for considerably longer as a common law offence, making it one of the more established of crimes. Assaults may take place in a range of situations, from brawls in nightclubs, to fights between rival teams at football matches, amongst gangs establishing territory or imposing control and in the context of domestic violence. According to government statistics, just under 2% of the adult population are assaulted each year and, although the percentage is lower than the high of nearly 5% in 1995, for each person this is a significant event. It should also be borne in mind that this represents the national average so the figure would be much higher or lower in some areas. Dealing with such behaviour is important from a social policy perspective to ensure that people may go about their daily lives without fear.

This chapter will explore the main non-fatal offences against the person. There are a number of such offences ranging in severity from the infliction of really serious injuries to causing mental harm to simply instilling fear. Indeed, assault is best understood as a generic term referring to a category of related offences rather than a single crime.

3.2 Hierarchy of assaults

The criminal law distinguishes between a defendant who so severely attacks a victim that they almost die and a defendant who merely pushes someone causing no injury at all. To recognise this differentiation, there is a sliding scale of offences dependent upon the degree of harm caused to the victim and, to a lesser extent, the mens rea of the perpetrator.

In order of severity, beginning with the least serious, the offences are:

- Assault
- Battery
- Assault occasioning actual bodily harm
- Maliciously wounding or inflicting grievous bodily harm
- Wounding or causing grievous bodily harm with intent

The classification and maximum sentences reflect this hierarchy as illustrated below. 'Summary only' means the offence can only be dealt with in the magistrates' court, whereas an either way offence may be tried in either the magistrates' or the Crown Court. Indictable only offences are the most serious and must be heard in the Crown Court.

Table 3.1 Hierarchy of assaults

Offence	Statute	Classification	Sentence (maximum)
Assault	Common law offence but charged under s 39 CJA 1988	Summary only	6 months' imprisonment and/or a fine
Battery	Common law offence but charged under s 39 CJA 1988	Summary only	6 months' imprisonment and/or a fine

Offence	Statute	Classification	Sentence (maximum)
Assault occasioning actual bodily harm	s 47 OAPA 1861	Either way	5 years' imprisonment
Maliciously wounding or inflicting grievous bodily harm	s 20 OAPA 1861	Either way	5 years' imprisonment
Wounding or causing grievous bodily harm with intent	s 18 OAPA 1861	Indictable only	Life imprisonment

3.3 Common law assaults

There are two assaults that derive from the common law, namely:

- simple assault – also known as 'technical' assault; and
- battery – which may be referred to as 'physical' assault.

These two offences are collectively known as common assault and the main difference between them is that, for the offence of simple assault, the accused need not make any physical contact with the victim at all. In practice, assault and battery normally happen together so that, for example, the defendant may raise their fist as a threat before actually hitting the victim.

Although they are referred to in statute, s 39 of the Criminal Justice Act (CJA) 1988 merely confirms that the offences are summary only offences triable in the magistrates' court and provides the maximum sentence; no definition is included.

3.4 Simple assault

Simple assault occurs where the assailant intentionally or recklessly causes the victim to apprehend immediate and unlawful personal force. The defendant does not need to actually touch the victim at all. If they do, this is the entirely separate common law offence of battery.

Figure 3.1 Simple assault

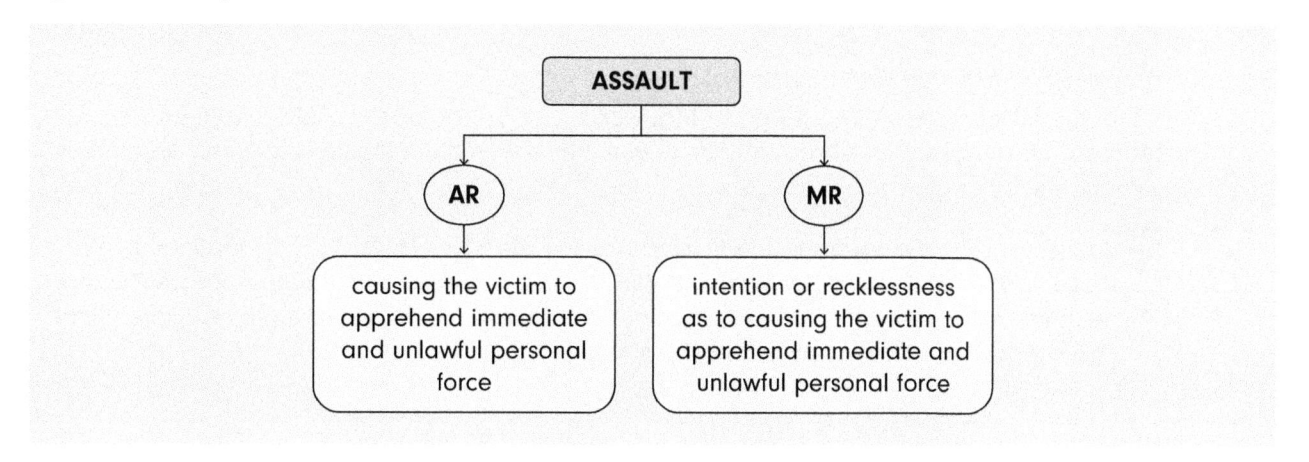

```
                    ASSAULT
                   /        \
                 AR          MR
                  |           |
        causing the victim   intention or recklessness
        to apprehend         as to causing the victim to
        immediate and        apprehend immediate and
        unlawful personal    unlawful personal force
        force
```

Criminal Law

3.4.1 Actus reus

To determine whether the accused has satisfied the actus reus of simple assault, namely causing the victim to apprehend immediate and unlawful personal force, the offence must be broken down into its constituent parts.

3.4.1.1 Unlawful

The first point to bear in mind is that not all assaults are unlawful. A police officer may use reasonable force to make an arrest, perhaps to apprehend someone running away from a crime scene; and an individual may use reasonable force to defend themselves, or others, or indeed their property.

3.4.1.2 Apprehension

The actus reus requires the victim to apprehend unlawful force or violence, but what does this actually mean? An assault may be committed in a variety of ways and those set out below are just some suggestions.

> ⭐ *Example*
>
> *Rhys is a violent young man. He:*
>
> *(a) chases after Liam threatening to slash his face;*
>
> *(b) pulls a gun and points it at Madesh;*
>
> *(c) raises his arm as if to strike his mother, Nancy; and*
>
> *(d) sends a text message to Oliver stating 'u r dead'.*
>
> *In all these situations, Rhys has committed the actus reus of assault as it is the apprehension of unlawful force that is important. Thus, the fact that there is no violence or touching is irrelevant as this is not a requirement. As a consequence, for simple assault, no injury or harm actually needs to be caused.*
>
> *What if Rhys:*
>
> *(e) threatens to push Pip, a martial arts expert who is not afraid of Rhys; and*
>
> *(f) creeps up behind Hamish unnoticed and jumps on his back?*
>
> *In scenario (e), the actus reus of assault is satisfied. This is because the victim is only required to apprehend the force, in other words, be aware of it. They do not have to fear it in the sense of being frightened. As long as Pip believes he is about to be unlawfully touched, that is sufficient.*
>
> *With regard to scenario (f), because Rhys has approached unnoticed, Hamish did not apprehend any unlawful force at all so Rhys is not guilty of simple assault (although he may be liable for battery as discussed later in this chapter).*

3.4.1.3 Assault by words or silence

Although this may seem illogical given that words can be far more intimidating than actions, for many years there was uncertainty as to whether words alone could amount to an assault without any other gesture.

> *In the combined appeals of* R v Ireland *and* R v Burstow *[1998] AC 147, the law on this issue was settled. The defendant in* Ireland *made repeated silent telephone calls to three women over a period of months. The calls were generally made at night and sometimes the women could hear heavy breathing.*

In R v Burstow, the defendant harassed a woman over an eight-month period. In addition to making silent (and abusive) telephone calls to her, he distributed offensive cards in the street where she lived, turned up uninvited at her home and place of work and surreptitiously took photographs of her.

In both cases, the victims suffered psychiatric illness as a result of this unwanted attention. In confirming the defendants' guilt, the House of Lords held that:

- *Words alone can amount to an assault as 'a thing said is also a thing done'.*
- *A silent telephone call may be an assault depending upon the facts of the case.*

The justification for the decision was the impact of the repeated calls on the victims; hence, a pattern of contact is likely to be required.

3.4.1.4 Immediacy

For simple assault, the actus reus is only satisfied where the defendant causes the victim to apprehend *immediate* and unlawful personal violence. As a consequence, realising that someone may inflict such force in the future will not suffice. Thus, if the defendant says: 'I'll be around next week to give you a kicking', they are not guilty of assault as the force will not occur for several days.

However, it will be enough if the victim fears that force *could* occur immediately. This applies particularly where modern technology is used, such as a mobile telephone, as the defendant may in fact be very close to the victim when making the threat of violence, meaning they could strike at any time.

3.4.1.5 Conditional threats

There are occasions where the defendant will make a conditional threat, for example: 'If you don't shut up, I'll slap you!' Although, to some extent, whether the victim is hit or not is in their own hands, the law takes the view that the unjustified restriction on their personal liberty is unwarranted. As a consequence, the defendant could still be liable for assault provided that the conditional threat also satisfies the 'immediacy' requirement.

3.4.2 Mens rea

For the mens rea, the prosecution must establish that the defendant intended to cause the victim to apprehend immediate and unlawful personal force, or was reckless as to whether such apprehension is caused.

The test for recklessness is subjective and so the defendant must personally foresee the risk and go on to take it.

⭐ Example

Brendan is of low intelligence. He fires his air rifle across a field towards a tree to practise his shooting skills, narrowly missing his young cousin (Molly) who is on her way to feed her horses. He is only liable for assault if the prosecution can prove that Brendan himself was aware of the risk of causing Molly to apprehend unlawful force as, on the evidence, it was clearly not his intention to do so.

3.4.3 Summary of assault

Figure 3.2 Assault

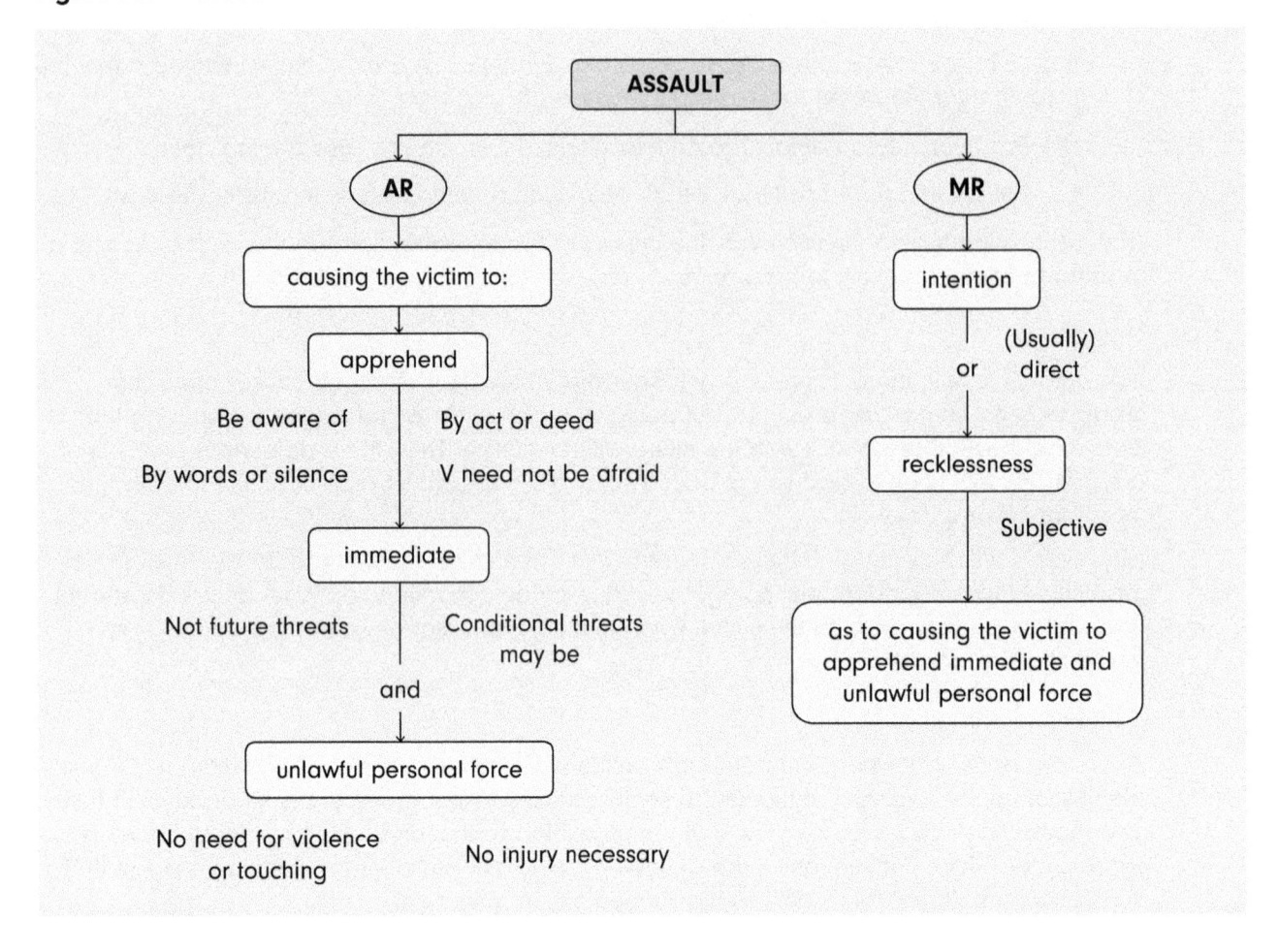

```
                           ASSAULT
                   ┌─────────┴─────────┐
                  AR                   MR
                   │                    │
         causing the victim to:      intention
                   │                    │     (Usually)
               apprehend             or    direct
                   │                    │
  Be aware of    By act or deed    recklessness
                   │                    │
By words or silence  V need not be afraid   Subjective
                   │                    │
               immediate          as to causing the victim to
                   │              apprehend immediate and
Not future threats  Conditional threats    unlawful personal force
                   │     may be
                  and
                   │
          unlawful personal force

   No need for violence      No injury necessary
      or touching
```

3.5 Battery

If simple assault is causing the victim to apprehend immediate and unlawful personal force, physical assault is the infliction of that force. Because any unlawful touching may suffice, the offence is also referred to as 'physical assault'.

Figure 3.3 Battery

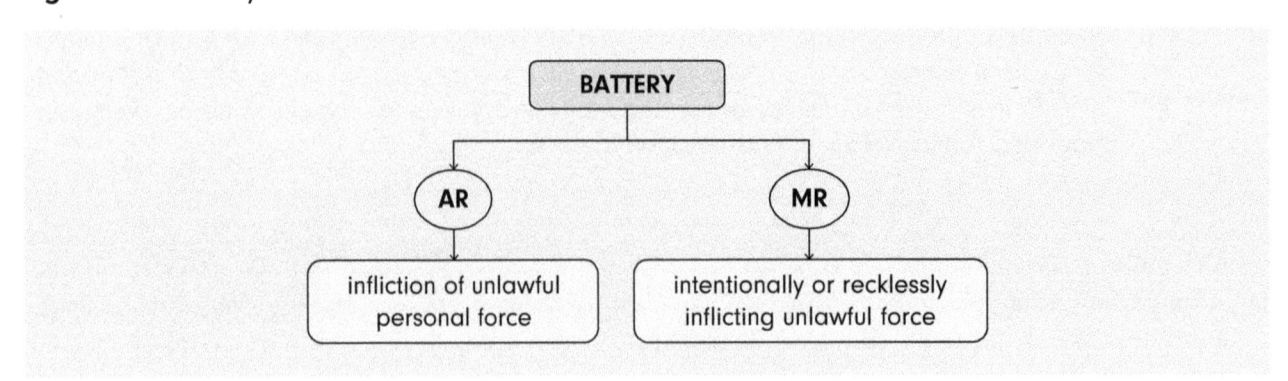

```
                    BATTERY
              ┌────────┴────────┐
             AR                 MR
              │                  │
     infliction of unlawful   intentionally or recklessly
        personal force         inflicting unlawful force
```

3.5.1 Actus reus

For the offence of battery, the actus reus is the *infliction* of unlawful personal force by the accused upon the victim. However, force may be applied in a variety of ways.

(a) By direct bodily contact between two people including pushing, prodding or hitting. This can be with, or without, a weapon such as a knife or a stick.

(b) The application of force may not involve direct contact and may include where the defendant throws an object or spits at a victim, or even purposely cycles over their foot.

(c) A defendant who sets their dog on the victim or who deliberately places an obstacle behind a door so that the victim trips over it are examples of the indirect application of force.

However the force is applied, what is apparent is that the degree required is very slight and even the least touching will satisfy the actus reus. The prosecution do not need to establish that any harm is suffered by the victim.

3.5.2 Mens rea

The mens rea of battery is intention or recklessness in relation to the infliction of unlawful force on another person. As with simple assault, the subjective standard of recklessness applies. However, for the prosecution to succeed in convicting the accused of battery, the defendant must have intended or foreseen the actual *infliction* of force, not just the victim's apprehension of this. Furthermore, there is no need to show intent or recklessness as to causing any injury.

3.5.3 Practical application of assault and battery

Usually the two offences of assault and battery will go together so that the victim believes they are about to be hit, and then they are. However, there can be a physical assault alone, for example, where the defendant approaches the victim from behind, unheard, and then hits them over the head. Because the victim did not apprehend the force (as they did not hear the defendant), there is no simple assault – just a physical one.

Whether one or both of these common law assaults have been committed will depend upon the particular facts.

⭐ *Example*

(a) *Craig tells his teenage daughter, Fay, that if she continues to see her girlfriend, Tilly, he will break every bone in Tilly's body. Has Craig committed simple assault? Although there is a clear threat:*

- *Fay does not apprehend any violence against her as the threat is directed against her girlfriend; and neither does Tilly as she was not present when the words were spoken.*

(b) *What if Craig speaks these words to Tilly?*

- *It may be simple assault but only if Tilly apprehends* immediate *unlawful violence. Craig's threat is a conditional one – he will only attack Tilly* if *she continues to see Fay so it is not immediate.*

The effect is that Craig is not guilty of simple assault. This is an unusual example and most common law assaults are much more straightforward, with a clear threat by the defendant to the victim causing them to fear immediate violence.

(c) *Fay ignores her father. In anger, Craig seeks out Tilly and punches her in the face.*

- *Now Craig has committed an offence – that of battery – because he has actually inflicted unlawful force on Tilly.*

Although this scenario raises a number of issues, in reality, most common law assaults are quite clear on the facts.

3.6 Statutory assaults

For the remainder of this chapter, the statutory offences of assault will be explored. All of these offences may be found in the OAPA 1861. Because of this, some of the original language is rather old-fashioned but, fortunately, the terms have been given modern meanings.

Note that, in this context, the word 'assault', is used to mean either of the common law offences of simple assault or battery unless clearly stated to the contrary.

3.7 Assault occasioning actual bodily harm (OAPA 1861, s 47)

The first of the statutory offences is contained in s 47 of the OAPA 1861 and it creates the offence of assault occasioning actual bodily harm. This is an either way offence, which means it can be tried either in the magistrates' or the Crown Court.

Section 47 provides that:

> Whosoever shall be convicted upon an indictment of any assault occasioning actual bodily harm shall be liable...to be imprisoned for any term not exceeding five years.

3.7.1 Actus reus

The actus reus is that the defendant commits a simple assault or battery that causes (occasions) actual bodily harm. In other words, it is a common law assault with the added 'extra' of injury.

3.7.1.1 Assault or battery

A s 47 assault is an aggravated form of common assault as it requires proof, not only that an assault or a battery has been committed, but also that *harm* has been caused to the victim. Because of this, it is a more serious crime.

3.7.1.2 Occasioning

The second element of the actus reus is that the assault or battery *causes* harm and the usual rules on causation (factual and legal) will apply – see **Chapter 1** for further details on this aspect.

3.7.1.3 Actual bodily harm

Although the wording of s 47 makes it clear that the assault or battery must cause harm, there is no further guidance in the statute as to how serious the injury must be to satisfy this offence. Fortunately, case law provides some assistance.

> According to R v Miller [1954] 2 QB 282, actual bodily harm means any hurt or injury calculated to interfere with the health or comfort of the victim. The injury need not be serious or permanent in nature, but it must be more than 'transient or trifling'.

Each case will be decided on its facts and even a bruise or swelling may suffice, depending upon the severity.

⭐ Examples

The defendant causes actual bodily harm where they:

- *give the victim a split lip;*
- *stab the victim's arm so that the injury requires three stitches;*
- *cause significant bruising to the victim's face;*
- *kick the victim's leg causing swelling to the knee;*
- *cut a substantial piece of the victim's hair; or*
- *cause a temporary loss of consciousness;*

but not where the victim only suffers:

- *a very small bruise;*
- *a minor scratch; or*
- *a red mark on the skin, from a slap, which quickly fades.*

3.7.1.4 Mental harm

The question of whether harm could include psychiatric injury was considered in the combined appeals of *Ireland* and *Burstow* (referred to at **3.4.1**). The judges confirmed that it could, with the severity of the psychological harm determining the statutory assault for which the defendant is liable. On a practical point, medical evidence will be required by the prosecution to establish a more serious assault and, in this context, it would almost certainly be from a psychiatrist.

Table 3.2 contains some examples of the types of mental harm that may be caused and an indication of whether this is likely to be sufficient to satisfy the actus reus of a s 47 assault.

Table 3.2 Examples of mental harm

Actual bodily harm	NOT actual bodily harm
• anxiety neurosis • reactive depression	• strong emotions such as rage, extreme fear or distress • a panic attack

For the actus reus of a s 47 assault, the psychiatric condition must be a recognisable clinical condition, thus (for example) an hysterical or nervous disposition is unlikely to suffice.

3.7.2 Mens rea

The mens rea is that the defendant must intend or be reckless as to a simple assault or battery only. Specifically, there is no need to show the defendant intended additionally to cause actual bodily harm.

> *This principle of law was confirmed by the case of* R v Savage; R v Parmenter [1991] 1 AC 699. *The defendant intended to throw a pint of beer over the victim, but the glass also left her hand and broke and a piece of glass cut the victim's wrist. Despite the defendant's lack of desire to cause harm, she was convicted of the offence.*

The effect of this ruling is that all the prosecution have to prove is that the accused (for example) hit the victim deliberately and, provided injury is caused of sufficient gravity, they will be guilty of a s 47 assault.

⭐ Example

Gavin punched Kayden in the face causing him a black eye (bruising around his eye). In his police interview, he stated: 'I admit I intended to hit Kayden but I didn't mean to injure or harm him and the thought never entered my head that I might'.

Gavin has satisfied the actus reus of an assault under s 47 because:

- *he has punched Kayden (the assault), and*
- *this caused (occasioned)*
- *a black eye – an injury that would interfere with Kayden's health and comfort (actual bodily harm).*

With regard to the mens rea, Gavin must intend or be reckless as to the assault only:

- *Gavin admits that he intended to assault Kayden and the fact that he did not intend or foresee the risk of any harm or injury is irrelevant as this is not required. Gavin is liable for this offence.*

To conclude, there is no difference between the mens rea for simple assault or battery and the mens rea for s 47 of the OAPA 1861. The only difference between the offences is in relation to the actus reus – for s 47 some bodily harm must be caused.

3.7.3 Summary of s 47 assault

To be criminally liable for a s 47 assault, the defendant must cause some harm (actual bodily harm) but, crucially, it is not necessary to intend or be reckless as to the specific injury suffered, or indeed any injury at all. The defendant need only intend or be reckless as to the assault or battery.

Figure 3.4 Assault occasioning actual bodily harm

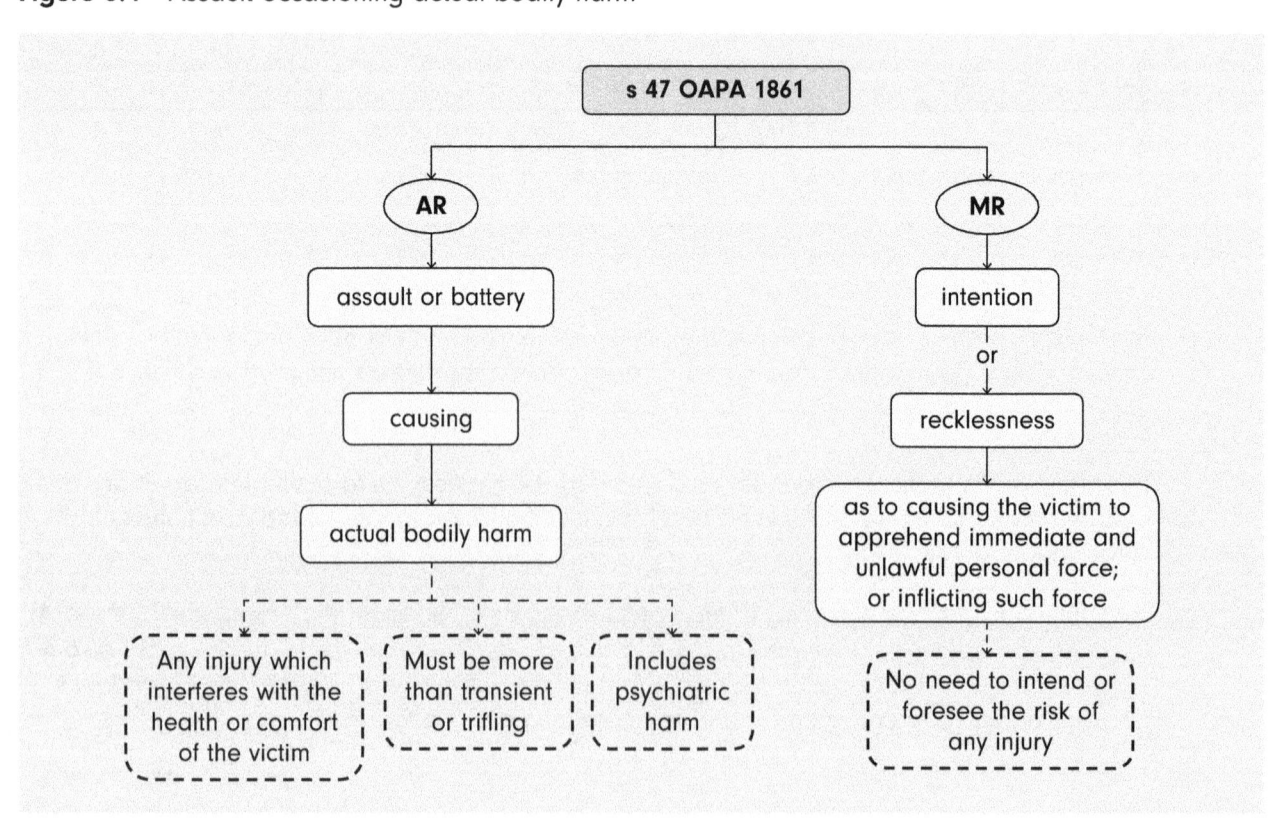

3.8 Wounding or inflicting grievous bodily harm (OAPA 1861, s 20)

Section 20 of the OAPA 1861 is the next most serious assault and it creates offences of inflicting grievous bodily harm or wounding. The statute provides:

> Whoever shall unlawfully and maliciously wound or inflict any grievous bodily harm upon any other person ... shall be liable ... to imprisonment for a term not exceeding five years.

As with the s 47 assault, the offence is triable either way so may be heard in the magistrates' or the Crown Court. Even though it is a more serious offence as wounding or grievous bodily harm must be established rather than just actual bodily harm, it carries the same maximum penalty of five years' imprisonment.

3.8.1 Actus reus

The actus reus is that the defendant unlawfully wounds *or* unlawfully inflicts grievous bodily harm on the victim.

3.8.1.1 Grievous bodily harm

Grievous bodily harm is defined in the case of *DPP v Smith* [1961] AC 290 as 'really serious harm'. The judges were of the view that the term should be given its ordinary and natural meaning. This is a question of fact for the jury, which considers the effect of the injuries on the particular victim, taking account of their age and health; thus, it will be whatever the magistrates or the jury regards as serious enough.

Examples of grievous bodily harm would include:

- a fractured skull
- severe internal injuries
- broken limbs
- disfigurement caused by acid being thrown on the victim
- really serious psychiatric injury.

The statute refers to grievous bodily harm being 'inflicted' rather than 'caused'. However, the courts have confirmed that, for the purposes of the criminal law, these words may be taken as having the same meaning.

In R v Dica [2004] EWCA Crim 1103, the defendant, knowing he was HIV positive, was found guilty of a s 20 assault after having unprotected consensual sexual intercourse with two women, who were unaware of his medical condition. He was found to have inflicted grievous bodily harm after they both later tested positive for the virus.

3.8.1.2 Wounding

Wounding is rather different. It is defined as the breaking of both layers of the skin resulting in bleeding – *Moriarty v Brookes* (1834) 6 C&P 684. Because there is no reference to the wound being serious, rather oddly, a minor cut would be sufficient.

For example, a wound would include:

- a cut of any size or severity
- a scratch that draws blood
- a cut to the inside of the mouth

  but not

- bruising or internal bleeding
- a rupture of the blood vessels in the eye.

Differentiating between different types of injury can be very important in establishing which offence is appropriate and may be somewhat problematic. To assist, the Crown Prosecution Service provides some guidance on what injuries would be sufficient to be charged under s 20 of the OAPA 1861. Indeed, it is at this point that academic and practical law diverge as, although a small cut would satisfy the actus reus for this serious offence, it is very unlikely to be charged as such.

3.8.2 Mens rea

The mens rea required for the s 20 offence is to 'maliciously' wound or inflict grievous bodily harm on the victim. However, this rather archaic word has been given a more modern interpretation and is now taken to mean intention or recklessness.

3.8.2.1 What must the defendant intend or foresee?

The question as to what degree of harm the accused must intend or be reckless as to, before being liable for a s 20 assault, has been determined by the judges.

Returning to the case of R v Savage; R v Parmenter, the House of Lords stated that the defendant need only intend or be reckless as to causing some bodily harm or, in other words, actual bodily harm. It is not necessary for the prosecution to prove that the defendant intended or foresaw really serious harm (grievous bodily harm) or the exact nature of the harm that in fact occurred.

As with s 47, for the more serious s 20 offence, the defendant must intend or be reckless as to a *different* injury to that which resulted. Whilst the actus reus requires a wound or grievous bodily harm, the defendant need not intend or be reckless as to an injury of this gravity. It is sufficient that they have foreseen a risk that *some* physical harm to some person will result.

3.8.3 Summary of s 20 assault

Figure 3.5 provides an overview of the elements required for an assault under s 20 of the OAPA 1861. The offence appears inconsistent in that the smallest cut (such as the pricking of a finger with a pin) will satisfy the actus reus provided it draws blood, but if not, really serious harm is required. For the mens rea, the level of harm anticipated by the accused is lower – actual rather than grievous bodily harm.

Assaults

Figure 3.5 Maliciously wounding or inflicting grievous bodily harm

```
                          s 20 OAPA 1861
                         /              \
                       AR                MR
                      /  \                |
                 wound    grievous     intention
                   |      bodily harm     or
            cutting of both  |         recklessness
            layers of the   really         |
            skin            serious     as to causing
                            harm        actual bodily harm
                                             |
                                       anything which interferes
                                       with the health or comfort
                                       of the victim
```

3.8.4 Practical application of s 20 assault

Whether a defendant is liable for a s 20 offence will depend, to a considerable extent, upon what was going through their mind at the time of the assault.

⭐ *Example*

Lukas is involved in an argument with Ahmed in a restaurant, during which he punches Ahmed in the face. Ahmed stumbles backwards, falls over and hits his head on the corner of a table, fracturing his skull. Lukas is questioned by the police and his comments are recorded as set out below.

Table 3.3 Examples of mens rea for s 20 assault

Extracts from Lukas' police interview	Does this satisfy the mens rea for a s 20 assault?
Ahmed was asking for it! I punched him very hard as I wanted him to really suffer!	Yes: Lukas wanted to inflict really serious harm – this is sufficient as the defendant need only intend some bodily harm for s 20.
I admit I punched Ahmed really hard. I thought I would break his jaw but I never intended to fracture his skull. I feel so bad about that.	Yes: Lukas intended grievous bodily harm. The fact that he envisaged a broken jaw and not a fractured skull is irrelevant. The defendant need not intend the precise injury that is caused.

(continued)

Table 3.3 (*continued*)

Extracts from Lukas' police interview	Does this satisfy the mens rea for a s 20 assault?
I never meant to hurt Ahmed so badly. I suppose I realised that I might harm him, but I didn't want it to happen.	Yes: Although Lukas did not foresee the actual injury caused nor its severity, he is still liable for a s 20 assault. By stating that he realised he might harm Ahmed, Lukas is admitting that he foresaw the risk and went on to take it. Thus, he is reckless as to causing some bodily harm and this is sufficient for the mens rea of a s 20 assault.
I agree I intended to hit him but it honestly never entered my head that there was any chance of causing him an injury.	No: Lukas is admitting that he intended the assault but he did not foresee the risk of any harm. Hence, there is no mens rea for s 20 as intention or recklessness as to causing some harm or injury is a vital element of the mens rea. (Note that Lukas could, however, be charged with a s 47 assault in these circumstances.)

3.9 Wounding or causing grievous bodily harm with intent (OAPA 1861, s 18)

The most serious of the assaults is to be found in s 18 of the OAPA 1861. To reflect this, s 18 offences are indictable only and must be sent to the Crown Court for trial. The grave nature of the offence is also demonstrated by the maximum sentence, which is life imprisonment. The statute provides:

> Whosoever shall unlawfully and maliciously by any means whatsoever wound or cause any grievous bodily harm to any person with intent to do some grievous bodily harm to any person or with intent to resist arrest or prevent the lawful apprehension or detainer of any person, shall be guilty of an offence, and being convicted thereof shall be liable to imprisonment for life.

Understanding the non-fatal offences is not easy given that they tend to overlap, as demonstrated by s 47 where the definition of the assault includes the common law offences within it. This issue is also apparent with s 18 where the actus reus is actually the same as for s 20, namely, wounding or causing grievous bodily harm. However, once the mens rea is taken into account, s 18 is even more confusing as it creates multiple offences – four variations in total.

3.9.1 Actus reus

The actus reus of this offence is unlawfully wounding or causing grievous bodily harm to a person. This is almost identical to the definition of s 20 with the only difference being the use of the word 'cause' rather than 'inflict'. However, case law has established that these terms are interchangeable.

As a consequence, there are two ways in which a defendant may commit the actus reus of a s 18 offence, either:

(a) by wounding or

(b) by causing grievous bodily harm.

The definitions of these are discussed above at **3.8** in the context of s 20 of the OAPA 1861.

3.9.2 Mens rea

The mens rea of s 18 may also be satisfied in two distinct ways:

(a) with intent to cause grievous bodily harm; or

(b) with intent to resist or prevent the lawful apprehension or detention of any person, coupled with the intention or recklessness as to causing some bodily harm.

3.9.2.1 Intention to cause grievous bodily harm

In most prosecutions for s 18 assault, the defendant will be charged on the basis that they intended to cause grievous bodily harm. It is important to note that an intention to cause lesser harm or a wound will not suffice; and nor will recklessness.

★ Example

Valerie lunges at Samrita with a kitchen knife causing a deep cut to her face.

(a) Valerie admits that her aim or purpose was to scar Samrita permanently. She has the (direct) intent to cause grievous bodily harm and satisfies the mens rea for s 18.

(b) Valerie states that her aim was only to cut Samrita in a very minor way. Although she has an intention to wound, this is not sufficient for a s 18 assault. Furthermore, although she may be reckless as to causing grievous bodily harm in such circumstances, again, this would not satisfy the mens rea.

When deciding whether to charge a defendant with a s 18 offence, there are practical difficulties for the prosecution to overcome in establishing the mens rea as the threshold is so high. Evidence of clear planning, the use of a weapon, or repeated punching or stamping would all suggest an intention to cause grievous bodily harm but each case will turn on its facts.

3.9.2.2 Intention to resist or prevent arrest

The alternative mens rea applies where the defendant intended to resist or prevent the lawful apprehension of any person. In simple terms, the accused intended to resist or prevent an arrest. However, this is only one of the requirements and the other element needed to satisfy this mens rea is that the defendant intended or foresaw that some harm would be caused.

★ Example

PC Gore is called to attend a fight outside the Red Lion public house. He tells Tracey that he is arresting her for a public order offence. She panics in response and, in an effort to escape, she lashes out at him, causing a deep scratch to PC Gore's face, which draws blood.

- *Actus reus: Tracey satisfies the actus reus of a s 18 assault as she has wounded the officer by scratching him.*

- *Mens rea: Tracey did not intend grievous bodily harm as her intention was to escape. However, she did have the intention to resist arrest and, whilst she may not have intended some bodily harm, she was reckless as to this by lashing out at PC Gore.*

Thus, the only time a defendant who is reckless as to causing some bodily harm or worse may be successfully prosecuted for a s 18 assault is if the prosecution can also prove the ulterior intent, namely an intention to resist or prevent arrest of any person. This will be a rare event in practice, particularly as there are a number of other offences with which a defendant could be charged in such circumstances.

3.9.3 The four ways of committing a s 18 assault

The effect of the wording of s 18 is that there are four different ways of committing this most serious of assaults and these are summarised below. Note that, although the options have been categorised into 'ordinary' victims and 'police officers' as victims, this is to assist understanding and is an over-simplification. For example, a police officer may be assaulted in the same way as any other member of the public, in which case the prosecution would need to prove that the accused intended grievous bodily harm. However, this summary provides an overview of the correct approach to take when analysing a defendant's liability.

Four varieties of s 18 of the OAPA 1861:

'Ordinary' victim

1. AR – wound;   MR – intention to cause GBH
2. AR – GBH;   MR – intention to cause GBH

'Police officer' victim

3. AR – wound;   MR – intention to resist/prevent arrest <u>and</u> intention/recklessness as to causing ABH
4. AR – GBH;   MR – intention to resist/prevent arrest <u>and</u> intention/recklessness as to causing ABH

3.9.4 Summary of s 18 assaults

- Unlawfully wounding or causing grievous bodily harm with intent is a statutory offence under s 18 of the OAPA 1861.
- The only difference to s 20 lies in the mens rea as both require a wound or grievous bodily harm for the actus reus.
- The mens rea is intention to cause grievous bodily harm unless the circumstances are such that the accused is resisting or preventing an arrest, where the defendant may intend or be reckless as to causing some bodily harm.

Figure 3.6 Wounding or causing grievous bodily harm with intent

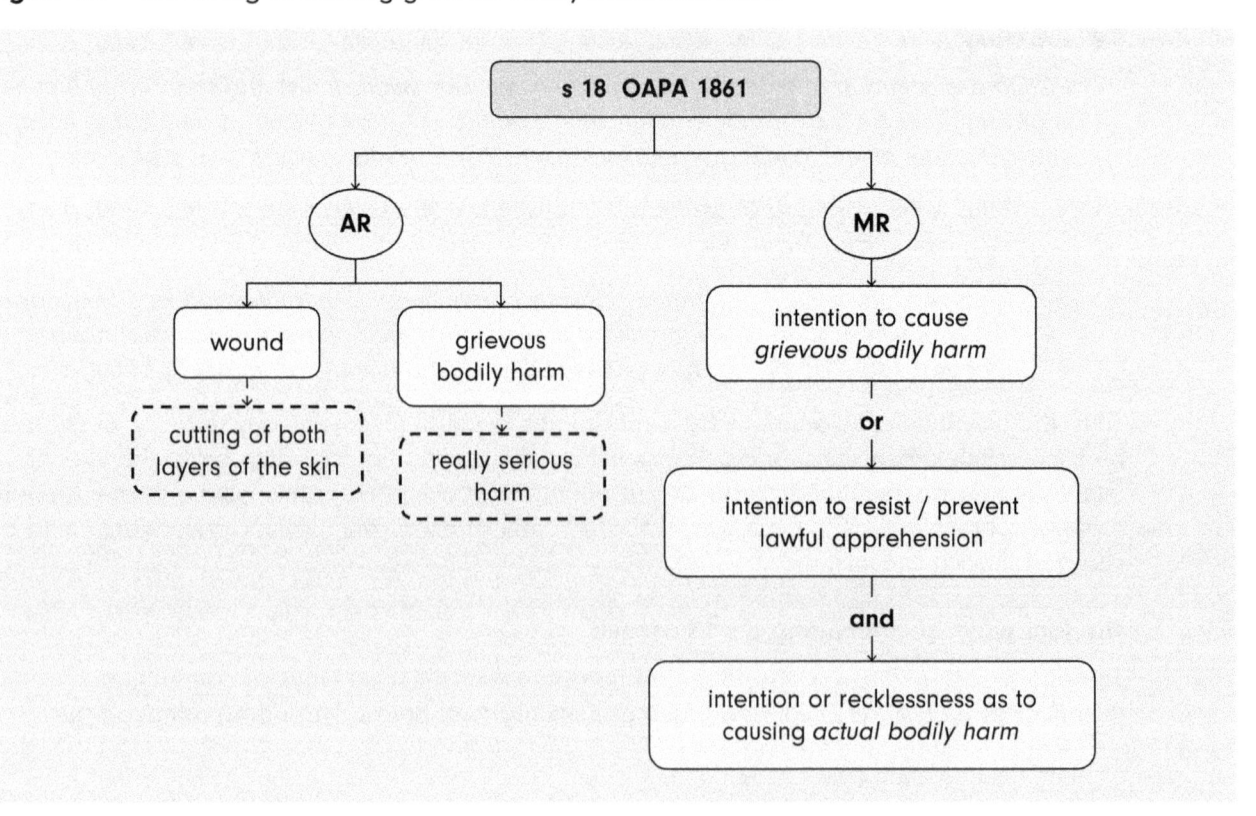

3.10 Overview of the non-fatal offences against the person

It is easy to confuse the different elements of the non-fatal offences and so, to assist, **Table 3.4** summarises the main requirements of each.

Table 3.4 Actus reus and mens rea of assaults

Offence	Actus reus	Mens rea
Simple assault – s 39 CJA 1988 and common law	Acts or words that cause the victim to apprehend immediate and unlawful personal force	Intention or recklessness as to causing the victim to apprehend immediate and unlawful personal force
Battery (physical assault) – s 39 CJA 1988 and common law	Infliction of unlawful personal force upon the victim	Intention or recklessness as to the infliction of unlawful personal force
s 47 OAPA 1861	Simple or physical assault causing actual bodily harm (which can include psychiatric harm)	Intention or recklessness as to the simple or physical assault (no need for the defendant to have intended or foreseen the actual bodily harm)
s 20 OAPA 1861	To wound or inflict grievous bodily harm (which can include really serious psychiatric harm)	'Maliciously' ie intention or recklessness as to actual bodily harm
s 18 OAPA 1861	Wound or cause grievous bodily harm (as for s 20)	Intention to cause grievous bodily harm *or* 'Maliciously' ie intention or recklessness as to actual bodily harm plus an intent to resist/prevent arrest

Identifying which of the assaults is the most suitable charge for a defendant will vary according to the particular facts and will require practise. However, the starting point should be the injury. If none, consider the offences of simple assault or battery depending upon whether the defendant touched the victim in any way. If injury is caused, it is likely the accused could be charged with a s 47 offence – an assault occasioning actual bodily harm. If the injury is serious or the victim is cut in any way, the prosecution will analyse the evidence to determine if a s 20 or s 18 offence is the most appropriate. Illustrations of how this would apply in practice are set out below.

Criminal Law

Table 3.5 Examples of non-fatal offences against the person

Scenario	Offence and application to the facts
Abigail shakes her fist at Betsy.	Simple assault (common law and CJA 1988, s 39) – Abigail causes Betsy to apprehend unlawful and personal force and intends this, as her gesture is a clear threat.
Candice slaps Debbie on the cheek during an argument.	Physical assault / battery (common law and CJA 1988, s 39) – Candice inflicts unlawful and personal force on Debbie and intends to do so as the slap is deliberate.
Errol hits Favour in the face causing him to suffer bruising to his jaw.	s 47 OAPA 1861 – Errol causes actual bodily harm and intends a battery as he hits Favour in the face.
Gerry punches Howard once intending to hurt him but causes Howard to suffer from a severely fractured cheek bone.	s 20 OAPA 1861 – although Gerry inflicts grievous bodily harm, his intention is only to cause Howard to suffer some bodily harm, as evidenced by the single punch.
Ivor stabs Jenny intending to really hurt her.	s 18 OAPA 1861 – Ivor wounds Jenny and does so intending grievous bodily harm.
In attempting to prevent his friend being arrested, Kamal pushes PC Lyle who falls onto the floor. Kamal is careless as to whether he injures the officer but PC Lyle suffers a fractured skull.	s 18 OAPA 1861 – Kamal causes grievous bodily harm to PC Lyle and does so intending to prevent an arrest. He does not intend actual bodily harm, but may be reckless as to it.

3.11 Consent as a defence

Consent (or rather the lack of it) is a crucial aspect in the prosecution proving the offence. Usually, this issue will be raised by the defence, with the aim of persuading the court that the circumstances are such that the accused should not be found guilty of the assault for which they have been charged.

3.11.1 Simple assault and battery

It has long been established that consent can amount to a defence to simple assault or battery, and this is a common sense approach in a modern society where people interact with each other on a frequent basis. Indeed, it would be nonsensical if every touch involved the criminal law as it would be very difficult to travel by public transport or socialise in a crowded bar without coming into contact with anyone. Also, normal social conduct requires touching such as shaking hands, or a kiss on the cheek as a sign of welcome. To cover these situations, it is the law that people impliedly consent to the inevitable physical contact that occurs as part of everyday life.

3.11.2 The statutory assaults

However, the same legal principle of consent does not apply to the more serious offences.

3.11.2.1 The general rule

The general rule is that consent is *not* available as a defence to any assault where harm is intended or caused.

Assaults

> *In* Attorney General's Reference (No. 6 of 1980) *[1981] 2 All ER 1057, two youths decided to settle their differences by means of a fist fight. The outcome was that the victim sustained bruises to his face and a bleeding nose. The court held that his consent was not a defence to a charge under s 47 of the OAPA 1861, as 'it is not in the public interest that people should try to cause, or should cause, each other actual bodily harm for no good reason' – Lord Lane CJ.*

However, there are several exceptions to this rule and establishing the scope of these has been the subject of much judicial scrutiny.

3.11.2.2 Exceptions to the general rule

There are a number of established examples where consent is valid to an assault that causes harm. In these situations, the defendant must be acquitted.

- Surgery, as otherwise, operations and other essential medical examinations and procedures could not be carried out lawfully and doctors would be at constant risk of being prosecuted.
- Dangerous exhibitions (such as circus acts).
- Sport provided it is properly conducted; whilst it is accepted that, in highly competitive sport, conduct outside the rules might be expected to occur in the heat of the moment, consent will not defend all behaviour in a sporting environment.
- Ear-piercing and tattooing.

A more controversial exception is that of 'rough and ill-disciplined behaviour', which is also known as 'horseplay'. The justification for this is that youngsters messing around is part of growing up, but quite where to draw the line in determining criminal liability can be problematic.

In summary, the law is:

> Consent as a defence?
> - Simple assault and battery ✓
> - Sections 18, 20 and 47 of the OAPA 1861 ✗
>   unless
> - one of the recognised exceptions.

3.11.2.3 Limits to the exceptions

Deciding what harm individuals may consent to is a question that has come before the courts on many occasions. Public policy is the determining factor and this underpins the recognised exceptions, although some are easier to justify than others. For example, behaviour that might previously have been classified as horseplay may, in a modern society, be viewed as bullying. With regard to tattoos and piercings, these are not actually beneficial to society but they are not harmful either. In any event, it would be difficult on a practical level to make such common body decorations illegal. However, the judges must draw the line somewhere and, as a consequence of the emphasis on public interest, it has been ruled that:

- sado-masochism and
- body modifications (such as nipple removal and the division of a victim's tongue)

are *not* exceptions.

3.11.3 Valid consent

What if the victim is tricked into giving their consent, perhaps because they are very young or suffer from a mental disability? The law does not provide any detailed guidance on this issue and deciding whether the consent is valid will be a question of fact in each case. However, the present position is that:

- Consent is only *valid* if it is freely given by a fully informed and competent adult.
- Consent is *not* valid if it is obtained by fraud as to the identity of the defendant or fraud as to the nature and quality of the act.

⊛ Examples:

(a) *Zara, who has severe learning difficulties, willingly allows her friend to practise his tattooing skills upon her arm. Because Zara thinks that the ink will wash off, her consent is not valid.*

(b) *Harriet agrees to a breast examination believing Clarence is a doctor doing so for medical purposes. In fact, Clarence is not medically qualified and touches Harriet's breasts for his own sexual gratification. Although Harriet knows the identity of the defendant and the nature of the act, the consent is invalid as she is deceived as to the quality of the act.*

Consent to a non-fatal offence must be informed. Thus, a victim who agrees to have sexual intercourse with a person unaware they are HIV positive, would not satisfy this test. The reason is that there is a critical distinction to be drawn between taking the risk of potentially adverse consequences of sexual intercourse, and giving an informed consent to the risk of what may be a fatal condition.

3.11.4 Summary of consent

- Consent must be valid.
- Consent is implied to simple or physical assault provided no harm is intended or caused.
- Consent is not a defence to an assault under ss 47, 20 or 18 of the OAPA 1861 unless the behaviour comes within one of the exceptions.

Summary

Understanding the definitions of the various non-fatal offences against the person can be challenging as the different elements that make up these assaults appear more than once but in different contexts. However, adopting a clear and logical approach will assist.

- To determine the offence with which a defendant is likely to be charged, start with the most sensible one based upon the injury inflicted. This will be a s 18 assault if the injury is significant, but may only be a common assault if the victim is simply threatened.
- Next, identify the actus reus and apply each element to the facts to determine if all the constituent parts of the offence have been satisfied. This may be clear on the evidence provided; alternatively, the answer may require some analysis of whether the injury is (for example) actual or grievous bodily harm.
- If the actus reus is present, determine the mens rea – specifically whether the facts provided support the mental elements of the particular assault under consideration.
- If either the actus reus or the mens rea of the assault are not satisfied, analyse the next assault down in severity to see if this applies. For example, if the prosecution cannot realistically establish a s 18 assault, s 20 should be discussed, followed by s 47 and so on. Alternatively, if the facts suggest the most serious offence is a s 47 assault but there is some doubt as to whether the evidence supports this, consideration should be given to simple assault or battery.
- Finally, if there is potential liability for an assault, consider any possible defences, in particular, whether the victim has given valid consent.

Sample questions

Question 1

The defendant has been told that his next door neighbour is a convicted paedophile. He is concerned about his son, aged eight years, who often plays outside. He approaches the neighbour in the street and says: 'If you go near my son, I'll break your legs!' The neighbour is frightened and runs back into his house.

Has the defendant committed the offence of simple assault?

A   Yes, because the defendant makes a deliberate threat to break the neighbour's legs.

B   Yes, because the neighbour clearly apprehends unlawful personal force as he is frightened.

C   Yes, because the defendant intends the neighbour to apprehend unlawful force to ensure that the neighbour stays away from his son.

D   No, because the threat of force must be an immediate one and here it is conditional upon the neighbour going near the man's son.

E   No, because words alone will not suffice and the defendant did not hit the neighbour.

Answer

Option D is correct. The actus reus of simple assault requires the victim to apprehend immediate and unlawful personal force and both A and B demonstrate the requirement for the neighbour to apprehend such force. However, because the apprehension must be of immediate force, the threat does not satisfy the actus reus as it is a conditional one to break the neighbour's legs only 'if' he goes near the defendant's son. This is why D is the correct answer.

Option B refers to the neighbour being afraid, but this is not actually a requirement of the actus reus of assault, although it would be evidence that he apprehends the infliction of unlawful force. Option C is wrong because, although this may satisfy the mens rea of the offence, the actus reus is not complete. Option E is wrong as words alone can satisfy the actus reus of simple assault.

Question 2

A woman is playing in a football match against a rival team. The match is important as it is the final game in the league and hotly contested on both sides. The teams are level at one goal each when, just before full time, the woman (legitimately) tackles an opposing player to stop her shooting at goal. The opposing player trips and falls awkwardly to the floor as a result of the impact. Her right arm is badly broken in the fall.

Which of the following best describes the woman's liability for inflicting or causing grievous bodily harm (GBH) to the opposing player?

A   The woman is liable for causing GBH as she caused the opposing player to suffer a fractured arm and, by tackling the opposing player, she intended to cause grievous bodily harm.

B   The woman is liable for causing GBH as she caused the opposing player to suffer really serious harm and, when tackling her, was reckless as to causing the injury.

C   The woman is liable for inflicting GBH if the injury is classified as actual bodily harm and the woman was at least reckless as to causing such harm.

D   The woman cannot be liable for a statutory assault because the injury occurred in the context of a football match and this will always provide an accused with a complete defence.

E   The woman is unlikely to be liable for inflicting or causing GBH because consent will operate as a defence provided the football match was properly conducted, which it appears to be.

Answer

Option E is the correct answer because by taking part in a football match, the opposing player has given valid consent to harm but such consent will not defend all behaviour in a sporting environment. In this instance, the woman 'tackled' the opposing player 'legitimately' during play and the opposing player fell 'awkwardly'. Given this, it is likely the defence of consent would succeed.

Option A is wrong as although a broken arm may well be grievous bodily harm (defined as 'really serious harm'), the prosecution is unlikely to establish an intention to cause grievous bodily harm in the context of a contact sport such as football where the participant is focused on the game. Option B is wrong because the mens rea for s 18 GBH in this context does not include recklessness. Option C is wrong as the actus reus of a s 20 GBH is the same as for s 18, namely a wound or grievous bodily harm – not actual bodily harm. The mens rea is accurately described.

Option D is wrong because a person can be criminally liable for injuries incurred in a sporting event such as a football match. Although the general rule is that a victim cannot consent to actual bodily harm or above, there is an exception for injuries which occur in sport. However, this only applies if the sport is properly conducted and so does not 'always' provide the accused with a defence.

Question 3

A man who is standing on a train objects when another passenger sits down on the last remaining seat. He begins shouting and swearing at the passenger, who becomes nervous and anxious. A police officer who is also on the train goes to the passenger's assistance. When the man shows no signs of calming down, the officer tries to arrest him. During the scuffle, the officer is bitten on her finger, an injury which draws blood and requires four stitches. In interview, the man states that the officer put her hand over his mouth, so he could not breathe, and he bit the officer to make her let go. He denies intending to cause her really serious harm, but accepts that he knew she would suffer some harm by biting her in this way.

The prosecution have advised that they intend to charge the man with the most serious offence of assault in relation to the passenger and the police officer which can be justified on the evidence.

Which of the following best describes the man's potential liability in relation to the passenger and the police officer?

A   The man is liable for battery in relation to the passenger and intentionally causing a wound to the officer.

B   The man is liable for simple assault in relation to the passenger and wounding the officer intending to resist arrest and intending to cause her some harm.

C   The man is liable for simple assault in relation to the passenger and inflicting grievous bodily harm on the officer.

D   The man is not liable for an assault in relation to the passenger and liable for inflicting grievous bodily harm on the officer.

E   The man is liable for battery to the passenger and causing actual bodily harm to the officer.

Answer

The best answer is option B. With regard to the incident with the passenger, the man did not apply any unlawful force and so cannot be charged with battery. For this reason, options A and E are both wrong. The relevant assault would be a simple assault as the man caused the passenger to apprehend immediate and unlawful personal physical force and intended or was reckless as to doing so. This is apparent from the evidence that the passenger was 'nervous and anxious'.

The most serious offence with which the man could be charged for the assault on the police officer is a s 18 assault. The actus reus is to wound or cause grievous bodily harm. The man has caused a wound to the officer as he bites her finger drawing blood; this is apparent as the injury required four stitches. Although the man's intention was not to cause grievous bodily harm, just to stop the officer from suffocating him, he is liable under the alternate mens rea. He has an intention to resist arrest and an intention (or recklessness) as to causing actual bodily harm.

Options C, D and E are wrong because the question required the most serious assault to be identified. Thus, although the man could be charged with either a s 20 or a s 47 assault, this does not meet that criteria. Furthermore, option D states (wrongly) that the man is not liable for an assault in relation to the passenger, whilst E suggests that he would be liable for battery.

4 Homicide I: Murder and the Partial Defences

4.1	Introduction	70
4.2	Homicide	70
4.3	Murder	71
4.4	Manslaughter	73
4.5	Voluntary manslaughter	73
4.6	Diminished responsibility	74
4.7	Loss of control	78

SQE1 syllabus

By the end of this chapter you will be able to apply relevant core legal principles and rules appropriately and effectively, at the level of a competent newly qualified solicitor in practice, to realistic client-based and ethical problems and situations in the area of **murder and the partial defences**.

Note that, as students are not usually required to recall specific case names, or cite statutory or regulatory authorities, these are provided for illustrative purposes only.

Learning outcomes

The learning outcomes for this chapter are:

- to explain the definitions of murder and voluntary manslaughter and understand how these offences are applied in practice; and
- to appreciate the circumstances in which the partial defences of diminished responsibility and loss of self-control may apply.

4.1 Introduction

Homicide is the collective term for unlawful killings. It includes murder, which is one of the most serious of crimes as it involves the deliberate taking of a human life. It also covers voluntary manslaughter, where the law recognises certain mitigating factors that, to some extent, excuse the defendant's actions. Both of these will be analysed in this chapter. In addition, homicide includes the offence of involuntary manslaughter, which applies where the accused causes the death of another without the necessary mens rea for murder. In such situations, the offence will either be unlawful act manslaughter or gross negligence manslaughter, both of which are covered in **Chapter 5**.

4.2 Homicide

Homicide is the unlawful killing of another human being and is an umbrella term used to encompass situations where the defendant is criminally liable for either murder or manslaughter.

4.2.1 Actus reus of homicide

The common element in all homicide cases is that the accused unlawfully causes the death of the victim. In most cases, the prosecution will have no difficulty in establishing this because, for example, there is clear evidence that the defendant shot or stabbed the victim who immediately dies of their injuries. However, there are occasions where this will not be so straightforward.

4.2.1.1 Unlawful

Homicide requires that the death of the victim is unlawfully caused. Thus, if a police officer shoots a terrorist just as they are about to detonate a bomb, this would be a lawful killing as it is justified to prevent a crime and to defend others. As a consequence, there is no 'homicide' and the officer would not be guilty of a criminal offence.

4.2.1.2 Victim

The defendant will only be guilty of murder or manslaughter if the victim is a human being. Although the definition of murder refers to a 'reasonable creature in being', this is a rather old-fashioned phrase and is rarely used. Only very occasionally will this aspect be disputed. The law provides that:

- as soon as a baby is born and has an existence independent of the mother it is protected by the law of homicide; and
- it does not matter whether the injury occurred in the womb; it is the time of death that is relevant.

Occasionally, there may be a dispute as to when the victim died, perhaps because they have been so severely assaulted they are in a coma. The generally accepted legal definition of death is that it occurs where the brain stem, which controls the basic functions of the body such as breathing, has died. Thus, it is irrelevant that the task of switching off a victim's life support machine falls to the medical staff – the perpetrator of the injuries remains liable for the death.

4.2.1.3 Causes death

The final element that is common to all offences of homicide is that the accused must *cause* the death of a human being. The usual rules of causation apply and these may be found in **Chapter 1**. This means that the prosecution must prove that the defendant was both the factual and legal cause of the victim's death. This is a question for the jury to determine.

4.3 Murder

Murder is a common law offence and one of the most serious in the criminal justice system. This is reflected by the mandatory life sentence imposed on anyone who is convicted. However, this does not mean that an individual will spend the rest of their life in prison (although the most dangerous offenders may receive a whole life sentence). The judge will decide the minimum term that a defendant must serve and thereafter, if deemed no longer a threat to society, they will be released. Once back in the community, they are subject to a life licence, which means they can be recalled to prison if they commit a further offence.

4.3.1 Definition

Although there are two statutes (the Homicide Act 1957 and the Coroners and Justice Act (CJA) 2009) that deal with the partial defences to murder, the crime itself is from the common law. The definition of the offence dates back to the 17th century and is credited to Judge Coke who stated that murder is:

> The unlawful killing of a reasonable creature in being under the Queen's [or King's] peace with malice aforethought.

4.3.2 Actus reus

It is apparent from this definition that the actus reus of murder is satisfied when a defendant causes the death of a human being (as covered at **4.2.1**). The killing must take place in peacetime; thus, where the defendant kills an enemy combatant during times of war, they have a defence to a charge of murder.

4.3.3 Mens rea

The mens rea for murder is 'malice aforethought', but this term is rather misleading as no 'malice' is required. Even if a defendant kills with benevolent intentions to put a dying relative out of their misery (so-called 'mercy' killings), they will still be guilty of murder. The modern definition of the mens rea for murder is an intention either to kill or to cause grievous bodily harm.

Intention to kill does not require any further explanation and will obviously depend upon the facts, but what does grievous bodily harm mean? Case law has established that it means 'really serious harm' so the question is whether the accused intended to really hurt the victim.

> *In R v Moloney [1985] 1 AC 905, the defendant had been drinking with his stepfather when the latter challenged him to a competition to see who could load, draw and fire a shotgun in the shortest time. During this 'game', Moloney killed the victim with whom he had a loving relationship. The defendant claimed that, in his drunken state, he was unaware the gun was aimed at his stepfather.*
>
> *The court took the opportunity to provide guidance on how the issue should be approached. Lord Bridge stated that, when determining if the accused had the necessary intent, the judge should 'leave it to the jury's good sense'.*

Murder is an example of an offence of specific intent as it cannot be committed recklessly. Because of this, it may be necessary to consider indirect or oblique intent if the defendant's evidence is that their objective was not to kill or cause serious harm. This topic is discussed in more detail in **Chapter 2**.

- Direct intent means that death or grievous bodily harm was the defendant's aim or purpose (the ordinary meaning of 'intention').
- Indirect or oblique intent applies where death or serious harm is not the defendant's primary aim, but is a virtually certain consequence of their actions and the defendant appreciates this.

⭐ *Example*

Toby has just been released from prison for abusing children at a local sports club. Parman, who lives next door, and his friend, Rick, decide to push a firework through Toby's letter box. Parman's aim is to drive his neighbour out of the area but Rick hates Toby as he was abused by him as a child and wants to burn him to death. The firework explodes in the house setting fire to it and killing Toby.

(a) Rick directly intends Toby to die – he desires this outcome.

(b) Parman's aim or purpose is to pressurise Toby into leaving the area but, if he foresees death or serious injury as a virtually certain consequence of his actions, the jury may find that he intended it. This will depend upon factors such as what time of day the firework was pushed through the letter box, how powerful it was, whether Parman was aware that Toby was in the house and so on.

4.3.4 Summary of murder

- The actus reus for murder is the unlawful killing of a human being (not a foetus) under the King or Queen's peace. This is common to all homicides.
- The mens rea for murder is the intention to kill or cause grievous (really serious) harm. It is an entirely subjective test – did this particular defendant have the relevant intention?
- Murder is a crime of specific intent so it cannot be committed recklessly.
- Either direct or indirect intent will satisfy the mens rea for murder.

Figure 4.1 Murder

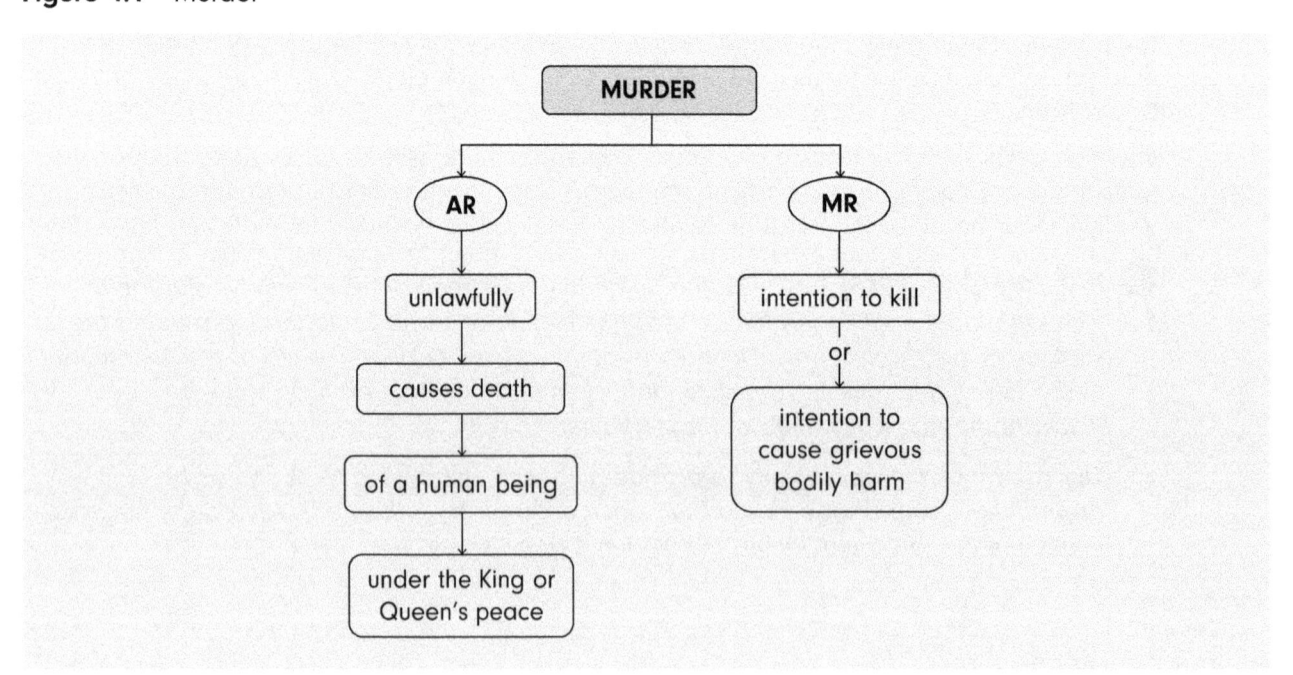

```
                        MURDER
                       /      \
                     AR        MR
                     |          |
                unlawfully   intention to kill
                     |          or
                causes death    |
                     |     intention to
                     |     cause grievous
              of a human being  bodily harm
                     |
              under the King or
                Queen's peace
```

4.4 Manslaughter

Some may consider that taking another person's life can never be excused and, it is fair to say, in most homicides the defendant deserves little or no sympathy. However, the reality is that there are degrees of culpability for this offence.

The case of R v Ahluwalia (1993) 96 Cr App R 133 illustrates this point. The defendant had been violently abused by her husband for over 10 years until she could take no more. One night, she poured petrol over her sleeping victim and then set fire to him. The victim died from his burns.

Most people would sympathise with Ahluwalia's predicament and even the fact that she killed her husband; after all, she was reacting to a violent bully. Arguably, she is not morally culpable at all because she was provoked by the abuse she received over a period of time. However, although the law recognises a defence for those who are pushed to the edge so they lose their self-control, the means adopted were extreme, particularly as Ahluwalia's husband was asleep at the time.

This case illustrates the complexity of the issues that may arise. On the one hand, Ahluwalia has taken a life but, on the other, she herself is clearly a victim. This case was adopted by women's groups who were pressing for a change in the way the courts dealt with domestic violence cases and her conviction for murder was subsequently reduced to manslaughter.

The case of R v Martin (Anthony) [2002] EWCA Crim 2245 is another example. Martin's home, known as Bleak House, had been plagued by burglars over the years. One night, he confronted a burglar in his house; then, as the burglar was fleeing his property, he shot him dead with a gun he used for shooting rabbits. Although there was much sympathy for Martin, he remains morally culpable. The fact that the victim was running away from him at the time of the shooting demonstrates that this is not a case of self-defence or prevention of crime.

Both of these defendants were subsequently convicted of manslaughter of which there are two different types – voluntary and involuntary manslaughter – and it is important to be able to distinguish them. The significance of being found guilty of manslaughter rather than murder is that the judge has discretion in sentencing and, thus, can take account of all the relevant circumstances. In particular, there is no mandatory life sentence so that although life imprisonment may be appropriate, often a less severe penalty is imposed.

4.5 Voluntary manslaughter

Before considering voluntary manslaughter, the jury must conclude that the defendant has satisfied the elements of the crime of murder; if not, voluntary manslaughter is irrelevant. Only if the actus reus and mens rea of murder have been proved should the evidence be analysed to determine whether the offence can be reduced to manslaughter.

The three situations where the law recognises that a person who has killed another with the necessary mens rea for murder should be treated differently are:

(a) diminished responsibility;

(b) loss of control; and

(c) suicide pact.

Criminal Law

It is important to note that:

- None of these reasons provide a true defence since, even if successful, the accused is still liable for an offence, that of voluntary manslaughter. Hence, why the reasons are known as 'partial defences'.
- They are defences *only* to murder and should not be considered in relation to any other offence.

Suicide pact is very rarely raised as a defence and is outside the scope of this manual.

The flowchart in **Figure 4.2** illustrates whether the defendant has committed murder and the relationship between this offence and manslaughter.

Figure 4.2 Murder and voluntary manslaughter

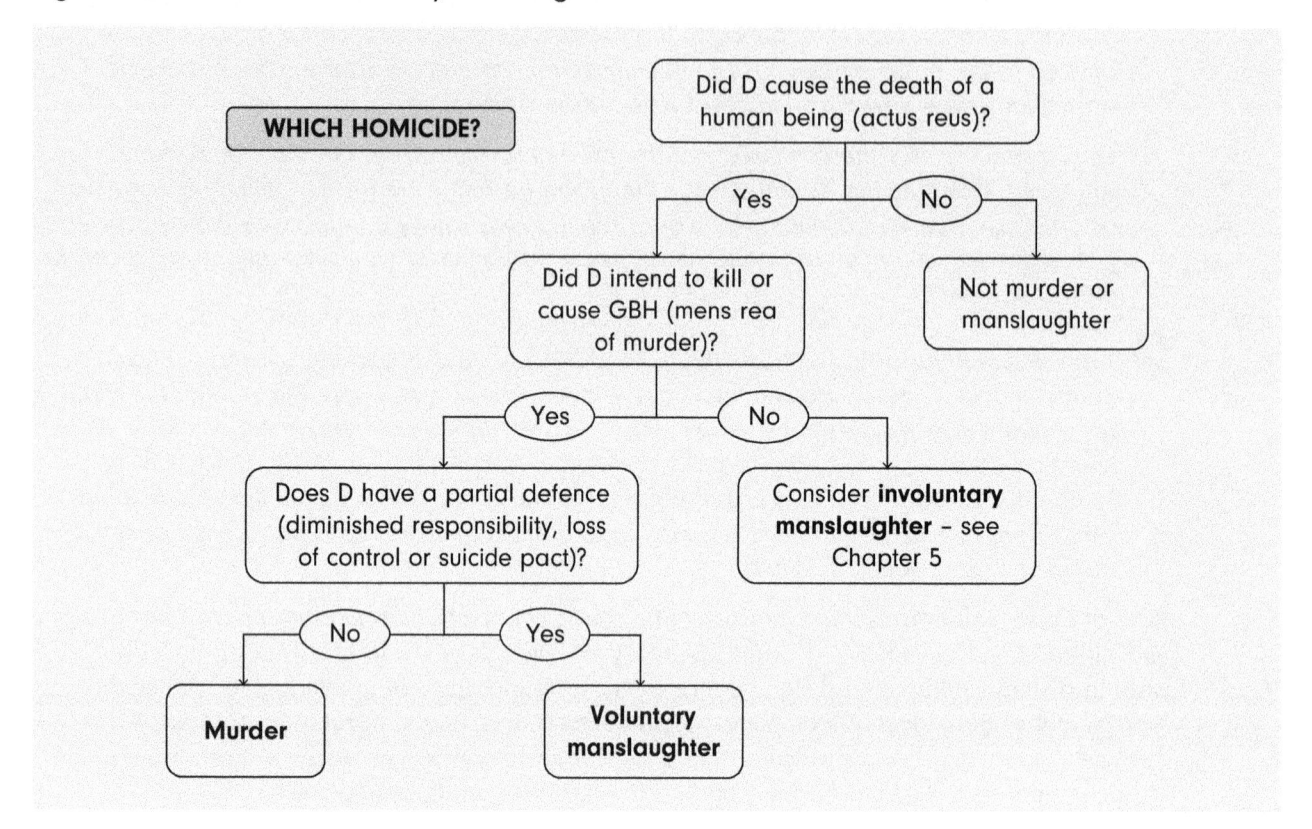

```
WHICH HOMICIDE?
                    ↓
        Did D cause the death of a human being (actus reus)?
           Yes ↓              ↓ No
    Did D intend to kill or     Not murder or
    cause GBH (mens rea         manslaughter
    of murder)?
       Yes ↓    ↓ No
                Consider involuntary
                manslaughter – see
                Chapter 5
    Does D have a partial defence
    (diminished responsibility, loss
    of control or suicide pact)?
       No ↓     ↓ Yes
      Murder    Voluntary
                manslaughter
```

4.5.1 Actus reus and mens rea

The actus reus and mens rea of voluntary manslaughter are the same as for murder. Hence, for voluntary manslaughter, the prosecution must prove that the defendant:

- has unlawfully caused the death of a human being (actus reus); and
- did so with an intention to kill or cause grievous bodily harm (mens rea).

Only then will the court consider whether any of the partial defences apply.

4.6 Diminished responsibility

Diminished responsibility is a statutory defence, which is set out in s 2 of the Homicide Act 1957, as amended by s 52 of the CJA 2009.

There are four elements to the defence that need to be proved:

(a) an abnormality of mental functioning; which

(b) arose from a recognised medical condition; and

(c) substantially impaired the defendant's ability to understand the nature of their conduct, and/or form a rational judgment and/or exercise self-control; and

(d) provides an explanation for the defendant's act or omission in doing the killing.

The defendant cannot be convicted of murder if these elements are successfully pleaded.

4.6.1 Evidential issues

The prosecution are required to prove the actus reus and mens rea of homicide beyond a reasonable doubt. Having done so, the legal burden of proving all the elements of diminished responsibility switches to the defendant. This is unusual in the criminal law as the prosecution are generally required to *disprove* any defence raised; however, the standard of proof required from the defendant is only on a balance of probabilities. In other words, the accused must show that it is more likely than not they were suffering from diminished responsibility at the time of the killing.

4.6.2 Abnormality of mental functioning

The first question for the jury to consider is whether the defendant was suffering from an abnormality of mental functioning when they killed their victim. There is no further definition in the Act as to what this actually means, although it tends to be interpreted widely, and the jury will make its decision having heard expert medical evidence.

The term 'abnormality of mental functioning' was introduced to ensure consistency with the medical profession as it is a phrase commonly used in this context. Given that medical experts will be providing the evidence that will determine whether a defendant can rely on diminished responsibility, this seems logical.

4.6.3 Recognised medical condition

The second requirement for diminished responsibility is that the abnormality of mental functioning must arise from a recognised medical condition. This means that it must be supported by medical evidence and will generally be found in accepted classification systems such as the World Health Organisation's International Classification of Diseases. However, this is not a closed list and what counts as a recognised medical condition will evolve over time as medical understanding increases. Examples are set out in **Table 4.1** and include physical conditions that may impact upon the defendant's mental state.

Table 4.1 Examples of recognised medical conditions

Psychiatric conditions	Physical conditions
depression	alcohol dependency syndrome
schizophrenia	diabetes
post-traumatic stress disorder	epilepsy
battered person's disorder	
phobic anxiety	

Deciding whether an accused is suffering from an abnormality of mental functioning arising from a recognised medical condition may be challenging at times and even controversial.

In the case of R v Blackman [2017] EWCA Crim 190, the defendant, then a member of the Royal Marines, shot and killed a badly wounded rebel while serving in Afghanistan. At his trial, Blackman was found guilty of murder as the evidence was that he was acted calmly and deliberately. However, his original conviction for murder was overturned on appeal as a result of psychiatric evaluations that suggested the defendant was suffering from an adjustment disorder, compounded by the presence of several 'exceptional stressors'. As a consequence, Blackman was incapable of making rational judgments or exercising self-control and a finding of manslaughter was substituted.

4.6.3.1 Diminished responsibility and intoxication

It is not unusual for offences to be committed while the defendant is under the influence of alcohol and there have been a number of cases in which the judges have considered the relationship between intoxication (whether from alcohol or any other substance) and the partial defence of diminished responsibility.

Examples

Dwayne stabbed and killed his friend, Lionel, during a violent argument.

(a) During the evening, Dwayne consumed a cocktail of illegal substances causing him to become acutely intoxicated. Because he does not suffer from alcoholism or a dependency-related condition, he cannot rely on diminished responsibility. For public policy reasons, an offender who voluntarily takes alcohol or drugs and then behaves in a way they would not have done when sober is not excused from responsibility.

(b) Dwayne suffers from schizophrenia, which is a recognised medical condition. His psychotic state of mind at the time of the fatal act was triggered by his voluntary intoxication. Because the medical evidence confirms that it was the abnormality of mental functioning that caused him to kill Lionel, he may successfully plead the partial defence of diminished responsibility. The law does not require the abnormality of mind to be the sole cause of the defendant's acts.

(c) Dwayne finds it almost impossible not to drink vodka every day and, once he has had his first drink, he cannot control his urges to drink more. If he resists, he suffers from headaches, nausea, uncontrollable shaking and other symptoms. He has been diagnosed with alcohol dependency syndrome. The court hears evidence that Dwayne was also drunk at the time he killed Lionel. Dwayne is not necessarily precluded from pleading diminished responsibility just because he has consumed alcohol voluntarily. In deciding whether his mental responsibility for the killing was substantially impaired as a result of his dependency on alcohol, the jury should focus exclusively on the effect of the alcohol consumed as a result of his illness and disregard the effect of any alcohol consumed voluntarily. Given the difficulties of such a task, medical evidence is likely to be crucial.

4.6.4 Substantial impairment of the defendant's ability

Once the defendant has satisfied the court that they have a recognised medical condition, they must also demonstrate that this impaired their ability to do one of the three things set out in s 2(1A) of the Homicide Act 1957, specifically:

(a) to understand the nature of their conduct; and/or

(b) form a rational judgment; and/or

(c) exercise self-control.

It is clear from the wording of the statute that any one, or combination of more than one, of these will enable the defendant to establish the required impairment.

4.6.4.1 'Substantial'

It is not sufficient for the abnormality of mental functioning to impair the defendant's ability – it must do so substantially. Whether there has been a substantial impairment is a question of fact for the jury.

> *In R v Golds [2016] UKSC 61, the Supreme Court gave some consideration to the meaning of 'substantial' and concluded that this word means 'important or weighty'. This is, perhaps, not surprising when the context is borne in mind; the partial defences only come into play when the prosecution have proved that the defendant has committed murder. As such, the judges ruled that there must be a 'weighty' impairment of the defendant's abilities before this grave offence may be reduced to the lesser offence of manslaughter; a reason that is so minor it just passes the trivial will not be enough.*
>
> *The judges agreed that, ordinarily, there will be no need to direct a jury on the meaning of 'substantial'. It is clearly a question of degree, which can only be determined when all the facts have been made apparent.*

4.6.4.2 Impairment of the defendant's ability

Under s 2 of the Homicide Act 1957, the defendant's ability to do *particular things* must be substantially impaired. Considering these in a practical scenario gives assistance into the meaning of each.

⭐ Examples

(a) Shuhab enjoys playing violent computer games. He stabs his friend, Yasser, in the heart believing that he will come back to life as the victims do when he replays his computer games. Shuhab does not understand the nature of his conduct. He fails to realise that stabbing someone in the heart has fatal consequences and that his 'real life' victim will remain dead.

(b) Humphrey is obsessed with the mistaken belief that his daughter, Elisabeth, is trying to evict him from the family home and move him into a care home. One day, when Elisabeth calls by to visit Humphrey, he shoots her in the chest, killing her instantly. Humphrey appears to be suffering from some sort of neurosis, which impairs his ability to form a rational judgment.

(c) Daphne falls into a jealous rage and hits her boyfriend over the head with an iron after he receives a number of texts from a work colleague. Daphne appears to lack the ability to exercise self-control. There is nothing to suggest that she does not understand the nature of her conduct or is incapable of forming a rational judgment.

4.6.5 Provides an explanation for the defendant's acts or omissions in killing

Having reached this stage, the defendant must also establish that the medical condition from which they are suffering provides an explanation for their act of killing. In other words, there is a causal link between the defendant's medical condition and their behaviour. This is important because, otherwise, anyone who suffers from a psychiatric condition would automatically succeed in this defence even if the condition has no bearing whatsoever on their fatal act.

Determining this question will involve considering the extent to which the defendant is answerable for their behaviour in light of their state of mind and ability to control their physical actions. Realistically, the jury will not be able to answer these questions without medical evidence. For example, even the phrase 'abnormality of mental functioning' would be difficult for a lay person to interpret as it requires an understanding of the processes going through the defendant's mind – something that only an expert is likely to have.

⭐ Example

*Returning to the case of Daphne – example (c) above at **4.6.4.2** – medical evidence has now been obtained that confirms she suffers from a paranoid personality disorder. The expert's report concludes that she has an abnormality of mental functioning arising from a recognised medical condition sufficient to satisfy these aspects of the legal test for diminished responsibility. However, because Daphne kills her boyfriend in a fit of rage that is unrelated to this condition, she will not be able to rely on this partial defence. For the defence to succeed Daphne must show that the homicide was caused by her mental abnormality, and, on these facts, it was not.*

4.6.6 Summary flowchart of diminished responsibility

Figure 4.3 Diminished responsibility

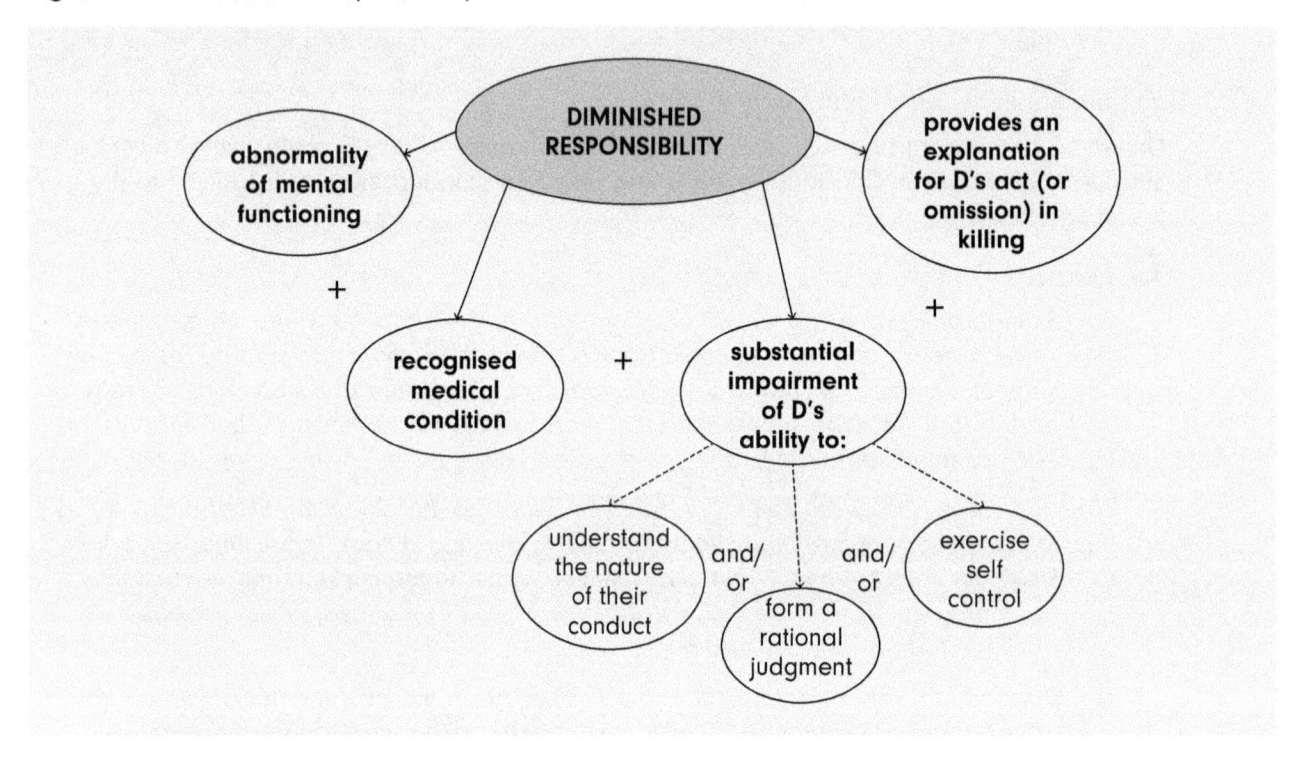

4.7 Loss of control

Loss of control is the second partial defence that, if successful, reduces murder to voluntary manslaughter. As with diminished responsibility, this defence only applies to murder and no other crime; thus it should not be pleaded if the defendant is charged with an assault, for example. Loss of control is also defined by statute, specifically sections 54 and 55 of the CJA 2009.

The rationale behind the defence is an acceptance by the law that everyone has a breaking point and circumstances may arise that push people so far they lose control. Providing this defence acknowledges that such defendants are less morally culpable than deliberate murderers. However, not every situation will allow an accused to rely on this partial defence.

The definition of loss of control is contained within s 54 of the CJA 2009, which sets out the three components:

(a) the defendant must lose self-control;

(b) the loss of control must have a qualifying trigger; and

(c) a person of the defendant's sex and age, with a normal degree of tolerance and self-restraint and in the circumstances of the defendant, might have reacted in the same or in a similar way as the defendant did.

Only if the accused successfully overcomes all three hurdles will their conviction for murder be reduced to manslaughter.

4.7.1 Evidential issues

There is one important difference between the two partial defences. Unlike diminished responsibility, the conventional burden of proof in criminal cases applies to loss of control. The effect is that, provided the accused can produce some evidence that raises the defence, the burden will revert back to the prosecution to disprove loss of control beyond reasonable doubt. If the prosecution fail to do so, the jury must assume the defence is satisfied. Some 60% of those accused of murder rely upon the defence of loss of control and, to succeed, all three elements listed in s 54 of the CJA 2009 must be satisfied.

4.7.2 Loss of control

First it must be established that the defendant lost self-control and this is a question of fact for the jury to decide. Because the issue is subjectively assessed, the jury must be satisfied that this particular defendant lost self-control; it is not enough that the reasonable person would have done so but the accused actually did not.

✪ Example

Felipe's wife, Moira, constantly criticises him both in public and at home. As soon as he steps through the front door, he faces a torrent of abuse. Moira has also thrown saucepans at Felipe and scratched his car when she is angry. Felipe is an exceptionally calm individual but he decides that he can no longer tolerate her behaviour. However, he does not want to pay his wife a divorce settlement, so he decides that the next time she begins to insult him, he will kill her. Two days later, he strangles Moira to death.

Even though a reasonable person may well have 'cracked' under the continuous verbal onslaught, Felipe cannot rely upon the partial defence of loss of control. This is because Felipe, in fact, did not because he planned Moira's death.

Although the statute does not define the term loss of control, the judges have provided some assistance.

In R v Jewell [2004] EWCA Crim 404, the accused shot and killed a work colleague. He alleged that the victim had intimidated and threatened him the previous evening and that he had armed himself for protection. He claimed that, when he saw the victim, he could not control himself. The Court of Appeal approved the meaning of loss of control as a loss of the ability to act 'in accordance with considered judgement, or a loss of normal powers of reasoning'. However, in this instance, the degree of planning was such that the defendant was convicted of murder.

4.7.2.1 No need to be sudden

Although the court must be satisfied that the defendant did indeed lose control, there is no requirement for this to be sudden.

Returning to the case of R v Ahluwalia, *which was covered earlier in this chapter, the defendant set fire to her husband and killed him while he slept. Initially, Ahluwalia was unsuccessful in her attempt to reduce her criminal liability to manslaughter. This was because, under the test that applied at the time, the loss of control had to be sudden. However, more understanding of how domestic violence victims react to their abusers led to a change in the law so that (now) the defendant need only prove they actually did lose control at the time of the killing.*

As a consequence, killings that occur in the domestic violence context, where the defendant's reaction builds up over a period of time, are not excluded. Nevertheless, in reality, the greater the level of deliberation the less likely it is that the killing followed a true loss of self-control.

In summary, there may be a loss of control where:

- the defendant 'snaps'; or
- their reaction is a response to a culmination of events, such as incidents of abuse, that occur over time.

4.7.2.2 Considered desire for revenge

Whilst the loss of self-control need not be sudden and without warning, it will not apply where the defendant acted in a considered desire for revenge (CJA 2009, s 54(4)). Although it may be difficult for the jury to distinguish between a planned attack and the reaction of a victim of abuse, this is a decision it is required to make. It is important that defendants who take deliberate steps to kill the victim should be distinguished from those who act on impulse or in fear or both.

As to what qualifies as a 'considered' desire for revenge, there is no guidance in the statute but factors that may satisfy the test could include where:

(a) the defendant arms themselves with a weapon;

(b) there is evidence of planning; or

(c) there is a significant delay between the provoking words or conduct and the killing.

4.7.2.3 Practical application

As is often the way with the partial defences, whether the defendant lost control is a question that must be decided by the jury after considering the evidence put before it. However, some situations will be much easier to determine than others.

Example

Eithne is 35 years of age. She has been married to Aaron for 10 years and they have a six-year-old daughter, Iona. Eithne is significantly overweight and was bullied at school because of this. Furthermore, during the marriage, Aaron has punched and kicked Eithne on a frequent basis, and constantly taunted her about her weight.

In each of the scenarios below, the jury must consider whether Eithne lost control when she carried out the fatal act.

(a) One evening, Aaron returns from work in a foul mood. He starts shouting at Eithne, calling her an 'ugly fat bitch' before grabbing her hair and slapping her face. This is usually the prelude to a violent assault. Eithne is chopping vegetables when Aaron enters the kitchen and she uses the knife to stab him to death. Here, there is a clear loss of control – Eithne 'snaps' and reacts instantly to Aaron's assault.

(b) As for scenario (b) above, except that Eithne does not respond immediately. Aaron continues with the violence, punching his wife in the face and then repeatedly kicking her as she cowers on the floor. When he leaves the kitchen, Eithne hides in the understairs cupboard and waits until Aaron falls asleep in front of the television, which he does two hours later. When she emerges, she sees him lying there and, unable to take any more, Eithne grabs a kitchen knife and stabs him to death.

In this example, there is not (on the face of it) a lack of control because Eithne did not react spontaneously to the assault but, instead, waited for a couple of hours until Aaron was asleep. However, her action was a response to an accumulation of years of provocation, something that has been described as 'a snapping in slow motion, the final surrender of frayed elastic'. It is now established that certain defendants, such as those who have been the victim of domestic violence, may lose control in a manner that is not obviously so.

(c) One morning during breakfast, Aaron looks at Eithne and says contemptuously: 'You really could make a bit of effort – you look a right state!' Eithne storms out of the kitchen and grabs Aaron's golf club, which is in a bag in the hallway. She runs towards him and smashes Aaron repeatedly over the head with the club, killing him. Here, the evidence is clear that Eithne lost her temper when she killed her husband, satisfying the test for loss of control. The fact that the final comment on its own may not be the most offensive does not matter as it can be the so-called 'straw that breaks the camel's back'.

(d) As for scenario (c) above, but instead of reacting immediately, Eithne walks out of the house to go to work. During the day, she plans how she is going to kill Aaron. That evening, she goes into the garage and finds a hammer and then, while he is playing computer games, she hits Aaron repeatedly over the head, killing him. On this evidence, the jury would not find a loss of control at the time of the fatal act. Not only has Eithne had time to 'cool down' but she planned the attack and carried it out deliberately.

When determining if there has been a genuine loss of control, the jury will need to consider all the facts. In particular, evidence of there being a delay does not automatically preclude a defendant from relying upon the partial defence of loss of control, but it may mean that the defence is less likely to succeed.

4.7.2.4 Summary diagram of loss of control

Figure 4.4 Loss of control

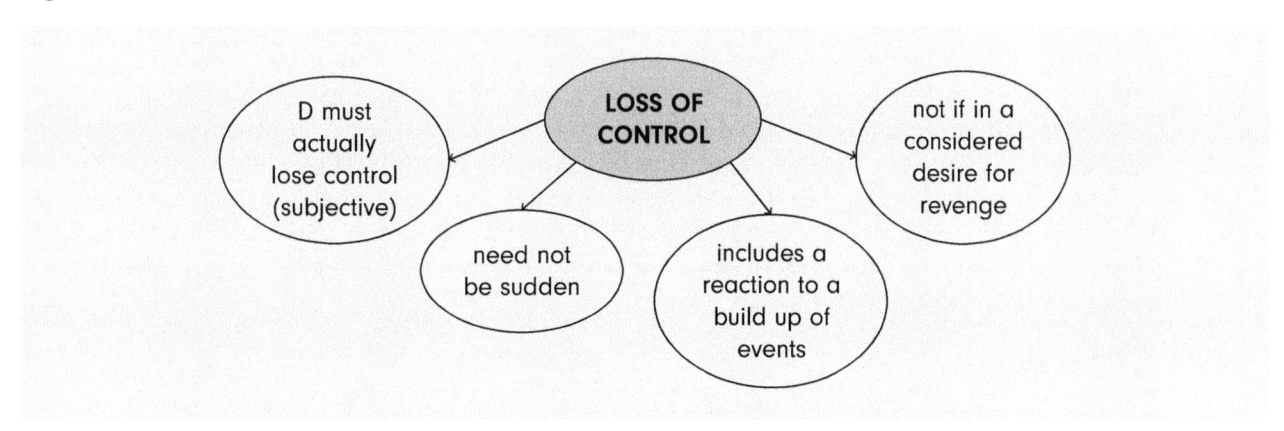

```
                    LOSS OF
   D must           CONTROL        not if in a
   actually                        considered
   lose control                    desire for
   (subjective)                    revenge

          need not        includes a
          be sudden       reaction to a
                          build up of
                          events
```

4.7.3 The qualifying trigger

The historical rationale behind an accused being able to lower their culpability from murder to manslaughter was that there were certain situations regarded as so provocative it was excusable for the defendant to react in anger. However, when the CJA 2009 was drafted, it was acknowledged that insufficient consideration had been given to those who are responding out of fear. To overcome this, 'qualifying triggers' were introduced, respectively known as the 'fear' and 'anger' triggers. The loss of control must be the result of one of these or a combination of both. The effect is that, unlike the previous law, a defendant may no longer rely upon the partial defence for killing a baby due to its persistent crying.

It is important to note that the defendant cannot rely on the triggers where they have incited the situation to provide them with an excuse to use violence in response.

⭐ Example

Ivan is an avid football fan. He insults a rival football club in front of their supporters in order to provoke a fight. Dave responds by shouting that Ivan's team are 'cheating bastards' and that he is 'a son of a whore'. Ivan is incensed and rushes at Dave, fatally stabbing him with a flick knife. The law takes the view that Ivan's behaviour is such that he should not be able to avail himself of an excusatory defence in these circumstances, and so he is precluded from relying on loss of control.

4.7.3.1 The fear trigger

The 'fear trigger' under s 55(3) will apply where the loss of control 'was attributable to the defendant's fear of serious violence from the victim against the defendant or another identified person'.

The defendant's fear of serious violence is subjectively assessed so that the jury must be satisfied the accused was genuinely afraid of such violence even if the fear is not reasonable. The fear of serious violence must be from the victim against the defendant or another identified person, rather than a more general fear.

⭐ Example

Returning to the case of Eithne, which was considered earlier in this chapter, in scenarios (a) and (b), Eithne would be able to rely upon the fear trigger. She kills Aaron because she is afraid that serious violence will be inflicted upon her by her husband. He has punched and kicked her on a frequent basis in the past and she is aware that when Aaron grabs her hair, this signals the start of another assault.

4.7.3.2 The anger trigger

The 'anger trigger' under s 55(4) applies where the defendant's loss of control was attributable to things said and/or done that amounted to circumstances of an extremely grave character and caused the defendant to have a justifiable sense of having been seriously wronged. No definitions are included in the Act. Whether the defendant's sense of being seriously wronged is justifiable is an objective question to be determined initially by the judge, who must decide whether a properly directed jury could reasonably conclude that it was. Only then should the judge leave the question as one of fact to be decided by the jury. Effectively, the judge is acting as a filter here.

⭐ Examples

(a) *Carlos arrives home to find his 17-year-old daughter, Yolanda, being raped by a student from her class, Antonio. Carlos is horrified and attacks Antonio so severely that he dies of his injuries.*

Carlos has lost his self-control and this would be attributable to the anger trigger. Seeing his daughter being raped would amount to a circumstance of an extremely grave character, as he is witnessing a serious crime being committed against a close relative. Carlos would have a justifiable sense of being seriously wronged, as indeed would the reasonable person, and so he could rely on the partial defence to reduce his criminal liability to manslaughter.

(b) *Deepak discovers that his sister, Amina, has a boyfriend. She has kept this a secret as she is aware her family will be extremely angry. In a fit of rage, Deepak kills Amina because of her relationship as he believes it will bring shame to his family (a so-called 'honour killing').*

Deepak may personally feel that his sister's relationship brings dishonour to the family, thus constituting circumstances of an extremely grave character and causing him to have a justifiable sense of being seriously wronged. However, he would not be able to rely on s 55(4) as a qualifying trigger because of the objective elements within the Act.

i   *Whether or not the circumstances are of an 'extremely grave character' is to be decided by the jury. It is doubtful they would consider that Amina's relationship meets this requirement.*

ii *The sense of being 'seriously wronged' must be 'justifiable' and a jury is unlikely to share Deepak's belief in this regard.*

As a consequence, Deepak is guilty of murder.

4.7.3.3 Sexual infidelity

Historically and statistically, the partial defence of loss of control (or its equivalent) was used by defendants who reacted violently to their partner's adultery. To combat this, the statute deliberately excludes such an excuse, providing that:

- the fact that a thing done or said constituted sexual infidelity is to be disregarded (s 55(6)(c)).

However, although understandable, such a rigid approach is perhaps not realistic. Difficulties arise where, for example, the victim taunts the defendant with their infidelity amongst a torrent of other abusive comments. Should one be ignored and others taken account of?

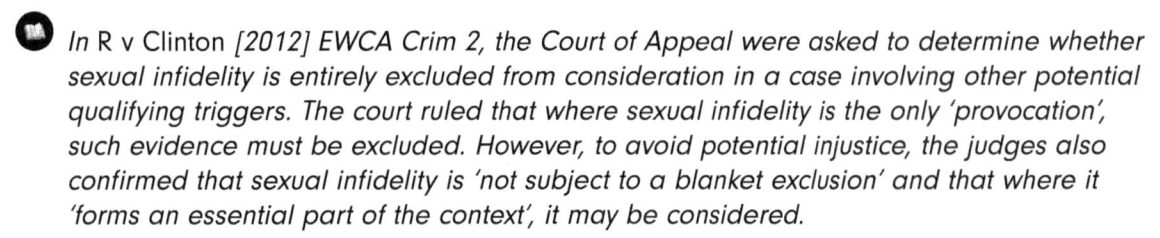

In R v Clinton [2012] EWCA Crim 2, the Court of Appeal were asked to determine whether sexual infidelity is entirely excluded from consideration in a case involving other potential qualifying triggers. The court ruled that where sexual infidelity is the only 'provocation', such evidence must be excluded. However, to avoid potential injustice, the judges also confirmed that sexual infidelity is 'not subject to a blanket exclusion' and that where it 'forms an essential part of the context', it may be considered.

The effect of this decision is that where the sexual infidelity is part of the background or context to other possible triggers, then evidence relating to it may be relevant when assessing the other potential qualifying trigger.

In summary:

- Sexual infidelity cannot be relied upon on its own as a qualifying trigger, but its existence does not prevent reliance on the defence where there are other qualifying triggers.

- Where other factors suggest a qualifying trigger, sexual infidelity may also be taken into account in assessing whether things done or said amounted to circumstances of an extremely grave character and gave the defendant a justifiable sense of being seriously wronged.

Criminal Law

- Sexual infidelity can be taken into account in the third component of the defence in examining whether a person of the defendant's sex and age, with a normal degree of tolerance and self-restraint and in the circumstances of the defendant, might have reacted in the same or in a similar way.

✪ Examples

(a) Dewi returns home to find his partner, Steve, having sex with another man. He loses his temper and attacks Steve ferociously, killing him instantly. Dewi has clearly lost his self-control. However, sexual infidelity on its own is to be disregarded as a qualifying trigger and, thus, he is liable for the offence of murder.

(b) Gawain and his wife, Jody, have been married for eight years and have three young children. However, Jody wishes to separate and has contacted a lawyer about divorce proceedings. Gawain is devastated about the break-up of his marriage and tries to dissuade her. The two begin to argue and Jody taunts Gawain about a range of matters including her repeated sexual infidelity, his visits to suicide websites, specifically that he did not have the courage to kill himself, and also her lack of care for their children. Gawain suddenly flips, beating Jody to death.

Jody's sexual infidelity may be considered as part of the background but it cannot be the qualifying trigger on its own. In Gawain's case there are other factors, namely the taunts about his suicidal thoughts and his wife's attitude to the children, that can (in the context of the sexual infidelity) count as a potential trigger. Combined together, the things said and done were such as to constitute circumstances of an extremely grave character, which caused Gawain to have a justifiable sense of being seriously wronged. The effect is that Gawain's conviction for murder may be reduced to voluntary manslaughter.

The fact that sexual infidelity cannot be relied upon on its own as a qualifying trigger, but may be taken into account as one of a number of factors, is generally regarded as a sensible compromise reflecting the complexities of relationships and the fact that murders are often committed when passions are roused, which may be for several reasons.

4.7.3.4 Summary flowchart of qualifying triggers

Figure 4.5 Qualifying triggers for loss of control

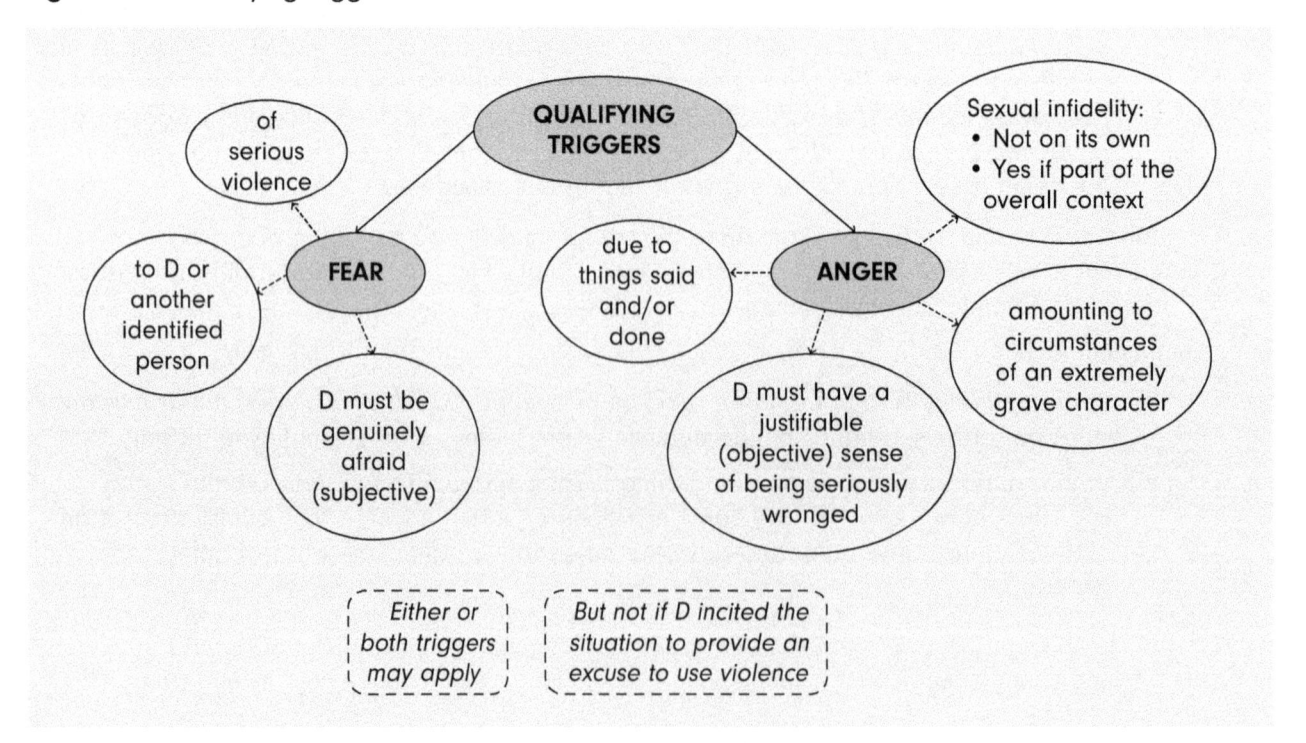

4.7.4 Similar reaction of a person of the same age and sex

Loss of control is subject to a third element, which is primarily objective in content. The reason is to maintain the rule of law and a peaceful society, there are standards of behaviour that must be adhered to whenever possible. The partial defences provide a compassionate outcome to those who are unable to meet this standard in particular circumstances but it does not mean the killing is acceptable.

The third element of the defence is set out in s 54(1)(c) of the CJA 2009:

- A person of D's age and sex, with a normal degree of tolerance and self-restraint and in the circumstances of D, might have reacted in the same or a similar way to D.

The effect of this provision is that the law accepts that a 'normal' person may intentionally kill another in certain circumstances. In doing so, the statute aims to put 'clear water' between the two partial defences of loss of control and diminished responsibility.

4.7.4.1 A person of the defendant's age and sex

The Act includes age and sex as general characteristics to be taken into account, although the relevance of both has been questioned. It is particularly unclear as to what role gender plays in this evaluation as it suggests that the different sexes have differing levels of self-control. However, the most likely scenario in which the defendant's sex may apply is where they react to a threat of violence – required for the 'fear' trigger. Although no justification is provided, this is presumably on the basis that females are generally less physically powerful than men.

With regard to the second characteristic, some argue that age is not really the issue – maturity is. However, age is an objective, if somewhat crude, way of measuring this. The argument for the inclusion of age is that a younger person generally has a lower capacity to control themselves and their emotions than an adult. Thus, to judge a child defendant against the level of control expected of an adult would be unjust.

4.7.4.2 The defendant's circumstances

The 'circumstances' of the defendant are defined in s 54(3) of the CJA 2009 as:

- All of D's circumstances other than those whose only relevance to D's conduct is that they bear on D's general capacity for tolerance and self-restraint.

Thus, if the defendant is particularly aggressive or short tempered, they will not be able to rely upon these characteristics as an excuse for the killing.

4.7.4.3 Practical application of same reaction

Set out below are three examples of how this element of the offence would apply in practice.

⭐ Examples

(a) Jay, who is 19 years of age, is waiting for a train with his girlfriend, Alex. As they enter the train, Tobias, who is boarding at the same time, smiles at Alex. Jay is convinced that Tobias is flirting with Alex despite his protestations to the contrary. Jay becomes more and more agitated and then loses his control completely, stabbing Tobias to death with a flick knife.

In this scenario, a 19-year-old male with a normal degree of tolerance and self-restraint would not have stabbed Tobias to death just because he smiled politely at the defendant's girlfriend, so the partial defence would fail.

(b) Ariana is a 14-year-old girl who has been sexually abused by Richard for over two years. One day, after she has been drinking heavily, Richard sexually assaults Ariana and then laughs at her distress. Ariana hits Richard with a vase and kills him.

Ariana must satisfy the jury that a 14-year-old girl with a normal degree of tolerance and self-restraint might have killed her abuser when taunted in this way. Her voluntary intoxication will not be taken into account and she will be assessed as if she were sober. Even so, the defence is likely to succeed.

(c) *Nyofi is 25 years of age and recently entered into a civil partnership with her girlfriend, Marnie. However, Marnie has just announced that she is leaving Nyofi and taking their five-year-old daughter, Jemma, with her. The two argue and Marnie screams at Nyofi that she is sick of her partner's 'disapproving African family' and that she does not want to be in a lesbian relationship any longer. Nyofi is devastated as she has cut all ties with her family to be with Marnie. As Marnie is leaving the house, she yells: 'Lesbians are all bitchy and African ones are the worst – I need to get Jemma out of this toxic atmosphere'. Nyofi grabs a kitchen knife and fatally stabs Marnie.*

To satisfy the test for manslaughter, it must be shown that a person of the defendant's sex and age with a normal degree of tolerance and self-restraint might have reacted in the same or a similar way in the circumstances. In making this assessment the 'normal' person will have the same history and characteristics as the defendant in so far as they are relevant to the qualifying triggers that prompted the loss of self-control.

Nyofi would have to establish that a 25-year-old female with a normal degree of tolerance might *have reacted by stabbing her partner to death, when taunted about being a lesbian and about her African heritage and confronted with the loss of her daughter. Because Nyofi is being taunted about her sexual orientation and racial origin, the normal person will have the same sexual orientation and racial origin. It is likely that Nyofi could rely successfully upon the partial defence of loss of control to reduce her criminal liability to manslaughter.*

4.7.4.4 Summary flowchart of similar reaction

Figure 4.6 Similar reaction for loss of control

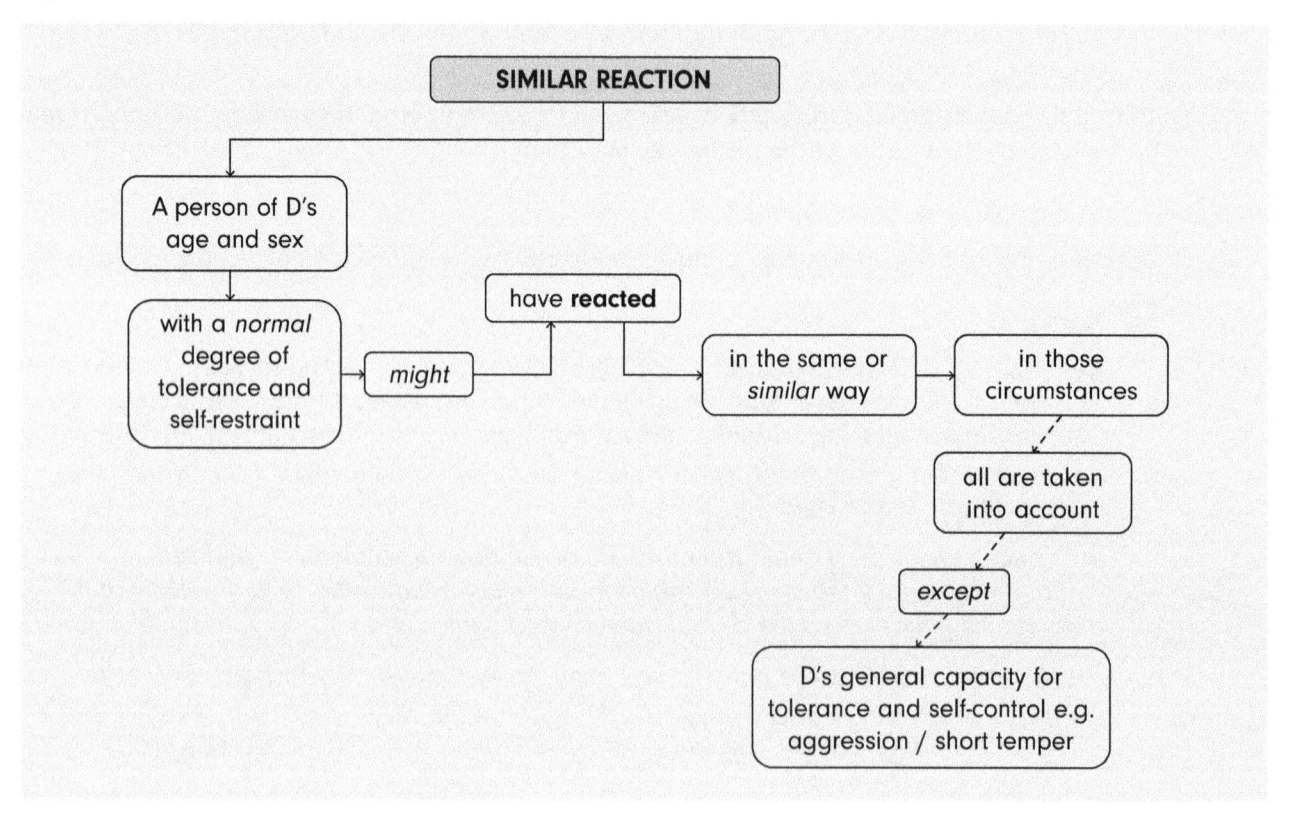

4.7.5 Summary of the partial defence of loss of control

- The defendant must actually lose control.
- The loss of self-control must be attributable to a qualifying trigger so that:
  - i the defendant feared serious violence from the victim against either the defendant or another identified person; and/or
  - ii something was said or done that constituted circumstances of an extremely grave character and that caused the defendant to have a justifiable sense of being seriously wronged.
- Sexual infidelity cannot be relied upon on its own as a qualifying trigger, but it can be taken into account as one of a number of factors. Thus, its mere presence does not prevent reliance on the defence where there exist other qualifying triggers.
- It must be shown that a person of the defendant's sex and age with a normal degree of tolerance and self-restraint might have reacted in the same or a similar way in the circumstances.

4.7.6 Sufficiency of evidence

In the past, if the defendant raised any evidence of provocation, the judge had no choice but to allow the matter to be put before the jury. However, there is now a filter on whether this occurs. Under s 54(5) of the CJA 2009, the defence of loss of control can only be presented to the jury if there is sufficient evidence that:

- in the opinion of the trial judge, a jury, properly directed, could reasonably conclude that the defence might apply.

How this works in practice is that, at the conclusion of the evidence, the trial judge will consider whether enough evidence has been raised in respect of all the components of the defence. If any one element is missing, that is the end of the matter and the partial defence will not apply. The jury will have no involvement at this stage.

In R v Jewell (see earlier in this chapter), when giving evidence, the defendant recited as if from legal textbooks: 'I did it because I lost control. I could not control my actions.' The Court of Appeal judges confirmed that a mere assertion by the defendant that he had lost control was not on its own sufficient evidence upon which a jury could reasonably conclude that the defence might apply. As a consequence, the defendant was convicted of murder.

Other examples of circumstances where the judge could or did intervene to remove the partial defence entirely from consideration by the jury include deaths in response to:

(a) a baby's persistent crying

(b) so-called 'honour killings'

(c) a conditional threat to prevent the defendant seeing his children unless he agreed to the victim's divorce settlement terms.

However, these would rarely arise in practice.

Summary

- The actus reus and mens rea for voluntary manslaughter and murder are the same. The victim must be unlawfully killed and the defendant must do so intending to kill or cause grievous bodily harm.

Criminal Law

- In certain situations, the law accepts that the accused's culpability should be reduced. The defendant remains liable for causing the death, but their behaviour is excused in some way. These are referred to as the partial defences.
- This is significant as the sentence for voluntary manslaughter is at the court's discretion and does not necessarily involve imprisonment at all, let alone life imprisonment.
- The most commonly pleaded partial defences are where the defendant was acting under diminished responsibility or suffered from a loss of self-control.

Figure 4.7 Summary of murder and the partial defences

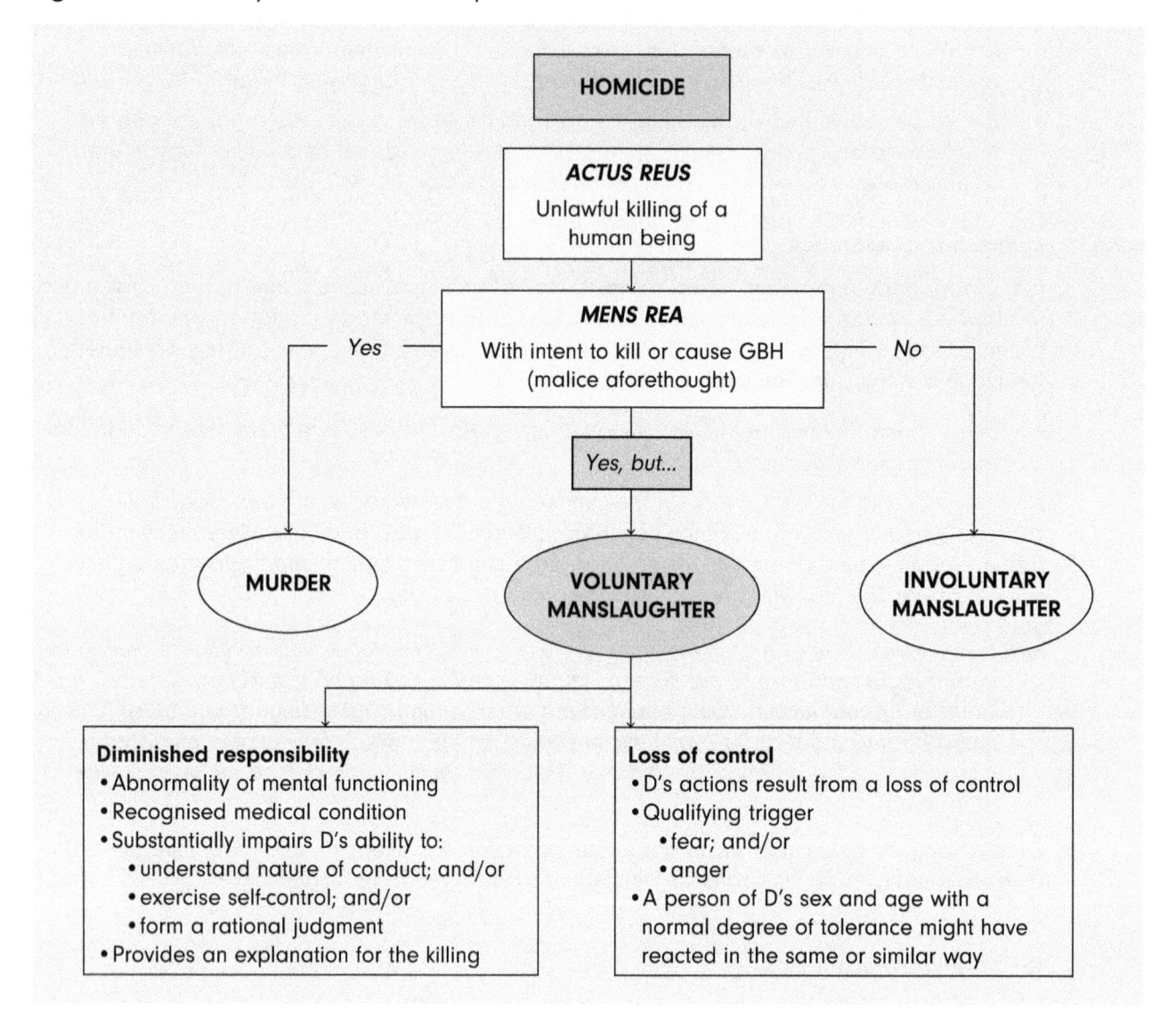

```
                          HOMICIDE
                              |
                         ACTUS REUS
                      Unlawful killing of a
                         human being
                              |
                          MENS REA
        Yes ─── With intent to kill or cause GBH ─── No
                     (malice aforethought)
                              |
                          Yes, but...
                              |
         ┌────────────────────┼────────────────────┐
      MURDER            VOLUNTARY            INVOLUNTARY
                       MANSLAUGHTER         MANSLAUGHTER
                              |
              ┌───────────────┴───────────────┐
```

Diminished responsibility
- Abnormality of mental functioning
- Recognised medical condition
- Substantially impairs D's ability to:
  - understand nature of conduct; and/or
  - exercise self-control; and/or
  - form a rational judgment
- Provides an explanation for the killing

Loss of control
- D's actions result from a loss of control
- Qualifying trigger
  - fear; and/or
  - anger
- A person of D's sex and age with a normal degree of tolerance might have reacted in the same or similar way

Sample questions

Question 1

The defendant's house has been burgled seven times in the past three years and he is unable to afford the increased premium for home insurance. One night, he is awoken by a noise. He picks up the shotgun that he keeps by his bed and goes downstairs to investigate. He sees a burglar trying to break into a window in the kitchen and angrily fires the gun towards him. The shell from the shotgun breaks through the glass and kills the burglar instantly. The defendant is shocked by the burglar's death. He believed the glass would deflect the shot because the gun is not very powerful and is only used for sport. He is adamant that he only intended to frighten the burglar.

Which statement provides the best assessment of the defendant's potential liability for murder?

A   The defendant had neither direct nor indirect intent to kill the burglar or cause him grievous bodily harm.

B   The defendant had direct intent to kill the burglar.

C   The defendant had direct intent to cause grievous bodily harm to the burglar.

D   The defendant had indirect intent to kill the burglar.

E   The defendant had indirect intent to cause grievous bodily harm to the burglar.

Answer

The best answer is option A. The defendant does not have the direct intent to kill or cause grievous bodily harm as he states that he only intended to frighten the burglar, so options B and C are wrong. He does not have indirect intent either because the evidence suggests that he does not foresee death or serious injury as a virtually certain consequence of his action. The defendant thought that the glass would deflect the shot and his knowledge that the gun is not powerful and only used for sport supports this view. Hence, options D and E do not provide the best assessment of the evidence.

Question 2

A woman is 40 years of age and has been married to a man for 15 years. During this time, the man has subjected his wife to frequent and serious violent attacks and daily verbal abuse. She also suspects the man of having an affair with her best friend and she is furious about this. One evening, the man returns home and immediately begins to complain about how untidy the house is and what the woman has cooked for their evening meal. As the man is sitting eating his dinner with his back to her, the woman throws a pan of boiling water over him. The man subsequently dies from his injuries.

Which of the following best describes the woman's liability for the man's death?

A   The woman is liable for murder because of the manner in which she kills the man particularly as he was no threat to her at the time she attacks him.

B   The woman cannot argue the partial defence of loss of control because it is unreasonable to lose control just because the man complains about the state of the house and what has been cooked for dinner.

C   The woman cannot rely on the anger trigger because sexual infidelity must be disregarded as a thing said or done and this is a factor in her response.

D   The woman may rely on the qualifying trigger of fear because she is afraid of serious violence from the man as his abuse occurs on a frequent basis.

E   The woman may rely on loss of control as a partial defence because a 40-year-old woman with a normal degree of tolerance and self-restraint and in her circumstances would have reacted in the same or similar way.

Criminal Law

Answer

The correct answer is option D. One of the qualifying triggers for loss of control is that a defendant feared serious violence from the victim against either themselves or another identified person. This would apply here as the woman suffered abuse from the man on a frequent basis.

Option A is wrong because it is irrelevant that the man was no threat to her at the time she attacks him provided that she is genuinely in fear of serious violence (the fear trigger). The method the woman uses would be relevant to the third element when the jury consider how a person of her age and sex with a normal degree of tolerance and self-restraint might have reacted in those circumstances.

Option B is wrong because the final incident need not be significant in itself; for loss of control, the defendant may rely upon an accumulation of events to explain their reaction to the final one. Option C is wrong because, although sexual infidelity on its own may not be relied upon for the anger trigger, it can be as part of the overall context. Here, there are other factors, primarily the man's physical and verbal abuse. Option E is wrong due to the inclusion of the word 'would'. The jury must be satisfied that a 40-year-old woman 'might' have reacted in the same or similar way.

Question 3

A man is charged with murder after he kills his neighbour during an argument over loud music. In a fit of rage, the man grabbed a spade which was lying on the lawn and hit the neighbour over the head with it. The man was convinced that the neighbour was spying on him and trying to get him evicted from his property. The man supplies a medical report to the court which concludes that he is suffering from paranoia.

Which of the following best describes how this affects the man's liability for his neighbour's death?

A   The evidence suggests that the man killed the neighbour in a fit of rage so he cannot succeed in his partial defence of diminished responsibility.

B   Although paranoia is an abnormality of mental functioning arising from a recognised medical condition, the man cannot plead the partial defence of diminished responsibility as well as loss of control.

C   The man need only prove that he is suffering from a recognised medical condition to ensure that he is found not guilty of murder but only of voluntary manslaughter.

D   As the man acted quite deliberately in picking up the spade and hitting his neighbour with it, he cannot demonstrate an impairment of his ability to do various things as required for diminished responsibility.

E   The man's paranoia substantially impairs his ability to exercise self-control and/or form a rational judgment and so he will be able to establish this element.

Answer

Option E is the correct answer. The other requirements, including that the paranoia is an abnormality of mental functioning arising from a recognised medical condition, would also need to be established.

Option A is wrong because whether the man was in a fit of rage is not the question for the court when determining if the partial defences apply. Option B is wrong as the man may plead both loss of control and diminished responsibility, although he is only likely to succeed with one. Option C is wrong as there are other elements that must be proved by the defendant before successfully pleading diminished responsibility, specifically that the medical condition substantially impaired his ability to do various things and provides an explanation for the killing. Option D is wrong; just because the man acted deliberately does not in itself preclude him from relying upon his medical condition provided he can establish the other elements of the partial defence.

5 Homicide II: Involuntary Manslaughter

5.1	Introduction	94
5.2	Murder, voluntary and involuntary manslaughter	94
5.3	Unlawful act manslaughter	95
5.4	Gross negligence manslaughter	99

SQE1 syllabus

By the end of this chapter you will be able to apply relevant core legal principles and rules appropriately and effectively, at the level of a competent newly qualified solicitor in practice, to realistic client-based and ethical problems and situations in the area of **involuntary manslaughter**.

Note that, as students are not usually required to recall specific case names, or cite statutory or regulatory authorities, these are provided for illustrative purposes only.

Learning outcomes

The learning outcomes for this chapter are:

- to understand unlawful act manslaughter and gross negligence manslaughter and explain the elements of these offences; and
- to appreciate how involuntary manslaughter is applied in practice.

5.1 Introduction

This chapter deals with situations where a defendant kills the victim but does so without intending either death or grievous bodily harm. Thus, although they have committed the actus reus of murder, they have not satisfied the mens rea. The accused may only have intended minor harm, or indeed no harm at all but, despite this and perhaps due to pure misfortune, they cause the victim's death.

In these situations, the defendant may be guilty of involuntary manslaughter of which there are two types. The first is unlawful act manslaughter and the other is manslaughter by gross negligence.

5.2 Murder, voluntary and involuntary manslaughter

For all homicides, the defendant must unlawfully cause the death of a human being. However, a murder conviction is reduced to voluntary manslaughter if the defendant has the benefit of an excuse, in the form of a partial defence, as covered in **Chapter 4**. Involuntary manslaughter is distinguished by the mens rea as there is no requirement to prove that the defendant intended to kill or cause grievous bodily harm.

The flowchart in **Figure 5.1** summarises the three types of homicide.

Figure 5.1 Types of homicide

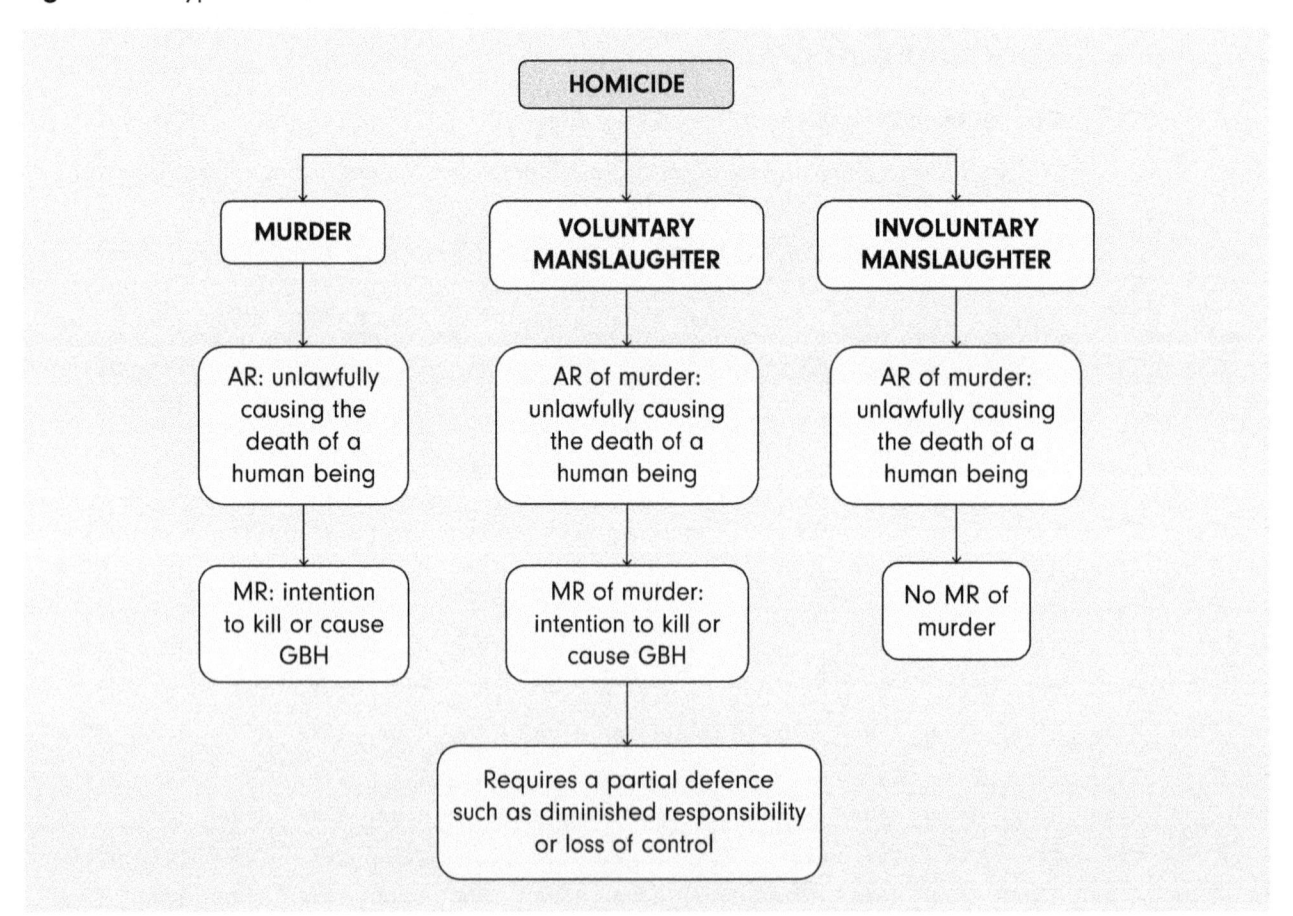

5.3 Unlawful act manslaughter

Unlawful act manslaughter is also referred to as unlawful and dangerous act manslaughter – a title that includes many of the elements required to establish the offence. There is also an alternate description of the offence as constructive manslaughter because liability for the death is 'constructed' from the fact the defendant has committed a lesser crime. However, it is important to remember that these are just different names for the same offence.

> *In the case of* DPP v Newbury and Jones *[1977] AC 500, the defendants pushed a paving stone over a bridge into the path of a train, smashing the train window and killing the guard. They were convicted of manslaughter and appealed unsuccessfully. The Court of Appeal took the opportunity to define this manslaughter and identified the elements that must be proved by the prosecution to secure a conviction.*
>
> *It was held that, provided the defendant commits a crime (an unlawful act) that is objectively dangerous and that causes the victim's death, the defendant will be guilty of manslaughter. The unlawful act in this case was never clearly established, although it was likely to have been criminal damage. The importance of this ruling was the clarification that the unlawful act does not need to be an assault – it may be burglary, robbery, theft and so on.*

Consequently, the actus reus and mens rea of unlawful act manslaughter may be summarised as in **Table 5.1**.

Table 5.1 Actus reus and mens rea of unlawful act manslaughter

Actus reus	Mens rea
The defendant must: • do an unlawful act; which • is dangerous; and • causes the victim's death	• of the unlawful act

5.3.1 Unlawful act

The first element that the prosecution must prove is that the defendant has committed an unlawful act, namely a crime with a mens rea of intent or recklessness. Crimes of negligence, such as careless driving, do not qualify.

There must be an unlawful *act*, so it follows that a failure to act cannot give rise to a charge of this type of manslaughter. There must be some form of positive action by the defendant.

> ⭐ **Example**
>
> *Vera's one-year-old son, Jonny, dies as a result of her neglect. Although Vera may be criminally liable for other offences, she cannot be convicted of unlawful act manslaughter.*

In most cases, the unlawful act will be one of the assaults although, as mentioned previously, it does not have to be. When dealing with a case where the unlawful act is a non-fatal offence, there is no need to worry about which type – the prosecution will choose the easiest level of assault to prove and this will usually be what is known as a physical assault.

✪ Examples

(a) Solly is unhappy with Benjy, a member of his team, who arrives late for an important rugby match. They begin arguing and Solly pushes Benjy in the chest, causing him to fall backwards and strike his head on the concrete floor. Benjy dies as a result of a bleed to the brain.

The unlawful act here is battery (the application of unlawful personal force). As this is an offence that may be committed either intentionally or recklessly, it counts as an unlawful act for the purposes of unlawful act manslaughter.

(b) Dawood breaks into his neighbour's property in the middle of the night. The house is owned by Harold, a frail 85-year-old man with chronic asthma. Harold hears a noise and comes out of his bedroom where he is confronted by Dawood. Harold is terrified and suffers a severe asthma attack from which he dies.

The unlawful act here is the burglary. As it causes Harold's death, Dawood is likely to be convicted of manslaughter.

The only requirement is that the unlawful act is a criminal offence in law; only rarely will there be occasions where this element is not satisfied.

In R v Lamb [1967] 2 QB 981, the defendant and the victim were fooling about with a revolver. As a practical joke, and unaware the bullets rotated in the chamber, the defendant pointed the gun at his friend. He pulled the trigger and shot the victim dead. Lamb was found not guilty of unlawful act manslaughter on appeal because there was no assault. The reason was that by simply pulling the trigger of a revolver, the defendant did not commit an unlawful act. He believed they were just playing a game and this in itself was not a criminal offence.

5.3.2 Dangerous act

In addition to being unlawful, the act must also be dangerous – a question that falls to be determined by the jury.

5.3.2.1 Test for dangerousness

Exactly how dangerous the unlawful act must be has been considered in case law.

In R v Church [1966] 1 QB 59, the Court of Appeal held that the unlawful act must be one that:

> *all sober and reasonable people would inevitably recognise must subject the other person to, at least, the risk of some harm ... albeit not serious harm.*

This is an objective test, as is apparent from the reference to reasonable people. Thus, it is not necessary for the prosecution to prove that this particular defendant realised the act was dangerous. Whether they have done an unlawful dangerous act is ultimately a question of fact for the jury to determine based upon the evidence put before it. In simple terms, the act must be dangerous from the point of view of the (ordinary) reasonable person.

5.3.2.2 Knowledge required

In determining whether the reasonable person would have recognised a risk of some harm, they are deemed to have the knowledge the defendant had, or should have had, at the time of the offence.

In R v Dawson [1985] 81 Cr App R 150, three defendants attempted to rob a petrol station wearing masks and armed with a pickaxe handle and replica guns. The petrol attendant was aged 60 and suffered from heart disease. After the defendants fled, he suffered a heart attack and died.

The defendants' conviction for manslaughter was quashed because, although the jury was aware of the attendant's heart condition, a sober and reasonable person present at the time of the robbery would not have been. The reasonable person has the same knowledge as the defendants, and none of them knew of the victim's vulnerability.

This outcome differs from the Dawood and Harold example in **section 5.3.1** above. The reason is because Dawood was Harold's neighbour and so he is likely to be aware of Harold's age and frailty. Such knowledge would have made the burglary dangerous from the outset. Even if not, Harold's condition would have been obvious at the time Dawood was disturbed and so the unlawful act (of burglary) becomes dangerous at this point.

Whether an act is categorised as objectively dangerous will depend upon the particular facts. A burglary that took place at a property situated in a remote rural location was found to be dangerous when the defendants ran over and killed the victim as they were fleeing the scene. The reason was that access to the premises was restricted to a single lane track. The unlawful act was held to be objectively dangerous because a reasonable and sober person would recognise that, if anyone tried to intervene in these circumstances, there would be the risk of them suffering some harm.

Case law establishes that the knowledge held by the reasonable person may be apparent in advance or gleaned during the crime. Because of the isolated location and single means of escape, this particular burglary was found to be dangerous from the outset.

5.3.2.3 Summary of 'dangerous'

- 'Dangerous' means the act carries the risk of some harm to some person, but not necessarily serious harm.
- The defendant need not foresee the precise form or sort of harm that ensues.
- The test is entirely objective, namely, whether all sober and reasonable people would think the act was dangerous; not whether the defendant themselves did.
- The reasonable person is deemed to have the knowledge the defendant had, or should have had, at the time of the offence, had they been present at the scene of the crime and watched the whole act being performed.

5.3.3 Causes death

The final element of the actus reus of unlawful act manslaughter is that the unlawful act causes the victim's death. The usual rules of causation apply so it must be proved that the defendant was both the factual and legal cause of the victim's death. These principles are analysed in detail in **Chapter 1**. If the prosecution are unable to do so, the accused will not be liable for either murder or manslaughter, although they may be guilty of another criminal offence, for example an assault.

This requirement has caused some difficulties in the drugs offences, where the defendant supplied the victim with illegal drugs from which they die. If the victim freely and voluntarily injected themselves, the chain of causation will be broken and the defendant will not be guilty of unlawful act manslaughter.

5.3.4 Mens rea

The mens rea of unlawful act manslaughter will change depending upon the circumstances as it will be linked to the particular unlawful act. Although it will usually be the mens rea of an assault, it need not be.

Example

Keni sets fire to the council house in which he and his family live because it is too small for them and he wants to be rehoused. Unfortunately, and unknown to Keni, his wife and child have returned early from their holiday. He is horrified to discover that the house is not empty and, although he manages to rescue his wife, sadly his son dies in the fire.

Although Keni thought his family were on holiday, he remains criminally responsible for his son's death. To be guilty of manslaughter, the prosecution must first identify the unlawful act and, in this instance, the crime is that of arson. Arson is objectively dangerous as all sober and reasonable people would regard it as such, particularly when it relates to a domestic property. The unlawful act causes the boy's death.

There is no single definition of mens rea for this type of manslaughter – it simply needs to match the unlawful act. Thus, Keni must have the mens rea for arson, which he does as he intentionally sets fire to the property. In legal terms he has the direct intent to destroy the house that belongs to another, here the local authority.

In summary, Keni's liability for unlawful act manslaughter is:

<u>Actus reus</u>

- *unlawful act: arson*
- *dangerous: setting fire to a house is objectively dangerous*
- *causes death: Keni's son dies*

<u>Mens rea</u>

- *of the unlawful act of arson: Keni intentionally damages by fire property belonging to another (the local authority)*

5.3.5 Practical application of unlawful act manslaughter

Example

Caspian and Lola are standing beside a waterfall at a well-known beauty spot. Lola wants a selfie for her Instagram account and asks Caspian to photograph her with her phone. Lola keeps posing and, eventually, Caspian begins to lose patience. He lunges at Lola, intending to frighten her into believing that he is about to push her over but, unfortunately, Lola steps back in response, trips on a tree root and falls over the cliff dying instantly.

(a) Caspian is not guilty of murder as he does not have the requisite mens rea of an intention to kill or cause grievous bodily harm. He only intended to frighten Lola.

(b) If Caspian is charged with manslaughter, the prosecution must prove an unlawful act. Caspian does not have the mens rea for either s 18 of the OAPA 1861 (intention to cause grievous bodily harm) or s 20 (intention or recklessness as to causing some harm). However, all that is required is for the prosecution to establish any unlawful act even if this does not seem to match the seriousness of the event. Caspian caused Lola to apprehend the application of unlawful force and did so intentionally, as his stated aim was to frighten her. Thus, he satisfies both the actus reus and the mens rea of the offence of simple assault.

(c) The unlawful act must be objectively dangerous. Given that Lola was standing at the edge of a waterfall, Caspian's act would be regarded by all reasonable people as carrying the risk of some harm to some person, in this case, Lola.

(d) The unlawful and dangerous act caused Lola's death as she fell over the cliff and died from her injuries.

In this instance, Caspian would be criminally liable for unlawful act manslaughter.

5.3.6 Summary of unlawful act manslaughter

Having considered the components required for unlawful act manslaughter, it becomes apparent why it is also known as unlawful dangerous act manslaughter, as this closely mirrors its definition. **Figure 5.2** summarises the main issues that arise when analysing whether the defendant is guilty of this offence.

Figure 5.2 Unlawful act manslaughter

```
                    UNLAWFUL ACT
                    MANSLAUGHTER
                         |
              ┌──────────┴──────────┐
              AR                    MR
              |                     |
   Not an ─── D must do an    The MR of the
   omission   unlawful act    unlawful act
              |                     |
   A crime with a                Changes to 'fit
   MR of intention or ──┐        in' with the
   recklessness         |        unlawful act
                        |
   Objective: sober ──  which is dangerous
   and reasonable             |
   people would think   causes V's death
   the act dangerous          |
                              |
   Dangerous: the         Usual rules of
   act carries the risk   factual and legal
   of some harm to        causation apply
   some person
```

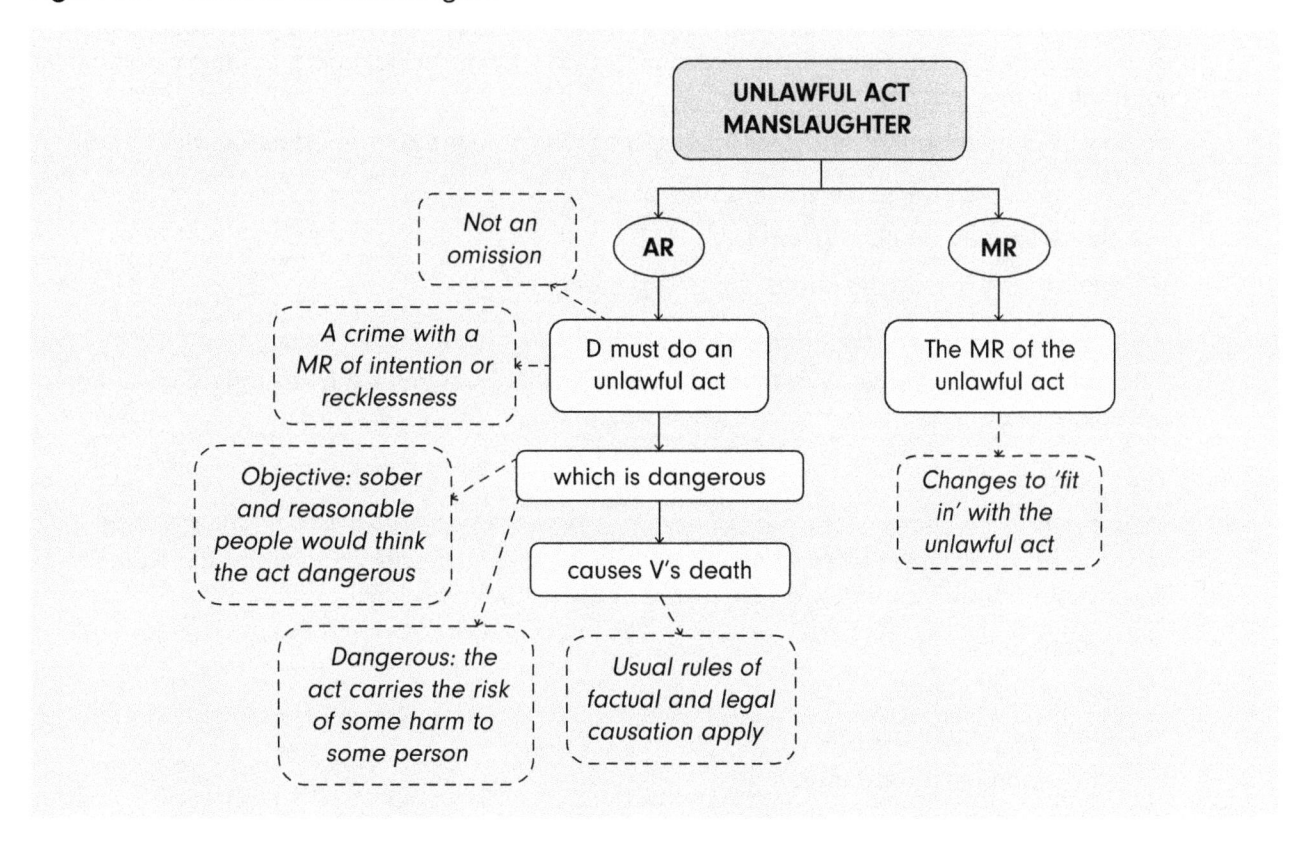

5.4 Gross negligence manslaughter

There is a second type of involuntary manslaughter, that of gross negligence manslaughter. As with unlawful act manslaughter, the accused does not intend either to kill the victim or to cause them serious bodily harm. However, there are some key differences as outlined in **Table 5.2**.

Table 5.2 Comparison of unlawful act and gross negligence manslaughter

Similarities	Differences
In both gross negligence and unlawful act manslaughter: • D unlawfully causes the death of V • D does not intend to kill V or to cause serious bodily harm	Unlawful act manslaughter: • only applies where D has a criminal state of mind (intention or recklessness) • cannot be committed negligently • requires an act Gross negligence manslaughter: • only requires negligence • may be committed by an act or by omission

Gross negligence manslaughter is unusual in that it 'mops up' defendants who would not normally expect to be caught by the criminal justice system, including professionals doing their job such as medical practitioners.

To convict a defendant of gross negligence manslaughter, the court must be satisfied that:

- the defendant owed the victim a duty of care;
- the defendant breached that duty;
- the breach caused the death of the victim; and
- the defendant's conduct was grossly negligent.

This definition looks very similar to the civil wrong of tort, but there is a key difference – the breach must be gross.

5.4.1 Duty of care

That a duty of care is owed by the defendant to the victim is a prerequisite of this offence. In most cases, determining whether there is a duty to act is quite straightforward; for example, it is well established that a duty of care exists between the following:

- parent and child
- doctor and patient
- employer and employee
- driver and other road users
- occupier and visitor.

However, some situations are rather less clear cut and, in these rare cases, the court must decide.

5.4.1.1 Approach taken by the courts

A defendant will only be liable for gross negligence manslaughter if a duty exists. Determining this issue is a matter of both law and fact.

- Where there is a clear duty, as between a medical practitioner and a patient, or a statutory duty, the judge can direct the jury that a duty of care exists.
- Where the existence of a duty is not clear, the judge must decide whether there is any evidence that is capable of establishing one. If not, the offence falls at the first hurdle.
- If there is such evidence, the jury will determine whether a duty of care is present in the scenario before it.

⭐ Example

Olivia supplied her friend, Lydia, with heroin. Lydia overdosed but, instead of seeking medical assistance, Olivia just kept her under observation overnight as she was afraid of getting into trouble. Lydia died. As this situation was not covered by the established duties, the court was required to determine the issue. After some consideration, Olivia was held to owe a duty of care on the basis that she had created or contributed to a state of affairs that was life-threatening and ought to have taken reasonable steps to save Lydia's life.

5.4.1.2 Omissions

Unlike unlawful act manslaughter, gross negligence manslaughter can be committed by omission, as well as where the defendant does a positive act or behaves negligently. Indeed, in practice, it is more commonly applied to situations where the defendant is under a duty to act but fails to do so. The situations in which a defendant may be liable for their omission to act are covered in **Chapter 1**. The general rule is that the criminal law does not impose a duty on a person to act. However, there are a number of exceptions to this rule including where there is a special relationship, a voluntary assumption of responsibility, a contractual or statutory duty and a duty to avert a danger created by the defendant.

5.4.2 Breach of duty

The prosecution must also prove that the defendant breached their duty of care towards the victim, either by the performance of a positive act or by a failure to act. The ordinary principles of negligence will apply to ascertain whether a breach has occurred.

- A defendant will breach their duty of care to the victim where their conduct falls below that expected of a reasonable person. There is no need to establish that the defendant was aware their conduct may fall below this standard – just that it did.

- Where the defendant has special knowledge or expertise, such as a doctor, they will be expected to meet the standard of care expected of a reasonable person with that knowledge or expertise.

The ordinary principles of the law of negligence apply to ascertain whether the accused breached their duty of care to the victim.

5.4.3 Causes death

It must be shown that the defendant's breach of duty caused the death of the victim and the usual rules of causation will apply here. These are set out in detail in **Chapter 1**. In practice, this aspect will not usually cause any significant difficulties to the jury. Indeed, it is the final part of the test that makes the difference between a negligent act and a criminal one.

5.4.4 Gross negligence

The breach of duty must be grossly negligent. This means that the conduct of the defendant must be sufficiently bad as to justify the law imposing a criminal penalty.

In the case of R v Bateman [1925] All ER 25, a patient died following negligent treatment and the doctor was charged with gross negligence manslaughter. Lord Hewart CJ stated that:

> *in order to establish criminal liability the facts must be such that, in the opinion of the jury, the negligence of the accused went beyond a mere matter of compensation between subjects and showed such disregard for the life and safety of others as to amount to a crime against the State and conduct deserving punishment.*

A simple lack of care, sufficient for the tort of negligence, will not satisfy the test for negligence in the context of manslaughter.

It is for the jury to determine whether as a matter of fact the defendant's breach of duty was serious enough to be grossly negligent.

> *The leading case on gross negligence manslaughter is that of* R v Adomako [1995] 1 AC 171 *involving an anaesthetist who failed to notice that the oxygen supply to a patient had become disconnected. As a consequence, the patient suffered a cardiac arrest and died. Lord Mackay confirmed that:*
>
>> *The essence of the matter ... is whether, having regard to the risk of death involved, the conduct of the defendant was so bad in all the circumstances as to amount in [the jury's] judgment to a criminal act or omission.*

The Court of Appeal's judgment clarified that one aspect in deciding whether the defendant's conduct was so bad as to be worthy of criminal sanction is the risk of death involved.

5.4.4.1 Risk of death

For the defendant to be criminally liable for gross negligence manslaughter, there must be a risk their conduct could cause death.

> *In R v Singh [1999] Crim LR 582, the court held that to establish gross negligence manslaughter:*
>
>> *the circumstances must be such that a reasonably prudent person would have foreseen a serious and obvious risk not merely of injury or even of serious injury but of death.*

The test was satisfied where:

- A defendant who was smuggling illegal immigrants into the country in the back of his lorry sealed the air vent to reduce the risk of discovery. The immigrants died of suffocation.

This test was *not* satisfied where:

- A doctor failed to attend a 12-year-old boy who subsequently died from a very rare disease; the mere possibility that an assessment may reveal something life-threatening is not the same as an obvious risk of death.

5.4.4.2 How does the jury approach the meaning of 'gross'?

The prosecution do not need to provide evidence that the defendant acted either intentionally or recklessly because there is no requirement for a 'criminal' state of mind to secure a conviction for gross negligence manslaughter.

Whether the breach of duty is gross will depend upon its seriousness and this is clearly a question of degree. The jury will need to consider 'grossness' in light of the circumstances in which the defendant found themselves at the time when the breach occurred.

Whilst experts may guide the jury on what behaviour is expected in that situation, the question of whether the defendant's negligence is gross is one for the jury to decide. It will have to determine the extent to which the defendant's conduct departed from the proper standard of care expected. Serious or even very serious mistakes are unlikely to be sufficient for a conviction of gross negligence manslaughter; the accused's behaviour must be exceptionally bad and such a departure from, for example, a competent doctor, that it becomes criminal as a consequence.

> In R v Zaman [2017] EWCA Crim 1783, the defendant was found guilty of gross negligence manslaughter. Zaman owned a restaurant in which a customer died after eating a meal. The defendant had persistently failed over a period of several months to take steps to ensure customers suffering from a peanut allergy were not served food containing peanuts. Moreover, the supplier of the mixed nut powder that proved to be fatal had warned him that he should advertise the presence of nuts in his menu; but rather than do this, Zaman had reassured his customers that his menu did not contain any nuts.

5.4.5 Practical application of gross negligence manslaughter

Both Maisie and Barney are doctors on duty at their local hospital.

(a) Maisie is suffering from a hangover and lack of sleep after an all-night party. She administers a fatal dose of morphine to a seriously ill patient (Ivy) who dies a few hours later as a result of the overdose. Maisie misread the instructions as to the correct dosage to be administered.

(b) Barney is a junior doctor who has been working without sleep for 36 hours. In the early hours of the morning, in the absence of a consultant, he is asked to examine a patient, Roy, who appears to have a minor head wound. The patient is slurring his speech and, believing him to be intoxicated, Barney leaves him to sober up while he treats other patients as the department is severely short staffed. Unfortunately, Roy has suffered a fractured skull and dies from a bleed on the brain. He would have survived if Barney had identified the issue and arranged for appropriate treatment.

Maisie and Barney are not guilty of murder as they did not intend to kill or to cause grievous bodily harm. Furthermore, Maisie cannot be guilty of unlawful act manslaughter as she has not committed an unlawful act (she was acting with the consent of the patient in administering morphine and thus does not commit an assault). Neither can Barney because, in his case, the death was caused by a failure to act and unlawful act manslaughter requires a positive act.

What about gross negligence manslaughter? Both doctors owe a duty of care to their patients. It is also apparent that both have breached their duty and in doing so caused the death of Ivy and Roy. As there was a clear risk their conduct could cause death, the factor that will determine whether they are criminally liable for manslaughter is whether their negligence is gross. In other words, is their conduct so bad in all the circumstances as to make them criminally liable?

This is a matter that will be determined by the jury, whose members may legitimately have differing views. However, it is likely Barney will attract far more sympathy given that he was doing his best while working excessively long hours in a pressurised and short-staffed environment, with little support. In contrast, Maisie has acted irresponsibly in turning up to work while hungover and tired due to her attendance at a party.

5.4.6 Summary of gross negligence manslaughter

Manslaughter by gross negligence can be established if all the elements in **Figure 5.3** are present.

Figure 5.3 Gross negligence manslaughter

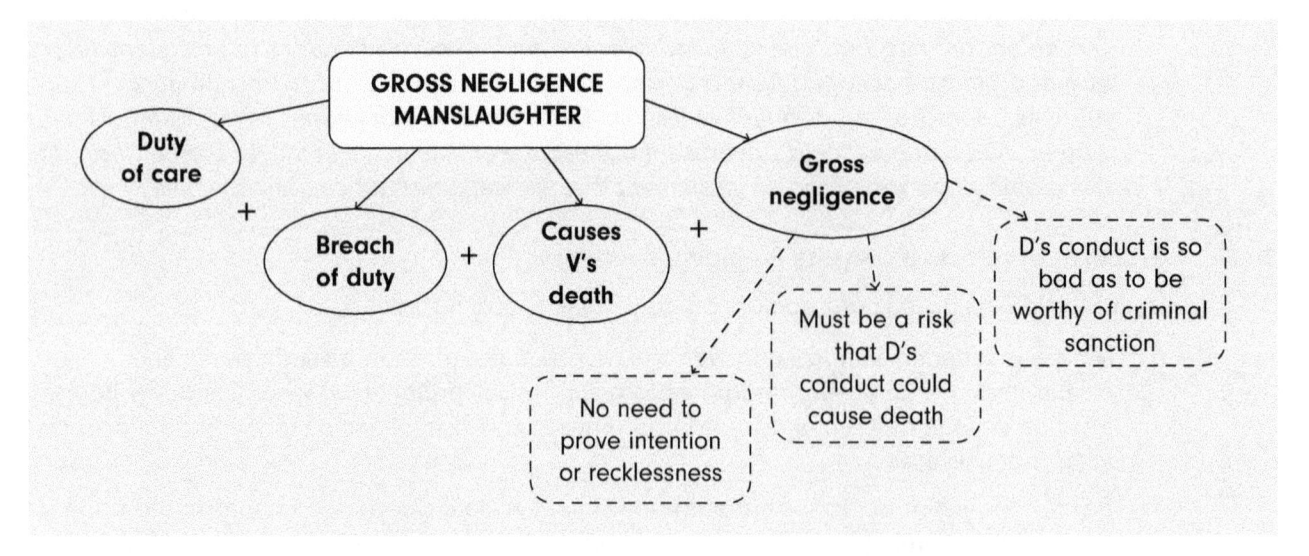

[Flowchart: GROSS NEGLIGENCE MANSLAUGHTER = Duty of care + Breach of duty + Causes V's death + Gross negligence. Gross negligence notes: No need to prove intention or recklessness; Must be a risk that D's conduct could cause death; D's conduct is so bad as to be worthy of criminal sanction.]

To establish gross negligence manslaughter, the prosecution must prove:

- A duty of care was owed by the defendant to the victim; in most instances, there will be a clear and established duty of care.
- The duty was breached; this will be determined based upon the particular facts of the case.
- There was a risk that the defendant's conduct could cause death.
- The breach of duty did cause the victim's death.
- The defendant fell so far below the standards of the reasonable person that they can be labelled grossly negligent and deserving of criminal punishment.

However:

- There is no need for the prosecution to establish intention or recklessness – the defendant is punished for their negligence.
- Liability for gross negligence manslaughter may be incurred through the defendant's omission to act (if they have a duty to do so) as well as by a positive act.

Summary

Having considered the involuntary manslaughters of unlawful act and gross negligence manslaughter, these have now been added to the flowchart (**Figure 5.4**) to provide a complete picture of homicide.

Figure 5.4 Summary of homicide

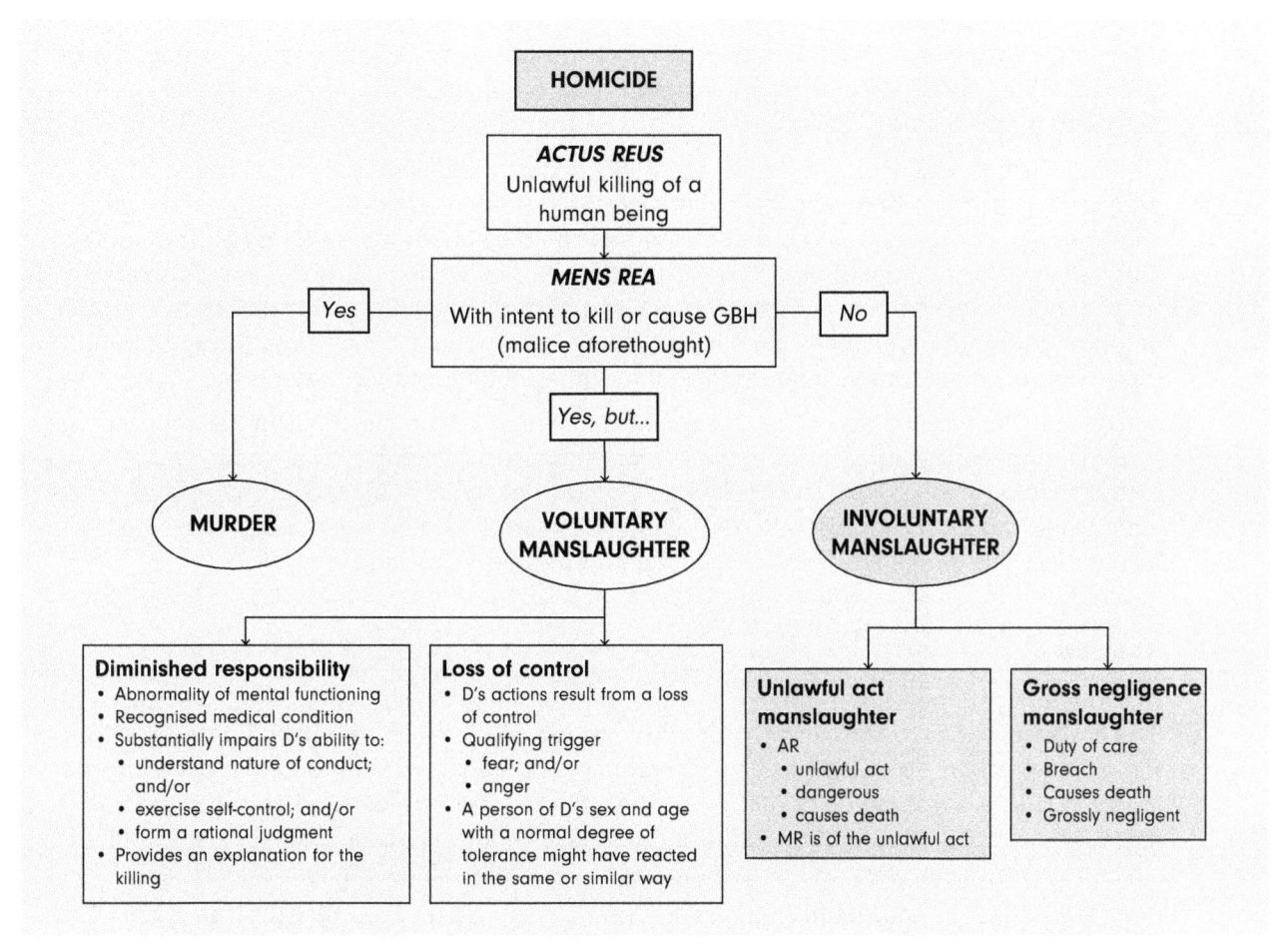

```
                        ┌──────────┐
                        │ HOMICIDE │
                        └────┬─────┘
                             │
                    ┌────────▼─────────┐
                    │   ACTUS REUS     │
                    │ Unlawful killing │
                    │  of a human being│
                    └────────┬─────────┘
                             │
              ┌──────────────▼──────────────┐
              │          MENS REA           │
    Yes ◄─────│ With intent to kill or cause│─────► No
              │  GBH (malice aforethought)  │
              └──────────────┬──────────────┘
                             │
                         Yes, but...
                             │
    ┌────────┐       ┌──────────────┐       ┌──────────────┐
    │ MURDER │       │  VOLUNTARY   │       │ INVOLUNTARY  │
    │        │       │ MANSLAUGHTER │       │ MANSLAUGHTER │
    └────────┘       └──────────────┘       └──────────────┘
```

Diminished responsibility	Loss of control	Unlawful act manslaughter	Gross negligence manslaughter

• Abnormality of mental functioning
• Recognised medical condition
• Substantially impairs D's ability to:
  • understand nature of conduct; and/or
  • exercise self-control; and/or
  • form a rational judgment
• Provides an explanation for the killing
	• D's actions result from a loss of control
	• Qualifying trigger
	  • fear; and/or
	  • anger
	• A person of D's sex and age with a normal degree of tolerance might have reacted in the same or similar way
		• AR
		  • unlawful act
		  • dangerous
		  • causes death
		• MR is of the unlawful act
			• Duty of care
			• Breach
			• Causes death
			• Grossly negligent

Sample questions

Question 1

A lawyer in the Crown Prosecution Service is asked to provide charging advice to the police in relation to a number of defendants.

A man sees a six-year-old child struggling in a swimming pool at a holiday park. The child is clearly in distress, but the man does nothing to help and the child drowns. A mother leaves her 18-month-old son unattended in a bath for 30 minutes while she talks to a friend on the telephone. The child drowns. A heating engineer fails to notice he has wrongly connected a customer's boiler when he services it because he is in a rush to finish work. The householder dies in her sleep from carbon monoxide poison that is leaking from the boiler. A woman drops her cigarette onto the ground and walks away as she believes (wrongly) that it has been extinguished. The ensuing fire destroys a nearby building.

Which defendants are most likely to be liable for gross negligence manslaughter?

A The man, the mother and the woman.

B The man and the heating engineer.

C The mother and the heating engineer.

D The mother, the heating engineer and the woman.

E All of them.

Criminal Law

Answer

Option C correctly lists the defendants who are most likely to be liable for gross negligence manslaughter. All the other answers either include a defendant who is not liable or miss one who is.

The mother has a duty of care to her son – this is both a statutory duty and a special relationship and she breaches this by leaving the child unattended for so long in a bath. Given his young age there is a risk her conduct could cause death and it does. The heating engineer has a contractual duty towards his customer to service the boiler with reasonable care and skill, and he breaches this by allowing carbon monoxide – a toxic gas – to leak. In both cases, the defendant's conduct is likely to be regarded as so gross (bad) as to be deserving of criminal punishment sufficient for gross negligence manslaughter.

In contrast, the man would not be liable for his failure to rescue the child. This is because there is no general duty to act and the law only imposes such a duty in exceptional circumstances – none of which apply here. Similarly, the woman is not under a duty of care when she drops her cigarette as, although she created a dangerous situation, she is unaware of this as she thought the cigarette had been extinguished.

Question 2

The defendant is out with a group of friends at a pub. She sees a woman, with whom she suspects her husband is having an affair, sitting on a stool at the bar and decides to confront her about the situation. An argument ensues, during which the defendant raises her hand to slap the woman across the face. The woman jerks backwards, overbalances and causes the stool to topple over. She falls onto the ground awkwardly and suffers a fractured neck from which she dies. The defendant is charged with unlawful act manslaughter.

Which statement correctly describes whether the defendant may be guilty of this offence?

A   Yes, because the act of raising her hand was dangerous as the woman was sitting on a stool.

B   Yes, because she was reckless as to causing death.

C   No, because the defendant did not touch the woman.

D   No, because the defendant did not intend to cause the woman's death.

E   No, because the defendant's act did not cause death as the woman died as a result of falling off the stool.

Answer

Option A is correct because raising a hand to slap someone who is sitting on a stool at a bar is objectively dangerous given the likelihood of injury if they fall off.

Options B and D are wrong as the prosecution do not need to establish that the woman either intended or was reckless as to causing the death. The mens rea required is that of the unlawful act – in this instance, intention or recklessness as to causing the victim to apprehend unlawful personal force. Option C is wrong as any unlawful act will satisfy the actus reus, including simple assault as here. Option E is wrong because the rules of factual and legal causation apply. But for the defendant's act, the woman would not have fallen off the stool and hit her head, and the defendant's conduct was also an operating and substantial cause of her death.

Question 3

A defendant is angry at the proposal by the local authority to build houses on local fields, as it will involve the destruction of the habitats of rare birds. He climbs up to the roof of the Town Hall and hangs a banner of protest onto the railings. As he is attaching it, the metal spike comes loose and falls towards the ground. A pedestrian who is passing is hit by the spike and killed by the impact. The defendant is horrified by what has happened as he thought the spike was secure.

Which of the following statements correctly describes the court's approach when determining the defendant's liability for unlawful act manslaughter?

A   Criminal damage is not an unlawful act for unlawful act manslaughter so the defendant cannot be liable.

B   The court will apply a subjective test in deciding whether the act was dangerous and the defendant thought the spike was secure.

C   For the act to be dangerous, it must carry a risk of death and this would be satisfied by the spike falling to the ground.

D   The defendant must have intended a physical assault which he did not on these facts.

E   The defendant is liable for causing the pedestrian's death even though he was horrified by what happened.

Answer

The correct answer is option E because the usual rules of factual and legal causation apply. But for the spike falling the pedestrian would not have died as and when they did, and the defendant's action was an operating and substantial cause of the death. The mens rea of the unlawful act is satisfied as he was reckless as to causing criminal damage.

Option A is wrong as criminal damage can be the unlawful act. Option B is wrong as the test for dangerousness is objective; whilst option C is wrong because to satisfy this test, the act must carry the risk of some harm – not death. Option D is wrong because, for unlawful act manslaughter, the mens rea must match the actus reus of the unlawful act, namely criminal damage on these facts. There is no requirement that the mens rea is of an assault, although it usually is.

6 The Property Offences

6.1	Introduction	110
6.2	Theft	110
6.3	Robbery	122
6.4	Burglary	125
6.5	Aggravated burglary	133

SQE1 syllabus

By the end of this chapter you will be able to apply relevant core legal principles and rules appropriately and effectively, at the level of a competent newly qualified solicitor in practice, to realistic client-based and ethical problems and situations in the area of **property offences**.

In this chapter, the test for dishonesty is commonly referred to as the '*Ivey* test' or the 'test in *Ivey v Genting*' from the authority which established it. In addition, burglary with intent is often referred to by reference to the statute, namely, 's 9(1)(a) burglary'; and burglary as 's 9(1)(b) burglary'. Otherwise, references to case names, or statutory or regulatory authorities, are provided for illustrative purposes only.

Learning outcomes

The learning outcomes for this chapter are:

- to understand and apply the elements of theft and robbery;
- to understand and apply the elements of burglary and aggravated burglary; and
- to appreciate how these offences are applied in practice.

6.1 Introduction

There are a number of property offences, many of which are set out in the Theft Act 1968. This chapter will consider four such crimes, beginning with theft and robbery and then moving on to consider burglary and its aggravated form.

6.2 Theft

The offence of theft is one of the most commonly reported crimes and it covers a wide range of criminal activity from simple shoplifting to sophisticated conduct, such as the taking of thousands of pounds of stock as a result of organised theft from a factory.

There are five key elements to theft and ss 2 to 6 of the TA 1968 give guidance on the interpretation of this offence. However, the statutory provisions have been supplemented by a considerable amount of case law, particularly in relation to dishonesty which is usually the most important requirement for the prosecution to prove. Theft is an either way offence, which means that it may be tried in either the magistrates' or the Crown Court and, if convicted, the defendant faces imprisonment of up to seven years.

6.2.1 Definition

The definition of theft is contained in s 1 of the TA 1968, which provides:

> A person is guilty of theft if he dishonestly appropriates property belonging to another with the intention of permanently depriving the other of it.

The actus reus is the appropriation of property belonging to another, whilst the mens rea is dishonesty coupled with an intention to permanently deprive. Thus, in the statutory definition, the mens rea effectively sandwiches the actus reus.

Having defined what theft is, the next five sections of the TA 1968 go on to explain these terms in more detail, although some are more successful than others in achieving this.

Elements of theft	Theft Act 1968
Dishonesty	s 2
Appropriation	s 3
Property	s 4
Belonging to another	s 5
An intention to permanently deprive	s 6

6.2.2 Actus reus

The features that make up the actus reus of theft are highlighted in bold in the above list and these will be considered in turn.

6.2.3 Appropriation

The physical act required by a defendant in order to establish the actus reus of theft is known as an 'appropriation' and this is usually easy to establish. According to s 3, appropriation is any assumption of the rights of an owner. This is extremely widely interpreted so that everyone spends much of their day assuming such rights. Consider these scenarios:

- Kathryn sells a book
- Laura eats a meal in a cafe
- Mo selects a birthday card from the local shop
- Narina grabs a £10 note from her classmate
- Otis pickpockets a wallet.

Taking something from someone is a clear example of an appropriation and this is what most people would consider as theft. However, in all these examples, there is an appropriation of property because the phrase 'any assumption ... of the rights of an owner' goes well beyond simply taking. Indeed, case law has developed the concept of appropriation so that this will rarely be an issue for the prosecution.

Appropriation includes:

(a) A shopper switching a price label on a piece of meat – *R v Morris* [1984] AC 320.

(b) Property passing with the consent of the owner – *DPP v Gomez* [1993] AC 442 (where a shop manager handed over goods on receipt of a fraudulent cheque).

(c) The receipt of a gift – *R v Hinks* [2000] UKHL 53.

The combined effect of these cases is that it is difficult to imagine a situation where a person is not appropriating property if it is dealt with in any way at all. This is because, to be an appropriation, the defendant need only assume any *one* right of the owner.

The examples (above) are appropriations because they are acts that an owner is entitled to carry out. How the person came to deal with the property (whether with or without the consent of the owner) is irrelevant to the issue. However, just because an appropriation occurs does not necessarily mean the individual is guilty of theft. This is because the offence is committed only when all five elements are satisfied at the same time and, in most instances, the person will not be dishonest.

6.2.3.1 Later assumption of the rights of an owner

Appropriation will usually occur at the time when the defendant first deals with the property, but the Theft Act's influence extends further. Section 3(1) states that appropriation includes where the defendant has come by the property (innocently or not) without stealing it, but later keeps or deals with it as an owner.

⭐ *Examples*

(a) *Suki borrows a book from the university library in February. In March, she decides to keep it permanently.*

(b) *Guy accidentally picks up his friend's watch. When he discovers his mistake, instead of returning it, Guy decides to sell the watch on Ebay.*

6.2.3.2 Can property be stolen more than once?

As it is possible to commit appropriations on a frequent basis, the question arises as to whether a defendant can be charged with more than one offence of theft.

In the scenario below, each time Ian deals with the car, there is an appropriation, as he is assuming a right of the owner. However, the case of *R v Atakpu* [1994] QB 69 confirms that the defendant can only commit theft of the property once.

Figure 6.1 Multiple appropriations

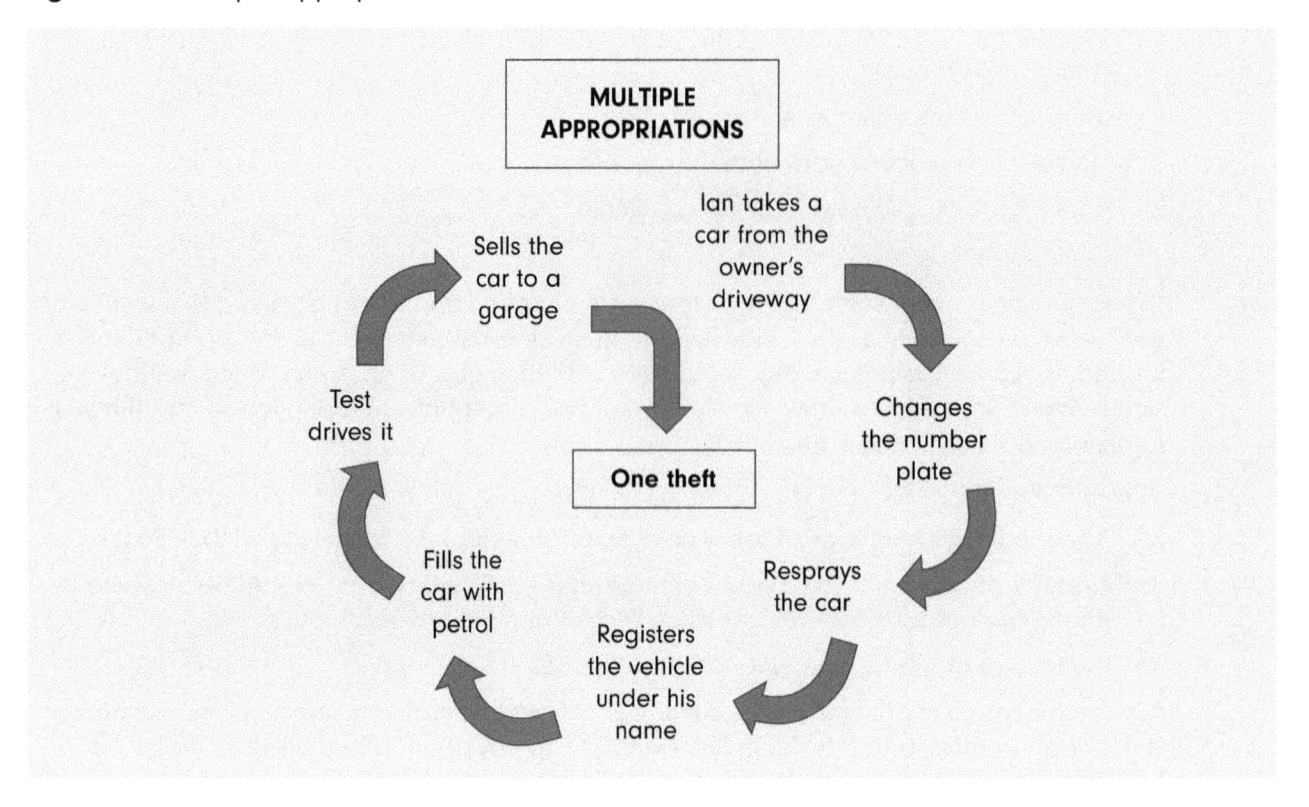

```
                    MULTIPLE
                  APPROPRIATIONS

                                    Ian takes a
         Sells the                  car from the
         car to a                   owner's
         garage                     driveway

  Test                                          Changes
  drives it                                     the number
                        One theft               plate

         Fills the                              Resprays
         car with                               the car
         petrol         Registers
                        the vehicle
                        under his
                        name
```

6.2.4 Property

The next requirement for the actus reus of theft is that there must be an appropriation of 'property'. This is defined in s 4 of the TA 1968 as:

> Money and all other property, real or personal, including things in action and other intangible property.

Most of the items in the list are fairly self-explanatory but others require further consideration.

- *Money*: Currency – notes and coins (cash).
- *Real property*: Land and things attached or fixed to it, such as a house, the plot of land on which it is built, and a garage.
- *Personal property*: This is the category most commonly stolen and would include, for example, cars, jewellery, clothes, mobile phones – the list is endless.
- *Things in action*: These are also referred to as 'chose in action'. They are things that cannot be physically seen or touched but are nevertheless of value and can be legally enforced, such as a right arising under a trust. Money in a bank account is another such example. If the account is in credit, the bank owes the account holder that money and the legal right to reclaim it is a thing in action. If money is transferred electronically, this could be theft of a thing in action.
- *Other intangible property*: An example would be a patent for a new drug.

6.2.4.1 When can land be stolen?

Despite its inclusion in s 4(1), land can only be stolen in exceptional circumstances.

(a) By a trustee in breach of trust

⭐ Example

Florence dies leaving her house, Bramble Cottage, to her granddaughter, Emma, who is aged 12. In her will, she appoints her brother, Ray, as executor to hold the property on trust for Emma until she reaches 18 years of age. Ray forges a signature on the documentation and transfers the cottage to his own name. Ray may be liable for theft of the land.

(b) By a person who is not in possession of the land if they appropriate anything forming part of the land either by severing it or after it has been severed

⭐ Example

Jade is annoyed that her neighbour is refusing to cut down a bush that overhangs her garden. She leans over the fence and chops down the bush. Jade may be guilty of theft as she has severed the bush from her neighbour's land.

Later the same day, Jade is walking through her local allotments when she sees a pile of vegetables that one of the gardeners has just dug up. She picks up a number of carrots and walks away. As Jade is not in possession of the allotment, she has committed theft because the carrots have been severed from the land.

(c) By a tenant who takes something fixed to the land that they are not supposed to take

⭐ Example

Gethan rents a house in the country. When he leaves the property, he takes the shelving from the kitchen (a fixture) and the greenhouse from the garden (a structure). Subject to the prosecution establishing the other four elements of the offence, Gethan is guilty of theft of these items.

6.2.4.2 What cannot be stolen?

Some things cannot be stolen and these include electricity and confidential information.

In Oxford v Moss [1979] Crim LR 119, a university student who saw his exam paper in advance was not guilty of theft because the exam questions were information, which cannot be stolen. The outcome would have been different if he had removed the paper itself, rather than just reading it, as he would have been liable for theft of the piece of paper.

Other items that cannot usually be stolen are:

(a) Mushrooms, flowers, fruit or foliage growing wild on land

A person who picks these items is innocent of theft provided this was not done for reward, sale or other commercial purposes. Thus, if a person picks a bunch of buttercups growing by the roadside, the flowers will not be 'property' under s 1 of the TA 1968 unless they intend to sell them.

(b) Wild creatures

Although wild creatures are excluded as property, there are exceptions. If a wild animal is tamed or ordinarily kept in captivity, for example a lion in a zoo, it may be stolen. Similarly, a wild creature that has been reduced into possession may be stolen; this would apply if the owner of land had snared a wild rabbit and someone else then took it.

6.2.5 Belonging to another

For an offence of theft to be committed, the property must belong to another according to s 5(1) of the TA 1968. Property will be regarded as belonging to another where any person has:

- possession;
- control; or
- any proprietary right or interest in the property in question.

Set out below are illustrations of this point.

⭐ Examples

(a) Cheung lends his mobile phone to his friend, Liu. Liu hands the phone to his partner, Xi, to look at Instagram. Joel grabs the phone from Xi and runs off. Joel has taken the property from Cheung (the owner) but also from Liu, as he has possession of the phone at the time of the theft, and Xi, who has control of it.

(b) Cheung and Liu set up a business partnership together. Liu withdraws money from the joint business account and spends it on a holiday. Liu has stolen from Cheung as they each have a proprietary right or interest in the property (the money).

Establishing whether property belongs to another is usually straightforward but, on occasion, the courts have been confronted by more unusual circumstances.

6.2.5.1 Theft of own property

Can a person steal their own property? This question has been considered by the courts and answered in the affirmative.

In R v Turner (No2) [1971] 2 All ER 441, the defendant's car was at his local garage overnight having been repaired. The arrangement with the garage was that it would be collected the following day. Instead, Turner sneaked onto the garage forecourt that night and drove his car away as he did not want to pay the repair bill. He argued that the vehicle did not belong to another but the Court of Appeal disagreed. As the garage was owed money by the defendant, it was lawful for them to retain possession of the car; hence, they had possession and control and so it 'belonged' to them under s 5. As a consequence, Turner was found guilty of theft.

6.2.5.2 When does ownership in property pass?

For the offence of theft to be committed, the property must belong to another, so determining who owns the property is crucial. This is particularly problematic with items such as food – because obviously it disappears into the defendant's stomach – and petrol, which mixes with the petrol inside the vehicle's tank. If the property does not belong to another, the defendant cannot be guilty of theft as one of the essential elements required for the offence is missing.

This issue was considered in the case of Edwards v Ddin [1976] 1 WLR 942. The defendant filled his car with petrol intending to pay for it, but then realised he did not have the means to do so. He drove away from the petrol forecourt without paying.

Deciding who owned the petrol was key to whether the defendant committed theft. The judges concluded that, as soon as the petrol entered the tank, the defendant had ownership, possession and control of it. Thus, the property no longer belonged to another. Because it was only at this point that the defendant decided not to pay, he could not be guilty of theft as, whilst he had the mens rea for the offence, one of the elements required for the actus reus was missing.

Although an interesting legal point, this question will rarely arise in practice as it only really applies to items such as food, which becomes part of the body once eaten, or petrol, which becomes an integral part of the vehicle.

6.2.5.3 Obligation to deal with property in a particular way

In certain situations, a person is given money by another for a particular purpose, such as for a school trip or to pay for competition entry fees in a sports club. If the normal rule applied, once handed over, the money would no longer belong to another and so the defendant could not steal it. To overcome this, s 5(3) states that:

> Where a person receives property from or on account of another, and is under an obligation to the other to retain and deal with that property or its proceeds in a particular way, the property or proceeds shall be regarded (as against him) as belonging to the other.

This issue has arisen in case law and the facts of two authorities are set out below to aid understanding of the circumstances in which such an obligation will apply.

Table 6.1 Obligation to deal with property in a particular way

Obligation under s 5(3)	No obligation under s 5(3)
Facts: D raised money by organising events for a charity. He paid it into a special bank account but then, rather than pay the sponsorship money over to the charity, he spent it on himself. *Judgment*: Although the sponsorship money had been given to the accused, he was under an obligation to deal with it in a particular way (to pay to the nominated charity). *Conclusion*: The property *did* belong to another – *R v Wain* [1995] 2 Cr App R 660.	*Facts*: D was a travel agent and received money from various clients to pay for flights, which went into his general business account. The flights were not booked and no monies were refunded. *Judgment*: D was not obliged to use the money that had been given to him for that specific purpose. This was because he was under no obligation to preserve the money in a separate fund. *Conclusion*: The property did *not* belong to another – *R v Hall* [1973] 1 QB 126.

6.2.5.4 Abandoned property

Such property does not belong to another and, provided it has been genuinely abandoned, no offence will be committed.

⭐ Examples

(a) *Seamus is walking home one evening when he passes a charity shop. He sees a bin bag full of clothing lying next to the door of the shop. Because it is very cold, Seamus selects a jumper from the bag, puts it on and then continues on his way.*

The courts are reluctant to treat property as abandoned and, in this particular case, it was held that the owner had not abandoned the bag as they intended the charity shop to have the items. This approach is evident in the next scenario.

(b) *Leon goes to a local golf club at night with sub-aqua diving equipment and retrieves a large number of golf balls from a lake on the course, which he sells online. His submission that the golf balls have been abandoned by the owners fails as, although the individual golfers may have abandoned the balls, they remain the property of the golf club itself.*

This issue has caused some controversy in relation to supermarket bins where out of date food is often discarded by the retailer. However, although individuals have been charged with theft after having removed food in these circumstances, the cases tend not to reach court, partly due to the adverse publicity generated.

Criminal Law

6.2.6 Summary of actus reus

The flowchart in **Figure 6.2** summarises the issues that may arise in relation to the actus reus of theft.

Figure 6.2 Actus reus of theft

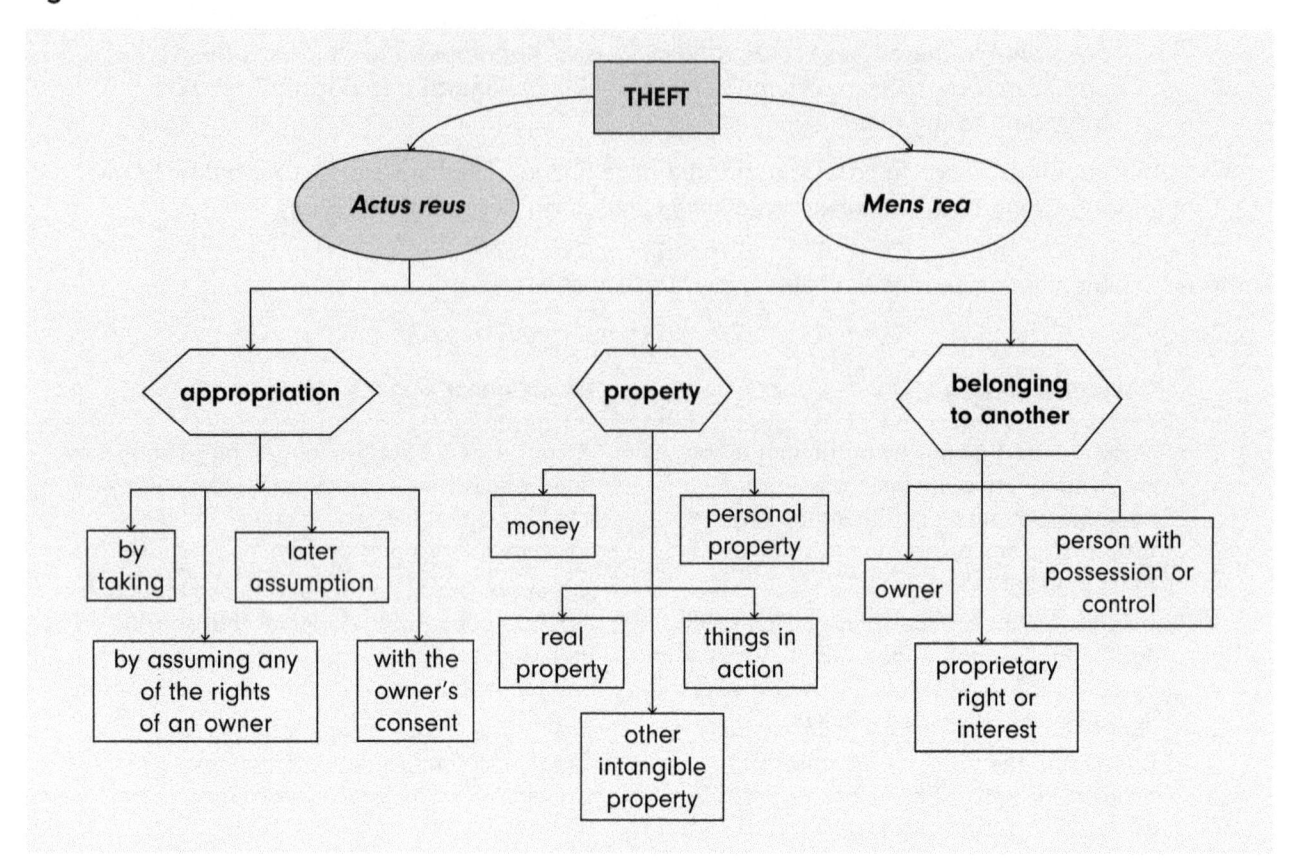

```
                            THEFT
                          /       \
                    Actus reus    Mens rea
                    /    |    \
         appropriation  property  belonging
                                  to another
         /    \         /    \      /    \
      by    later    money  personal  owner  person with
    taking  assumption      property         possession or
                                              control
   /    \              /    \
by assuming  with the  real  things in   proprietary
any of the   owner's   property action    right or
rights of    consent                       interest
an owner              other
                      intangible
                      property
```

6.2.7 Mens rea

For an accused to be guilty of theft, the prosecution must also prove mens rea beyond a reasonable doubt. The mens rea of theft is made up of two elements – dishonesty and an intention to permanently deprive.

6.2.8 Dishonesty

The effect of the wide interpretation of appropriation is that everyone appropriates frequently throughout the day, whether this be filling their supermarket trolley with food or selecting books from a library. However, this does not mean the entire population are thieves, as the offence also requires the person to have been dishonest when doing so. Although the TA 1968 provides no working definition of this key term, it does give a partial definition of three circumstances that will *not* amount to dishonesty and one circumstance that *may* still be regarded as dishonest. These are all contained in s 2.

The three situations listed in the TA 1968 where the defendant is not regarded as dishonest are defined in s 2(1). In each, the person believes:

- he has the right in law to the property (s 2(1)(a))

⭐ *Example*

Musa has lent £10 to Taiwo. Taiwo has not repaid Musa despite constant requests to do so. Musa therefore takes £10 from Taiwo's wallet without his knowledge. In this instance,

The Property Offences

Musa may argue that he does have the right in law to deprive Taiwo of the £10 because it was a debt owed to him.

- the owner would have consented had they known of the circumstances (s 2(1)(b))

✪ Example

Suki shares a flat with Dana. She has run out of food and her welfare benefits are not due to be paid until the next day and so she eats some of Dana's food from the fridge. Suki believes that Dana would have consented to this had she known of the circumstances.

- the owner cannot be discovered by taking reasonable steps (s 2(1)(c))

✪ Example

Ari picks up a £20 note that he finds on a busy high street pavement and decides to keep it. Realistically, he will not be able to find out who the owner is by taking reasonable steps. In contrast, if Ari had found a purse with bank cards inside, he would have been able to trace the owner and, thus, would almost certainly be regarded as dishonest.

Note that the test is a purely subjective test, so the question is what this particular defendant believed and not whether the belief was reasonable or not. However, the more unreasonable the belief, the less likely it is that a jury will accept the defendant did actually believe it.

The TA 1968 also gives limited assistance on who actually *would* be dishonest.

- a person may be dishonest even though they were willing to pay for the property (s 2(2))

✪ Example

Lucy is desperate to see her favourite music band play but the tickets have sold out. Her friend Anya has a ticket for the concert. Lucy takes this and leaves Anya an amount of money in excess of the ticket value, even though she knows Anya would not have agreed to sell her the ticket. Lucy is dishonest in this scenario.

It is up to the defendant to raise these issues but, having done so, the prosecution will then have to *disprove* them beyond a reasonable doubt.

Figure 6.3 Section 2 of the Theft Act 1968

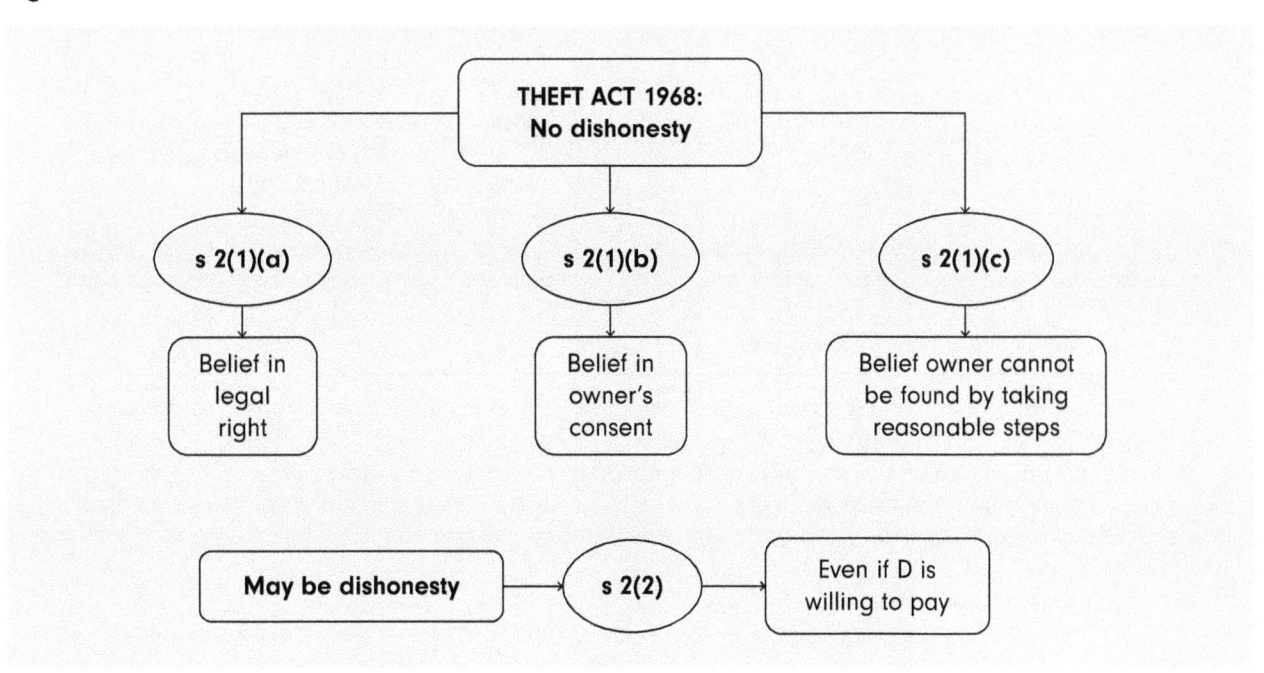

```
                    THEFT ACT 1968:
                    No dishonesty
          ┌──────────────┼──────────────┐
       s 2(1)(a)      s 2(1)(b)      s 2(1)(c)
          │              │              │
       Belief in      Belief in     Belief owner cannot
        legal          owner's       be found by taking
         right         consent       reasonable steps


       May be dishonesty  →  s 2(2)  →   Even if D is
                                         willing to pay
```

Criminal Law

In the absence of a definition of dishonesty in the statute, and as a consequence of the issues this has created, case law has developed to provide further guidance.

In the important case of Ivey v Genting Casinos (UK) Ltd *[2017] UKSC 67, the Supreme Court took the opportunity to revisit the issue of dishonesty. The claimant, Phil Ivey, sued Genting Casinos for over £9 million, which he won over two days playing a cards game called Punto Banco. The casino refused to pay him the money, claiming that he had cheated. The court agreed but, more importantly, the judges went on to declare specifically that the civil test for dishonesty should also apply to criminal cases. The effect of this is that the magistrates or jury must:*

(a) *ascertain (subjectively) the actual state of the defendant's knowledge or belief as to the facts; and then*

(b) *determine whether their conduct was honest or dishonest by the (objective) standards of ordinary, decent people.*

To secure a conviction, the prosecution must put before the court the facts of what the accused did and thought, and then leave it to the jury to decide whether it believes what was done was dishonest or not.

Set out below are various scenarios together with a consideration of whether the accused is likely to be found dishonest under the *Ivey* test.

Table 6.2 Examples of dishonesty

Scenario	Dishonest under *Ivey*?
Alicia takes £10 from the till at the shop where she works to buy cigarettes.	Alicia's actions are clearly dishonest by the standards of ordinary, decent people.
Alicia takes £10 from the till because she has forgotten her bus fare. She leaves a note for her boss explaining the situation and that she will repay the money the next day.	This example is less clear. Factors such as whether Alicia actually intends to repay the money as soon as she can, whether she knows if borrowing from the till is allowed under any circumstances and her relationship with her boss would all be relevant to her (subjective) view of the facts. Having determined this, the question is whether Alicia was (objectively) dishonest, and this will depend upon the jury's assessment of the situation.
Alicia takes £10 from the till because she has forgotten her bus fare. She is aware from company policy that it is forbidden to take money from the till under any circumstances.	In this scenario, Alice is aware of the company policy forbidding the taking of the money, so she is likely to be found dishonest.
Alicia takes £10 from the till because her bus is not running due to poor weather. Her route home, had she walked, would have been through a crime-ridden area late at night. She is aware from company policy that it is forbidden to take money from the till under any circumstances, but she repays the £10 the next day.	The outcome of this scenario would depend upon the weight the court gives to Alicia's particular circumstances given that she knows of the company policy forbidding the taking of money from the till.

To conclude, when deciding if the accused is dishonest, the court should first determine if the dishonesty is clear, for example, a shoplifting scenario. If so, that is the end of the matter and the defendant will be guilty of theft. If not, the court will then refer to the partial definitions contained in s 2 of the TA 1968 for guidance; only if these do not assist should the jury or magistrates turn to the common law test from the *Ivey* case. Thus, the relevant order in which the courts will approach dishonesty is:

- Clear dishonesty
- TA 1968, s 2
- *Ivey* test

6.2.8.1 Summary flowchart of dishonesty

Figure 6.4 Dishonesty

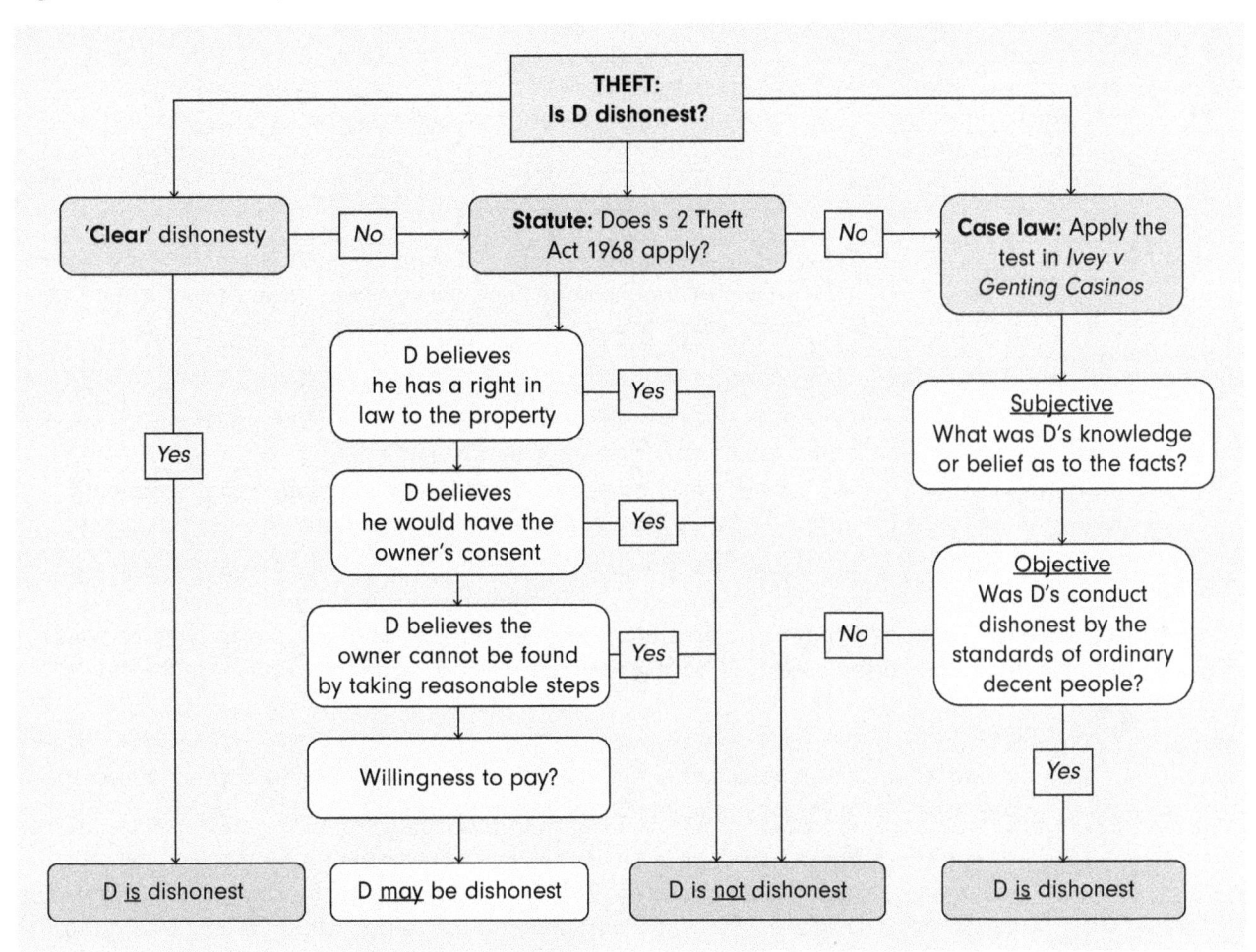

6.2.9 Intention to permanently deprive

The final element the prosecution must prove is that the accused intended to permanently deprive another of the property in question. Usually this will not be an issue and the ordinary meaning of intention to permanently deprive, as set out in s 1 of the TA 1968, will suffice.

Examples

(a) Zac steals a sandwich to eat for lunch – he clearly has no intention of returning it.

(b) Yvonne takes £5 from her friend intending to return it the next day. She has an intention to permanently deprive as, even though Yvonne intends to repay the money, she cannot do so with the same notes and coins that she took.

However, there are some situations that are problematic and s 6 provides assistance here. These are summarised in the flowchart below.

Figure 6.5 Intention permanently to deprive

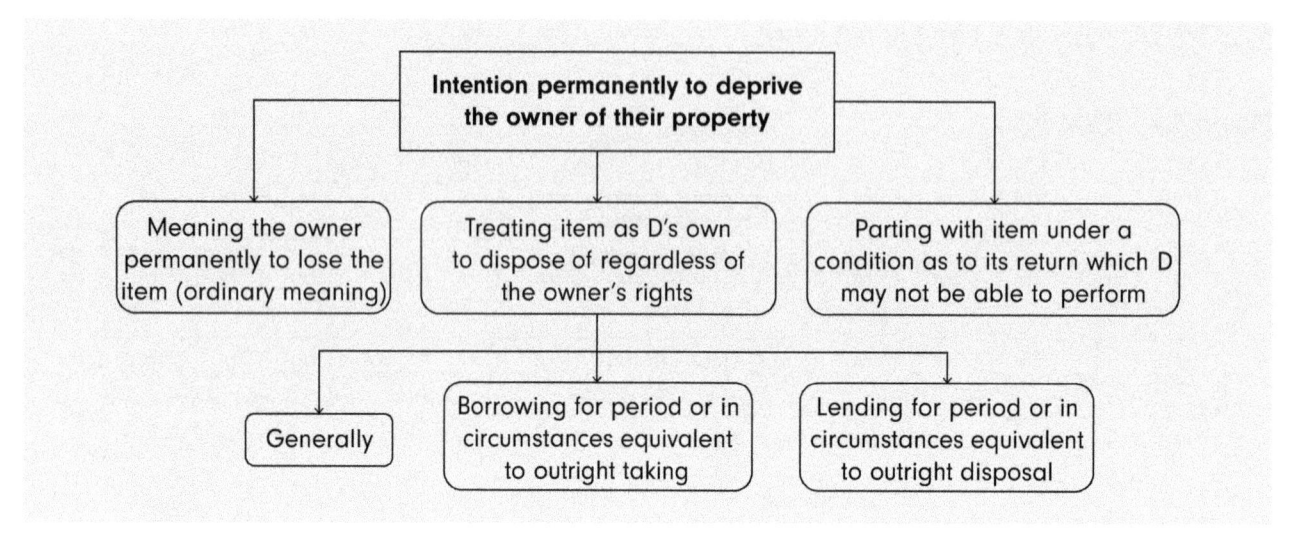

```
                    Intention permanently to deprive
                    the owner of their property
        ┌───────────────────┼───────────────────┐
Meaning the owner    Treating item as D's own    Parting with item under a
permanently to lose the  to dispose of regardless of  condition as to its return which D
item (ordinary meaning)   the owner's rights     may not be able to perform
        │                   │
    Generally     Borrowing for period or in    Lending for period or in
                  circumstances equivalent      circumstances equivalent
                    to outright taking             to outright disposal
```

6.2.9.1 Treating the property as the defendant's own

Section 6(1) of the TA 1968 provides that an accused will have an intention to permanently deprive if 'he treats the property as his own to dispose of regardless of the owner's rights'.

Despite the wording of the statute, the defendant does not actually need to dispose of the property to satisfy the test and the definition is perhaps best understood by removing the reference to this phrase. Indeed, a defendant who intends to return the property to its owner, but only after it has been used, will have an intention to permanently deprive on this basis.

Examples

(a) Julia takes a debit card but only returns it once she has bought a coat. She treats the card as her own by using it to purchase the clothing.

(b) Marshall acquires used but unexpired tickets from passengers on the London Underground and sells them on. The tickets are returned to the Underground after the second wave of passengers have used them. Despite this, Marshall has treated the tickets as his own by acquiring and re-selling them.

(c) A company accountant writes out (unauthorised) cheques for his own benefit. He submits that he did not intend to permanently deprive his employers of the money because he believes – correctly – that the bank will reimburse the company as the money was taken by fraud. The argument fails because the accused treated the credit balance in the company account as his own by using it to transfer money from the company account to his – Chan Man-sin v A-G of Hong Kong *[1988] 1 All ER 1.*

6.2.9.2 Borrowing in circumstances making it equivalent to an outright taking

Simple borrowing will not make someone a thief as there is no intention to permanently deprive. Thus, if A borrows B's lawnmower to cut their grass and then returns it in the same state, this does not satisfy the mens rea for theft. However, there are occasions where the borrowing has a greater effect, for example, if A takes B's concert ticket and only returns it after the performance. Although the ticket has been physically returned, it is of no value as the concert is over.

> *In R v Lloyd [1985] QB 829, the defendant worked as a projectionist at a cinema. He loaned a film to his friend to make an illicit copy. When interviewed, Lloyd explained the arrangement with his friend was that the film would be returned after only a few hours and before the next showing.*
>
> *The Court of Appeal confirmed that a mere borrowing will never constitute the requisite intention to permanently deprive unless it could be said that all the 'goodness and virtue had gone'. Given that the film was returned within a few hours ready to be shown to the paying public, this was not the case here.*

6.2.9.3 Parting with the property under a condition as to its return

Finally, s 6(2) states that there will be an intention to permanently deprive if the person parts with the property under a condition as to its return that they may not be able to perform. The clearest example of where this section applies is in relation to pawning.

⭐ Example

Khadija takes her mother's ring and pawns it. She has parted with the property – the ring – under a condition as to its return, the condition being that she will pay the pawnbroker money to redeem it. Khadija has an intention to permanently deprive her mother of the ring as she may not be able to repay the loan. It is irrelevant whether the prospects of her doing so are extremely good or very poor.

6.2.10 Summary of theft

Figure 6.6 Overview of theft

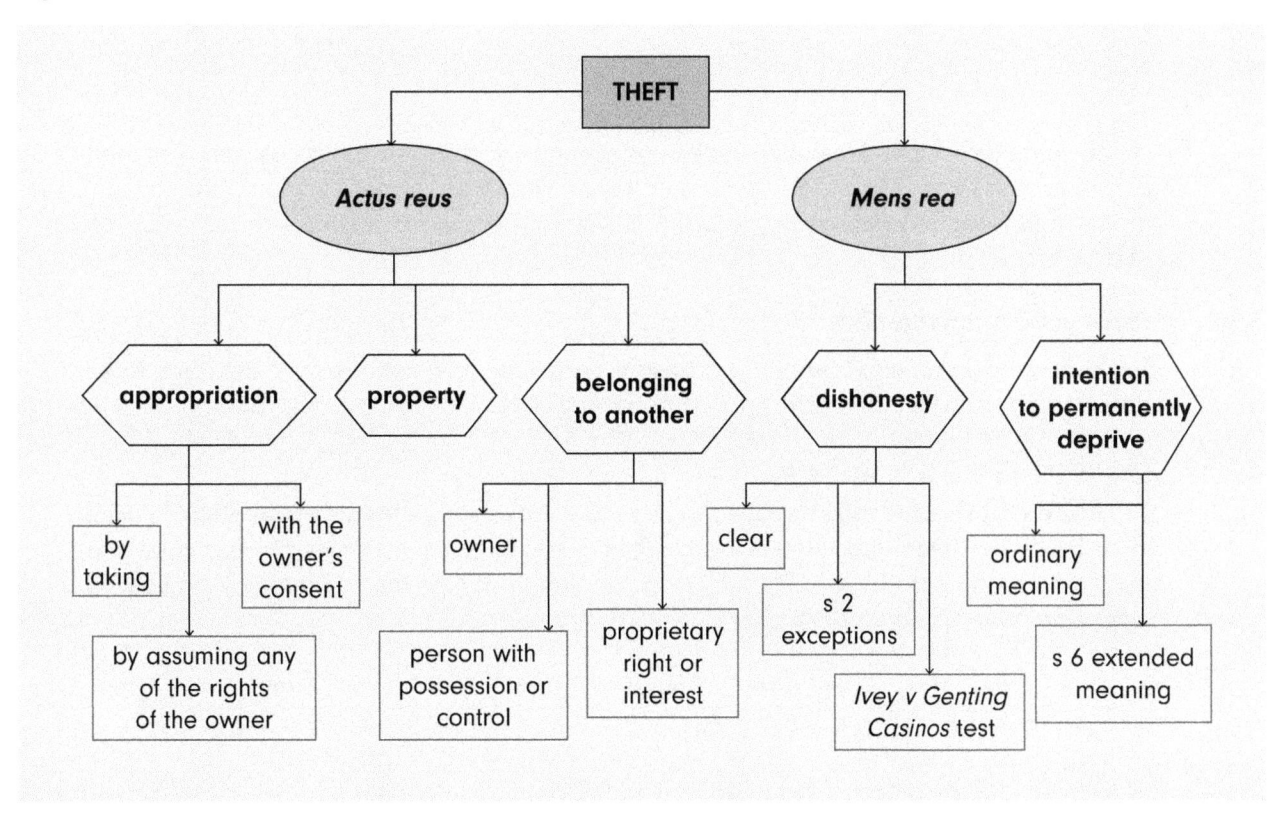

Criminal Law

In most cases, the prosecution will have little difficulty in proving an allegation of theft against the accused. However, unusual or problematic situations do arise and lawyers should be ready to deal with them. The key is to look out for the less obvious points – those which are not immediately apparent, but which could make the difference between a conviction or an acquittal.

6.3 Robbery

6.3.1 Introduction

Robbery covers a wide spectrum of criminality from an armed gang of robbers who actually use their weapons during the commission of the offence, to a teenager threatening a classmate to make them hand over their mobile phone. According to the Home Office Report 'Crime in England and Wales', robberies (including so-called 'muggings' where force and/or intimidation are used to steal property) are the most common type of street crime, meaning those offences that affect people going about their daily lives.

The offence of robbery is contained in s 8 of the TA 1968, which provides:

> A person is guilty of robbery if he steals, and immediately before or at the time of doing so, and in order to do so, he uses force on any person or puts or seeks to put any person in fear of being then and there subjected to force.

Robbery is an indictable only offence, which means it must be tried in the Crown Court.

There are four key components to the offence of robbery:

(a) The actus reus and mens rea of theft.

(b) The defendant uses or threatens force.

(c) This occurs immediately before or at the time of the robbery.

(d) The motivation is in order to steal.

6.3.2 Theft

The first requirement for robbery is the commission of a theft and so the accused must have stolen something. As a consequence, the prosecution must prove all the elements of theft before robbery can be considered as an offence. However, robbery is more than this. The use or threat of force is a vital aspect and this is why robbery is sometimes referred to as a form of aggravated theft.

6.3.3 Force used or threatened

This was considered in a number of cases. In particular, how serious does the force need to be and against whom or what should it be directed?

6.3.3.1 The meaning of the word 'force'

Guidance on this issue may be found in case law. However, determining whether sufficient force is used or threatened depends upon the particular circumstances of each case and, according to the case of *R v Dawson* [1976] 64 Cr App R 170, this is ultimately a question of fact to be determined by the jury.

Table 6.3 Comparison of force in robbery and theft

Robbery	Not robbery (theft only)
Two people gently jostle the victim to distract him so that another member of their gang can take the victim's wallet from his trouser pocket.	A pickpocket slips his hand into the victim's pocket with only slight touching.
A man grabs hold of an elderly lady's bag and snatches it from her hands before running away.	A woman snatches a cigarette from the victim without touching her.

It is apparent from the examples in **Table 6.3** that violence is not required – a simple nudging or slight pushing of the victim will suffice. Defendants have also been found guilty of robbery despite not touching the victim, where the force was directed against property, such as a bag. Nevertheless, there comes a point at which the contact cannot justify the more serious offence and the accused would only be liable for theft.

6.3.3.2 Against whom must force be used or threatened?

Usually, the threat or use of force will be against the person to whom the property belongs, but it need not be so and may be against 'any person' according to s 8.

Figure 6.7 Direction of force for robbery

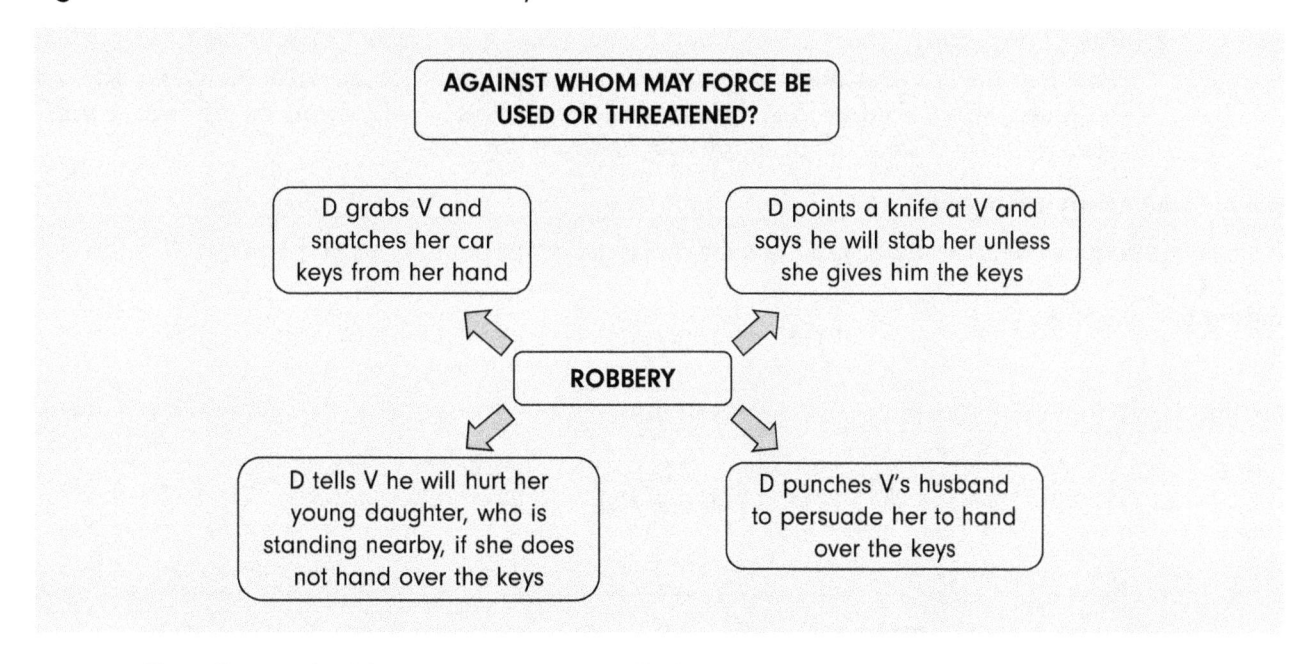

AGAINST WHOM MAY FORCE BE USED OR THREATENED?

- D grabs V and snatches her car keys from her hand
- D points a knife at V and says he will stab her unless she gives him the keys
- D tells V he will hurt her young daughter, who is standing nearby, if she does not hand over the keys
- D punches V's husband to persuade her to hand over the keys

ROBBERY

The offence of robbery is committed in all of the scenarios in **Figure 6.7**, provided the other required elements are also present. This is because the force used or threatened does not need to be against the owner of the property. However, if a third party is the subject of the threat, the intended victim must be aware of the threat.

In summary:

- whether the defendant has used or threatened the victim is ultimately a question of fact for the jury;
- the force need not be substantial;
- it does not matter against whom the force is used or threatened; and
- the force can be directed against property.

6.3.4 Timing of the force being used or threatened

The use or threat of force must be 'immediately before or at the time' of the theft. In other words, it must be broadly simultaneous with the act to satisfy the definition of robbery. In most instances, this will be clear and so it may be more helpful to give an example of where this requirement is not satisfied.

✪ Example

Zeenat is at a nightclub and has a fight with Victoria who has been flirting with Zeenat's boyfriend. During the fight Zeenat notices that Victoria has dropped her mobile phone onto the floor and so, after the fight has ended, she picks up the phone and keeps it. Zeenat is not guilty of robbery as the theft takes place after *the use of force.*

In R v Hale (1978) 68 C App R 415, the Court of Appeal held that the issue to be determined was whether the appropriation was still continuing at the time the force was used. In this case, the defendant stole various items from the victim's home and then, on the way out, threatened her young son if she rang the police within five minutes of his leaving. The court held that at the time the threat of force was made, the theft was continuing and, therefore, the defendant was guilty of robbery.

This outcome accords with a 'common-sense' view of the requirement.

6.3.5 The force must be in order to steal

To satisfy the offence of robbery, the force used or threatened must be in order to steal and for no other reason.

✪ Example

Paul punches Tony because he dislikes him. He then takes Tony's wallet from the pocket of his jacket, which is hanging on the back of a chair. This is not robbery as the force is not used in order to steal but because Paul does not like Tony.

6.3.6 Summary of robbery

Set out below is a summary of the elements required for the offence of robbery.

Figure 6.8 Robbery

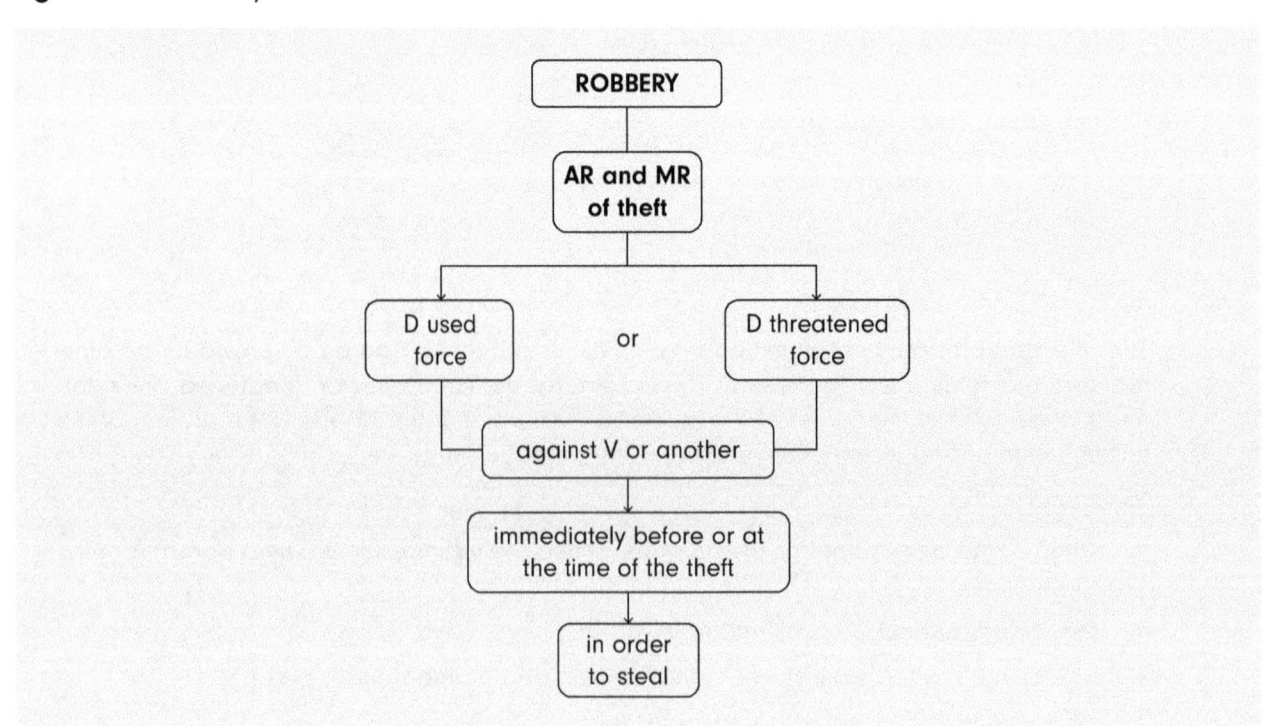

```
                    ┌─────────┐
                    │ ROBBERY │
                    └────┬────┘
                    ┌────┴────┐
                    │ AR and MR│
                    │ of theft │
                    └────┬────┘
         ┌───────────────┼───────────────┐
    ┌────┴────┐          │          ┌────┴─────┐
    │ D used  │    or    │          │D threatened│
    │  force  │          │          │   force   │
    └────┬────┘          │          └────┬─────┘
         └───────────┐   │   ┌───────────┘
                ┌────┴───┴───┴────┐
                │against V or another│
                └────────┬────────┘
                ┌────────┴────────┐
                │immediately before or at│
                │ the time of the theft │
                └────────┬────────┘
                    ┌────┴────┐
                    │ in order│
                    │ to steal│
                    └─────────┘
```

When faced with a scenario involving robbery, instead of working through the actus reus and then the mens rea of the offence, consider taking a less traditional approach. It may be preferable to discuss the elements of theft first and then focus on the three issues relating to the use or threat of force. The flowchart in **Figure 6.9** gives a complete picture of the elements the prosecution need to prove to convict a defendant of robbery.

Figure 6.9 Flowchart of theft and robbery

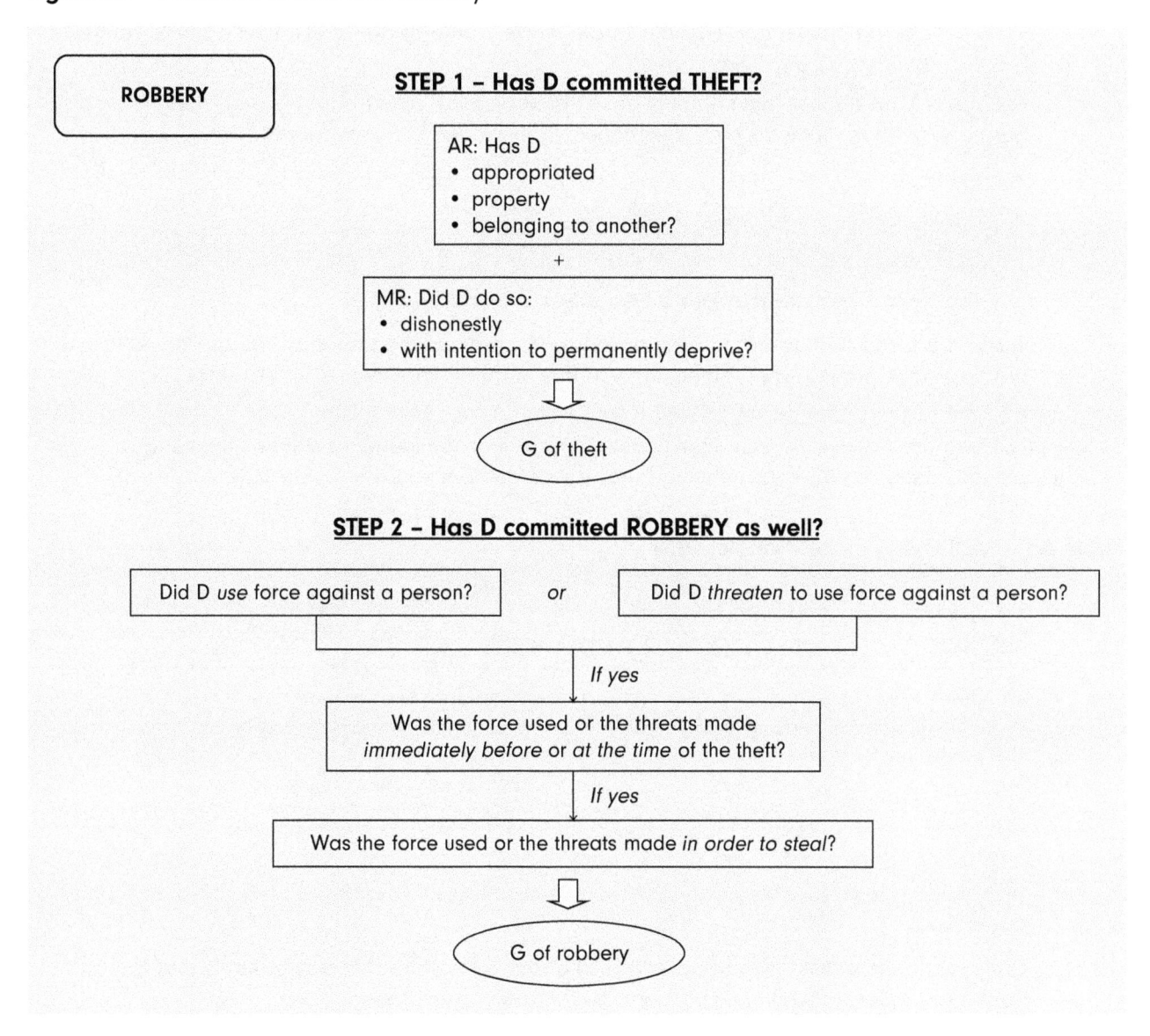

ROBBERY

STEP 1 – Has D committed THEFT?

AR: Has D
- appropriated
- property
- belonging to another?

+

MR: Did D do so:
- dishonestly
- with intention to permanently deprive?

⇩

G of theft

STEP 2 – Has D committed ROBBERY as well?

Did D *use* force against a person?   or   Did D *threaten* to use force against a person?

If yes

Was the force used or the threats made *immediately before* or *at the time* of the theft?

If yes

Was the force used or the threats made *in order to steal*?

⇩

G of robbery

6.4 Burglary

6.4.1 Introduction

Burglary is a statutory offence found under s 9(1)(a) and (b) of the TA 1968. It is an either way offence that carries a maximum sentence of 10 years' imprisonment in the Crown Court, increasing to 14 years' imprisonment in the case of burglary of a dwelling (TA 1968, s 9(3)), reflecting public concern about safety in the home.

Under s 9:

(1) a person is guilty of burglary if—

(a) he enters any building or part of a building as a trespasser and with intent to commit any such offence as is mentioned in subsection (2) below; or

(b) having entered any building or part of a building as a trespasser he steals or attempts to steal anything in the building or that part of it or inflicts or attempts to inflict on any person therein any grievous bodily harm.

(2) The offences referred to in subsection (1)(a) above are offences of stealing anything in the building or part of a building in question, of inflicting on any person therein any grievous bodily harm ... and of doing unlawful damage to the building or anything therein.

Because of the distinct requirements of s 9(1)(a) and (b), effectively, there are two types of burglary, although they do have similarities. Both require the defendant to:

- enter
- a building (or part of a building)
- as a trespasser, and
- know or be reckless they are a trespasser.

There are also key differences. Section 9(1)(a) focuses on the thoughts that are going through the defendant's mind when doing so, whereas criminal liability in s 9(1)(b) rests upon the defendant's actions once inside the property.

Furthermore, there is no consistency as to which offences the defendant must intend or actually carry out when committing burglary, as demonstrated in **Table 6.4**.

Table 6.4 Section 9(1) of the Theft Act 1968

s 9(1)(a)	s 9(1)(b)
The defendant must *intend*... • theft, infliction of grievous bodily harm or criminal damage.	The defendant must *commit*... • theft or infliction of grievous bodily harm or *attempt*... • theft or grievous bodily harm.

6.4.2 Actus reus

Common to the actus reus of both s 9(1)(a) and s 9(1)(b) are the requirements that the defendant enter a building or part of a building as a trespasser.

6.4.2.1 Entry

Although 'entry' is a word that is in everyday use, there are a number of cases that have considered its meaning in the context of burglary. Usually, it is clear the defendant entered the property, for example, if they walk through the door of a stranger's house or break into a school premises at night. However, on occasion, this is not so.

> *In the rather bizarre case of R v Collins [1973] QB 100, the defendant climbed up a ladder to the window of the victim who was asleep in her bedroom, after having removed all his clothes except his socks (which he kept on believing this would enable him to escape more quickly!). The victim awoke and, adding to the already unusual circumstances of the case, invited Collins in assuming (despite the odd means of entry) that the defendant was her boyfriend and the two went on to have sexual intercourse.*

At the time of the incident, burglary could be committed by entry as a trespasser with intent to rape.

The crucial question for the jury in deciding guilt was where Collins was at the time he was invited in. If he was outside the building kneeling on the window sill, he was innocent of burglary; however, if he had entered the room before being invited in, he was guilty. The case went to the Court of Appeal, which held that the defendant should not be convicted unless the jury was satisfied Collins had made 'an effective and substantial entry' into the room.

Although this authority provides some assistance the facts of each particular case will be crucial to the outcome. Fortunately, case law has clarified the issue further.

⭐ Example

Table 6.5 Examples of entry

Abraham...	Entry?
• climbs through the open window of a factory.	Yes
• breaks down the door of an office building and goes inside.	Yes
• leans through a shop window and searches through the shelves inside. The lower part of his body stays outside the shop.	Yes: these facts are based upon the case of *R v Brown* [1985] Crim LR 212, which confirms that the entry need only be 'effective'.
• is discovered by a householder, firmly stuck with just his head and arm inside the window.	Yes: it is irrelevant that the defendant was incapable of committing a crime – *R v Ryan* [1996] Crim LR 320.
• inserts a wire hanger through a letter box and hooks the keys that are hanging near the door.	Maybe: if an instrument is used to commit an offence, such as the theft of keys, it may be treated as an extension of the defendant's body.
• pushes his fingertips through the door of a house, which is slightly ajar.	No: if only fingertips are inserted, the entry would not be 'effective'.

It is apparent that there are occasions when entry is clear and this will apply in the majority of instances. However, there are others where the law lacks clarity; for example, there is no recent case law on how an instrument is treated in the context of burglary.

6.4.2.2 Building

The word 'building' is only partially defined in the TA 1968. However, case law suggests that a building is a structure of significant size with some degree of permanence; this would include, for example, houses, offices and warehouses but also garden sheds. These fall within the definition of a building whether or not someone is actually living there or occupying the property.

Section 9(4) provides further guidance on the definition of a building by confirming that inhabited vehicles and vessels, such as houseboats, are included. However, further enquiries would need to be carried out to determine whether a person lives in the structure; if so, it is irrelevant whether anyone is actually there at the time of the burglary.

Criminal Law

> ⭐ **Example**
>
> Is a camper van a building under s 9 of the Theft Act 1968?
>
> - Lived in as a permanent home. ✓
> - Being used as a holiday home at the time of the burglary. ✓
> - Parked on the owner's drive for use at a future date. ✗

A summary of what constitutes a building for the purposes of an offence of burglary is set out in **Figure 6.10**.

Figure 6.10 Definition of building for burglary

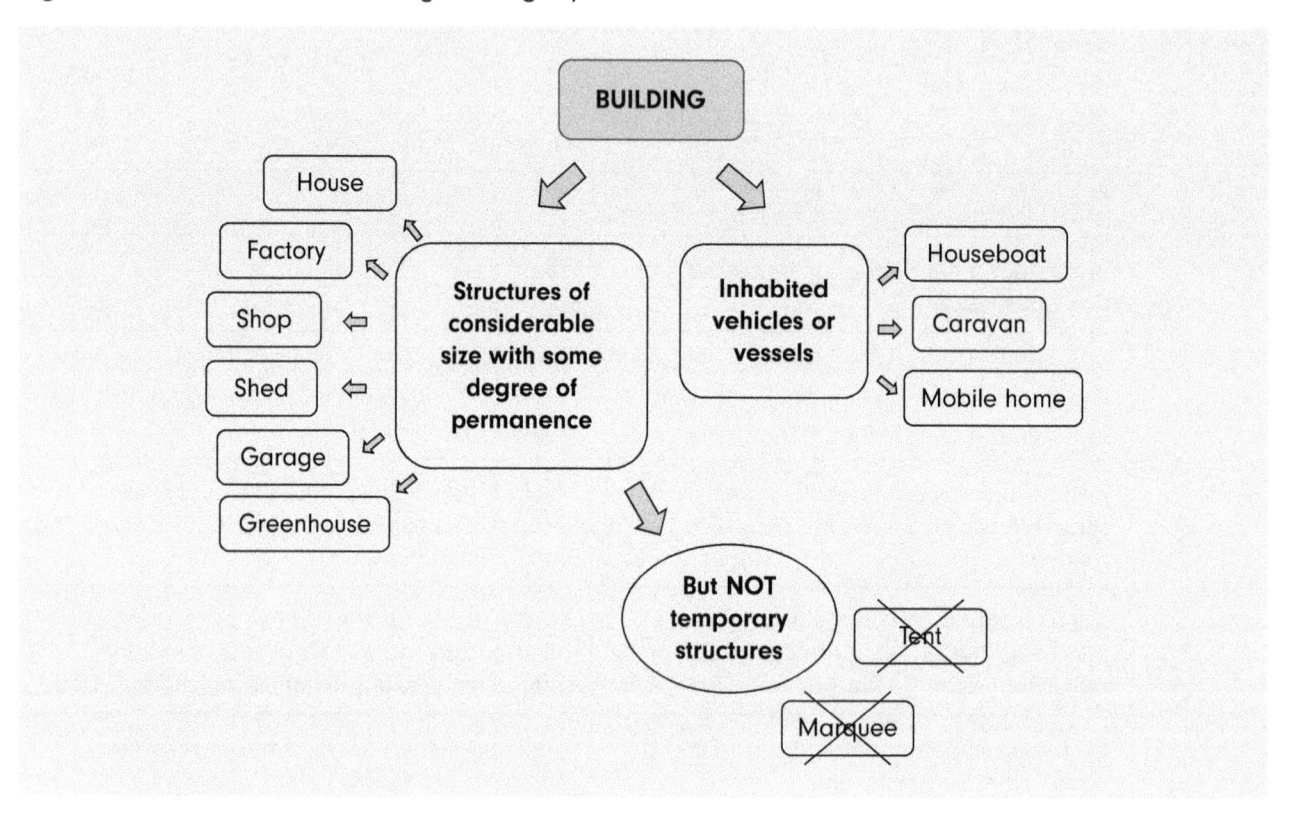

```
                            BUILDING
                         ↙          ↘
    House
    Factory                                      Houseboat
                 Structures of      Inhabited
    Shop    ⇐   considerable    ⇒  vehicles or  ⇒  Caravan
                 size with some      vessels
    Shed    ⇐   degree of                          Mobile home
                 permanence
    Garage
    Greenhouse
                              ↓
                         But NOT
                         temporary    ⊗ Tent
                         structures
                              ⊗ Marquee
```

6.4.2.3 Part of a building

A defendant may be criminally liable for burglary not only if they enter a building but also if they enter a *part* of a building. This would include a defendant who enters a building lawfully but who then moves to another part where they do not have authority to go.

> ⭐ **Examples**
>
> (a) Gerry is living in student accommodation. As he walks down his corridor to the shared kitchen, he sees his flatmate's door is open and goes inside to have a look.
>
> (b) Hal has been invited to his friend's house for a drink. However, the two men have an argument and Hal is told to leave immediately. On the way out, he decides to go upstairs to use the toilet.
>
> (c) Irem is looking for clothes in a high street shop. She sees a jumper she wants inside a storeroom and goes inside despite the door being labelled: Employees Only.
>
> (d) Jacqui is wandering around a department store. She goes behind the perfume counter to see if she can access the till.

In all of these examples, the defendant has moved from one area to another. Entering a different flat or a separate room of a building would be sufficient to satisfy s 9, but what about going behind the counter in example (d)?

> In the case of R v Walkington [1979] 1 WLR 1169, the defendant entered a department store just before closing time and went behind a three-sided, movable counter into an area reserved for staff. It was held that the counter was 'a physical demarcation' and was sufficient to count as a part of a building.

Given the decision in *Walkington*, it is likely that Jacqui has entered a separate part of the building sufficient to satisfy s 9 of the TA 1968. However, the decision would, ultimately, be a matter for the jury and would depend upon the layout of the store.

6.4.2.4 Trespasser in fact

It is an essential element of burglary that the defendant enters as a trespasser. If this is not established, there cannot be a conviction for burglary. Trespass requires proof that the defendant entered without consent or permission and, usually, this will be straightforward. If the accused breaks a window to gain access to a stranger's house at night, they will clearly be a trespasser. However, other instances are less apparent.

> **Example**

Table 6.6 Examples of trespass

Kaye...	Trespasser?
• has been banned from a local library but, by covering her face with a scarf, she manages to get inside.	Yes: she has no express or implied permission to enter the library.
• falsely tells Alfred that she is a police officer to gain access to his house.	Yes: she has obtained permission by deceiving the owner. Although the TA 1968 does not state that gaining entry by fraud is sufficient to establish trespass, previous case law is clear that it is. Alfred's permission is not a true one as he would not have let Kaye in had he known she was lying as to her status.
• enters a supermarket intending to steal bottles of alcohol.	Yes: although Kaye has permission of the shop owners to enter, this is only to browse the products on display and to purchase items legally. She goes beyond this permission when she enters in order to steal.

These examples demonstrate that a person may be a trespasser in fact despite, apparently, having permission to enter.

> In R v Jones and Smith [1976] 1 WLR 672, Smith entered his father's house and stole two television sets. He was found guilty of burglary as, although he had a general permission to enter the house, he exceeded that permission when he entered with the intention to steal the items.

What if a person is asked to leave a property? In the example above, Hal has been invited to his friend's house for a drink but, when the two men argue, he is told to leave immediately.

Had he done so, Hal would not have been a trespasser as he has an implied licence to leave by the most direct route. However, on the way out, Hal decided to go upstairs and, as a consequence, he is a trespasser.

6.4.2.5 Additional actus reus requirements for s 9(1)(b) burglary

Under s 9(1)(b) of the TA 1968, the defendant must also commit the actus reus of theft, attempted theft, grievous bodily harm or attempted grievous bodily harm.

6.4.2.6 Summary of actus reus of burglary

- For both s 9(1)(a) and s 9(1)(b) burglary, the defendant is required to enter a building or part of a building as a trespasser.
- For s 9(1)(b), there is an additional actus reus requirement that the defendant actually commits or attempts to commit theft or grievous bodily harm.

6.4.3 Mens rea

As with the actus reus there are some elements that are common to the two types of burglary but others that are not.

6.4.3.1 Knowledge or recklessness as to being a trespasser

For both s 9(1)(a) and (b) burglary, the defendant must either know they are a trespasser or foresee a risk they do not have permission to enter and go on, without justification, to take that risk. When must the accused have this awareness?

- It is clear that for burglary under s 9(1)(a), the defendant must have the mens rea for entry as a trespasser at the time of entry into a building or part of a building as the offence is complete at this point.
- With regard to s 9(1)(b), as the statute refers to the defendant 'having entered' as a trespasser, they must also have the mens rea on entry.

This may be apparent in a number of ways. Apart from a clear admission from the accused, the prosecution may establish that the defendant knows they are a trespasser or are reckless as to this fact by other evidence. A building may be locked or there may be signs excluding entry or, in the context of the defendant entering part of a building, the area may be roped off or separated by a counter.

6.4.3.2 Additional mens rea requirements for s 9(1)(a) burglary

Under s 9(1)(a) of the TA 1968, the defendant must enter with the intention to commit theft, grievous bodily harm or criminal damage in the building or *that part* of the building. In the examples above (at **6.4.2.3**):

- Neither Gerry nor Hal have an intention to steal from the part of the building they entered. Gerry's aim is just to have a look inside his flatmate's room, whilst Hal's intention is to use the toilet.
- Irem and Jacqui do intend to steal from the part of the building, namely the storeroom (to take a jumper) and the counter (to remove cash) respectively.

The defendant does not actually need to commit these offences; it is enough simply to enter as a trespasser with the intent to do so, hence:

- Irem would be guilty of burglary if she intends to steal the jumper from the storeroom even if she does not succeed. The offence is complete the moment she steps into the unauthorised part of the shop.

What about the accused who argues that their intent to steal, cause criminal damage or inflict grievous bodily harm was conditional?

- Jacqui is wandering around a department store where she has permission to be. When she goes behind the perfume counter, she becomes a trespasser. Her stated intention is to try to steal the cash if the till is open. She is guilty of burglary as a conditional intent will suffice; it is irrelevant that the till is locked and she is unsuccessful – *Attorney General's Reference (Nos 1 and 2 of 1979)* [1980] QB 180.

6.4.3.3 Additional mens rea requirements for s 9(1)(b) burglary

To be guilty of s 9(1)(b) burglary, the defendant must also have the mens rea for either theft or grievous bodily harm or for an attempt of one of these two offences, but *not* criminal damage. Note that the offence is satisfied if the defendant has the mens rea for either a s 18 or a s 20 assault under the OAPA 1861.

6.4.4 Comparison between the two types of burglary

The two burglary offences share elements but there are also key differences, such as which crimes the defendant intends to or does commit; these are listed in **Table 6.7**.

Table 6.7 Actus reus and mens rea for burglary

	s 9(1)(a)	s 9(1)(b)
Actus reus	Enter a building or part of a building as a trespasser	Same
		Commit the actus reus of: • theft; • attempted theft; • grievous bodily harm; or • attempted grievous bodily harm.
Mens rea	Knowledge / recklessness as to being a trespasser	Same
	Intend to commit: • theft; • grievous bodily harm; or • criminal damage.	Have the mens rea for: • theft; • attempted theft; • grievous bodily harm; or • attempted grievous bodily harm.

6.4.5 Summary of burglary

Burglary is an unusual offence in that it can be committed in two similar but slightly differing ways and the main points are summarised below, together with a diagram.

- For offences under both s 9(1)(a) and s 9(1)(b), the defendant must enter a building or part of a building.
- To satisfy the trespass element, the defendant must be a trespasser in fact – enter without permission or authority – and know or be reckless as to this on entry.

Criminal Law

- If the defendant enters a part of a building, they must intend to or actually commit the ulterior offence in that part.
- For s 9(1)(a), it is the defendant's intent (to steal, inflict grievous bodily harm or cause criminal damage) at the time of entry that makes them criminally liable. It is irrelevant that no such offence is committed.
- For s 9(1)(b), the prosecution must prove that, having entered as a trespasser, the defendant stole or inflicted grievous bodily harm or attempted these offences. The mens rea for the theft or assault (or attempt) can be formed once inside the property.

Figure 6.11 Summary of burglary

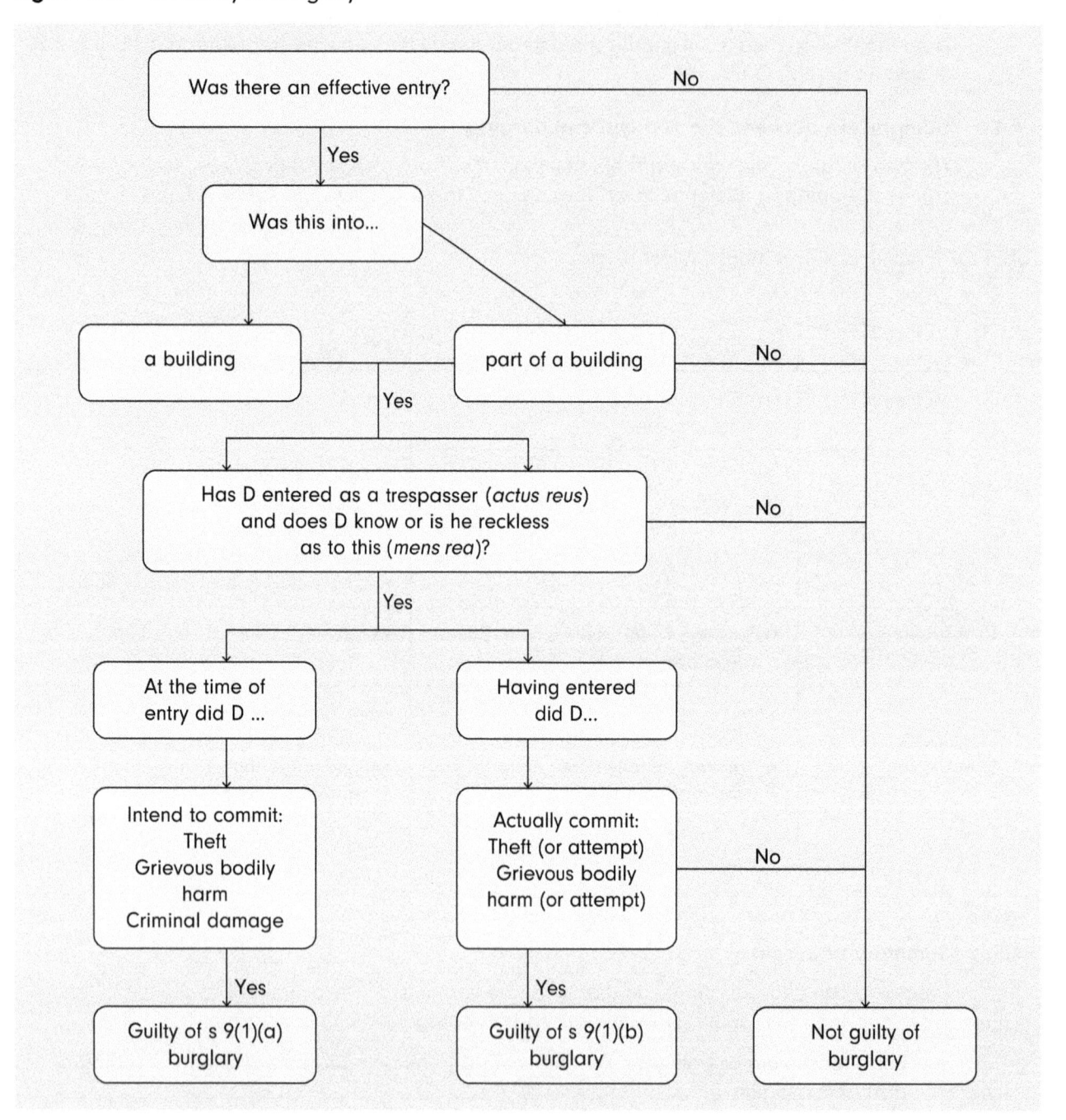

6.5 Aggravated burglary

6.5.1 Introduction

In addition to the 'basic' offence of burglary, the offence of aggravated burglary may be found in s 10(1) of the TA 1968. This provides:

> A person is guilty of aggravated burglary if he commits any burglary and at the time has with him any firearm or imitation firearm, any weapon of offence, or any explosive.

Aggravated burglary is an indictable only offence, meaning it can only be tried in the Crown Court, and carries a maximum sentence of life imprisonment to reflect the seriousness of criminals entering premises armed with weapons. The offence requires proof of all the elements of burglary for either s 9(1)(a) or s 9(1)(b) of the TA 1968 but, in addition, the defendant must be in possession of a weapon at the time of the burglary.

6.5.2 Weapons

The TA 1968 deems the following items to be weapons:

- firearms (including air guns, air pistols and imitation firearms whether capable of being discharged or not)
- a 'weapon of offence' (meaning any article made or adapted for use for causing injury to or incapacitating a person, or intended for such use)
- explosives.

A weapon of offence could include:

(a) a machete (made for causing injury)

(b) a broken bottle (adapted for use for causing injury)

(c) a hammer (intended for such use, namely causing injury)

(d) a length of rope (could be used to incapacitate a person)

(e) handcuffs (intended for use of incapacitating a person).

However, it would not include, for example, a fencing sword as this is made for sport and intended for use as such. The defendant must know they have the item with them.

6.5.3 'At the time'

The defendant must have the weapon with them at the time of committing the burglary and this varies depending upon the offence with which they are charged:

- s 9(1)(a) burglary: at the time of entry.
- s 9(1)(b) burglary: when the ulterior offence (theft, grievous bodily harm or attempted theft or grievous bodily harm) is committed.

In R v Francis [1982] Crim LR 363, the defendants entered a house armed with sticks then discarded them before committing theft. They were found not guilty of aggravated burglary on appeal as the prosecution could not prove that the accused had the sticks with them at the moment they intended to steal.

6.5.4 Summary of aggravated burglary

Before considering whether the defendant is guilty of an offence under s 10(1) of the TA 1968, the prosecution must prove there has been a burglary under s 9. If the defendant is armed in some way, aggravated burglary may be established.

Figure 6.12 Aggravated burglary

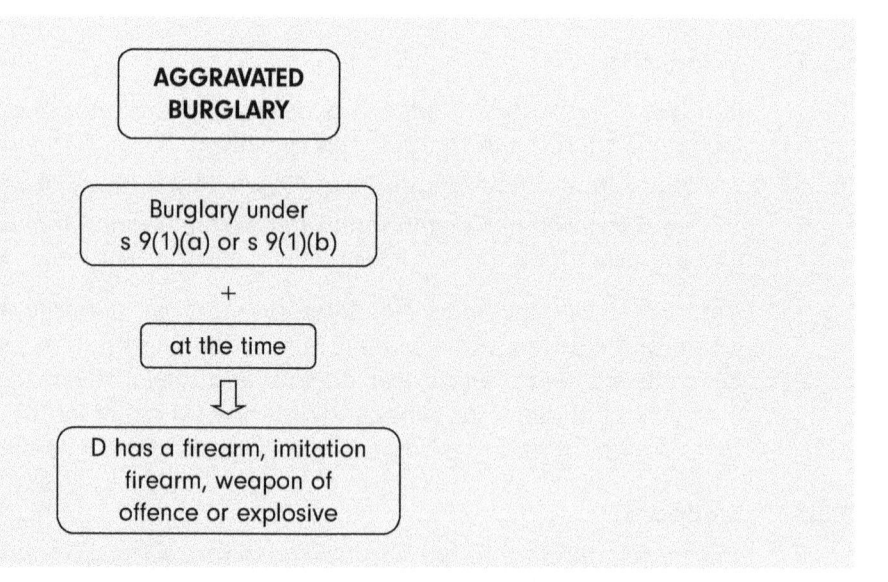

```
         AGGRAVATED
          BURGLARY

       Burglary under
      s 9(1)(a) or s 9(1)(b)
              +
          at the time
              ⇩
       D has a firearm, imitation
       firearm, weapon of
       offence or explosive
```

6.5.5 Summary of the property offences

- There are a number of property offences, with the most common being theft. Although there are five elements required to establish theft, dishonesty is usually the key factor.

- Robbery is an aggravated form of theft as it involves the use or threat of force in order to steal.

- An offence of burglary may be committed as soon as the defendant enters the property as a trespasser if they have the relevant mens rea, but also once the defendant is inside. In this instance, the defendant must commit or attempt to commit certain offences.

- The offence becomes aggravated burglary where the defendant has a firearm or other weapon with them at the time.

Sample questions

Question 1

A man enters his supervisor's office and sees a copy of the secret recipe that is used to make a vegan pie. He memorises it and leaves the office. On the way out, he picks up a black umbrella that he believes has been left by one of his colleagues; in fact, it is his own umbrella.

On walking home, the man picks and eats some blackberries that are growing on a bush by the side of the road. Nearby, he sees a wedding ring in the grass, which has been flung away by the owner with the intention of never retrieving it, after her husband asked for a divorce. The man puts the ring in his pocket. He then calls on his elderly aunt and drops off a loaf of bread that he has purchased for her. In confusion, she gives him a £50 note, which he decides to keep.

For which item has the man satisfied the actus reus of theft?

A   The secret recipe.
B   The umbrella.
C   The blackberries.

D The wedding ring.

E The £50 note.

Answer

The correct answer is option E. The man commits the actus reus of theft when he takes the £50 as the note is property belonging to another – his aunt – and gifts may be an appropriation (although it will only be theft if the defendant also satisfies the mens rea).

The man has not satisfied the actus reus of theft for the secret recipe in option A, as confidential information is not property within the meaning of the TA 1968. To be liable for theft, the man must steal property belonging to another and the umbrella (option B) belongs to him, even though he does not realise this. The blackberries are fruit taken from a plant growing wild so cannot be considered as 'property'; thus, option C is wrong. The wedding ring has been abandoned by the owner and so does not belong to another, hence, the actus reus is not complete in option D.

Question 2

A woman is sitting in her university library when she picks up a text book that is on the desk next to her. The text book is worth £30. She then leaves the library with the book.

In which of the following circumstances is she dishonest?

A She honestly and reasonably thinks it is her book.

B She honestly but unreasonably thinks it is her book.

C She leaves the sum of £30 in cash to pay for the book.

D She honestly believes the owner would consent to her taking the book as she thinks it belongs to a friend of hers.

E She honestly thinks that the book has been abandoned.

Answer

The correct answer is option C. The woman may be dishonest as s 2(2) of the TA 1968 states that a willingness to pay is not in itself proof of a lack of dishonesty.

The woman is not dishonest in options A or B because of the provisions contained in s 2(1)(a); the woman thinks it is her book and so she believes she has the right in law to take it. Provided the defendant's belief is honestly held, it does not need to be reasonable and the jury must acquit her of theft in these circumstances.

She is not dishonest in option D because of s 2(1)(b), as she honestly believes the owner would consent to her taking the book. With regard to option E, if she genuinely believes that the book has been abandoned she is not dishonest under s 2(1)(c).

Question 3

The defendant is in the final of a national sculpture competition. Realising that his sculpture is inferior to the work of the other finalist, a woman, he decides to ruin her work. He waits until the gallery is closed and smashes a window to gain access to the room where her work is displayed. Once inside, he breaks off part of his rival's sculpture, which is on display.

He then sees a painting that he likes and so he picks it up and places it in his bag. Suddenly, the security guard enters the room and, to ensure that he keeps the painting, the defendant pushes him away as hard as he can. The security guard falls and fractures his arm in several places as he lands on the floor. The defendant flees the gallery.

The defendant is charged with a number of offences. What is the only offence he should be acquitted of?

A   Burglary with intent in relation to the damaged sculpture.

B   Burglary in relation to the damaged sculpture.

C   Burglary when he takes the painting.

D   Burglary for the assault on the security guard.

E   Robbery for the assault on the security guard.

Answer

Option B is the only offence for which the defendant is not liable and, thus, should be acquitted. He is not guilty of burglary (contrary to s 9(1)(b)) as although he enters the gallery (the building) as a trespasser, the definition does not cover the commission of criminal damage (although he would be liable for the substantive offence).

The defendant is liable for the offence of burglary with intent in option A. The actus reus of s 9(1)(a) burglary is satisfied as the defendant enters the building as a trespasser and breaks a window in order to do so. He satisfies the relevant mens rea as he intends to enter as a trespasser as he 'waits until the gallery is closed'; and he has the ulterior mens rea of intent to commit criminal damage on entry which is sufficient for the s 9(1)(a) offence.

The defendant is also liable for the burglary offence in option C because, having entered as a trespasser, he steals (appropriates property belonging to another dishonestly and with the intention to permanently deprive) the painting. He is also guilty of this offence in option D as the security guard suffers grievous bodily harm and the defendant either intends or is reckless as to causing some bodily harm (the mens rea for an assault under s 20 of the OAPA 1861).

The defendant is criminally liable for robbery in option E when he assaults the security guard because the defendant commits theft of the painting and uses force at the time of the theft to do so.

7 Fraud

7.1	Introduction	138
7.2	Fraud	138
7.3	Definition	138
7.4	Fraud by false representation	138
7.5	Fraud by failing to disclose information	143
7.6	Fraud by abuse of position	145
7.7	Overlap between the fraud offences	147

SQE1 syllabus

By the end of this chapter you will be able to apply relevant core legal principles and rules appropriately and effectively, at the level of a competent newly qualified solicitor in practice, to realistic client-based and ethical problems and situations in the area of **fraud**.

Note that, as students are not usually required to recall specific case names, or cite statutory or regulatory authorities, these are provided for illustrative purposes only.

Learning outcomes

The learning outcomes for this chapter are:

- to define the elements of the offence of fraud; and
- to identify and understand the three ways in which fraud may be committed.

7.1 Introduction

Fraud is the most commonly experienced offence in the United Kingdom according to the National Crime Agency. Victims of fraud range from individuals to businesses to the public sector, and a recent report estimated the annual cost to the economy of this criminal activity as £190 billion each year.

7.2 Fraud

The offence of fraud was created by the Fraud Act (FA) 2006. It was introduced to replace the multiple deception offences that applied prior to its implementation, as these were regarded as too complex and out-dated. The offence has been widely drafted to ensure that a broad range of behaviour is caught within its provisions, with the aim of ensuring that the law can keep pace with developing technology and the increasingly inventive ways in which criminals are committing fraud. It is an either way offence with a maximum penalty of 10 years' imprisonment in the Crown Court or an unlimited fine or both.

7.3 Definition

The FA 2006 creates a general offence of fraud, which can be committed in three different ways. Section 1(1) provides for the offence of fraud, but does not define it, and s 1(2) sets out the methods by which fraud may be established. These are:

(a) by making a false representation (s 2);

(b) by failing to disclose information (s 3); and

(c) by abuse of position (s 4).

Sections 2, 3 and 4 contain information on specifically how the offence of fraud may be satisfied. In particular, there is no requirement for the prosecution to prove that the defendant actually obtained anything (such as goods or services) by their actions, just that they intended to do so. As with theft, dishonesty is a key element of the mens rea.

Figure 7.1 Types of fraud

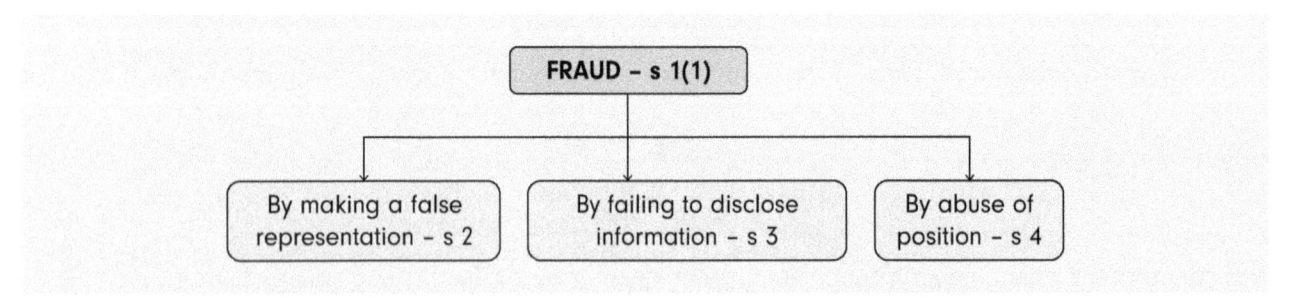

```
                    FRAUD - s 1(1)
          ┌───────────────┼───────────────┐
   By making a false   By failing to disclose   By abuse of
   representation - s 2   information - s 3     position - s 4
```

7.4 Fraud by false representation

Section 2(1) of the FA 2006 provides that a person commits fraud if they dishonestly make a false representation and intend, by making the representation, either to make a gain for themselves or another, or to cause loss to another or to expose another to a risk of loss.

The offence raises a number of issues but, before considering these in detail, the starting point is to identify the elements of the actus reus and the mens rea and these are summarised in **Figure 7.2**.

Figure 7.2 False representation

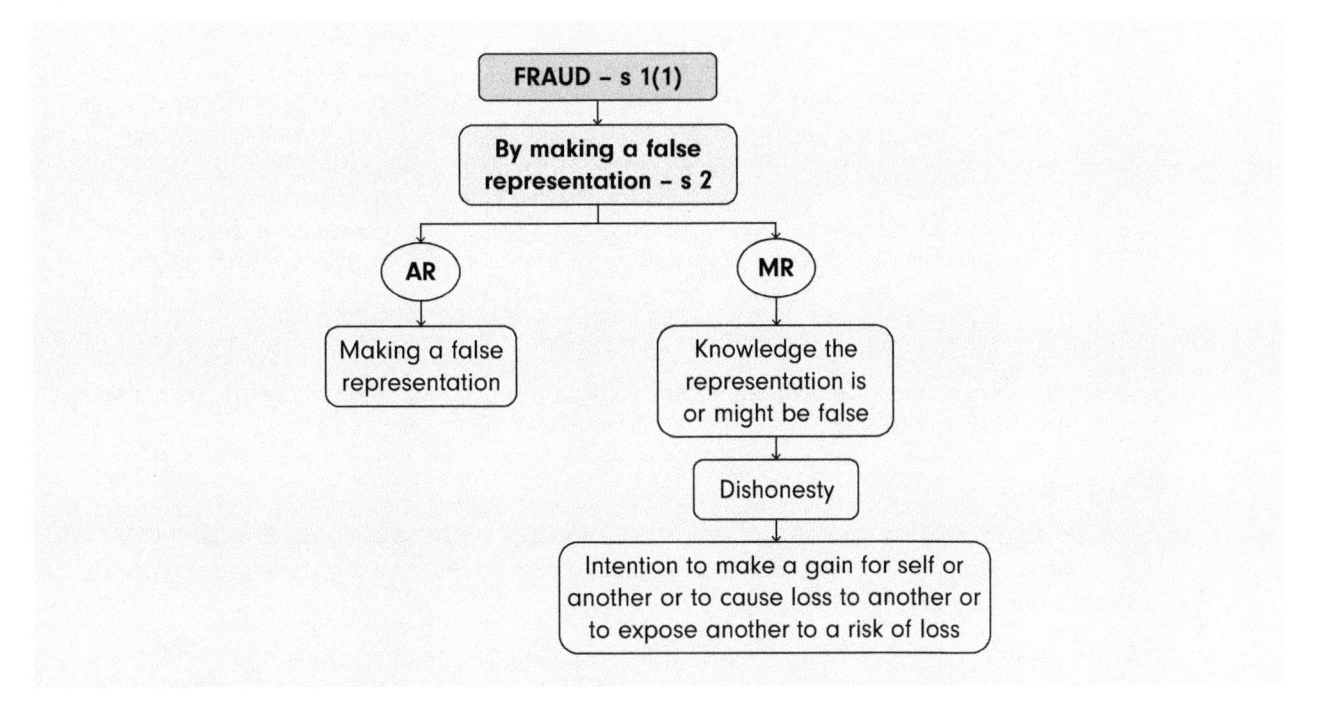

```
                    FRAUD – s 1(1)
                         │
              By making a false
              representation – s 2
                   ┌─────┴─────┐
                  AR           MR
                   │            │
           Making a false   Knowledge the
           representation   representation is
                            or might be false
                                 │
                            Dishonesty
                                 │
                    Intention to make a gain for self or
                    another or to cause loss to another or
                    to expose another to a risk of loss
```

7.4.1 False representation

Central to the commission of the offence is the requirement that a false representation should be made. Fortunately, the FA 2006 provides some assistance in interpreting this phrase. Section 2(2) states that a representation is false if:

(a) it is untrue or misleading; and

(b) the person making it knows that it is, or might be, untrue or misleading.

This definition includes elements of both the actus reus and the mens rea. First, the representation must actually be false or misleading; and secondly, the defendant must have some awareness of this.

7.4.1.1 What is a representation?

The FA 2006 and the Explanatory Notes to the Bill provide some detail as to what counts as a representation and these are summarised in **Table 7.1**.

Criminal Law

Table 7.1 Meaning of representation in the Fraud Act 2006

s 2(3)	s 2(4)	Explanatory Notes to the Bill
A representation may relate to: • a fact; • the law; or • the state of mind of the person making the representation and any other person.	A representation may be: • express; or • implied.	A representation may be: • in words; or • communicated by conduct. There is no limitation on how this is expressed, which may be: • in writing; • spoken; or • posted on a website.

Most representations will be representations of fact but there may, on occasion, be a false representation as to the law.

⭐ *Example*

A moneylender tells one of his debtors that she has no legal defence to a claim for payment, knowing full well that she does, perhaps because of the extortionate rate of interest imposed.

A representation as to the state of mind of the accused or any other person is also included. It would cover, for instance, if the defendant stated that they would do an act in the future, or that some event would occur in the future.

⭐ *Example*

Bernard, a wealthy farmer, promises to change his will to benefit his son, Adam. These words imply that he genuinely intends to do so, perhaps by leaving Adam the family farm; thus, the promise is a representation.

Furthermore, a representation may be express, such as a declaration on a job application form that the applicant has a degree, but it may also be implied.

⭐ *Examples*

(a) Jacinta orders a meal at a restaurant. She is making a representation that she is a legitimate customer willing to pay for her food.

(b) Hua uses her credit card to pay for her shopping. By offering the card as payment, she is representing that she has the authority to use it.

The Explanatory Notes provide more clarification on how representations may be made. Usually, a representation will be in words and this can be expressed in a variety of ways whether it be verbally, by email, in a text message, in a letter or even on an internet site.

7.4.1.2 When is a representation false?

Whether the defendant has made such a representation is a question of fact to be determined by the jury. However, it would usually involve a victim being deceived or misled by something said or written to or about them.

⭐ *Examples*

(a) Anton, a burglar, tricks his way into a property by telling the householder that he is a police officer investigating a crime that took place in the local neighbourhood. This is an express false representation by words.

(b) *Rehana uses a stolen debit card to purchase a mobile phone – by her behaviour (using the card) she is falsely representing she has the right to use it. Here, there is an implied false representation by her conduct.*

However, the requirement will not be satisfied if the defendant says something they believe to be false but that is, in fact, true.

✪ Example

Sebastian sells Violet a painting telling her that it is an undiscovered work of art from a famous painter. He believes that the painting is a fake but, in fact, it turns out to be genuine. In this scenario, there is no false representation and, thus, no s 2 offence.

Whilst juries should be capable of determining if a representation is 'untrue', the lack of a definition of the word 'misleading' can cause difficulties. The Home Office suggests that 'misleading' means 'less than wholly true and capable of an interpretation to the detriment of the victim' and gives the following scenario to illustrate what is meant by this phrase.

✪ Example

Dennis drafts an email with the heading 'Sponsored Swim to Support Cancer Research' and sends it to family, friends and neighbours. Dennis carries out the swim but only donates five per cent of the sponsorship money collected, keeping the rest for himself. Although Dennis has completed the swim and donated some money to the relevant charity, it is likely a jury would find his email to be misleading.

The effect of the use of the word 'misleading' and the related Home Office guidance is that, potentially, it opens up an extremely broad scope of behaviour to the criminal law. It has been argued that even street traders could be liable for fraud if they satisfy the other elements of the offence such as dishonesty.

In addition to the representation being false, s 2(2)(b) of the FA 2006 requires the prosecution to prove a mens rea requirement. The accused must either know the representation is false, or know that it might be. In most instances, this will be quite straightforward to establish as these cases demonstrate.

In Idress v DPP [2011] EWHC 624 (Admin), the defendant had failed his driving test on 15 occasions so he arranged for another, unknown, person to impersonate him to sit the test. It was held that the false representation was made by the defendant when he booked the test online.

In R v Nizzar (unreported, July 2012), the defendant worked on a till in a shop and informed a woman who had a £1 million winning lottery ticket that her ticket had not won any money.

In R v O'Leary [2013] EWCA Crim 1371, the defendant visited the homes of two elderly victims who suffered from dementia. He claimed he had completed roof repair work to their properties and demanded payment for this, despite not having done so.

7.4.1.3 Effect of a representation

For the offence of fraud under s 2 of the FA 2006, the prosecution need only prove that a false representation was actually made; there is no need to prove that anyone was actually deceived. As a consequence, it is possible to commit the offence by making a false representation to a machine. Section 2(5) provides that:

> a representation may be regarded as made if it (or anything implying it) is submitted in any form to any system or device designed to receive, convey or respond to communications (with or without human intervention).

The statute is drafted so that the representation need only be 'submitted' and not necessarily communicated. The reason was to ensure that the FA 2006 remains relevant in a modern society, enabling it to convict those engaged in fraudulent conduct in the context of ever-changing technology.

The practical effect is:

- A representation by email is made as soon as it is sent, whether the intended victim reads the contents or even receives it at all.
- Withdrawing money from a cash point machine is covered by the FA 2006 and the representation is made when the PIN (personal identification number) is inputted into the machine.
- Entering stolen bank details onto an internet site to purchase items is a representation.

7.4.2 Mens rea

For the offence to be committed, the defendant must know the representation is untrue or misleading, or know that it might be so. This element has already been discussed above.

In addition, the defendant must be shown to have acted dishonestly and to intend, by that representation, to make a gain for themselves or another, or to cause loss to another or to expose another to a risk of loss.

7.4.2.1 Dishonesty

Despite the importance of dishonesty in fraud, there is no definition in the Act. However, in most cases, dishonesty will be clear and the issue will simply be left to the common sense of the magistrates or the jury when considering the evidence presented to them.

However, if the court does need further assistance in determining this issue, it will be directed to the test in *Ivey v Genting Casinos*, which is discussed in **Chapter 6.** Having listened to the evidence and established the defendant's awareness of the facts, the court will determine whether the accused's conduct was honest or not by the (objective) standards of ordinary, decent people.

7.4.2.2 Intention to make a gain or cause loss

In order to be guilty of fraud, the defendant must intend by making the representation to make a gain for themselves or another, or to cause loss to another or to expose another to a risk of loss. The statute makes it clear that it is 'by' making the false representation that the defendant must intend to make the gain or cause the loss, so there must be a link between the two. In other words, the defendant must intend the gain or loss to be as a result of the representation.

Guidance on this aspect of the mens rea is to be found in s 5 of the FA 2006, the effect of which is summarised below.

Table 7.2 Meaning of gain and loss in the Fraud Act 2006

'Gain' and 'loss'	'Gain' includes:	'Loss' includes:
Extends only to money or property.	Keeping what one has.	Not getting what one might get.
May be real or personal property including things in action and other intangible property.	Getting what one does not have.	Parting with what one has.
May be temporary or permanent.		

The effect of this provision becomes clear when looking at various examples. In all of these, there is both a view to gain and an intent to cause loss and this will usually be the case. However, to establish criminal liability for fraud, only one or the other is required.

⭐ Example

Assume in each of these scenarios that Hannah has deliberately made a false representation to Noah and she has been dishonest.

(a) Hannah has lost her textbook but she tells Noah she has forgotten it and asks him to give her his copy. Hannah has a view to gain (by getting what she does not have – the textbook) and also intends to cause loss to Noah (by making him part with what he has).

(b) Hannah intends to return the book at the end of the day but the fact that the borrowing of the textbook is only temporary is immaterial – she still has the relevant view to gain and intent to cause loss.

(c) Hannah does not want to buy another textbook so, at the end of the day, she emails Noah to say that she has mislaid his. Hannah has a view to gain what she does not have (the textbook) and an intent to cause loss, by Noah not getting what he might get (the return of the book).

(d) Hannah then tells Noah that she has no money for her bus fare home and asks if he can lend her £5. Hannah has a view to gain and an intent to cause loss as this intent can relate to money as well as property.

7.4.3 Summary of fraud by false representation

In summary, the offence of fraud under s 2 FA 2006 is drafted very widely as the defendant need only make a false representation with the requisite mens rea. It is irrelevant whether anyone is misled by the representation, whether the victim relied upon it or whether the representation actually resulted in the defendant gaining anything or causing any loss. A defendant is convicted on the basis of the representation they make, rather than whether they were actually successful in their aim. This is because the offence occurs as soon as the representation is made.

7.5 Fraud by failing to disclose information

Under s 1 of the FA 2006, a person is guilty of fraud under s 3 if they:

(a) dishonestly fail to disclose to another person information which they are under a legal duty to disclose; and

(b) intend, by failing to disclose the information, to make a gain for themselves or another, or to cause loss to another or to expose another to a risk of loss.

As with other offences, the actus reus and mens rea elements must be proved by the prosecution and these are summarised in **Figure 7.3**.

Figure 7.3 Failing to disclose information

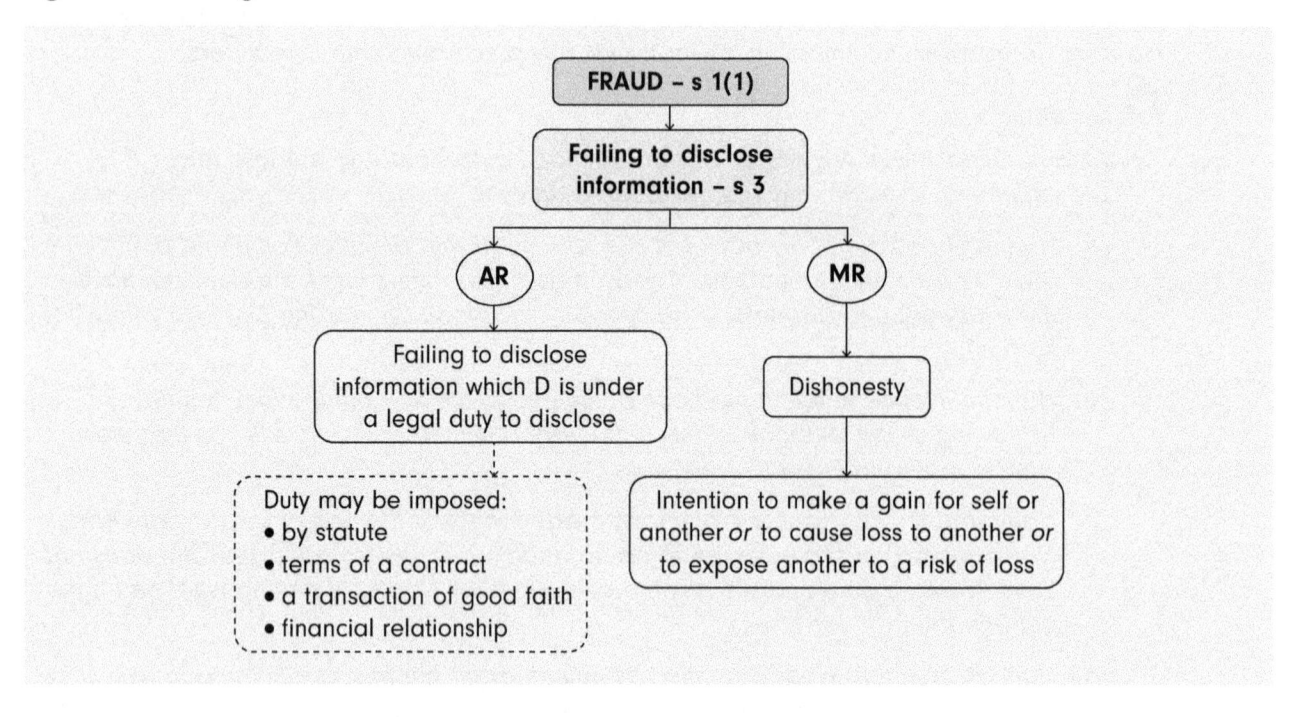

```
                    FRAUD – s 1(1)
                          ↓
                  Failing to disclose
                  information – s 3
                    ↓           ↓
                   AR          MR
                    ↓           ↓
          Failing to disclose
          information which D is under    Dishonesty
          a legal duty to disclose
                    ↓           ↓
          Duty may be imposed:     Intention to make a gain for self or
          • by statute             another or to cause loss to another or
          • terms of a contract    to expose another to a risk of loss
          • a transaction of good faith
          • financial relationship
```

7.5.1 Failing to disclose information

Not all information must be disclosed and it only becomes a criminal offence if the defendant fails to do so when under a legal duty.

The FA 2006 does not define a 'legal duty', but the Explanatory Notes state that it includes 'duties under oral contracts as well as written contracts'. Examples of where there is a legal duty to disclose would include those derived from:

- statute (such as the provisions governing company prospectuses or the requirement to notify a change in circumstances in relation to a welfare benefits claim);
- the fact that the transaction is one of utmost good faith (for example, contracts of insurance);
- the express or implied terms of the contract;
- the custom of a particular trade or market; and
- the existence of a fiduciary relationship between the parties (such as agent and principal).

There are various situations where a failure to disclose such information may arise.

⭐ Examples

(a) Chun applies for travel insurance to cover his trip to Hong Kong to see his family, but fails to disclose that he has previously been treated for a heart condition. Three days after arriving in Hong Kong he suffers a heart attack. The contract of insurance is a transaction of good faith, so Chun was under a legal duty to disclose his previous medical condition.

(b) Rachel applies for a post as a teacher of a school. An express requirement of the position is that the successful applicant is a person of good character. Rachel sends off her CV and is delighted to be awarded the job. In fact, she was disciplined for cheating in her first year at university. A legal duty to disclose arises due to the express term of the employment contract.

The legal duty to disclose information applies not only if the defendant's failure to disclose the relevant facts gives the victim a cause of action for damages, but also if the law gives the victim a right to set aside any change in their legal position to which they may consent as a result of the non-disclosure.

⭐ Example

Sadiq often travels abroad due to his employment and so he decides to appoint his brother, Aman, as a trustee of his young son. Aman fails to tell Sadiq that he has recently been made bankrupt.

- *Aman is being placed in a fiduciary position with Sadiq and, as a consequence, he is under a duty to disclose material information. His failure to do so means that Sadiq can rescind or cancel their contract and reclaim any monies transferred under it.*

- *If Aman has invested the trust fund unwisely, Sadiq may also have a claim for damages for the monies he has lost.*

7.5.2 Mens rea

The mens rea required for an offence of fraud by failing to disclose information under s 3 is dishonesty and an intention to make a gain for themselves or another, or to cause loss to another, or to expose another to risk of loss. These mirror two of the mens rea elements of the s 2 offence of making a false representation, which have already been discussed in this chapter.

7.6 Fraud by abuse of position

There is a further means of committing fraud, which covers those defendants who are in some form of privileged position in relation to the victim. This is dealt with in s 4 of the FA 2006, which provides that a person is in breach of this section if they:

(a) occupy a position in which they are expected to safeguard, or not to act against, the financial interests of another person;

(b) dishonestly abuse that position; and

(c) intend, by means of the abuse of that position to make a gain for themselves or another, or to cause loss to another or to expose another to a risk of loss.

The offence of fraud by abuse of position is made up of two actus reus and two mens rea elements.

Figure 7.4 Abuse of position

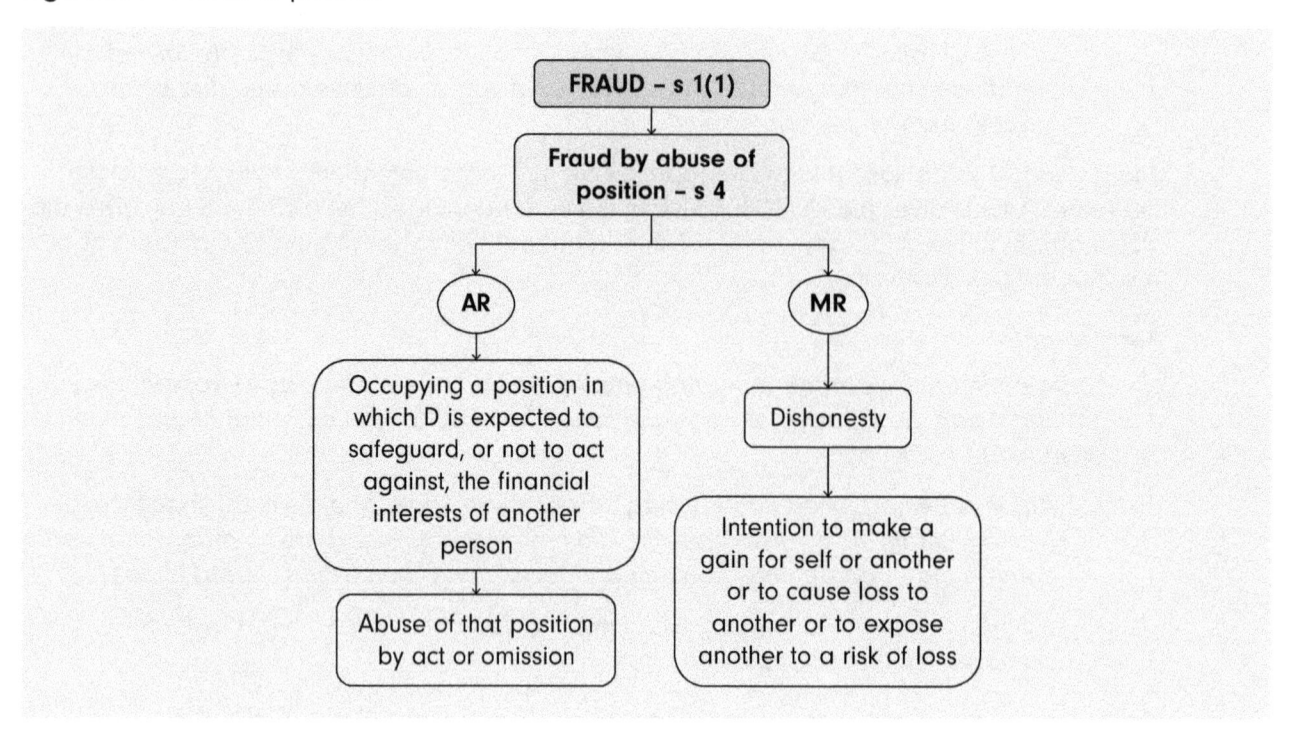

```
                    FRAUD – s 1(1)
                          │
                 Fraud by abuse of
                   position – s 4
                   ┌──────┴──────┐
                  AR             MR
                   │              │
      Occupying a position in    Dishonesty
      which D is expected to         │
      safeguard, or not to act       │
      against, the financial    Intention to make a
      interests of another      gain for self or another
           person               or to cause loss to
             │                  another or to expose
      Abuse of that position    another to a risk of loss
        by act or omission
```

7.6.1 Actus reus

The actus reus of fraud by abuse of position comprises two elements the first of which relates to the position held by the defendant, whilst the second concerns their behaviour.

7.6.1.1 Occupation of a relevant position

Fraud under s 4 requires the existence of a position of financial trust between the defendant and the victim. This is further defined as one in which the defendant is expected to safeguard or not to act against the financial interests of another person. The FA 2006 does not define the word 'position', but suggested examples are between:

- trustee and beneficiary;
- director and company;
- professional person and client;
- agent and principal;
- employee and employer.

A position of financial trust may also arise in other circumstances such as within a family, or in the context of voluntary work.

In all these examples, the victim has voluntarily placed the defendant in a privileged position with respect to their financial interests, so that the defendant is able to act in relation to those interests without reference to the victim. For example, an employee of a software company who is able to access his employer's databases to clone software products occupies such a position, as they could use their access to sell products to a rival business.

The offence is interpreted widely and may be committed in a number of ways, not just where the defendant owes a specific fiduciary duty to the victim, as demonstrated by the case considered below.

> In R v Valujevs [2014] EWCA Crim 2888, unlicensed gang-masters – who abused their position by exploiting migrant workers, making unlawful deductions from their wages and charging excessive rent payments – were found to occupy a position that was capable of being one in which they were expected to safeguard the financial interests of another.

7.6.1.2 Abuse of position

Many people are in positions of trust but, to be liable for fraud, the defendant must go on to abuse their position. Thus, the employee of the software company referred to in **7.6.1.1** must actually clone the software products with the intention of selling them on.

The abuse can be committed either by a positive act or by an omission.

> *In R v Rouse [2014] EWCA Crim 1128, the defendant was found guilty of fraud under s 4. He was the deputy manager of a care home with access to residents' bank and credit cards, and account details. As such he was in a position in which he was expected to safeguard, or not to act against, the financial interests of the residents. However, he abused that position by using the cards to withdraw money from a cash machine, which he then spent on himself and to pay his personal bills.*

Professionals such as lawyers and accountants clearly occupy positions in which they are expected to safeguard, or not to act against, the financial interests of another person – their clients. The criminal law will intervene when an abuse takes place and, in such instances, more than one offence may be committed.

7.6.2 Mens rea

The mens rea required for an offence of fraud by abuse of position under s 4 is dishonesty and an intention to make a gain for themselves or another, or to cause loss to another, or to expose another to risk of loss. These mirror two of the mens rea elements of the s 2 offence of making a false representation, discussed in **section 7.4.2**.

7.7 Overlap between the fraud offences

It is not unusual for a defendant to be criminally liable for different offences under the FA 2006 particularly as ss 2 to 4 describe three ways in which the offence of fraud may be satisfied.

> ★ *Examples*
>
> *(a) Lee is an estate agent who has been instructed by Danielle to market her property known as Packwood Cottage in Lichfield. Lee under-values the property and does not market it effectively so that his daughter may purchase it at the lower price.*
>
> *Lee is guilty of an offence under s 3 as he fails to disclose to the seller, Danielle, that a close family relative is the prospective purchaser. This is material information that he is under a legal duty to disclose.*
>
> *Furthermore, Lee is in a fiduciary position with the seller of the property (Danielle) in which he is expected to safeguard or not to act against his client. This would require him to market the cottage properly and to obtain the best price for it. Because he intends to make a gain for another (his daughter) and a corresponding loss to Danielle, provided the court is satisfied as to his dishonesty, Lee will also be guilty of an offence of fraud by abuse of position under s 4 of the FA 2006.*
>
> *(b) Nathan is a builder. He befriends an elderly woman, Polina, who believes him to be an honest tradesman. He carries out various work for Polina and also helps her with chores around her house. However, Nathan charges a grossly excessive sum for work carried out on her roof. He is liable under s 2 as there was an implied representation that the price would be fair and reasonable due to the relationship of trust between Nathan and Polina.*
>
> *However, Nathan may also be guilty under s 4 due to his commission of a fraud by abuse of position of financial trust.*

Summary

The flowchart in **Figure 7.5** summarises the actus reus and mens rea elements of ss 2, 3 and 4 of the FA 2006.

Figure 7.5 Summary of fraud

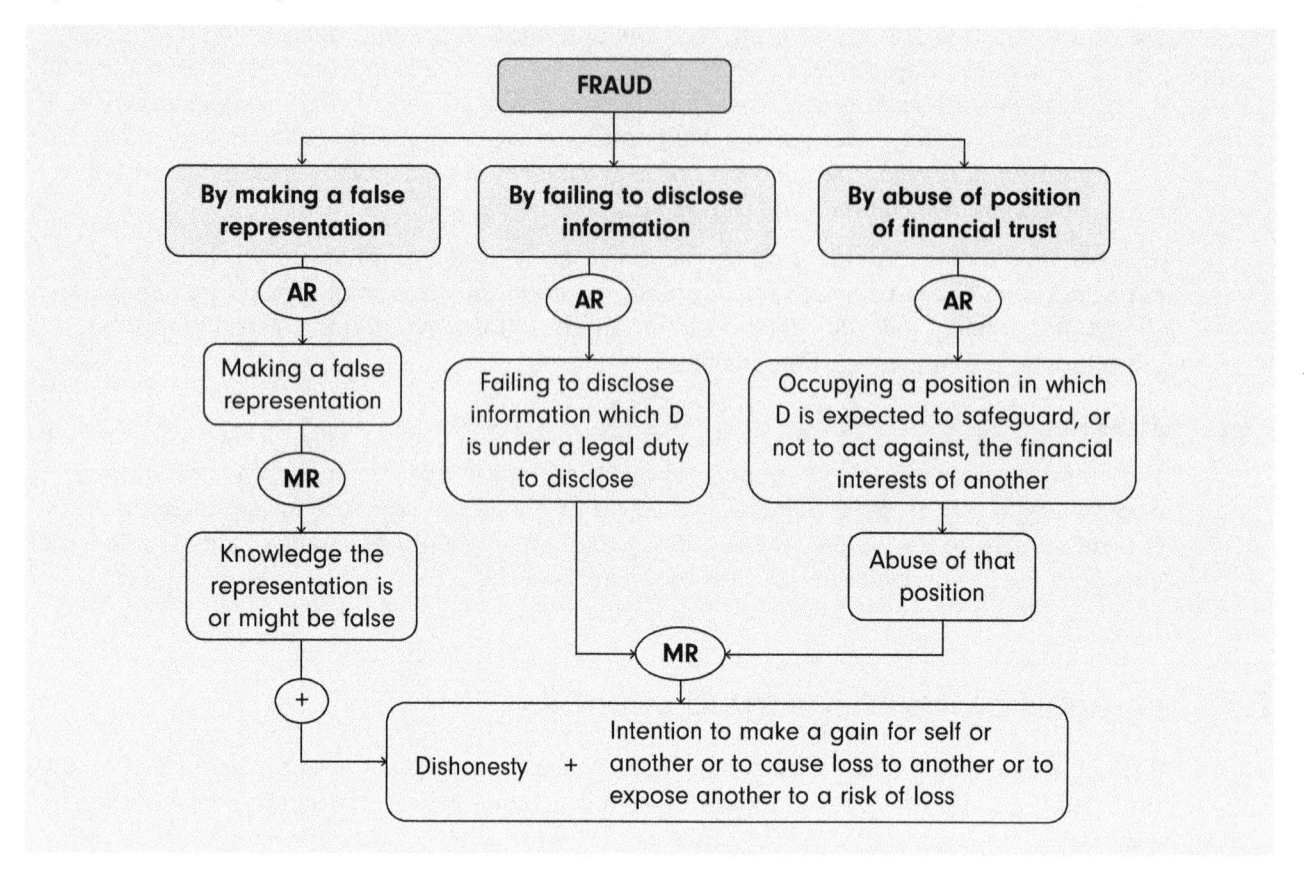

```
                              FRAUD
        ┌───────────────────────┼───────────────────────┐
  By making a false      By failing to disclose    By abuse of position
   representation              information          of financial trust
        │ AR                      │ AR                    │ AR
        ▼                         ▼                        ▼
   Making a false          Failing to disclose      Occupying a position in which
   representation          information which D      D is expected to safeguard, or
                           is under a legal duty    not to act against, the financial
        │ MR               to disclose              interests of another
        ▼                                                  │
   Knowledge the                                           ▼
   representation is                                  Abuse of that
   or might be false                                   position
                                   │ MR ◄──────────────────┘
        │ +                        ▼
        └──────────►  Dishonesty  +  Intention to make a gain for self or
                                     another or to cause loss to another or to
                                     expose another to a risk of loss
```

In conclusion, set out below is an overview of the offence of fraud.

- The FA 2006 creates a general offence of fraud under s 1 but it may be committed in three different ways: s 2 provides for fraud by false representation, s 3 by failing to disclose information and s 4 by abuse of position.
- All three types of fraud share the same mens rea although s 2 also has an additional requirement.
- Dishonesty is a key element; if the defendant is not clearly dishonest, the *Ivey* test will apply.
- The defendant must intend, by making the representation, to make a gain for themselves or another, or to cause loss to another or to expose another to a risk of loss. 'Gain' and 'loss' are defined under s 5 of the FA 2006.
- To be guilty of s 2 fraud, the defendant must make a false representation, knowing it to be untrue or misleading or that it might be.
- In order to be guilty of fraud by failing to disclose information under s 3, there must be a legal duty to disclose the information.
- To be guilty of fraud under s 4, the defendant must be in a position of financial trust, which is abused. Such a position is one in which the defendant is expected to safeguard or not to act against the financial interests of another person.

Sample questions

Question 1

A lawyer for the Crown Prosecution Service is asked to provide charging advice in relation to a defendant who has allegedly committed a number of offences of fraud. Having considered the evidence, the lawyer sends a report to the police informing them of the outcome of the review.

In which of the following scenarios is there insufficient evidence to establish that the defendant has made a false representation?

- A   The defendant states he is 18 years of age in order to purchase alcohol when he is aged only 16 years.
- B   The defendant uses his friend's identity card to gain entry to a night club.
- C   The defendant dresses as a police officer so that he is allowed into an elderly man's house.
- D   The defendant uses a stolen credit card to purchase goods from a shop by swiping it across the payment machine.
- E   The defendant uses his bank card mistakenly believing that the bank had frozen his account, but in fact, he has sufficient funds for the purchase.

Answer

Option E is correct. When using the card, the defendant represents that he has the means and authority to pay and he actually does; thus, there is no false representation. In all the other answers, the defendant makes a false representation in fact, either expressly in words (as in option A) or by his conduct (options B, C and D). It is irrelevant that the representation is made to a machine.

Question 2

A man drives onto a petrol station to buy fuel. He fills up his tank with petrol and walks towards the kiosk intending to pay. However, he then realises that he has left his wallet at home and so he decides to drive away. As he walks back across the forecourt towards his car, the man spots a bank card that has been dropped by its owner on the floor. He picks it up and decides to use it to pay for his petrol. He does this by swiping the contactless card across the payment machine.

Which answer best describes the man's liability for an offence of fraud by false representation?

- A   The man is not guilty of fraud when he fills his tank with petrol because he is not dishonest. However, he is guilty of fraud when he uses the bank card to pay for it as he is dishonest at this point.
- B   The man is guilty of fraud when he fills his tank with petrol because he did not have the means to pay. He is also guilty of fraud when he uses the bank card as it does not belong to him.
- C   The man is guilty of fraud when he fills his tank with petrol. He is not guilty of fraud when he uses the bank card as the transaction involves a machine.
- D   The man is not guilty of fraud for either event because he did not make an express false representation.
- E   The man cannot be liable for fraud for either event because fraud by false representation requires evidence that a person is deceived.

Criminal Law

Answer

Option A is the correct answer because, whilst the man's conduct in filling his tank with petrol impliedly represents that he has the means and intention to pay for it (a false representation in fact), he is not dishonest when doing so. This is because he only realises he has forgotten his wallet when he walks towards the kiosk; thus, after the event. When using the bank card, the actus reus is established by his conduct as he makes a false representation that the card is his and that he has the authority to use it. The mens rea is also satisfied because the man knows this representation is false, he is dishonest as he is aware the card does not belong to him and he intends to make a gain of the petrol and a corresponding loss to the owner of the petrol station.

Option B is wrong as the man is not guilty of fraud in relation to the filling of his tank with petrol, as discussed above. C is wrong for the same reason but also because it does not matter that the representation is to a machine. Option D is wrong because the man is guilty of fraud in relation to the use of the bank card; whilst option E is wrong as there is no requirement that a person is actually deceived.

Question 3

A woman has been appointed as a trustee for a charity. Her role is to set up and promote a series of sponsored events to raise money for the charity. She enters into a contract with a company to assist her in this task but does not mention to the other trustees that one of the directors is her husband. The charity is also unaware that the woman has an arrangement with the company whereby she receives a payment for each event that they organise.

Which of the following best describes how the woman has committed an offence of fraud?

A   Fraud by false representation.

B   Fraud by failure to disclose information.

C   Fraud by abuse of position.

D   Fraud by false representation and by abuse of position.

E   Fraud by failure to disclose information and by abuse of postion.

Answer

The correct answer is option E. The woman is guilty of an offence under s 3 as she fails to disclose to the other trustees that her husband is benefiting from the contract to set up and promote the sponsored events. This is material information that she is under a legal duty to disclose. In addition, the woman is also guilty of an offence of abuse of position under s 4 of the FA 2006. She is in a fiduciary position (as a trustee) in which she is expected to safeguard or not act against the financial interests of another, in this instance, the charity. This duty would require her to ensure that all profits from the events were given to the charity and not to her personally. As to the mens rea, the woman intends to make a gain for herself and another (her husband) and a corresponding loss to the charity, and the court is likely to be satisfied as to her dishonesty.

Option A is wrong because the woman does not make a false representation under s 2, as is option D for the same reason. Options B and C are wrong as they only identify one of the offences for which she may be liable rather than both.

8 Criminal Damage

8.1	Introduction	152
8.2	Simple criminal damage	152
8.3	Arson	158
8.4	Aggravated criminal damage	158
8.5	Aggravated arson	160

SQE1 syllabus

By the end of this chapter you will be able to apply relevant core legal principles and rules appropriately and effectively, at the level of a competent newly qualified solicitor in practice, to realistic client-based and ethical problems and situations in the area of **criminal damage**.

Note that, as students are not usually required to recall specific case names, or cite statutory or regulatory authorities, these are provided for illustrative purposes only.

Learning outcomes

The learning outcomes for this chapter are:

- to define simple and aggravated criminal damage and arson and explain how these are applied in practice;
- to explain the concept of lawful excuse and when this will operate as a defence to a charge of criminal damage; and
- to be able to advise on how to prosecute or defend a claim for criminal damage.

Criminal Law

8.1 Introduction

Criminal damage is one of the more common offences committed in society and ranges from the petty, such as the daubing of graffiti on trains, to the very serious, for example the damage resulting from full scale riots, as in 2011, which cost businesses millions of pounds. The motives of those who commit these crimes are equally varied, from boredom to anger to the political.

The relevant offences may be found in the Criminal Damage Act (CDA) 1971. They consist of:

- simple criminal damage (s 1(1))
- aggravated criminal damage (s 1(2))
- simple arson (s 1(3) and s 1(1))
- aggravated arson (s 1(3) and s 1(2)).

8.2 Simple criminal damage

The basic offence of simple criminal damage is defined as:

> A person who without lawful excuse destroys or damages any property belonging to another intending to destroy or damage any such property or being reckless as to whether any such property would be destroyed or damaged shall be guilty of an offence.

8.2.1 Actus reus

The actus reus of simple criminal damage is made up of four key elements. The defendant must:

(a) destroy or damage

(b) property

(c) belonging to another

(d) without lawful excuse.

8.2.1.1 Destruction or damage

The requirement to destroy or damage something is the first element. It includes physical harm, whether permanent or temporary, as well as the impairment of the value or usefulness of property – for example when a part is removed from a machine. Destruction has its normal English language meaning and would cover, for example, the demolition of a building or the burning of a field of crops.

However, what counts as 'damage' is less clear. Whether criminal damage has occurred is a matter of fact and degree but, usually, if expense is incurred in rectifying the consequences of the defendant's act, this will be sufficient. An example would be:

- drawing on a pavement using soluble chalks because the local authority would have to pay the clean-up costs – *Hardman v Chief Constable of Avon and Somerset Constabulary* [1986] Crim LR 330; but not
- spitting on a police officer's raincoat because this could simply be wiped off to restore the jacket to its previous condition – *A (a juvenile) v R* [1978] Crim LR 689. (The lack of any attempt to do so led to a small stain.)

Figure 8.1 Destroy or damage

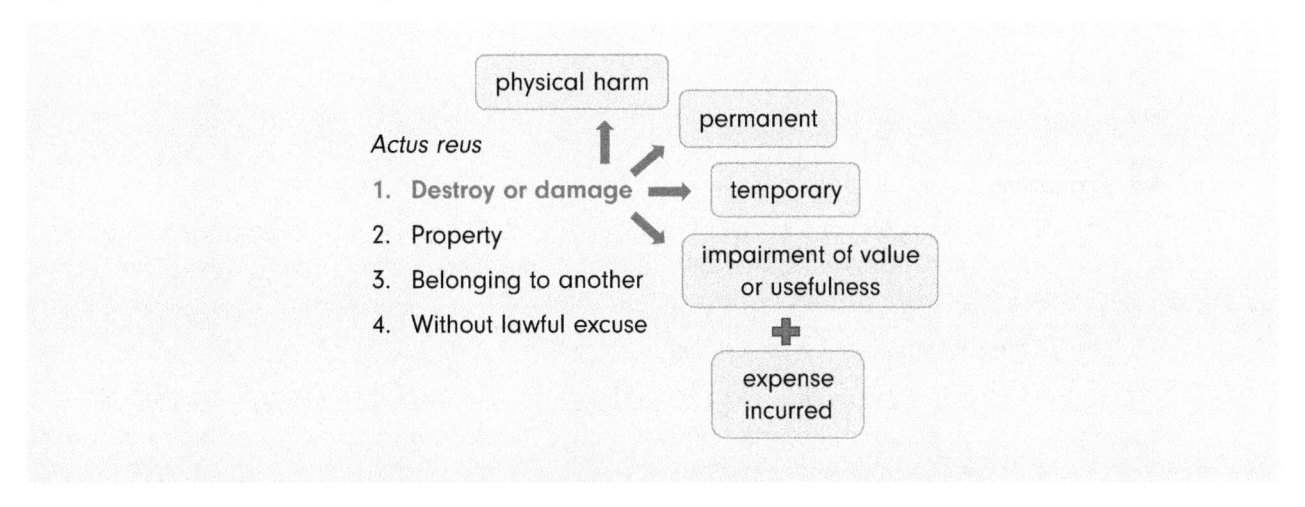

Actus reus
1. **Destroy or damage**
2. Property
3. Belonging to another
4. Without lawful excuse

→ physical harm
→ permanent
→ temporary
→ impairment of value or usefulness
+ expense incurred

8.2.1.2 Property

The criminal damage must be to property and this is defined in s 10(1) of the CDA 1971.

Only tangible property is covered so a thing in action, for example a bank account, cannot be damaged. It includes both real property, such as land and buildings, and personal property including money. With regard to animals and plants, the law takes account of the circumstances, primarily whether the item is wild or not.

Animals are included:

(a) if tamed or ordinarily kept in captivity (pets and zoo animals); or

(b) if they have been, or are being, reduced into possession (for example, a rabbit that has been snared).

A similar approach is taken to plants, so flowers growing in a local authority park may be damaged, but *wild* mushrooms, fruit, flowers, foliage and plants cannot.

Figure 8.2 Property

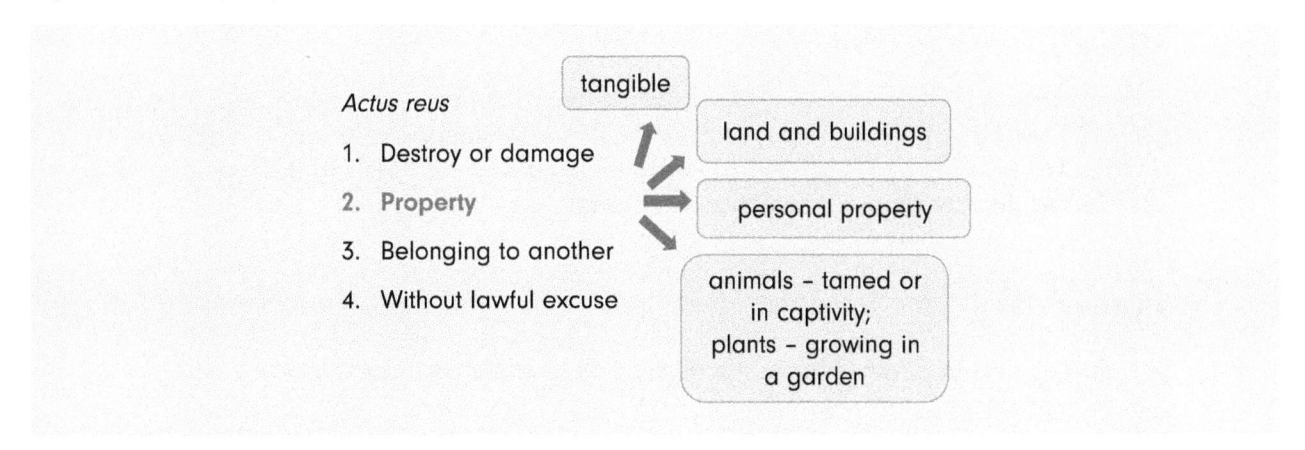

Actus reus
1. Destroy or damage
2. **Property**
3. Belonging to another
4. Without lawful excuse

→ tangible
→ land and buildings
→ personal property
→ animals – tamed or in captivity; plants – growing in a garden

8.2.1.3 Belonging to another

The simple offence of criminal damage cannot be committed against a person's own property and, usually, whether property belongs to another will be straightforward. Property will be treated for the purposes of the CDA 1971 as belonging to anyone who has legal ownership, for example the registered owner of a car or a house, but the definition is wider than this. Section 10(2) provides some additional guidance, specifically that it includes property over which the victim has:

Criminal Law

- custody or control;
- a proprietary right or interest; or
- a charge.

Set out below are some illustrations.

⭐ Examples

(a) Ayesha scribbles on a textbook that her friend, Patsy, has borrowed from the library. Patsy has custody or control, as she is in possession of the book. However, the library owns the textbook and has a proprietary right.

(b) Daljit kicks in the door of a house:
- If he owns the house, he cannot be liable for criminal damage; unless he owns it subject to a mortgage, in which case, the lending company has a charge (and also a proprietary interest).
- If he rents it, the landlord has a proprietary right.

Figure 8.3 Belonging to another

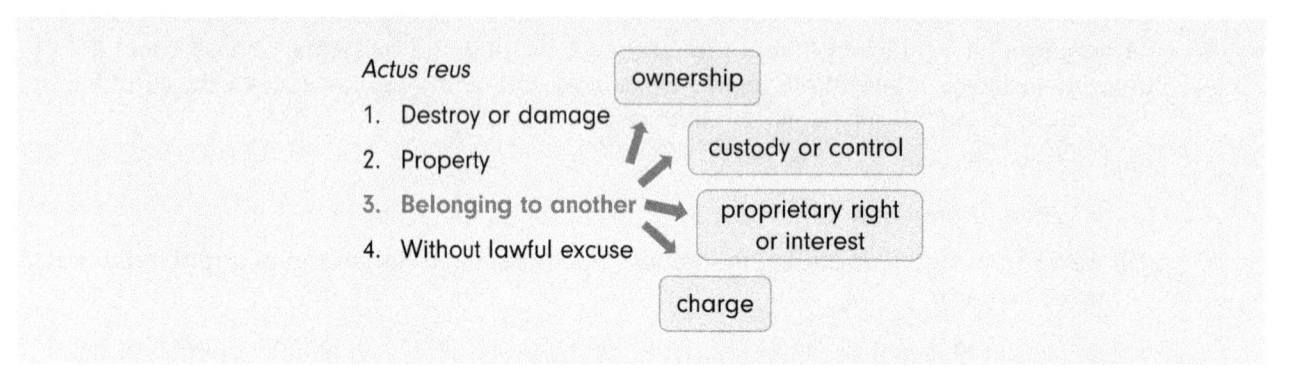

Actus reus
1. Destroy or damage
2. Property
3. Belonging to another
4. Without lawful excuse

→ ownership
→ custody or control
→ proprietary right or interest
→ charge

There is one other element of the actus reus of criminal damage to consider, that of lawful excuse, and this is dealt with later in this chapter (at **8.2.3**).

8.2.2 Mens rea

For the prosecution to succeed in establishing criminal damage, the mens rea must also be proved. For simple criminal damage, the destruction or damage to property belonging to another will only be an offence if it is done intentionally or recklessly and the defendant knew or believed that the property belonged to another.

Mens rea

- *Intention* or *recklessness* as to the destruction or damage of property belonging to another

  +

- *Knowledge* or *belief* that the property belongs to another

In many cases, the criminal damage will be deliberately inflicted, such as the smashing of a bus shelter or the writing of graffiti on a wall but, in other instances, the defendant may only be reckless. Nevertheless, this will be sufficient to satisfy the mens rea. The test for recklessness is subjective so that the accused is judged on the basis of their own state of mind. The question for the court is whether this particular defendant foresaw the (unjustified) risk of criminal damage and went on to take it.

> In R v G [2003] UKHL 50, the defendants, aged 11 and 12, set fire to newspapers in a yard behind a shop and then threw the newspapers under a wheelie bin, before running away. The fire spread to the shop causing significant damage. The House of Lords (as the Supreme Court was then called) ruled that the test of recklessness was subjective for criminal damage and, as the judges accepted that neither boy appreciated the risk of damaging property, the defendants were not guilty of this offence.

There is a second element to the mens rea and this is the requirement that the defendant must know or believe that the property belongs to another.

⭐ Examples

(a) Lottie cuts a designer dress, which she believes to be hers, into pieces because it has a stain on the front. In fact the dress is an identical one belonging to her flatmate.

(b) Jeffrey damages a radiator at the property he is renting, wrongly believing it is his.

The defendant is judged subjectively, on the basis of their honest belief, so neither of these individuals would be criminally liable.

There is one further aspect that needs to be considered. Section 1(1) of the CDA 1971 requires proof that the defendant intentionally or recklessly destroys or damages property belonging to another 'without lawful excuse'. This phrase will now be considered in more detail.

8.2.3 Lawful excuse

The law sets out two (non-exhaustive) situations where a defendant has a lawful excuse, and these can be found in s 5 of the CDA 1971. However, although an accused may rely upon the two statutory lawful excuses as a defence for simple criminal damage or arson, they do not apply to aggravated criminal damage.

Figure 8.4 Without lawful excuse

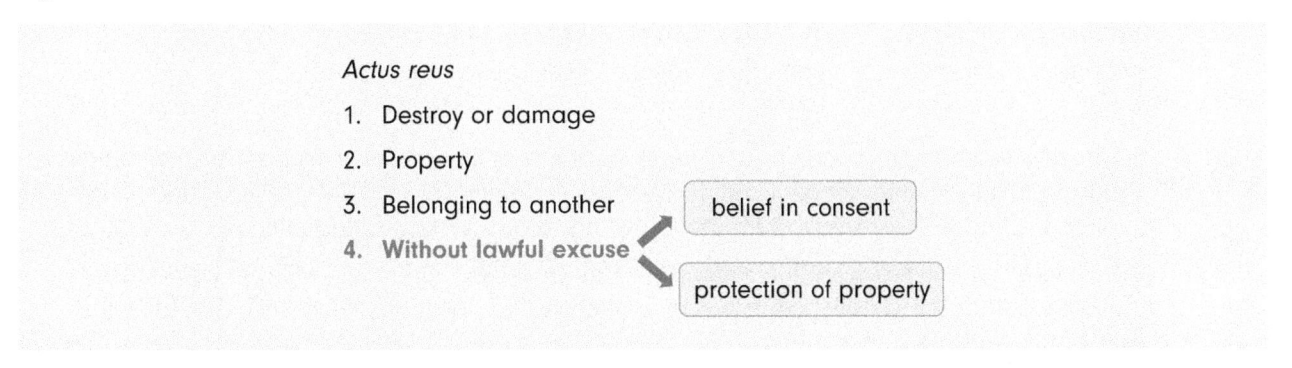

Actus reus
1. Destroy or damage
2. Property
3. Belonging to another
4. Without lawful excuse → belief in consent
                         → protection of property

8.2.3.1 Belief in consent

The first of these situations is contained within s 5(2)(a). The defendant will not be guilty of criminal damage if they had an honest belief that the person entitled to consent to the damage or destruction had consented or would have consented if they had known of the circumstances. This is a *subjective* test.

⭐ Examples

(a) Marietta sees a dog sitting in a car on a very hot day, looking distressed. She smashes the window in order to free the dog, believing that the owner would want the dog to be rescued in these circumstances.

(b) Sandy, an employee at a factory, sets fire to the factory because he believes his employer wanted him to do so in order to make a fraudulent claim.

In these situations, the defendant may rely upon the defence of lawful excuse.

Note that the 'circumstances' of the damage must be linked directly, so could include, for example, the time, place and extent of the damage.

⭐ Example

A protester caused thousands of pounds of damage to a bank's headquarters by shattering windows with hammers. The protester submitted that she honestly believed the bank would have consented if it had known more about the impact of climate change. The argument was rejected as 'circumstances' do not include the political or philosophical beliefs of the person causing the damage.

Whilst a defendant may simply have made a mistake, there will be occasions where they only did so because they were intoxicated.

In the case of Jaggard v Dickinson *[1980] 3 All ER 716, the judges were asked to consider this point. The defendant broke into a house that she thought belonged to her friend, believing (correctly) that her friend would not object because she had no way of getting home. Unfortunately, it was the wrong house. Despite only making the mistake because she was intoxicated, the defendant was able to rely on lawful excuse. This is consistent with the test being purely subjective – the requirement that the belief need only be honestly held.*

8.2.3.2 Need of protection

There is another form of lawful excuse and this may be found in s 5(2)(b). To succeed in establishing this defence, the defendant may argue that they believed the property was in immediate need of protection and that the means adopted were reasonable having regard to all the circumstances. This can be broken down into different elements.

Purpose?

The first question to be determined is whether the defendant's (real) purpose was the protection of their own or another's property. This is a two-stage process.

(i) The court must be satisfied that the accused honestly believed their action was protecting, or was capable of protecting, property (*subjective*). In other words, they are not simply using this reason to conceal a different one. A defendant who set fire to a room in a care home to raise awareness of the defective fire alarm system failed this test.

(ii) Having determined what the defendant's purpose was, the court will rule as a matter of law whether this amounts to a purpose of protecting property. This is an *objective* test.

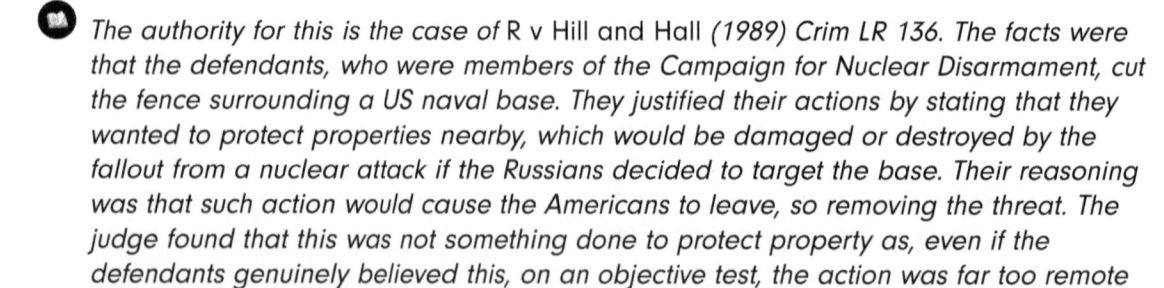

The authority for this is the case of R v Hill and Hall *(1989) Crim LR 136. The facts were that the defendants, who were members of the Campaign for Nuclear Disarmament, cut the fence surrounding a US naval base. They justified their actions by stating that they wanted to protect properties nearby, which would be damaged or destroyed by the fallout from a nuclear attack if the Russians decided to target the base. Their reasoning was that such action would cause the Americans to leave, so removing the threat. The judge found that this was not something done to protect property as, even if the defendants genuinely believed this, on an objective test, the action was far too remote from the eventual aim of protecting property.*

Lawful excuse has been used quite creatively over time. Greenpeace, for example, successfully argued this defence in 2000, after destroying genetically modified crops, by calling experts to support their case that they were trying to prevent genetic pollution to the environment.

However, others have questioned the defendants' motives and suggested that they were simply making a political statement and their real purpose was publicity for the cause. Ultimately, it will be for the judge to decide this question based upon the evidence.

Even if the defendant can overcome this hurdle, the remainder of the legal test must still be satisfied.

Immediate need of protection?

The defendant must also honestly believe that the property was in immediate need of protection. This is a *subjective* test.

In Johnson v DPP *[1994] Crim LR 673*, the defendant was squatting in a disused house in Leeds. He was charged with simple criminal damage after chiselling off the lock on the front door and replacing it with his own. Johnson admitted changing the lock but submitted that he only did so to secure the property and to prevent his possessions from being stolen. In other words, he was taking steps to protect his property.

Unfortunately for Johnson, the argument failed and he was found guilty of criminal damage. The reason was there was no evidence the house was in need of immediate protection and the future risk of theft was not sufficient.

Returning to the case of *Hill and Hall* (above), even if the defendants had succeeded in satisfying the objective test that they were protecting property, they would have failed on this subjective test as there was no immediate threat of a nuclear attack.

Reasonable?

Finally, the defendant would need to satisfy the court that they honestly believed the damage or destruction was reasonable in the circumstances. Again, this is a *subjective* test so the defendant will be judged on their own beliefs.

Example

Daniel has a right of vehicular access over his neighbour's land and is involved in a court dispute over this. One evening, he returns to find a gate has been built across the track, blocking his way. He needs to feed his horses which are in a field further on and so he removes the gate, causing damage as he does so.

To rely upon the defence of lawful excuse, Daniel would need to provide evidence that he caused the damage to the gate to protect his property (his horses) and not, for example, to pursue the neighbour dispute. The court must then be satisfied that, in law, his action was capable of doing so – an objective test.

Thereafter, Daniel would have to demonstrate that he honestly believed (a subjective test) that the property (his horses) were in immediate danger and that the means adopted were reasonable. This would depend upon the evidence.

(a) If Daniel's horses needed feeding, he may be able to prove that his property was in immediate danger; but he may fail if it could be established that he could gain access to the horses another way – perhaps by a different route.

(b) Similarly, with the means adopted. If Daniel damaged the hinges as he lifted the gate before setting it down on the side of the track, this would be reasonable; but not if he smashed into the gate with a tractor causing extensive damage.

In summary, although Daniel has intentionally damaged property belonging to another, he may have a lawful excuse for his actions under s 5(2)(b) provided he honestly believed he was protecting his horses and that there was no alternative to removing the gate to do so. Obviously in practice it would depend upon how convincing Daniel's evidence is and whether the prosecution could disprove it.

Criminal Law

> **Lawful excuse**
>
> **s 5(2)(a)** – Honest belief in the owner's consent – **subjective**
>
> **s 5(2)(b)** – Protection of property
> - Was D's (real) purpose the protection of property? – **objective**
> - If yes, did D honestly believe:
>   - the property was in immediate need of protection; and
>   - the means adopted were reasonable? – **subjective**

8.3 Arson

Criminal damage is committed where the defendant destroys or damages property belonging to another, either intentionally or recklessly and without a lawful excuse. This becomes the offence of arson when the method used is fire. Instead of being charged under s 1(1) of the CDA 1971, the offence is committed under s 1(3). All other elements discussed above apply to arson and so it is perhaps easier to think of it as 'criminal damage by fire'.

Arson is committed quite regularly and, indeed, there are some defendants who have a real fascination with fire. It is not uncommon for fires to be started deliberately in the summer on open ground and heathland, and the effect can be devastating.

Table 8.1 Simple arson

Actus reus	Mens rea
Destroy or damage	Intention or recklessness as to the destruction or damage of property belonging to another
Property	Knowledge or belief that the property belongs to another
Belonging to another	
Without lawful excuse	
By fire	

As with simple criminal damage, the defence of lawful excuse is available for arson.

8.4 Aggravated criminal damage

Section 1(2) of the CDA 1971 creates the offence of destroying or damaging property with intent to endanger life. This is more commonly referred to as aggravated criminal damage.

There are two key differences between the actus reus of simple criminal damage and the aggravated offence.

(a) The property that is damaged or destroyed may belong to either the defendant or to another. This contrasts with the actus reus for simple criminal damage where the property *must* belong to someone else.

(b) The statutory defence of lawful excuse does not apply even though, rather confusingly, these words appear in the statutory definition. However, this does not preclude the defendant from relying upon a general defence.

To be guilty of aggravated criminal damage, the defendant must either intend the damage or destruction, or be reckless as to it. However, there is an additional mens rea element for the prosecution to prove, namely that the defendant intended, by the destruction or damage, to endanger the life of another or is reckless as to whether the life of another would be thereby endangered.

Table 8.2 Aggravated criminal damage

Actus reus	Mens rea
Destroy or damage	Intention or recklessness as to the destruction or damage of property
Property	**Intention or recklessness as to the endangerment of life**
Belonging to *self* or another	
Section 5 lawful excuses do not apply	

As for simple criminal damage, the test for recklessness is subjective.

Quite what is required for endangerment to life was the subject of two important cases.

In R v Dudley [1989] Crim LR 57, the defendant had a grievance with the victim and threw a firebomb at his house. Fortunately, the victim and his family quickly extinguished the fire and only minimal damage was caused. The defendant submitted that he was not guilty of the aggravated offence of criminal damage because the fire did not spread. However, given that it is largely due to luck whether a fire takes hold or not, unsurprisingly, this argument failed. The court held that it was irrelevant whether life was actually endangered; the question is whether the defendant intended or was aware of a risk of danger to life at the time of doing the act, in this case throwing the firebomb.

The next case of R v Steer [1987] 2 All ER 833 established that, to satisfy the mens rea for the aggravated offence, the defendant must intend or be reckless as to the damage or destruction of property, but also intend by that damage to endanger life (or be reckless as to this). The facts of the case were that the defendant fired a shot through a window pane, behind which two people were standing.

It was accepted by the court at the trial that the defendant did not actually intend to endanger life, but he was convicted nevertheless because he was reckless. However, the House of Lords allowed the defendant's appeal on the basis that it must be shown that the endangering of life arose from the damage and not, as here, from the act that caused the damage. In other words, the endangerment to life must come from the broken glass and not from the firing of the gun. Note that, if followed through to its logical conclusion, in the context of arson, this would mean that the endangerment of life must arise from (for example) falling ceilings rather than the fire itself. However, the judge in R v Steer confirmed that the legal principle could include a victim overcome by smoke or incinerated by flames as it was 'absurd to suggest that this did not result from the damage to the building'.

This can be quite difficult to understand but the justification is that criminal damage is a property offence and there are many other offences that could be charged, such as assault or attempted assault. Some illustrations should assist:

⭐ Examples

(a) *Grigore rips out the copper wires from a signal box on a railway line, leaving live wires exposed. His actions endanger not only the engineers who repair the signals but also passengers on the trains as the damage to the signals may cause an accident. Grigore would be guilty of aggravated criminal damage if he is aware of this risk. Even if he did not intend to harm anyone, he is reckless as to the endangering of life.*

(b) *Georgia is involved in rioting. She throws bricks at the windscreen of a moving police car and one of the bricks smashes through the window, causing the glass to shatter. Shocked by the impact, the police officer immediately stops the vehicle. Georgia is guilty of aggravated criminal damage because she intends to damage property (the police car) and she is at least reckless as to endangering life. This is because the broken windscreen could have caused the officer to lose control and crash into pedestrians, particularly if the vehicle was being driven at speed. It is irrelevant that no-one is actually hurt.*

8.5 Aggravated arson

Adding in the ingredient of fire to an offence of aggravated criminal damage makes the offence one of aggravated arson. Thus, in the case of *R v Dudley* (above), the defendant was guilty of aggravated arson.

Table 8.3 Aggravated arson

Actus reus	Mens rea
Destroy or damage	Intention or recklessness as to the destruction or damage of property
Property	Intention or recklessness as to the endangerment of life
Belonging to self or another	
By fire	
Section 5 lawful excuses do not apply	

To conclude the analysis of aggravated criminal damage and arson, the key differences with the less serious simple offences are summarised below:

- The property damaged or destroyed does not have to belong to another.
- There is an 'extra' requirement to the mens rea of endangerment to life.
- The statutory defences of lawful excuses are not available, although the general defences are.

Summary

There are four distinct offences of criminal damage, ranging in severity up to aggravated arson. One approach to remembering these is to begin with the elements of simple criminal damage and then add in the 'extra' ingredients necessary to form others.

- Criminal damage
    - AR: destroy or damage property belonging to another
    - MR: intention or recklessness as to the damage/destruction and knowledge or belief the property belongs to another
- Criminal damage + **fire** = arson
- Criminal damage + **extra MR of intention or recklessness as to endangering life** = **aggravated** criminal damage
- Criminal damage + 'extra' MR of intention or recklessness as to endangering life + **fire** = aggravated **arson**
- NB: the s 5 lawful excuses only apply to **simple criminal damage or arson**

Figure 8.5 Criminal damage

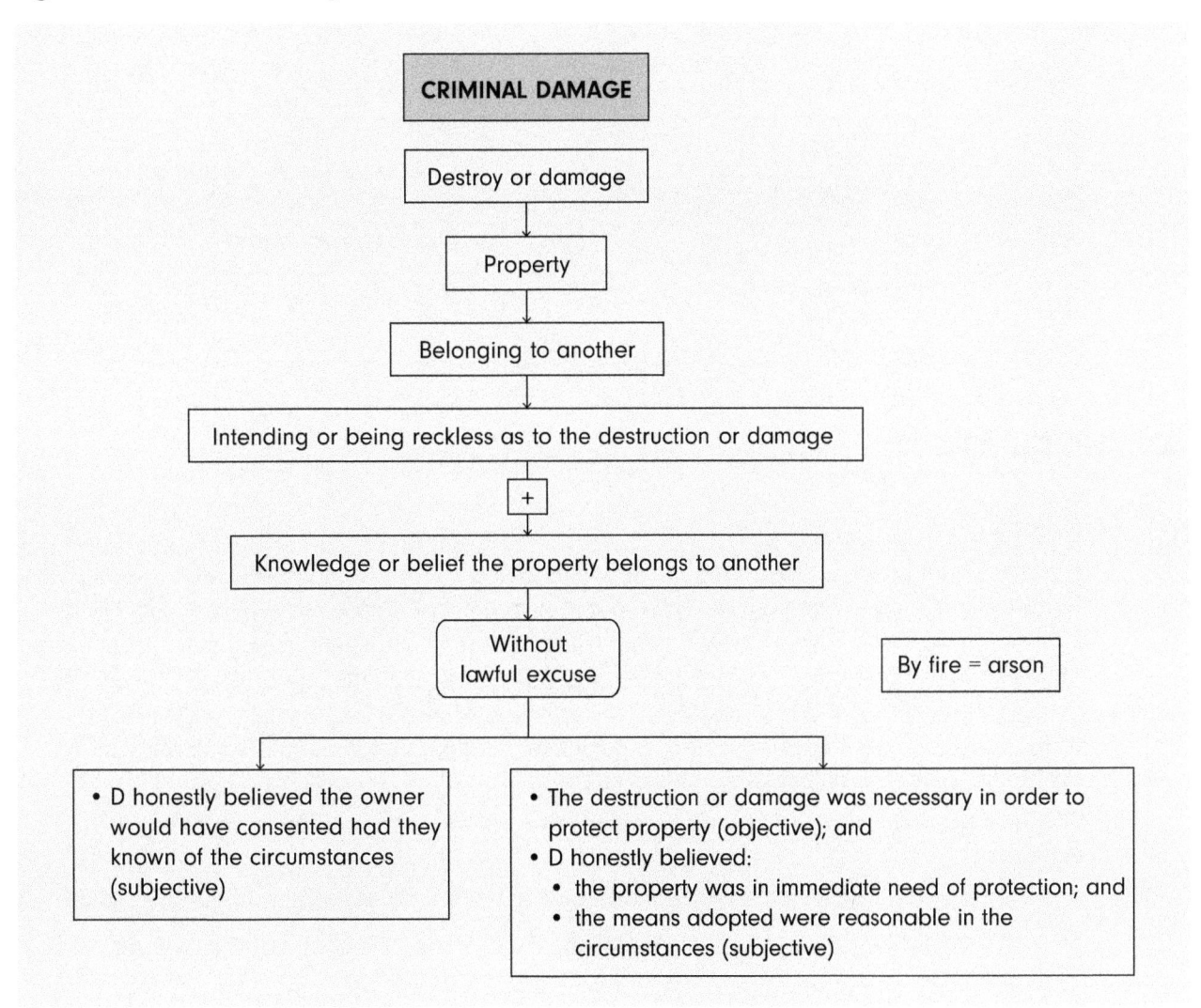

```
                    CRIMINAL DAMAGE
                           |
                    Destroy or damage
                           |
                       Property
                           |
                  Belonging to another
                           |
       Intending or being reckless as to the destruction or damage
                           +
           Knowledge or belief the property belongs to another
                           |
                    Without
                  lawful excuse            By fire = arson
```

- D honestly believed the owner would have consented had they known of the circumstances (subjective)

- The destruction or damage was necessary in order to protect property (objective); and
- D honestly believed:
    - the property was in immediate need of protection; and
    - the means adopted were reasonable in the circumstances (subjective)

Criminal Law

Figure 8.6 Summary of aggravated criminal damage

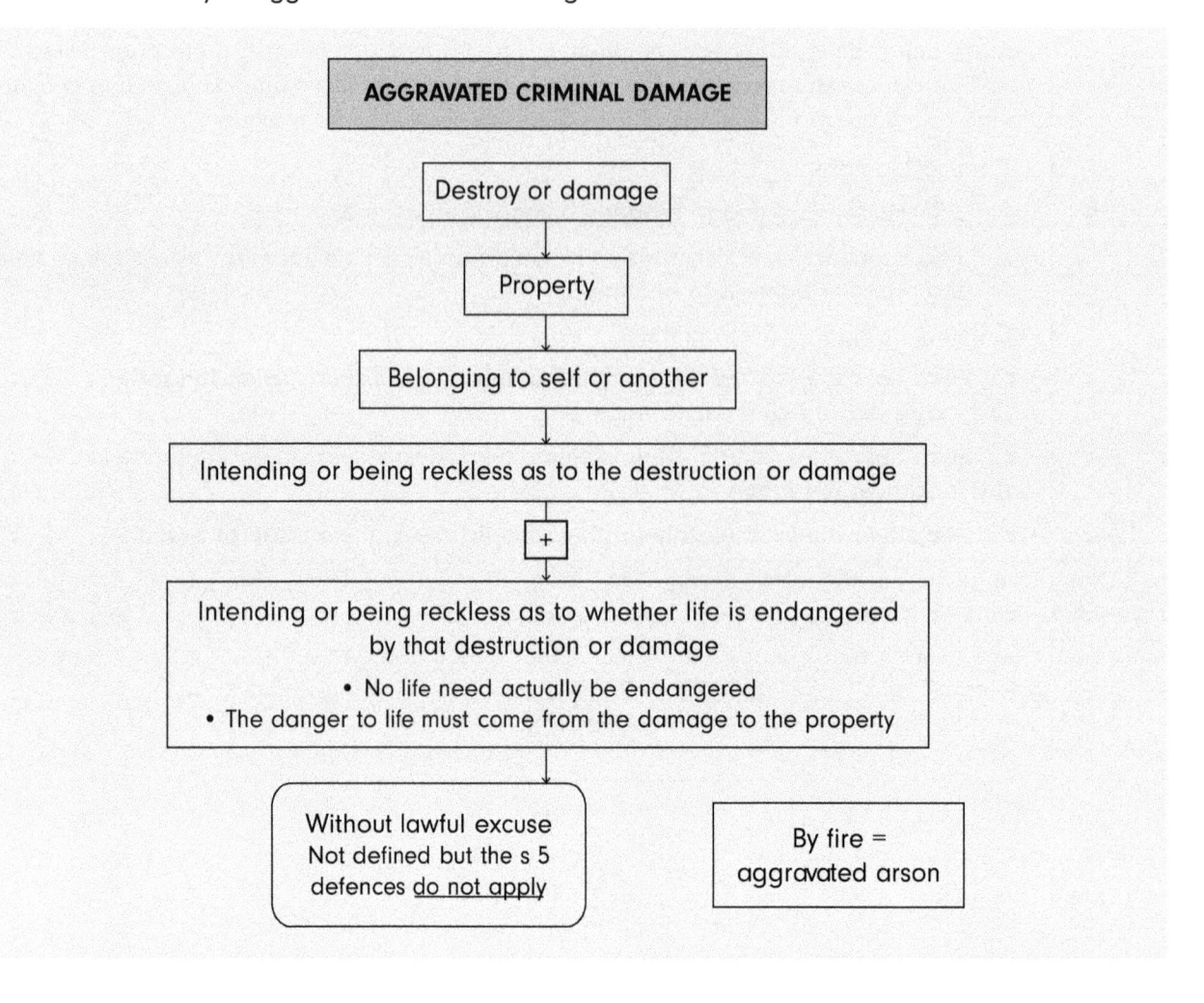

```
              AGGRAVATED CRIMINAL DAMAGE
                         │
                  Destroy or damage
                         │
                      Property
                         │
              Belonging to self or another
                         │
   Intending or being reckless as to the destruction or damage
                         │
                         +
                         │
   Intending or being reckless as to whether life is endangered
                  by that destruction or damage
              • No life need actually be endangered
     • The danger to life must come from the damage to the property
                         │
         ┌───────────────┴───────────────┐
   Without lawful excuse              By fire =
   Not defined but the s 5         aggravated arson
   defences do not apply
```

Sample questions

Question 1

The defendant receives a text from his girlfriend telling him she no longer wants to see him. He throws his mobile phone to the floor in anger and breaks the screen. On the way home from art class, he decides to try and win his girlfriend back by writing 'I love you' in chalk on the wall of her parents' house. He also leaves a bunch of bluebells, which he has picked from the roadside, in front of her door.

To remove the chalk, the parents had to purchase cleaning materials and scrub the wall although it only took a couple of minutes to do so.

Which of the following statements describes the defendant's liability for criminal damage?

A   The defendant is liable for criminal damage to the phone, the wall and the bluebells.

B   The defendant is liable for criminal damage to the wall and the bluebells, but not the phone.

C   The defendant is liable for criminal damage to the phone and the bluebells, but not the wall.

D The defendant is liable for criminal damage to the wall, but not the phone or the bluebells.

E The defendant is not liable for criminal damage to the phone, the wall or the bluebells.

Answer

The correct answer is option D. The defendant is liable for criminal damage for the chalk writing, despite the fact it could easily be removed, because expense was incurred in restoring the wall to its previous condition. He is not liable for the damage to the mobile phone as it is his own, so does not belong to another. Nor is the defendant criminally liable for picking the bluebells, as these are wild flowers growing by the roadside so not property within the definition of the CDA 1971. For these reasons, options A, B, C and E are wrong in some way.

Question 2

The defendant, aged 14 years, is at his friend's house. The boys are pretending they are on a survival camp in a forest and, as part of their play-acting, the defendant lights candles around the edge of the bedroom. Although his friend is worried about the risk of fire, the defendant reassures him they could easily put out any flames. Unfortunately, one of the candles falls over and sets light to the curtains, which burn fiercely as the material is particularly flammable. The boys are shocked and immediately flee the house. The fire causes considerable damage to the bedroom.

Which of the following best describes the defendant's criminal liability for an offence of arson?

A The defendant is liable for arson as he intentionally damaged property belonging to another by fire.

B The defendant is liable for arson as he recklessly damaged property belonging to another by fire.

C The defendant is liable for aggravated arson as he recklessly endangered life.

D The defendant is liable for aggravated arson as the risk of endangering life would be obvious to the reasonable person.

E The defendant is not liable for aggravated arson as no-one's life was actually endangered.

Answer

The correct answer is option B – the defendant is liable for arson as he recklessly damaged property belonging to another (his friend) by fire. Although he is a child, he was aware of his friend's concerns but took the risk regardless. Option A is wrong because he did not cause damage intentionally. His aim or purpose was to create the atmosphere of a survival camp.

Option C is wrong because the defendant was confident they could put out any flames, was 'shocked' by the fire and, furthermore, it appears the fire only took hold because the curtains were particularly flammable; thus, there is no evidence the defendant was aware of the risk of endangering life. Option D is wrong as the endangerment to life must be apparent to the defendant (subjective) rather than to the reasonable person. Option E is wrong as it is irrelevant whether anyone's life was actually endangered.

Question 3

A woman lives with her grandmother at her grandmother's house. She has left her key at work. On returning home she looks through the front window and is horrified to see her grandmother lying on the floor with a cigarette smouldering by her side. The woman grabs a large stone that she finds in the garden, smashes the window and climbs into the house. She stubs out the cigarette and immediately telephones for an ambulance. Her grandmother is admitted to hospital and makes a full recovery.

Has the woman committed an offence of simple criminal damage in these circumstances?

A   Yes, because the woman intentionally damaged property belonging to her grandmother.

B   Yes, because the woman has recklessly damaged property belonging to another and is aware that the property belongs to her grandmother.

C   No, because the woman may rely upon the defence of lawful excuse as a reasonable person would have consented to the damage had they known of the circumstances.

D   No, provided the court is satisfied that a reasonable person in the woman's position would have acted in the same way to save her grandmother.

E   No, because the woman honestly believed that the property was in immediate danger and the damage was reasonable in the circumstances.

Answer

The correct answer is option E as the woman honestly believed – a subjective test – that the property (the house) was in immediate danger from the cigarette and smashing the window was reasonable in these circumstances.

Option A is wrong because although the woman did intentionally cause criminal damage, she will be able to rely on the defence of lawful excuse. Option B is wrong as the defendant intentionally, rather than recklessly, damaged her grandmother's property as she smashed the window deliberately.

To establish the defence of lawful excuse under s 5(2)(a) of the CDA 1971, the woman's belief need only be an honest one (subjective) so option C is wrong. Option D is wrong as the court will decide – objectively – what the defendant's purpose was under s 5(2)(b) of the CDA 1971 and this must be to protect property (and not to save the grandmother). The statement in option D is not the correct definition of a lawful excuse.

9 Defences

9.1	Introduction	166
9.2	Intoxication as a defence?	166
9.3	Type of offence	166
9.4	Voluntary intoxication	168
9.5	Involuntary intoxication	170
9.6	Dutch courage	172
9.7	Intoxication and mistake	172
9.8	Intoxication and lawful excuse	173
9.9	Self-defence and prevention of crime	174
9.10	Section 76 of the Criminal Justice and Immigration Act 2008	175
9.11	Was force necessary?	175
9.12	Was the amount of force used reasonable?	177
9.13	Householder cases	179
9.14	No duty to retreat	181
9.15	The 'heat of the moment'	181
9.16	Pre-emptive strikes	182
9.17	Overview of self-defence	183
9.18	Summary	183

SQE1 syllabus

By the end of this chapter you will be able to apply relevant core legal principles and rules appropriately and effectively, at the level of a competent newly qualified solicitor in practice, to realistic client-based and ethical problems and situations in the area of **defences**.

Note that, as students are not usually required to recall specific case names, or cite statutory or regulatory authorities, these are provided for illustrative purposes only.

Learning outcomes

The learning outcomes for this chapter are:

- to understand and apply the principles relating to voluntary and involuntary intoxication; and
- to define the general defence of self-defence and/or the defence of another and understand how these absolve an accused of criminal liability.

9.1 Introduction

In many cases a defendant will seek to avoid criminal liability by presenting a defence. At its most straightforward, a defence is simply an assertion as to why the accused should not be convicted; for example, because they are claiming mistaken identity or denying they had the necessary mens rea. There are, however, a number of formal defences recognised by the law, with one of the more common being that of self-defence as discussed in this chapter. This defence is significant as, if successful, the defendant will be acquitted of the offence entirely.

Intoxication, whether from alcohol or drugs, is a significant, contributory factor to the commission of crime and dealing with such defendants is a regular experience for a criminal lawyer. Because of this, a key influence in the development of the common law in relation to intoxication has been public policy. Whether and in what circumstances a defendant should be able to avoid criminal liability because of their intoxication has involved a delicate balancing act by the courts.

9.2 Intoxication as a defence?

Intoxication is the cause of a great deal of offending behaviour. This includes crimes of violence covering the entire spectrum from homicide down to common assault and public disorder offences, often because people tend to lose their inhibitions and act very differently and more aggressively than when they are sober. There are also a variety of driving offences, including driving while over the permitted limit, driving while unfit through drink or drugs and being drunk in charge of a vehicle. However, only where the intoxication results in a loss of capacity to form the mens rea may there be a defence.

When advising a client, it is important to be clear that an accused who simply argues that they committed the offence while intoxicated will not have a defence; and nor will the defendant who says they acted out of character because they were intoxicated.

In R v Kingston [1995] 2 AC 355, the defendant was given a coffee that, unknown to him, had been spiked with drugs. Following this he indecently assaulted a young boy. The defendant was found guilty and appealed on the basis that he only committed the offence because he was acting under the influence of drugs. The court held that the absence of moral fault by Kingston was not sufficient to acquit him. All the prosecution were required to prove was that the defendant had the necessary mens rea and they had succeeded in this regard. In summary, a drugged intent is still an intent.

Intoxication only comes into play when the defendant is so intoxicated they lack the mens rea entirely. Because of this, it is not technically a defence at all; if successful, the legal outcome is that the prosecution are unable to prove mens rea. Nevertheless, it is usually treated as such.

9.3 Type of offence

There are two stages to determining whether a defendant may rely upon the defence of intoxication.

(a) The court considers whether the accused's intoxication was voluntary or not as the rules differ depending upon how the defendant became intoxicated.

(b) The type of offence with which the defendant has been charged must be identified. Offences are categorised into crimes of basic and specific intent.

To deal with the second question first, classifying a crime as one of either basic or specific intent is more difficult than it might first appear. This is because the test has developed from a mix of legal principle and public policy.

9.3.1 Offences of specific intent

The basic rule is that a specific intent crime is one where the mens rea, or part of the mens rea, is intention – recklessness will therefore not suffice. The most obvious example is murder as the mens rea is an intention to kill or cause grievous bodily harm. One cannot commit murder recklessly.

9.3.2 Offences of basic intent

In contrast, crimes of basic intent are those where the mens rea can be fulfilled with something less than intent. Most of the assaults come within this category, for example assault occasioning actual bodily harm, which merely requires the defendant to intend *or be reckless as to* the infliction of force.

As will be seen below, it is beneficial to a defendant if the offence they are facing is one of specific intent where they intend to rely on intoxication as their defence. However, in order to prevent too many defendants succeeding in this argument, the courts have tried to limit the scope, for example by categorising the sexual offences as being of basic intent. In the case of *R v Heard* [2007] 3 WLR 475, Lord Justice Hughes commented that there was:

> no universally logical test for distinguishing between crimes in which voluntary intoxication can be advanced as a defence and those in which it cannot;
> there is a large element of policy; categorisation is achieved on an offence by offence basis.

To assist, the table below summarises the distinction between basic and specific intent crimes.

Table 9.1 Basic and specific intent crimes

Type of crime	Definition	Examples
Specific intent	Offences where the mens rea is intention (and nothing less)	• Murder: intention to kill or cause grievous bodily harm • Assault – s 18 OAPA 1861: intention to cause grievous bodily harm • Theft – s 1 TA 1968: intention to permanently deprive
Basic intent	Offences where the mens rea includes recklessness	• Unlawful act manslaughter • Assault – s 20 OAPA 1861: intention or recklessness as to causing some bodily harm • Assault – s 47 1861: intention or recklessness as to assault or battery • Assault and battery: intention or recklessness as to assault or battery • Criminal damage: intention or recklessness as to destroying or damaging property belonging to another

9.4 Voluntary intoxication

In most cases, it will be clear that the defendant is voluntarily intoxicated, such as the person who:

- goes out with their friends and drinks several pints of beer; or
- takes cocaine to keep them awake during a company deal.

However, other situations may be less obvious including the defendant who:

- has a couple of glasses of wine, but underestimates the effect this has on them; or
- has alcohol with medication when they have been told not to.

⭐ Example

Lars smokes some cannabis that he has recently purchased. It turns out to be much purer (and therefore stronger) than he usually buys and after smoking three 'joints' he becomes very high. Despite this, Lars is voluntarily intoxicated. If the defendant knows they are taking drugs (or drinking alcohol) but are mistaken as to its strength, this does not make their intoxication involuntary.

9.4.1 Impact on criminal liability

The leading authority on how voluntary intoxication may impact on criminal liability is an appeal court decision dating back many years.

In DPP v Majewski [1976] 2 WLR 623, the accused was charged with assault occasioning actual bodily harm, having struck a police officer. He claimed that, at the time, he was so intoxicated from having consumed a quantity of drugs and alcohol that he was incapable of forming the necessary mens rea. Lord Elwyn was unimpressed by this argument:

> *If a man of his own volition takes a substance which causes him to cast off the restraints of reason and conscience, no wrong is done to him by holding him answerable criminally for any injury he may do while in that condition. His course of conduct in reducing himself by drugs and drink to that condition in my view supplies the evidence of mens rea, of guilty mind certainly sufficient for crimes of basic intent. It is a reckless course of conduct and recklessness is enough to constitute mens rea in assault cases.*

In other words, the defendant's conduct in getting intoxicated is itself reckless.

9.4.1.1 Intoxication and offences of basic intent

Following *Majewski*, it is clear that in cases of voluntary intoxication, a defendant will never be able to argue that they lacked mens rea when charged with an offence of basic intent. Quite simply, there is no defence of intoxication in these circumstances because becoming intoxicated will automatically satisfy the mens rea of any crime that can be committed recklessly.

- Voluntary intoxication => crime of basic intent => no defence

The judgment was based on public policy reasons rather than strict legal principles. However, this is unsurprising given the many and varied offences committed by those who allow themselves to get into this drunken or drugged state.

9.4.1.2 Intoxication and offences of specific intent

With regard to crimes of specific intent, such as murder, the rules are different.

Here, a defendant may use evidence of their voluntary intoxication to argue that they were so intoxicated at the time of the offence, they lacked the mens rea entirely. The effect was that they were incapable of forming the necessary intent to commit the relevant crime of specific intent and, thus, are not liable.

In R v Lipman [1970] 1 QB 152, the accused had taken the drug, LSD, causing him to hallucinate that he was being attacked by snakes and descending to the centre of the earth. While in this state, he killed the victim by cramming bed sheets into her mouth.

The appeal court held that the defendant's intoxication could be used to establish that he lacked the required mens rea. Murder is a crime of specific intent and the prosecution must prove that the defendant intended to kill or to cause grievous bodily harm. Because of Lipman's extreme intoxication, they were unable to do so.

It does seem somewhat illogical that the most reckless defendants, those who are so intoxicated they have no awareness of what they are doing, can literally 'get away with murder'. However, the reason is that, although the judges have some licence to interpret the law based on public policy, they do not have the power to actually change it, and murder cannot be committed recklessly.

However, Lipman did not walk away from his misdeed entirely. Although he could not be convicted of murder, he was found guilty of manslaughter. Because this is a crime of basic intent, his intoxication could not operate as a defence here. This provides another public policy justification for the decision, because virtually all defendants who can argue that they are not guilty of a specific intent offence due to intoxication will be guilty of an alternative, lesser, basic intent offence.

Example

Dorian drinks a bottle of brandy. When his wife, Louisa, expresses anger at his behaviour, he reacts by pushing her off the balcony of their third floor flat. Louisa breaks both legs and is left with a permanent limp. Dorian is charged with an offence of causing GBH with intent under s 18 of the OAPA 1861. His legal team concede that Louisa suffered really serious harm sufficient to satisfy the actus reus of this assault, but seek to rely upon his intoxication as a defence in the following scenarios:

(a) Dorian intended to cause Louisa serious harm but formed that intention only because he was drunk. His confession that he intended to cause his wife grievous bodily harm means that he satisfies the mens rea for a s 18 assault. The fact that he would not have acted in this way had he been sober is irrelevant.

(b) Dorian just wanted to push Louisa over but he was so drunk that he forgot they were not on the ground floor. Although Dorian committed the actus reus of grievous bodily harm, he did not have the specific intent required for the s 18 assault. However, he is guilty of an assault under s 20 of the OAPA 1861 as the mens rea may be satisfied by his (intention or) recklessness as to some bodily harm. Dorian's conduct in getting drunk was itself reckless so that he automatically has the mens rea for the lesser assault as it is a crime of basic intent.

(c) Dorian was so intoxicated that he lost control of his limbs and pushed Louisa off the balcony without intending to do anything at all. If believed, the evidence is that Dorian lacked the mens rea for the s 18 assault entirely and so he is not guilty of the offence. He may though be guilty of a s 47 assault as the mens rea can be satisfied simply by (intention or) recklessness as to the infliction of force.

Determining where in the range of intoxication an accused falls will have a significant impact on whether they are guilty of an offence at all and, if so, which one. This will be a matter for the jury to decide depending upon the evidence presented to the court.

Criminal Law

Figure 9.1 Spectrum of intoxication

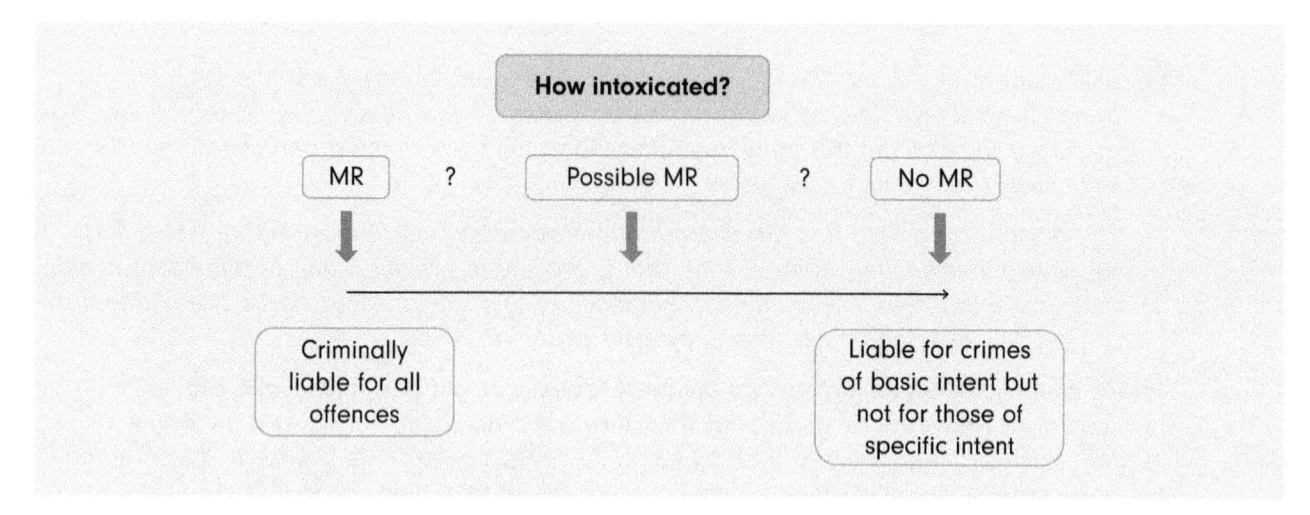

```
                        How intoxicated?

        MR          ?      Possible MR      ?      No MR
         ↓                      ↓                    ↓
    ─────────────────────────────────────────────────────→

     Criminally                                  Liable for crimes
     liable for all                              of basic intent but
     offences                                    not for those of
                                                 specific intent
```

9.4.2 Summary of voluntary intoxication

In summary:

- If the prosecution establish that the defendant has the required mens rea for the relevant offence, intoxication will not operate as a defence.

- At the other end of the spectrum, intoxication is a complete defence to crimes of specific intent provided the defendant is so intoxicated they are incapable of forming the mens rea.

- In direct contrast, intoxication is not a defence to crimes of basic intent even if the defendant lacks mens rea because, in simple terms, the defendant is reckless in getting intoxicated and this is sufficient to satisfy the mental element of the offence.

Figure 9.2 Voluntary intoxication

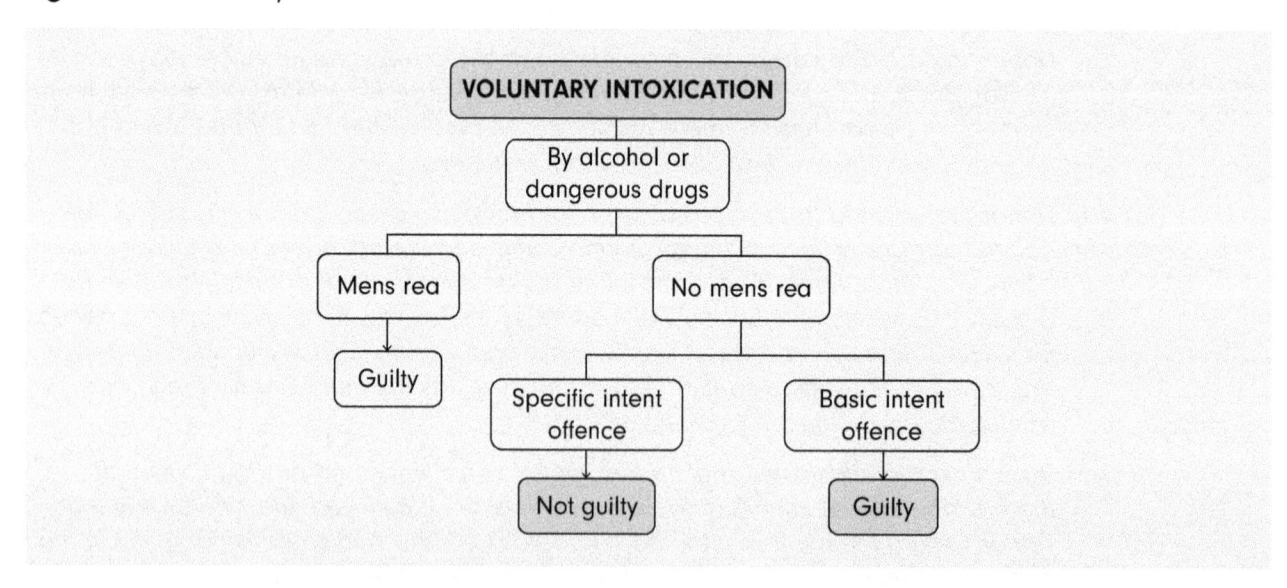

```
                    VOLUNTARY INTOXICATION
                            │
                    By alcohol or
                    dangerous drugs
                    ┌───────┴────────┐
                Mens rea          No mens rea
                    │                 │
                 Guilty       ┌───────┴────────┐
                         Specific intent   Basic intent
                           offence           offence
                              │                 │
                          Not guilty          Guilty
```

9.5 Involuntary intoxication

Thus far, the discussion has concentrated on how the criminal law treats defendants who have become voluntarily intoxicated. However, those who are involuntarily intoxicated are dealt with in a different way.

9.5.1 Meaning of 'involuntary'

The starting point is to identify what amounts to involuntary intoxication.

⭐ Example

Callum is out with friends. He needs to be up early the following day so decides to drink soft drinks all evening. Unknown to him, his friends put a triple vodka into his drink, which causes him to become drunk. Callum's intoxication is involuntary as his drink was spiked.

It seems only just that, in this situation, the defendant should not be regarded as harshly as those who are voluntarily intoxicated because it is not their fault they are in this drunken state. However, a less obvious example is where the person takes a non-dangerous or prescribed drug, which leads to unpredictable and aggressive behaviour that one would not normally expect. This may seem odd as the drug was taken voluntarily in the sense that no-one forced them to do so.

In R v Hardie [1985] 1 WLR 64, the defendant's relationship ended and, to calm his nerves, he took some of his girlfriend's Valium tablets that had been prescribed to her. Later that day, he started a fire and was charged with arson, but claimed not to know what he was doing because of the effect of the drug. Hardie was acquitted on appeal as his condition resulted from taking a non-dangerous drug that had an unusual effect on him.

The important question for the jury was whether the defendant's conduct in taking the Valium was itself reckless. As the drug is normally used as a sedative and Hardie had been informed by his girlfriend that the tablets would be harmless, he was found not to be reckless. Nevertheless, each case will be determined on its facts and there will be instances where the defendant will be found to be reckless in taking drugs that have been prescribed for someone else, without consulting their doctor.

9.5.2 Legal effect

Once the court is satisfied the defendant was involuntarily intoxicated, the next issue to determine is what effect this has on the legal outcome.

- Involuntary intoxication may be a defence to any offence, whether of basic or specific intent, but *only if* the defendant lacks mens rea.
- If there is clear evidence of mens rea, the defendant will not be able to rely on this defence.

⭐ Example

(a) Callum throws a brick at a window on the way home from the pub. He is involuntarily intoxicated as a result of his friends adding vodka to his orange juice. He accepts that he acted deliberately but claims he would never have done so had his drink not been spiked.

In this instance, Callum cannot rely on his involuntary intoxication because he had the mens rea to commit criminal damage. Although the alcohol may have caused him to act in a way that he would not otherwise, this is unfortunate but will not affect his guilt. In simple terms, Callum knew what he was doing.

(b) Joanna has taken a drug that belongs to her mother because she has been experiencing panic attacks due to her impending exams. Her mother suffers from anxiety and the medication was prescribed to improve her condition. Unfortunately, rather than calming Joanna down, the drugs have the opposite effect causing her to become aggressive. She argues with her mother and punches her in the face causing a large bruise to her cheek.

Joanna is arrested for an offence of assault occasioning actual bodily harm. She claims that she blacked out and did not intend or foresee any risk that she would hit her mother. Although the offence of s 47 of the OAPA 1861 is a crime of basic intent, Joanna may rely upon her intoxication because it was involuntary and it caused her to lack mens rea.

In summary, if the defendant is involuntarily intoxicated but still has mens rea, they are guilty, but if not, they will be acquitted.

The law in relation to involuntary intoxication is quite straightforward as demonstrated in the flowchart below; and whether the accused is guilty will depend upon how intoxicated they actually were at the time they committed the offence. The court will need to decide this after listening to the evidence.

9.5.3 Summary of involuntary intoxication

Figure 9.3 Involuntary intoxication

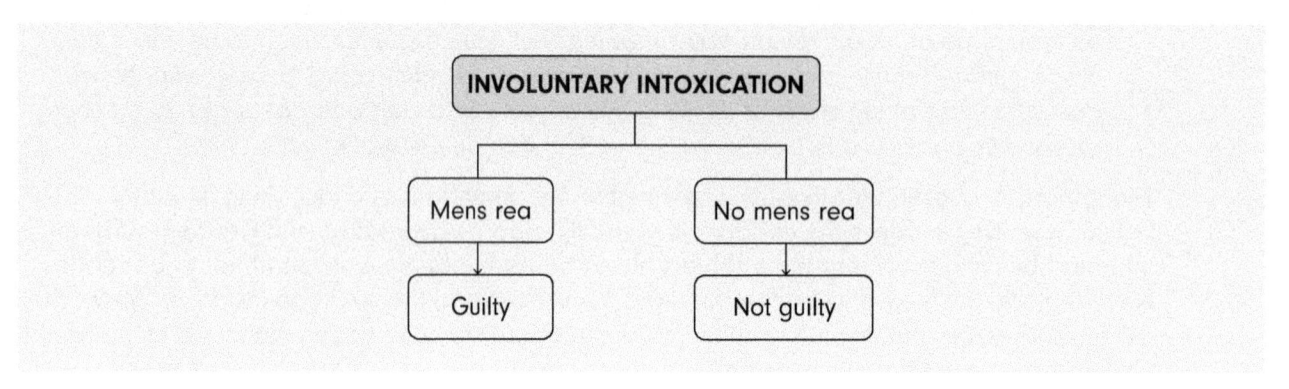

```
              INVOLUNTARY INTOXICATION
                    |
         _____|_____
        |                       |
    Mens rea                No mens rea
        |                       |
     Guilty                 Not guilty
```

9.6 Dutch courage

A defendant who deliberately consumes alcohol or drugs in order to gain the confidence to commit a criminal offence may not rely upon their intoxication to negate the mens rea of the offence. This is known as 'Dutch courage'.

In Attorney General for Northern Ireland v Gallagher [1963] AC 349, *the accused decided to kill his wife. He bought a knife and consumed a bottle of whiskey before stabbing her to death. Gallagher argued that, at the time he killed his wife, he was so drunk he no longer had the required mens rea for murder – a crime of specific intent. In refusing the appeal against conviction Lord Denning stated:*

> *The wickedness of [the defendant's] mind before he got drunk is enough to condemn him, coupled with the act which he intended to do and did do.*

The decision was reached despite there being no coincidence of actus reus and mens rea – a requirement of liability under the criminal law. Clearly, the justification was public policy as the alternative would have allowed anyone to go out and deliberately get very drunk before committing the crime in the hope of avoiding conviction.

9.7 Intoxication and mistake

If a defendant commits an offence while intoxicated, they cannot rely upon the defence for crimes of basic intent such as simple assault. However, what if the defendant only reacts because they make an error about the circumstances?

Example

Sonia consumes a number of illegal drugs during her night out in the local town. On the way out of the club, believing that the security guard man is about to sexually assault her, she hits him over the head with her stiletto shoe. Sonia admits to the police that she hit the victim but says that she only did so because she was drunk and (mistakenly) thought he was about to attack her.

In this situation, the accused is raising the defence of self-defence, which is discussed later in this chapter (at **9.10**). If the defendant makes a mistake about the need to defend themselves, they will be judged on the facts as they honestly believed them to be. However, Sonia's view of the events may be distorted by the drugs she had consumed. Case law establishes that she will not be able to rely upon any mistake that she makes as a consequence of her intoxication.

In R v O'Grady [1987] 3 WLR 321, the defendant and the victim had both drunk large quantities of alcohol before returning to O'Grady's apartment. During the night, a fight ensued and when O'Grady awoke in the morning, he discovered that the victim was dead. The defendant argued that he honestly thought he was being attacked but, despite this, his conviction for manslaughter was upheld by the appeal court.

Given that a person is regarded as reckless in getting intoxicated, it is logical that a defendant should not be able to rely on any mistake they make because of that same drunken or drugged condition. Thus, it is unsurprising that the judges ruled that, in this situation, there was no difference between offences of basic and specific intent and a mistaken belief caused by intoxication can never be relied on by an accused.

In summary:

- The defence of self-defence will fail where a defendant's mistaken belief is induced by voluntary intoxication.
- The defendant may only rely on self-defence if their reaction did not exceed that of a sober person in the same situation.

This decision has been described as one based on public policy and there is an underlying logic to the principle. Unfortunately, the situation is complicated by the rather different outcome where the defendant relies upon the defence of lawful excuse in criminal damage.

9.8 Intoxication and lawful excuse

Defendants accused of simple criminal damage or arson may avail themselves of a defence of lawful excuse under s 5(2) of the CDA 1971, which is covered in **Chapter 8**. This applies if the defendant honestly believed that the owner of the property had consented or would have consented to the damage had they known of the circumstances. Because the belief need only be genuinely held, it is irrelevant that the defendant came to it because they were intoxicated (see *Jaggard v Dickinson*).

This decision appears somewhat contradictory given that simple criminal damage is a crime of basic intent, so the defendant cannot rely on their intoxication to negate the mens rea part of the offence.

9.8.1 Comparison

The effect of the legal authorities is that if the defendant commits criminal damage in the mistaken but drunken belief that, for example, the owner would consent, they will not be convicted; but if the defendant punches their victim in the mistaken but drunken belief they are under attack, they are guilty of assault.

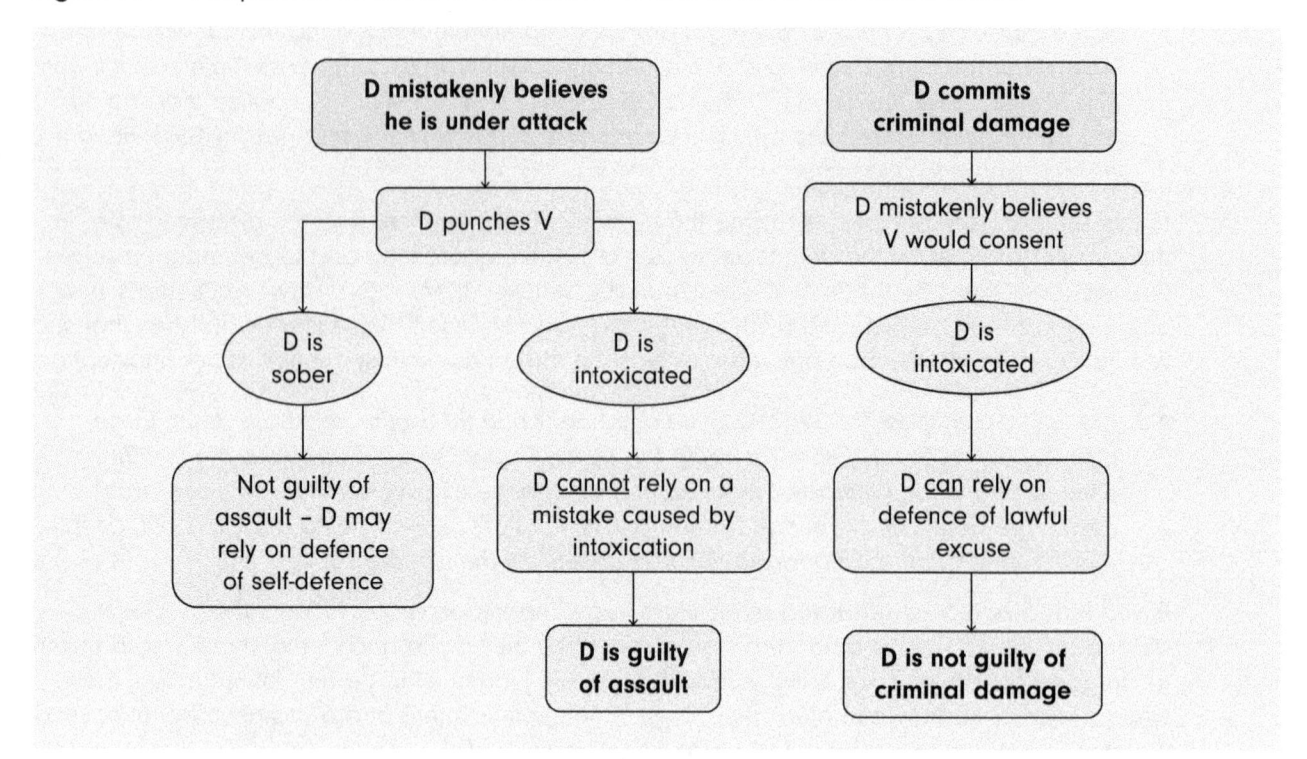

Figure 9.4 Comparison of effect of intoxication on self-defence and lawful excuse

```
         D mistakenly believes                D commits
          he is under attack              criminal damage
                    |                            |
             D punches V              D mistakenly believes
              /        \                V would consent
             /          \                       |
          D is         D is                   D is
         sober     intoxicated            intoxicated
           |            |                       |
    Not guilty of   D cannot rely on a      D can rely on
    assault – D may  mistake caused by    defence of lawful
    rely on defence   intoxication             excuse
    of self-defence        |                       |
                      D is guilty          D is not guilty of
                      of assault           criminal damage
```

The decision in *Jaggard v Dickinson* is clearly difficult to reconcile with *R v O'Grady* but is largely due to the development of the law on a case by case basis.

9.9 Self-defence and prevention of crime

There are certain circumstances in which the use of force may be justified. An accused may argue they did so to protect themselves, their property or others from attack, or to prevent a crime from being committed. In other words, the defendant is claiming that, although they used force on another person, it was lawful.

Self-defence is often highlighted as a defence in the media, leading to discussions on (amongst other aspects) how far a householder may go to protect their own property; indeed, there have been a number of high-profile cases in this regard. In situations where the defendant is held not to be to blame for their conduct, they will be excused from criminal liability altogether and will be acquitted of the charge. However, the law is far from straightforward and there are also some aspects that overlap, causing confusion at times.

- Historically, the common law defence of self-defence applied: 'the accused is entitled to be acquitted [if] the prosecution ... have failed to prove an essential element of the crime namely that the violence used by the accused was unlawful' – as explained by Lord Griffiths in the case of *Beckford v R* [1988] AC 130.

- Subsequently, an attempt was made to incorporate the defence into legislation, and s 3 of the Criminal Law Act 1967 provides that:

    A person may use such force as is reasonable in the circumstances in the prevention of crime, or in effecting or assisting in the lawful arrest of offenders or suspected offenders or of persons unlawfully at large.

- Finally, the two separate defences were codified into a more recent statute (Criminal Justice and Immigration Act (CJIA) 2008, s 76) with the stated aim being to clarify the law and to improve understanding.

For ease of reference, the defences will collectively be referred to as 'self-defence'.

Because of the piecemeal way in which the law has developed, the defences overlap and, in some situations, both may be available. Although this may be confusing at times, what they all have in common is the issue of reasonable force. If such force is used and the defence is successful, the accused will have a complete defence and must be acquitted.

⭐ Example

Len and his son are attacked by a rival football supporter, Billy. Len punches Billy in the face and breaks his nose.

(a) *Len is entitled to use reasonable force to defend himself and another (his son).*

(b) *He is also entitled to use reasonable force to prevent the crime of assault being committed on them both.*

Because these defences are general defences, they may operate as a defence to any offence. However, an accused who pleads self-defence is most likely to be charged either with an assault or a homicide offence.

9.9.1 The legal and evidential burden

Where an accused wishes to rely upon self-defence they have what is described as an evidential burden to discharge. In other words, whilst they do not need to prove the defence, they are required to raise it to make it a live issue at trial. Generally, this will be done by cross-examining prosecution witnesses, usually the alleged victim, and by the defendant themselves giving evidence that they acted in self-defence. Once the defence have discharged their evidential burden, the prosecution must disprove the defence beyond a reasonable doubt. If they fail to do so, the accused must be acquitted and will walk away from the court a free person.

9.10 Section 76 of the Criminal Justice and Immigration Act 2008

In response to media coverage, and a perceived lack of transparency in the existing law, s 76 of the CJIA 2008 was introduced. This clarified some of the legal principles that emerged from case law and put them on a statutory footing. The CJIA 2008 was a consolidating measure so it simply brought together the existing law rather than seeking to change it. However, it did set out some important principles, which will be explored in more detail below.

9.11 Was force necessary?

In determining if the accused can successfully argue self-defence, the first question is whether the use of force was necessary at all. A defendant may not rely on self-defence if they use force on another person out of revenge or in retaliation. Furthermore, the defence will only be available if the defendant's action was necessary to defend themselves or another from attack or to prevent the commission of a criminal offence. This question is subjectively assessed, so the important issue is whether the *defendant* believed the use of force was necessary.

Criminal Law

9.11.1 Mistaken belief

There may be circumstances in which the defendant is mistaken about what the other party is going to do, but allowance is made for the particularly stressful position the defendant finds themselves in. Specifically, where the defendant acts in self-defence due to a mistaken belief that the use of force is necessary, their mistake will not prevent them from relying upon the defence provided their belief was honestly held.

In the leading case of Williams (Gladstone) [1987] 3 All ER 411, M witnessed a youth rob a woman of her handbag. He chased the youth and knocked him to the ground. The defendant only saw the last part of the incident from his seat on a passing bus and, believing that he was defending the youth from an unlawful attack, he punched M in the face. In fact, M was a police officer trying to prevent the youth escaping criminal liability for the robbery.

The defendant argued that his mistaken belief that force was necessary to protect the youth did not preclude him from relying on the defence. The appeal court agreed and confirmed that it was sufficient for the defendant's belief to be honestly held.

The effect of this ruling is that:

(a) The defendant is judged on the facts as they honestly believed them to be, even if they are mistaken.

(b) This applies even if the defendant's belief was unreasonable.

(c) However, if the defendant's mistake was an unreasonable one to make, this may be a reason for the jury to conclude that the belief was not honestly held.

The principle contained in this case is now enshrined in the CJIA 2008:

- If it is determined that the defendant did genuinely hold that belief [that force was necessary] they are entitled to rely on it whether or not their understanding of the circumstances was mistaken or (if so) whether that mistake was a reasonable one to have made (s 76(4)).

Example

Steve mistakenly and unreasonably believes that he is about to be attacked by Bob and so pushes Bob away, causing him to fall over and break his wrist. Steve's belief need only be honest and genuine to satisfy this aspect of the defence.

9.11.2 Mistaken belief due to voluntary intoxication

However, where the defendant only made the mistake because they were *voluntarily* intoxicated, self-defence will not be available to them – see *R v O'Grady* [1987], which was discussed earlier in this chapter. Public policy considerations lie behind this decision, which is now dealt with specifically in the CJIA 2008:

- The defendant cannot rely on any mistaken belief attributable to intoxication that was voluntarily induced (s 76 (5)).

Examples

(a) Lawrence is drunk, having been out for the evening and consumed a significant quantity of alcohol. This causes him to mistakenly believe that Justin is about to attack him. In response, Lawrence grasps a nearby empty bottle and strikes Justin on the head. Because Lawrence's belief was induced by alcohol, he cannot argue self-defence.

(b) Ayo is drunk, having had his drinks spiked by an associate. He mistakenly and unreasonably believes that he is being attacked by Tom, whereas Tom has simply lost his balance and fallen onto him. Ayo lashes out to get Tom away from him, causing him a wound. In this situation, s 76(5) does not apply as Ayo's intoxication is involuntary and so he can rely upon his mistaken belief.

9.12 Was the amount of force used reasonable?

Whatever the situation, where a defendant raises self-defence, a key question for the court is whether the force used by the defendant was reasonable in the circumstances. What is regarded as reasonable is to be decided by the jury or magistrates but because the facts they may be required to consider are so varied, it is impossible to arrive at a specific definition. Consider the following:

⭐ Example

Brad sees a youth in his garden pick up some stones and start throwing them at his windows. One of the windows smashes. Brad chases after the youth and:

(a) grabs hold of him until the police arrive.

(b) gives him a couple of slaps around the face.

(c) gives him a severe beating.

(d) threatens to give him a beating until the youth promises to pay for the damage.

Whether the court considers that Brad acted reasonably in each situation will depend upon a number of factors, including the seriousness of the offence he was trying to prevent (here, criminal damage) and the degree of force he used to defend his property. Grabbing hold of the youth until the police arrive would clearly be reasonable whereas giving him a severe beating would not. With regard to the other two, people may have differing opinions.

9.12.1 On what basis is the defendant judged?

The defendant is judged on the basis of the facts as they honestly and genuinely believed them to be and this is confirmed by the CJIA 2008.

- Whether the use of force was reasonable in the circumstances will be decided on the basis of the circumstances that the defendant honestly believed to exist (s 76(3)).

Figure 9.5 Elements of self-defence

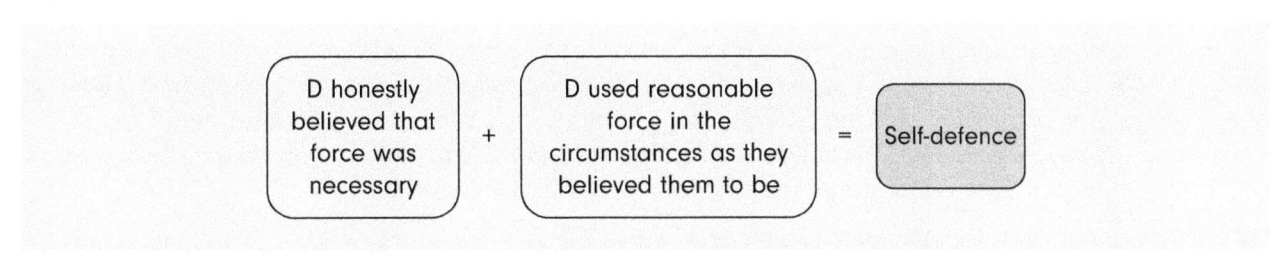

> D honestly believed that force was necessary **+** D used reasonable force in the circumstances as they believed them to be **=** Self-defence

⭐ Example

Warren pushes in front of Jin at a bus stop and Jin punches him on the nose. Unknown to Jin, Warren was about to threaten the bus driver and steal the fares. However, Jin cannot rely on facts of which he is unaware in deciding whether he used reasonable force. Thus, the question for the court is whether Jin used reasonable force in preventing Warren from queue jumping. As Jin did not know of the imminent robbery, this factor cannot be taken into account. Whilst it may be annoying if a person pushes in front in a queue, punching them on the nose would be excessive.

It is apparent, from this example, that a defendant cannot rely on facts of which they are unaware. Furthermore, just because a defendant says they perceived particular facts does not mean they will be believed.

- The reasonableness or otherwise of that belief is relevant to the question whether the defendant genuinely held it (s 76(4)).

⭐ Example

Ichika, a maths teacher, is passing Maya on her way to her next class, when she trips and loses her balance. Maya claims that she thought Ichika was lunging at her to push her against the wall and so she shoves Ichika away forcefully. In this situation, the court may question whether Maya genuinely believed that the teacher was about to push her. They were just passing each other in a school corridor and there is no reason to suggest that Ichika would behave in this way. Thus, the court may conclude that Maya's belief is so unreasonable that, in fact, she did not honestly hold it.

9.12.2 What does 'reasonable' mean?

Some guidance is provided in the CJIA 2008. Householders are dealt with differently and more generously than other defendants and will be considered later in this chapter.

- The degree of force used by the defendant is not to be regarded as having been reasonable in the circumstances as they believed them to be if it was disproportionate in those circumstances (s 76(6)).

The Crown Prosecution Service's website states that when dealing with cases of self-defence, account should be taken of the balance that needs to be struck between the public interest in promoting a responsible contribution on the part of citizens in preserving law and order, and in discouraging vigilantism and the use of violence.

In general, the greater the danger to the defendant, the more force they may use to repel an attack. However, if the jury or magistrates determine that the level of force is excessive, the defence will fail.

Evaluating this issue may prove difficult as much will depend upon the facts and some decisions of the courts have proved controversial.

In R v Clegg [1995] 1 AC 482, the defendant, a young soldier, was convicted of murder after shooting at a car being driven towards him while he was on duty during the conflict in Northern Ireland. It was held that the first three shots were legitimately fired in self-defence as the car approached Clegg and his colleagues at high speed. However, Clegg's final shot, which was fired at the car after it had broken through the checkpoint and after the danger had passed, amounted to excessive force.

Fortunately, other examples are less controversial:

⭐ Example

(a) *Ruth is out with some friends having a drink at a local bar. Jonah, who is sitting on a stool next to her, keeps touching her knee inappropriately. Ruth reacts by slapping Jonah across the face. This is a reasonable response to the sexual assault and Ruth would successfully argue self-defence.*

(b) *Albert is annoyed at Tanisha who has parked in a disabled space when she has no legal right to do so. He kicks her car and causes a small dent. Tanisha is furious and drives her car at Albert to prevent him from doing so again. Albert is hit by the vehicle and breaks his leg. Although Tanisha is acting to prevent the crime of criminal damage, her reaction is not a reasonable use of force.*

Given that the outcome is so reliant upon the specific facts, whether a defendant is convicted may lead to inconsistent decisions depending upon the particular magistrates or jury who consider the case.

9.12.3 Who decides reasonableness?

The test for reasonableness is objective, so the fact that the defendant themselves thought they used reasonable force is irrelevant. Whether the amount of force used by the defendant was reasonable is a question to be decided by the magistrates or the jury.

Thus, the question for the court is whether the degree of force is reasonable in the circumstances as the defendant honestly and genuinely believed them to be.

9.12.4 Defendant's characteristics

Which of the defendant's characteristics may be taken into account when determining if they acted reasonably? It is well established that evidence of the physical characteristics of the defendant are admissible; for example a threat to a frail elderly lady would seem greater than to a robust young person. In contrast, a defendant's psychiatric condition is not relevant to whether or not the defendant used reasonable force in self-defence.

*In the case of R v Martin (Anthony), which was considered in **Chapter 4**, the defendant was convicted of murder after shooting a burglar in the back as he fled the scene. On appeal, Martin put forward evidence that he suffered from a paranoid personality disorder that caused him to perceive a greater danger to his physical safety than the average person in his situation. The Court of Appeal ruled that psychiatric evidence on this condition was not admissible.*

9.13 Householder cases

The issue of self-defence in one's own home has attracted extensive media coverage from time to time.

In R v Martin (Anthony) (see above), there was a public outcry over the defendant's conviction and imprisonment despite the fact he shot and killed the burglar as the latter was running away from Martin's house.

As a result of public pressure, a provision was added to the CJIA 2008.

- In a householder case, the degree of force used by the defendant is not to be regarded as having been reasonable in the circumstances as they believed them to be if it was grossly disproportionate (s 76(5A)).

Thus, where a householder is involved, force will be classified as unreasonable if it is grossly disproportionate. In other words, a householder may use *more than* proportionate force provided they have not 'gone completely over the top'.

9.13.1 What is a 'householder'?

A 'householder' case is defined in the statute as one in which the defendant uses force in self-defence or in defence of another while in or partly in:

- a building or part of a building that is a dwelling;
- forces accommodation; or
- a vehicle or vessel that is a dwelling.

The defendant need not be the homeowner; all that is required is they are not a trespasser and are in or partly in a dwelling.

Example

In each case, Milly disturbs a burglar during the night and reacts by hitting Baz with a saucepan. Set out below is a table indicating when she would be able to rely upon the 'householder' defence.

Table 9.2 Examples of use of householder defence

Milly *can* rely on the 'householder' defence where she assaults Baz:	Milly *cannot* rely on the 'householder' defence where she assaults Baz:
In the bedroom of her detached property that she owns.	Outside her home on the driveway.
In her houseboat moored on the River Thames.	At the factory premises where she works.
In the army barracks where she is living on a temporary basis.	When she is trespassing in her neighbour's apartment.
In a campervan where she is staying on holiday.	
While halfway out of the door of her rented house.	
In her grocery shop, which is on the floor below the flat where she lives (because Milly's dwelling would be accessible from her place of work).	

9.13.2 When is force 'grossly disproportionate'?

The effect of this provision is that a householder may use force that is both reasonable and disproportionate. If the force is *grossly* disproportionate then it becomes unlawful.

Example

Tunji is woken at home in the middle of the night when he hears a smashing noise coming from downstairs. Tunji arms himself with a baseball bat and goes downstairs to investigate. He is confronted by Kola who is carrying Tunji's laptop. A struggle ensues but then Kola breaks free and starts to run away.

(a) Tunji hits Kola on the head with the bat, knocking him out.

This is a 'householder' case. Although Tunji may have used disproportionate force by hitting Kola on the head with his baseball bat as Kola is trying to leave the property, it is unlikely to be regarded as 'grossly disproportionate', although ultimately this is a question of fact for a jury to decide.

(b) Tunji hits Kola repeatedly with the bat, continuing even after Kola falls to the floor.

This would be regarded as grossly disproportionate due to the ferocity of the attack, particularly as Kola was trying to leave the premises at the time.

There have been few cases on this issue, primarily because it is so context dependent.

In R (Collins) v Secretary of State for Justice *[2016] EWHC 33 (Admin)*, Collins suffered serious injury when he was restrained by a householder in a headlock having unlawfully entered the property. The Crown Prosecution Service decided not to prosecute the householder – a decision that was unsuccessfully challenged by the victim. The court stated:

There may be instances when a jury may consider the actions of a householder in self-defence to be more than what might objectively be described as the minimum proportionate response but nevertheless reasonable given the particular and extenuating circumstances of the case.

This reflects the more sympathetic approach that is taken when determining if a householder may rely upon self-defence compared to other defendants.

9.13.3 Summary of householder cases

Figure 9.6 Householder cases

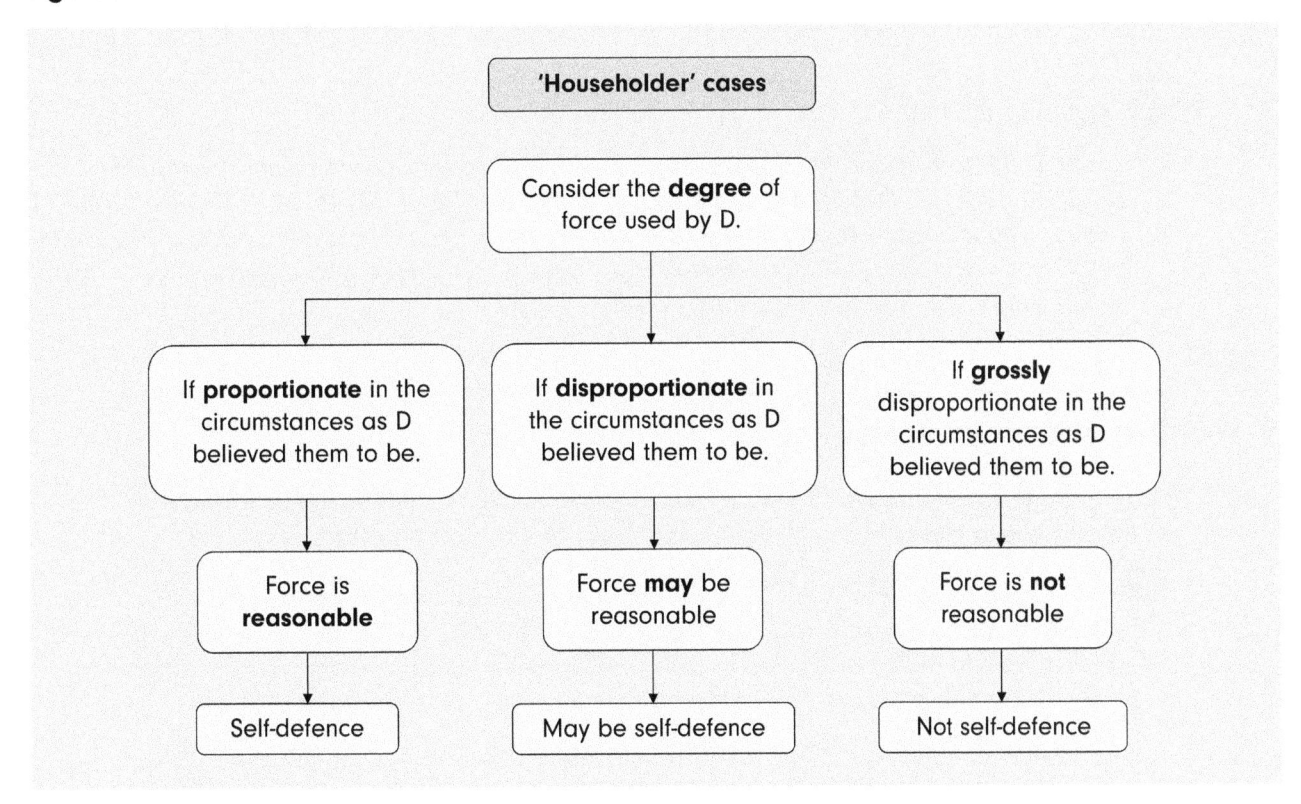

```
                    'Householder' cases
                           |
                Consider the degree of
                   force used by D.
        ┌──────────────────┼──────────────────┐
        ▼                  ▼                  ▼
If proportionate in    If disproportionate in    If grossly
the circumstances as D  the circumstances as D    disproportionate in the
believed them to be.    believed them to be.      circumstances as D
                                                  believed them to be.
        ▼                  ▼                  ▼
   Force is           Force may be          Force is not
   reasonable         reasonable            reasonable
        ▼                  ▼                  ▼
   Self-defence       May be self-defence   Not self-defence
```

9.14 No duty to retreat

There is no rule of law that states a defendant must retreat before resorting to action. When deciding whether the use of force was reasonable, the possibility that the defendant could have retreated is to be considered and taken into account, but no more (CJIA 2008, s 76(6A)).

9.15 The 'heat of the moment'

The law of self-defence demonstrates empathy with the defendant by acknowledging that the defendant may have little time to consider their response. Indeed, a person may have acted very differently with the benefit of hindsight. To deal with this factor, account is taken of the fact that the defendant may be under significant pressure to make up their mind quickly when deciding if force is necessary and to what degree.

> *In* Palmer v R *[1971] AC 814, Lord Morris stated that a defendant acting in self-defence in the heat of the moment may not always have time to make a rational decision, particularly bearing in mind that they are acting in 'a moment of unexpected anguish'.*

This view is now enshrined in statute. In deciding whether a defendant acted reasonably, the court must take into account that:

- a person acting for a legitimate purpose may not be able to weigh up to a nicety the exact measure of any necessary action (s 76(7)(a)); and
- evidence of a person's only having done what the person honestly and instinctively thought was necessary ... constitutes strong evidence that only reasonable action was taken by that person (s 76(7)(b)).

Legitimate purpose means acting in self-defence, the defence of another or the prevention of crime.

Example

Ariel is confronted and then grabbed by Juliet. Ariel instinctively punches Juliet in the face to protect herself. She later accepts that it might have been possible to have just pushed Juliet, who was smaller and lighter than her. However, Ariel appears to have acted for a legitimate purpose and will be assessed on what she honestly and instinctively did at the time rather than with the benefit of hindsight.

9.16 Pre-emptive strikes

A defendant does not have to wait to be assaulted to claim self-defence provided they honestly believe that the use of force is necessary to ward off an attack.

> *In the case of* Beckford v R *[1988] AC 130, the defendant was a police officer. He was sent to a house where it had been reported that the victim was terrorising his family with a gun. Beckford shot and killed a man who was running away from the house believing he was armed, although no gun was ever found. Lord Griffiths stated that:*
>
> > *a man about to be attacked does not have to wait for his assailant to strike the first blow or fire the first shot: circumstances may justify a pre-emptive strike.*

Although it is established that an attack need not be in progress before the defendant uses force, the danger they apprehend must be sufficiently specific or imminent to justify their actions.

9.17 Overview of self-defence

Figure 9.7 Self-defence

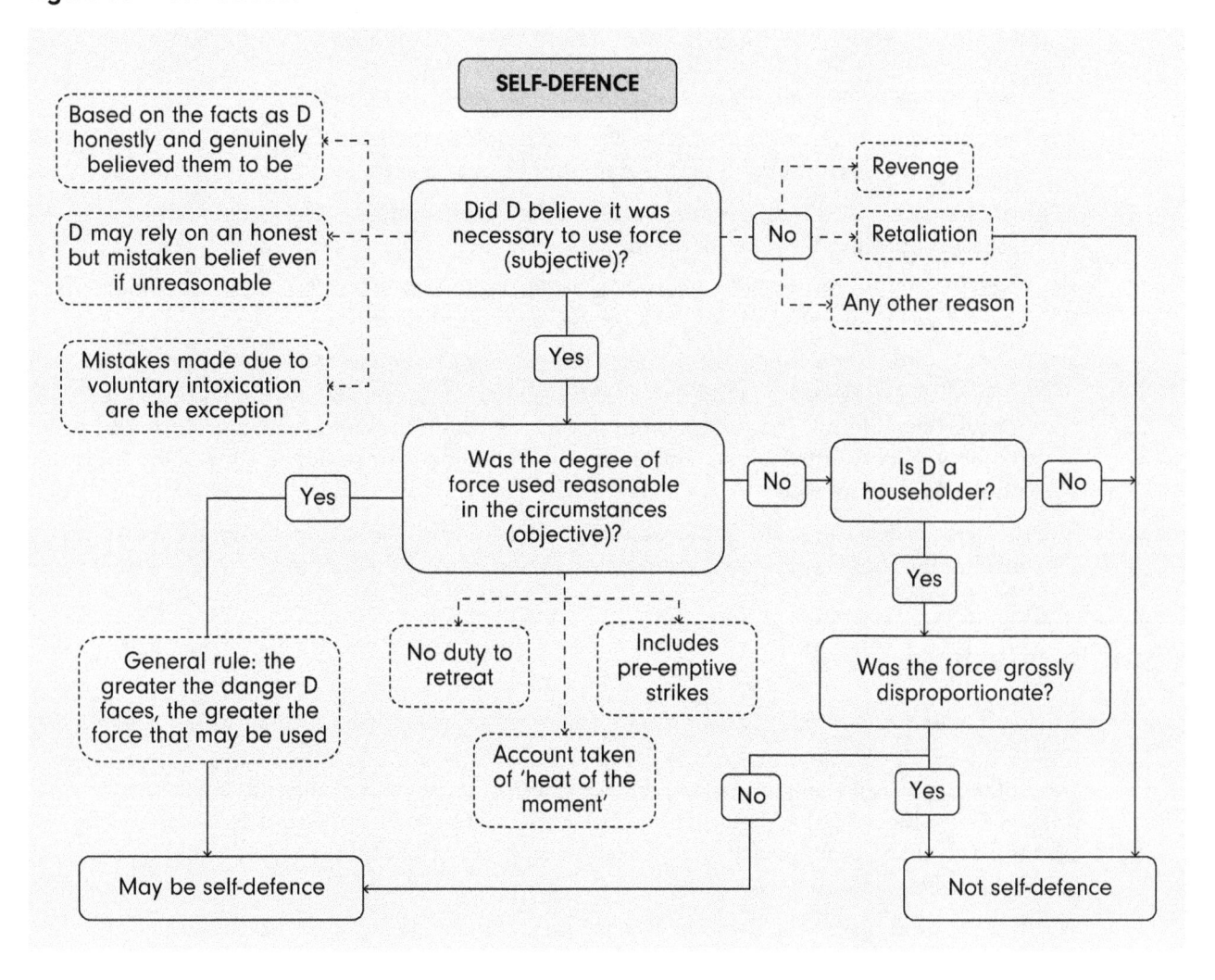

```
                              ┌─────────────┐
                              │SELF-DEFENCE │
                              └─────────────┘
  ┌─────────────────┐                │
  │Based on facts as│                │                    ┌─────────┐
  │D honestly and   │◄───┐           ▼                ┌──►│ Revenge │
  │genuinely        │    │    ┌──────────────┐        │   └─────────┘
  │believed them    │    │    │Did D believe │        │   ┌──────────┐
  │to be            │    │    │it was        │───No──►├──►│Retaliation│
  └─────────────────┘    │    │necessary to  │        │   └──────────┘
                         │    │use force     │        │   ┌──────────┐
  ┌─────────────────┐    │    │(subjective)? │        └──►│Any other │
  │D may rely on    │◄───┤    └──────────────┘            │ reason   │
  │an honest but    │    │           │                    └──────────┘
  │mistaken belief  │    │          Yes
  │even if          │    │           │
  │unreasonable     │    │           ▼
  └─────────────────┘    │    ┌──────────────┐
                         │    │Was degree of │                ┌───────────┐
  ┌─────────────────┐    │    │force used    │                │   Is D a  │     No
  │Mistakes made    │    │    │reasonable in │──No──────────► │householder│─────►
  │due to voluntary │◄───┘    │circumstances │                └───────────┘
  │intoxication are │         │(objective)?  │                     │
  │the exception    │         └──────────────┘                    Yes
  └─────────────────┘           │     │    │                       │
                              Yes    │    │                       ▼
          ┌───────────────────┘      │    │               ┌──────────────┐
          │                          ▼    ▼               │Was the force │
          │               ┌─────────┐  ┌──────────┐       │grossly       │
  ┌───────────────┐       │No duty  │  │Includes  │       │disproportion?│
  │General rule:  │       │to retreat│  │pre-empt  │       └──────────────┘
  │the greater    │       └─────────┘  │strikes   │          │        │
  │the danger D   │                    └──────────┘         No       Yes
  │faces, the     │            ┌──────────────┐              │        │
  │greater the    │            │Account taken │              │        ▼
  │force used     │            │of 'heat of   │              │  ┌────────────┐
  └───────────────┘            │the moment'   │              │  │Not self-   │
          │                    └──────────────┘              │  │defence     │
          ▼                                                  │  └────────────┘
  ┌────────────────┐                                         │
  │May be          │◄────────────────────────────────────────┘
  │self-defence    │
  └────────────────┘
```

9.18 Summary

The main provisions relating to the general defences covered in the chapter are as follows:

9.18.1 Intoxication

- Voluntary intoxication is a defence to crimes of specific intent, namely those offences where the required mens rea is intention (and nothing else). Even then, the defence will only succeed if the defendant lacked mens rea.
- Intoxication cannot be relied upon by the defendant for 'Dutch courage' cases nor is it available where the defendant is simply mistaken as to the strength of the alcohol.
- Voluntary intoxication is no defence to crimes of basic intent – those that can be committed recklessly.
- Involuntary intoxication may be a defence to crimes of both basic and specific intent, but only where the defendant lacks mens rea.
- Taking a non-dangerous drug that has unexpected consequences may count as involuntary intoxication provided the defendant was not reckless in taking the drug.
- A defendant who makes a mistake due to their voluntary intoxication may still rely on the defence of lawful excuse for criminal damage but a defence of self-defence would fail.

9.18.2 Self-defence

- There is a common law defence of reasonable force in self-defence, and a statutory defence under s 3(1) of the Criminal Law Act 1967 of reasonable force in the prevention of crime. In addition, many of the points from case law have been consolidated into legislation by virtue of s 76 of the CJIA 2008. These are general defences so they can apply to any crime and, if successful, result in a complete acquittal.

- The court must first consider whether the use of force was necessary at all, and this will be subjectively assessed based on the defendant's own beliefs.

- If so, the force used must be reasonable in the circumstances – a question that is assessed objectively by the magistrates or jury.

- Force will not be reasonable where it is disproportionate unless it is a 'householder' case where it will be unreasonable if it is grossly disproportionate.

- If the defendant made a mistake about the circumstances, the reasonableness of the force will be assessed on the basis of the facts as they honestly (even if unreasonably) believed them to be. The exception to this rule is where the defendant's mistake was due to their voluntary intoxication; here, they cannot rely on their mistaken view of the facts as a basis for self-defence.

- There is no duty to retreat and a defendant may act pre-emptively. Account will also be taken of the fact that the defendant acted in the 'heat of the moment'.

Sample questions

Question 1

The defendant is lying on the grass in the park having consumed an illegal, hallucinatory drug. He is approached by the victim, a park attendant, who is carrying a spike for picking up litter. Convinced that the victim is an alien who is about to attack him, the defendant grabs the spike and stabs her to death.

Which statement best describes the defendant's criminal liability for homicide?

A The defendant has a complete defence of intoxication to homicide because he lacked mens rea when he attacked the park attendant.

B The defendant can rely upon his intoxication for the offence of murder but will be liable for unlawful act manslaughter.

C The defendant cannot rely upon his intoxication as a defence to murder as he was reckless in becoming intoxicated.

D The defendant can rely upon his intoxication as a defence to homicide even though a sober person would not have made this mistake.

E The defendant cannot rely upon his intoxication as a defence to unlawful act manslaughter as it is a crime of specific intent.

Answer

The correct answer is option B. The defendant can rely upon his voluntary intoxication for murder as this is an offence of specific intent and he lacks the relevant mens rea because he believes he is killing an alien and not a human being. However, he would be guilty of unlawful act manslaughter as this is a crime of basic intent and the mens rea is satisfied by the defendant becoming voluntarily intoxicated.

Option A is wrong because the defendant does not have a complete defence to homicide as he will be liable for unlawful act manslaughter. Option C is wrong as the defendant can rely upon his voluntary intoxication for murder as it is a crime of specific intent and he lacks the mens rea. However, he cannot rely upon his mistaken belief that he is about to be attacked because he only made the error due to his intoxication; hence, option D is wrong. Option E is wrong because, although the defendant cannot rely upon his voluntary intoxication for unlawful act manslaughter, this offence is one of basic rather than specific intent.

Question 2

The defendant has unknowingly taken some amphetamines, which were added to her food as a 'joke'. She then discovers that the victim has stolen her mobile phone and loses her temper. She attacks the victim, intending to cause her really serious harm. The victim suffers a fractured jaw and a broken nose. The defendant is charged with intentionally causing grievous bodily harm. The defendant claims she would never have acted this way if she had not taken the drugs.

Can the defendant rely upon her intoxication as a defence to the charge?

A   No, because the defendant had mens rea when she attacked the victim.

B   No, because this is a 'Dutch courage' case.

C   Yes, because this type of assault is a crime of specific intent.

D   Yes, because the defendant was involuntarily intoxicated.

E   Yes, because the defendant would not have acted in this way had she not been intoxicated.

Answer

The correct answer is option A. Although this is a case of involuntary intoxication because the defendant unknowingly took amphetamines, she cannot rely on the defence as she still had mens rea at the time she attacked the victim. This is also the reason why Option D is wrong. Option B is wrong as the defendant did not become intoxicated in order to commit the offence and so this is not a 'Dutch courage' scenario.

The remaining answers are all wrong as the defendant cannot rely upon her involuntary intoxication as a defence. Furthermore, for option C, it is irrelevant whether the s 18 assault of causing grievous bodily harm is a crime of basic or specific intent, as the issue for involuntary intoxication is whether the defendant lacked mens rea at the time of the offence. Also, the fact that she would not have acted in this way without taking the drugs is irrelevant (option E).

Criminal Law

Question 3

A man and his family are awoken in the early hours of the morning by their dog barking. His wife and daughter are terrified, but the man is more annoyed and goes downstairs to investigate. He is confronted by an intruder, the burglar, in the kitchen. The burglar snatches a knife that is on the work surface and lunges at the man but the man manages to grab the burglar's wrist, forcing him to drop the knife. As the burglar tries to run away, the man smashes him over the back of the head with a plate, causing the burglar to fall to the floor. The man then kicks him hard in the ribs before standing on his other wrist to stop him getting away. The burglar suffers significant swelling to the back of his head and severe bruising to the ribs and his wrist.

Is the man able to rely on the defence of self-defence in relation to the degree of force he uses?

A No, a reasonable person would assess the degree of force used by the man as disproportionate.

B No, as hitting and kicking the burglar while he is trying to run away and then standing on his wrist will always be regarded as unreasonable.

C Yes, the man is entitled to use any force he regards as being reasonable given that the burglar tried to attack him with a knife.

D Yes, the degree of force used by the man was reasonable and not disproportionate.

E Yes, the degree of force used by the man was not unreasonable because his actions were not grossly disproportionate in the circumstances as he believed them to be.

Answer

Option E is correct. According to s 76(6) of the CJIA 2008, the degree of force will not usually be regarded as being reasonable where it is disproportionate. However, in 'householder' cases, s 76(5A) provides that disproportionate force may be regarded as reasonable; but if the force used is 'grossly' disproportionate then the defence will fail. In the man's case, hitting the back of the burglar's head with a plate while he is trying to run away, kicking him in the ribs and then standing on his wrist may be disproportionate, but it is unlikely that his actions will be regarded as grossly so. Hence, he may succeed in arguing self-defence.

Option D is wrong because the degree of force may well be regarded as disproportionate given that he kicked the burglar when he was on the floor – an action that was not necessary to detain him.

Options A and B are wrong as the man is likely to be able to rely on self-defence. As for option C, it is wrong to state that the man can use any force.

10 Attempts

10.1	Introduction	188
10.2	Attempts	188
10.3	Definition	188
10.4	Actus reus of attempt	188
10.5	Mens rea	190
10.6	Attempts and impossibility	191

SQE1 syllabus

By the end of this chapter you will be able to apply relevant core legal principles and rules appropriately and effectively, at the level of a competent newly qualified solicitor in practice, to realistic client-based and ethical problems and situations in the area of **inchoate offences**.

Note that, as students are not usually required to recall specific case names, or cite statutory or regulatory authorities, these are provided for illustrative purposes only.

Learning outcomes

The learning outcomes for this chapter are:

- to understand and apply the law in relation to attempted offences; and
- to appreciate how impossibility impacts upon criminal liability for attempts.

10.1 Introduction

Most defendants are convicted of a substantive offence such as assault, murder, theft, robbery or criminal damage. However, the scope of criminal liability is wider than this and includes individuals who try but fail to commit an offence. Even though nothing criminal has actually happened, the defendant may still be liable. This is for public policy reasons as, otherwise, unsuccessful defendants would evade responsibility. Furthermore, it would be absurd for the police to have to wait until the full offence was completed before being able to take action.

10.2 Attempts

An attempt to commit a crime is an offence in itself and is known as an 'inchoate' offence – one that is incomplete in some way. There are several inchoate offences but this chapter only deals with attempts. There may be a number of reasons why the accused fails to complete their crime, such as being arrested before they can do so or perhaps because the victim manages to escape or even because the defendant voluntarily withdraws from the plan.

10.3 Definition

The offence of attempt is defined in s 1(1) of the Criminal Attempts Act (CAA) 1981, which provides:

> If, with intent to commit an offence to which this section applies, a person does an act which is more than merely preparatory to the commission of the offence, he is guilty of attempting to commit the offence.

Almost all indictable offences (those that may be tried in the Crown Court) can be the subject of a charge of attempt. Summary only offences – those that must be dealt with in the magistrates' court – are excluded by the CAA 1981. The effect is that whilst a person may be convicted of an attempted murder, they cannot be charged with, for example, an attempted simple assault. Having said that, some of the statutes creating summary only offences specifically create an offence of attempt, for example attempting to drive a motor vehicle while over the prescribed limit for alcohol. These offences are, however, outside the scope of this manual.

10.4 Actus reus of attempt

As with other criminal offences, the prosecution are required to prove all the elements of the actus reus and the mens rea to establish criminal liability. It is apparent from s 1(1) of the CAA 1981 that, to satisfy the actus reus of attempt, the defendant must do an act that is more than preparatory to the commission of the full offence; but what does this actually mean?

10.4.1 Liability for actions

Because the statute specifically refers to 'an act', a person cannot be liable for their omissions.

✪ Example

Tammie, a care worker, fails to visit her elderly client as required and Marjorie almost dies of dehydration. As Tammie is under a contractual obligation to care for Marjorie, she would be liable for her failure to ensure her client has enough to drink. However, as Marjorie survives, the actus reus of attempted homicide cannot be established because there is no culpable act.

10.4.2 'More than merely preparatory'

The actus reus of an attempt requires an act that is more than merely preparatory to the commission of the crime. This is a question of fact that the jury must decide based upon the evidence provided in each particular case. However, guidance has been provided by the judges in determining quite when an act goes beyond the merely preparatory.

In R v Gullefer [1987] Crim LR 195, the defendant placed a bet on a dog at a greyhound racing track. During the race, it became clear the dog was not going to win and so the defendant jumped onto the track hoping that the stewards would declare the race void so he would be entitled to a refund of his bet. The defendant's conviction for attempted theft of the money was quashed on appeal on the basis that his act was merely preparatory.

In this instance, the defendant had not done enough to be criminally liable. So when can it be said that an accused has gone beyond mere preparation? In Gullefer, *Lord Lane indicated that this would be when the accused was effectively 'on the job', which:*

> begins when the merely preparatory acts have come to an end and the defendant embarks on the crime proper.

Whilst this provides some assistance, given that the facts will vary in every case, there is clearly scope for inconsistency. Gullefer's appeal was allowed because the Court of Appeal took the view that he was still only in the preparatory stages of stealing the money from the bookmaker. Although the judges did not list what the defendant needed to do to be liable for attempted theft, there were a number of steps outstanding before he was in a position to complete the full offence.

- *What Gullefer did:* Jumped onto the track.
- *What Gullefer needed to do to be liable for an attempt:* Climb back over the fence, go to the bookmakers, present his ticket and ask for a refund.

How does the court approach cases where there is a dispute as to whether the defendant's actions are more than merely preparatory sufficient to satisfy the statutory test?

- The judge assesses whether the prosecution evidence is such that a jury could reasonably conclude the defendant's acts were not simply preparatory acts but that they had actually embarked on the commission of the offence.
- If the answer to this question is 'no', in other words, the accused was clearly only in the early stages, the judge must withdraw the case from the jury.
- If yes, the jury will then decide whether, as a question of fact, what the defendant did was an attempt.

When this occurs may be surprisingly late.

In the case of R v Jones *[1990] 3 All ER 886, the jury had to decide at what stage the actus reus for attempted murder was complete; in other words, when did Jones cross what is known as 'the line in the sand' from preparatory steps to 'embarking on the crime proper'? Set out below are the steps that Jones carried out and the decision of the court.*

Figure 10.1 Steps taken in *R v Jones*

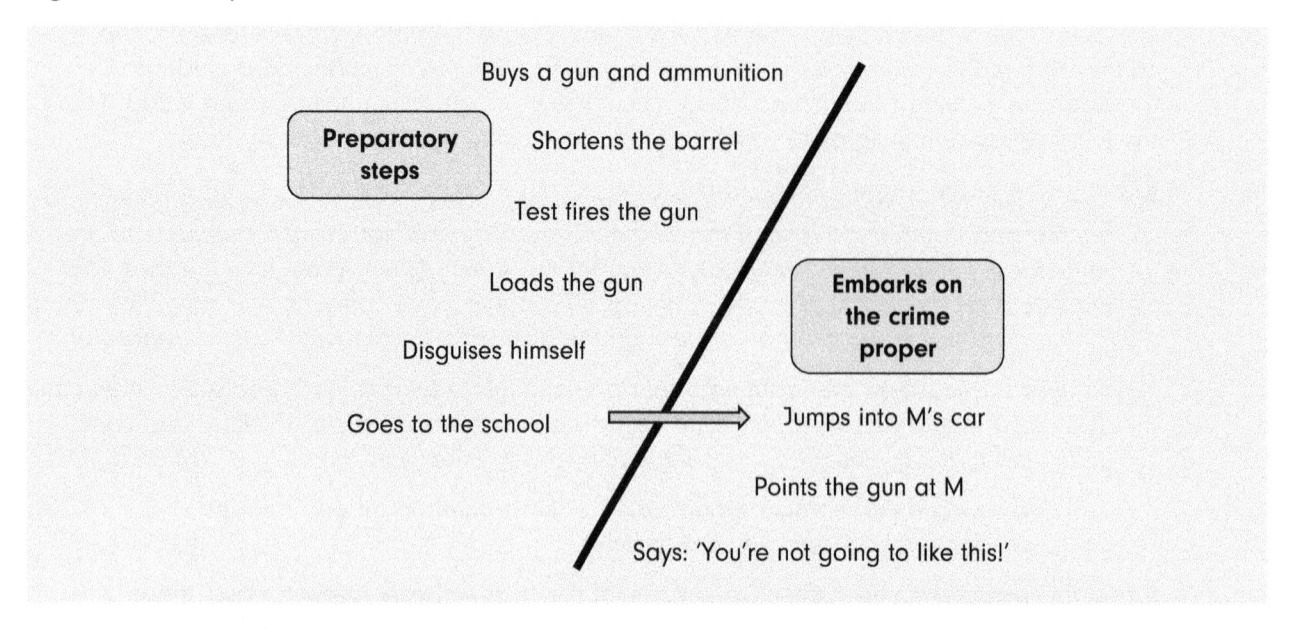

Preparatory steps:
- Buys a gun and ammunition
- Shortens the barrel
- Test fires the gun
- Loads the gun
- Disguises himself
- Goes to the school

Embarks on the crime proper:
- Jumps into M's car
- Points the gun at M
- Says: 'You're not going to like this!'

The Court of Appeal's view was that only when Jones climbed into the victim's car did he go beyond the merely preparatory. Indeed, at this point, the only reason the victim survived at all was because he managed to grab the gun from Jones and escape.

It is apparent that the stage at which the defendant is liable for attempt may be somewhat late in the process and this can cause difficulties for the law enforcement agencies. If they act too quickly, the defendant will be acquitted; if too late, the crime will be completed and the public may be put at risk.

10.5 Mens rea

Having established the actus reus of an attempt, the prosecution must also prove the mens rea. This is relatively straightforward as the defendant must intend to commit the specific offence attempted.

In R v Whybrow (1951) 35 Cr App R 141, the defendant wired up a soap dish to the electricity supply in order to electrocute and kill his wife. The Court of Appeal confirmed that the defendant must intend to kill the victim to be guilty of attempted murder. This is a higher level of mens rea than for murder, where an intention to cause grievous bodily harm is sufficient.

So far as intent is concerned, this can include both direct and indirect intent so the test in *R v Woollin* (considered in **Chapter 2**) applies. In other words, foresight (of death) as a virtual certainty is evidence from which the jury may find an intention.

Example

Larry lives with his partner, Janice. He has been told that Janice is having an affair and, when Janice returns home, he confronts her with the accusation. Janice denies it and the two have a heated argument during which Larry grabs a carving knife from the kitchen sideboard. In anger, he waves the knife at Janice and then launches himself at her causing a small cut to her face.

(a) *Larry could be charged with attempting to cause grievous bodily harm under s 18 of the OAPA 1861. His use of a weapon to cut Janice is evidence of his intent to cause really serious harm.*

(b) *If the prosecution decide to pursue Larry for the lesser s 20 assault, they still have to establish an intent to inflict grievous bodily harm, despite the full offence only requiring an intent or recklessness as to causing some harm. As a consequence, an accused in this situation would rarely be charged with an attempted s 20 assault.*

10.5.1 Offences with an ulterior mens rea

There are some offences where the prosecution must prove an ulterior mens rea and one such example is aggravated criminal damage (covered in **Chapter 8**). For this offence, the defendant must intend or be reckless as to destroying or damaging property, but also intend or be reckless as to endangering life. Effectively, the prosecution are required to prove two distinct elements to satisfy the mens rea. So how does the law of attempt deal with this?

According to the Attorney General's Reference (No.3 of 1992) [1994] 2 All ER 121, the intent that must be proved relates to the intent to cause criminal damage. So far as the ulterior mens rea (the secondary element) is concerned – namely, that relating to endangering life – all that needs to be established is the defendant either intended to or was reckless in endangering the life of another.

Example

The police receive a tip off that Junaid is planning to start a fire at a house where his ex-partner, Sunita and her two children are now living. The police covertly survey the property and see a car pull up outside the house at 6pm. Junaid is seen to go to the boot of his car, take out a can of petrol and walk towards the house. He is arrested halfway down the garden path. When searched, the police find a cigarette lighter and a cloth rag in his pocket.

Junaid admits driving to Sunita's house intending to cause a fire. However, he denies intending to endanger anyone's life as he believed his ex-partner and the children were out. In fact, they were inside the house having their evening meal. Junaid accepts that he did consider the risk they may have been at home but thought it very unlikely as Sunita takes the children to a swimming class at that time.

Junaid is charged with two offences:

(a) Attempted criminal damage by arson, contrary to s 1(1) of the CAA 1981

The actus reus is doing an act that is more than merely preparatory. In this instance, it is likely the jury would find that Junaid had moved from the preparation stage to the commission stage and that he had 'embarked on the crime proper'. The mens rea is satisfied as Junaid admits he intended to damage the house by fire – the offence of arson.

(b) Attempted aggravated criminal damage by arson, contrary to s 1(1) of the CAA 1981

The actus reus is the same as for attempted arson (above). With regard to the mens rea, in addition to the intention to cause damage by fire, the prosecution must prove that Junaid intended or was reckless as to endangering life. This is because aggravated arson is a crime of ulterior intent. Here, because Junaid admits to foreseeing a risk that Sunita and the children could be in the house and therefore presumably that their lives might be endangered, he is reckless as to this aspect.

10.6 Attempts and impossibility

An offence may be impossible:

- as to the end result (for example if the defendant pickpockets a victim only to find their pocket is empty); or
- as to the means (such as if the defendant tries to stab someone with a paper straw).

10.6.1 Actus reus and impossibility

In both these examples, impossibility will not prevent the establishment of the actus reus of attempt because s 1(2) of the CAA 1981 provides that:

> A person may be guilty of attempting to commit an offence ... even though the facts are such that the commission of the offence is impossible.

In simple terms, the defendant is guilty even if the crime they were intending to commit was actually impossible.

10.6.2 Mens rea and impossibility

The mens rea is covered by s 1(3) of the CAA 1981, which provides that the defendant is judged on the facts of the case as they believed them to be.

⭐ Example

Katrina intends to kill Roya by shooting her. She points the gun at her victim and only fails in her objective because there is no bullet in the gun. Although it is impossible for her to kill Roya, Katrina satisfies the actus reus of attempted murder because her actions have gone beyond the merely preparatory.

As far as the mens rea is concerned, Katrina is judged on the facts as she believed them to be and she thought the gun was loaded. Thus, she is regarded as having the relevant intent to commit the offence of murder.

Figure 10.2 Mens rea and impossibility

Katrina ⟹ pulls the trigger ⟹ no bullet

> AR: guilty of attempted murder even though commission of the crime is factually impossible
> s 1(2) of the CAA 1981

Katrina ⟹ intends to kill Roya

> MR: guilty of attempted murder as judged on the facts as Katrina believed them to be
> s 1(3) of the CAA 1981

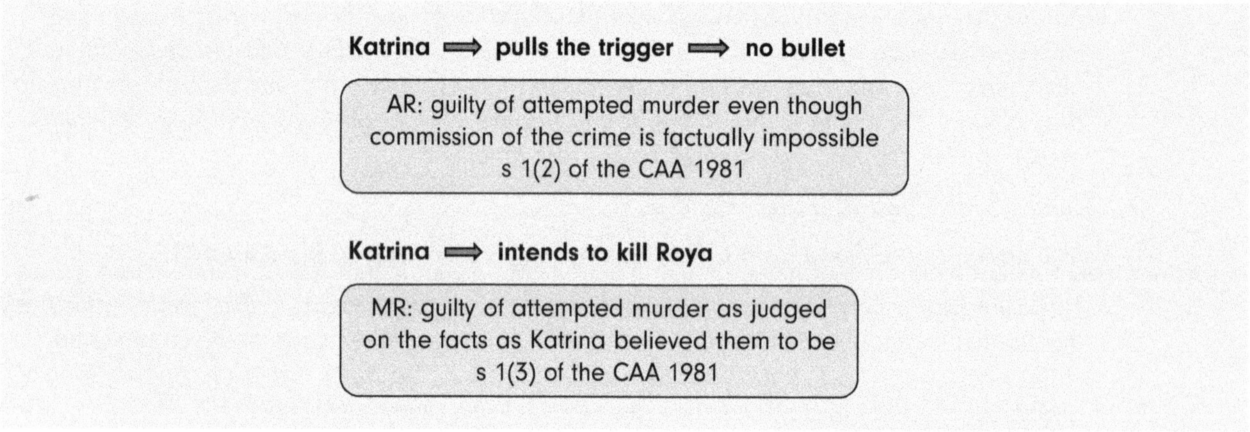

There is an underlying logic to this legal principle – it prevents incompetent offenders escaping criminal liability. The accused is tried on the basis of what they intended to do rather than what it was possible for them to achieve. Set out below is a case that illustrates this point.

📖 *In R v Shivpuri [1987] AC 1, the defendant was given a package to take with him on a flight from India to the United Kingdom. He was told the package contained heroin. Shivpuri was stopped at the airport, his bags were searched and the package was found. The defendant admitted he was carrying heroin but, when the substance was tested, it was found to be harmless and not an illegal drug at all.*

The defendant had clearly gone beyond the merely preparatory steps by arriving at the airport with the package. The fact that he could not actually have imported a class A drug was no defence. Furthermore, his intention to commit the offence was based on the facts as the defendant believed them to be and he thought he was smuggling heroin. As a consequence, he was guilty of attempting to commit the relevant importation of drugs offence even though it was impossible for him to do so.

Summary

The relevant statute is the CAA 1981 and it is important that the wording contained within this Act is used and not the definitions of the actus reus and mens rea of the full offence.

For the actus reus, there are three main points to remember when determining when the defendant has moved from the preparatory phase to the commission phase:

- An act (not an omission) is required that is more than merely preparatory to the commission of the full offence.
- Significant steps must be taken towards the completion of the full offence but it is not necessary to prove the defendant has done all they intend to do.
- Whether an act is more than merely preparatory will be a question of fact in each case, provided the judge believes there is some evidence that the defendant has 'embarked on the crime proper' so the matter can be left to the jury.

With regard to the mens rea:

- In most instances, the prosecution must establish that the defendant intended the consequences of their action, for example the death of the victim.
- If the full offence includes an ulterior mens rea, such as aggravated criminal damage, recklessness may suffice for this aspect.

Figure 10.3 Summary of attempts

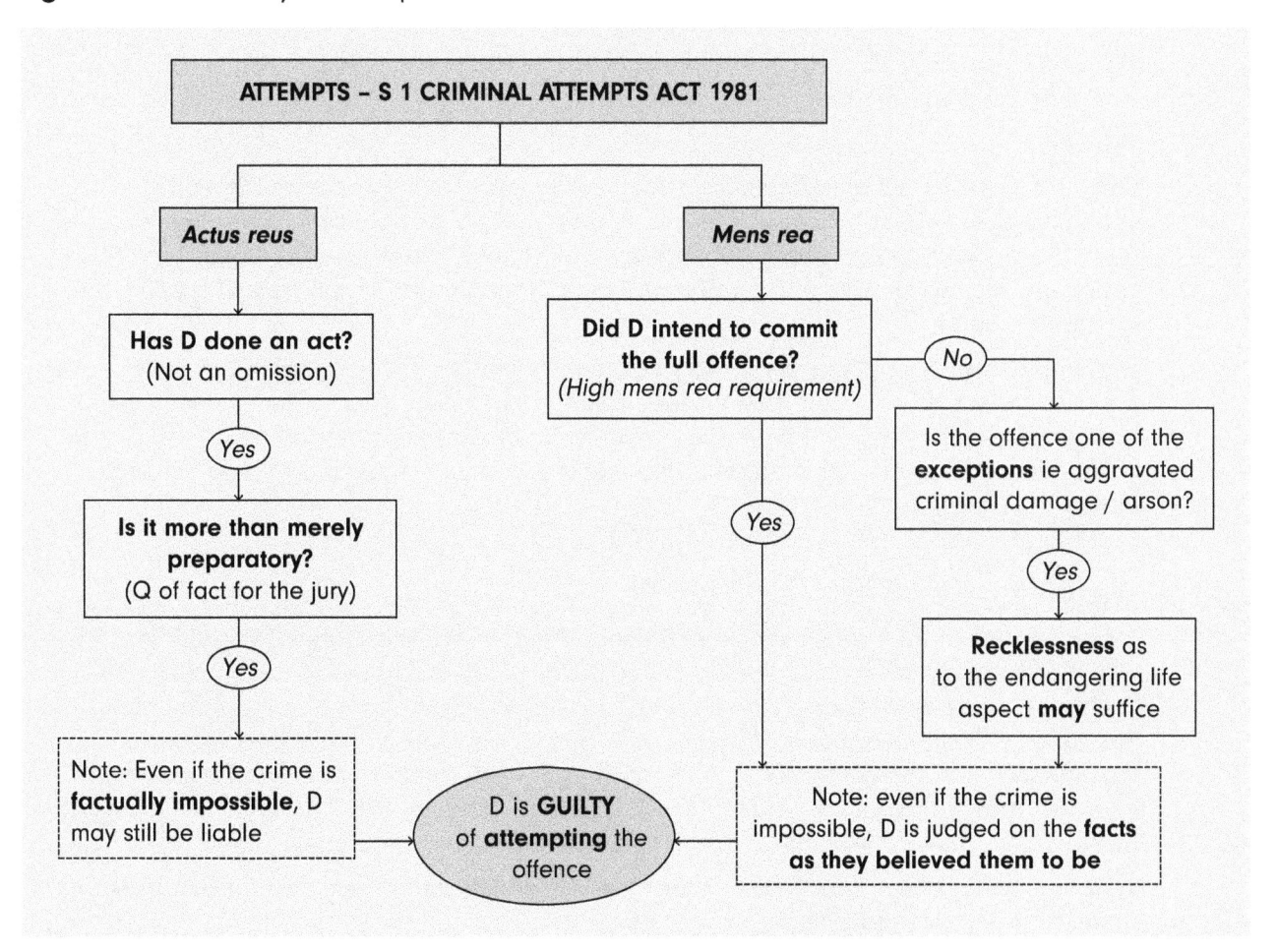

Criminal Law

Sample questions

Question 1

A man plans to carry out a robbery of a post office, but the police are tipped off and are lying in wait for him. In preparation, the man has located a post office to rob, obtained an imitation firearm, written a demand note which is in his pocket, been seen loitering outside the post office wearing sunglasses and carrying a heavy object (an imitation firearm), failed to give any warning about his intended actions and had just entered the post office when he was stopped and arrested.

Which of the following statements correctly describes whether the man satisfies the actus reus of attempted robbery?

A   The judge would not allow the matter to proceed to the jury as there is insufficient evidence that the man has moved from the preparatory stages to commit the full offence of robbery.

B   The jury must decide, as a question of fact, whether what the defendant has done is sufficient for the offence of attempted robbery.

C   The jury may take account of all the defendant's actions and omissions when determining if he is guilty of attempted robbery.

D   The jury is unlikely to conclude that the man satisfies the actus reus for attempted robbery as he has not completed the final act towards committing the full offence.

E   To be guilty of an attempted robbery the man must have embarked on the middle stages of the crime and the evidence provided suggests that he has.

Answer

Option B is the correct answer as this is the question for the jury to decide. Option A is wrong because, in a scenario such as this, there is sufficient evidence to allow the matter to go to the jury. Option C is wrong because the jury cannot take account of the defendant's omissions, such as his failure to give any warning, when determining if he is liable for attempted robbery.

Option D is also wrong. The jury is likely to conclude that the man has moved from the preparatory stage to the commission stage and the prosecution do not have to wait until he has completed the final act before the event. The man must have embarked on the 'crime proper' to be guilty of attempted robbery – not the 'middle stages of the crime' – hence, option E is wrong.

Question 2

A boy decides to set fire to his school late one afternoon as he is bored and thought it would be fun to watch the staff run out of the building. He purchases some matches and lighter fuel and approaches a litter bin that is full of paper. He pours the lighter fuel onto the paper and strikes a match. However, just as he is about to drop this into the bin, a teacher sees him and asks what he is doing. The boy panics and drops the match, which has now been extinguished, onto the floor causing no damage. He runs away but is caught by the teacher.

Which statement best describes whether the boy satisfies the mens rea for attempted arson and aggravated arson?

A   The boy is liable for both offences because he intended to damage property belonging to another by fire and intended to endanger life.

B   The boy is liable for both offences because he was reckless as to damaging property belonging to another by fire and reckless as to endangering life.

C   The boy is liable for both offences because he intended to damage property belonging to another by fire and was reckless as to endangering life.

D   The boy is liable for attempted arson as he intended to damage property belonging to another by fire, but he does not satisfy the mens rea for attempted aggravated arson.

E   The boy is not liable for either offence as he did not intend nor was he reckless as to endangering life.

Answer

The correct answer is option C. The boy intended to commit arson as he 'decides to set fire to his school' but was reckless as to endangering life (he was aware that staff were still in the building as he thought it would be fun to watch them run out). Options A and B are not the best answers because he intended the arson and was reckless as to the endangering life aspect, rather than intending or being reckless as to both. Option D is wrong because the boy does satisfy the mens rea for attempted aggravated arson and option E is wrong as he is criminally liable for both offences.

Question 3

A woman runs an air freight business, which has been struggling as a result of the downturn in exports. Her business has cash flow problems and she is worried that it will go into liquidation. Desperate to raise some cash, the woman plants a bomb on board one of her planes intending for it to explode while the plane is over the ocean, enabling her to claim a significant insurance payment. The bomb fails to detonate but is discovered when it lands at the airport. On closer inspection by the bomb disposal squad, it becomes apparent that the woman had not armed the bomb properly so it could never have detonated in its current state.

Is the woman liable for attempted murder?

A   No, because the substantive offence of murder could not have been committed as the bomb could never have detonated.

B   No, because planting a bomb is not an act that is more than merely preparatory to committing the full offence of murder.

C   No, because she does not intend to kill those on board the plane.

D   Yes, because the woman is reckless as to whether those on board the plane will be killed.

E   Yes, because the woman is judged on her own understanding of the facts and she thought she had armed the bomb properly so that it would explode over the ocean.

Answer

Option E is correct as the woman's intention to commit the offence will be based on the facts as she believed them to be; and therefore she is guilty of attempted murder even though the full offence of murder was impossible. Option A is wrong as the CAA 1981 provides that the accused may be liable for an attempt even if the crime is factually impossible.

Option B is wrong because, once she planted the bomb, the woman has clearly passed from the 'preparation phase' to the 'commission phase'; indeed, there was nothing more she could do to commit the substantive offence. Option C is also wrong as, although the woman's direct intent is for the plane to go down so that she can claim on the insurance, she has an indirect intent to kill (an intent to cause grievous bodily harm is not sufficient). In other words, even though the woman may not have desired the death of those on the plane, she must have foreseen this outcome as a virtual certainty had the bomb gone off over the ocean. This will be sufficient to fulfil the mens rea.

Option D is wrong because recklessness as to causing the death of those on board the plane is not sufficient to satisfy the mens rea of an attempted murder.

11 Parties to a Crime

11.1	Introduction	198
11.2	Terminology	198
11.3	Definition of accomplice liability	199
11.4	Actus reus	200
11.5	Links between the principal and the accomplice	203
11.6	Practical application of actus reus of accomplice liability	205
11.7	The relationship between the principal and the accomplice	207
11.8	Innocent agency	207
11.9	Summary of the actus reus of accomplice liability	208
11.10	Mens rea	208
11.11	Intention to do the act or say the words	208
11.12	Knowledge of the circumstances	209
11.13	Accomplice's liability for a different offence to the principal offender	211
11.14	Liability of the accomplice where the principal goes beyond the plan	213
11.15	Practical application of accomplice liability mens rea	215
11.16	Summary of the mens rea of accomplice liability	216
11.17	Withdrawing participation	217

SQE1 syllabus

By the end of this chapter you will be able to apply relevant core legal principles and rules appropriately and effectively, at the level of a competent newly qualified solicitor in practice, to realistic client-based and ethical problems and situations in relation to **parties to a crime**.

Note that, as students are not usually required to recall specific case names, or cite statutory or regulatory authorities, these are provided for illustrative purposes only.

Learning outcomes

The learning outcomes for this chapter are:

- to appreciate that the scope of criminal liability extends beyond those who commit a crime (the principal offender) to those who encourage or assist in the commission of the offence (secondary parties);
- to be able to identify the difference between principal and secondary offenders;
- to analyse effectively the criminal liability of an accomplice; and
- to understand the circumstances in which a secondary party may withdraw from the offence.

Criminal Law

11.1 Introduction

The scope of the criminal law, in relation to the parties involved, is intentionally wide for public policy reasons, to deter and punish those who are instrumental in the commission of crimes albeit in a rather less obvious way. Thus far, the focus has been on the potential criminal liability of someone who commits a substantive offence such as murder, theft, robbery or criminal damage. However, the law casts its net wider than this to catch those who simply assist or encourage. Effectively, they are involved, but on the fringes. Despite not actually committing the offence, such 'helpers' may attract criminal liability. Indeed, to reflect the responsibility of all those involved, the law allows for several people to be charged with the same offence, even though they have played very different roles in the crime.

11.2 Terminology

The language used in this area of the law can be somewhat confusing particularly as, for example, a person who assists a crime may be referred to as an accomplice, an accessory or a secondary party.

Table 11.1 Differences between the parties to a crime

Terminology	Definition	Example
Principal offender	The principal offender is the person who commits the actus reus of a substantive criminal offence with the necessary mens rea.	Pat snatches Vera's mobile phone and runs off with it. Pat is guilty of theft.
Joint principals (or co-principals)	Where two or more people perform the actus reus and the mens rea of an offence together.	Ian and Neil enter Ann's property as trespassers and steal her computer. Both are guilty of burglary under s 9(1)(b) of the TA 1968.
Secondary party (also referred to as an accomplice or an accessory)	Those who assist in the commission of an offence in some way, whilst not committing the actus reus of the offence themselves.	Shane stands outside Ann's property acting as a lookout. Shane is a secondary party to the burglary.

It is important not to become overwhelmed by this complex area of the law. Begin by analysing how each of the defendants are involved in the offence, as this will assist in keeping to the right path.

⭐ Example

(a) If Pat throws bricks at a window, he is liable as the principal offender for criminal damage.

(b) If Pat and Soji both throw bricks at the window, they are joint principal offenders.

(c) Only if one (or more) has a lesser involvement should accomplice liability be considered; perhaps if Arnie hands Pat the brick, but does not actually throw it himself.

Figure 11.1 Definition of principal and accomplice

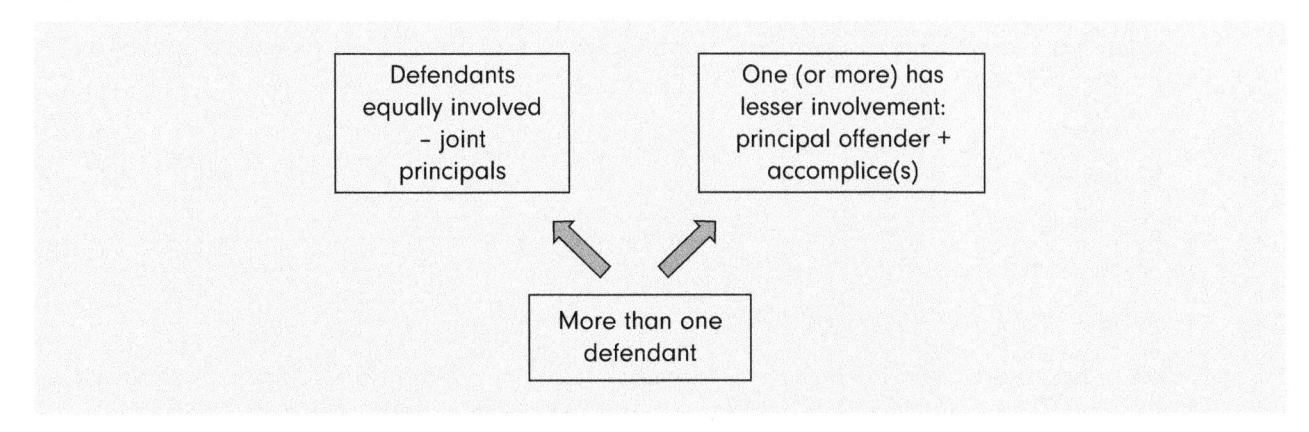

```
┌─────────────┐           ┌─────────────────┐
│ Defendants  │           │ One (or more) has│
│ equally involved│       │ lesser involvement:│
│   – joint   │           │ principal offender +│
│ principals  │           │   accomplice(s)  │
└─────────────┘           └─────────────────┘
         ↖                 ↗
           ┌──────────────┐
           │ More than one│
           │  defendant   │
           └──────────────┘
```

When analysing a scenario that involves more than one possible defendant, the first step is to identify the principal offender(s) and to consider their criminal liability, before moving on to those with lesser involvement.

11.3 Definition of accomplice liability

The law in relation to accomplice liability is set out in s 8 of the Accessories and Abettors Act 1861, which provides that:

> Whosoever shall aid, abet, counsel, or procure the commission of any offence, whether the same be an offence at common law or by virtue of any Act passed or to be passed, shall be liable to be tried, indicted and punished as a principal offender.

Unsurprisingly, given that the statute is over 150 years old, the language is rather archaic. In particular, the reference to being indicted is misleading as it is possible to be an accomplice to both either way and indictable only offences. There is a similar provision dealing with accomplice liability for summary only offences under s 44 of the Magistrates' Courts Act 1980.

It is apparent from these statutes that the law regards a person who assists in the commission of an offence to be as blameworthy as the person who actually commits the crime. As a consequence, conviction as an accomplice will attract the same powers of punishment as the principal offender.

⊛ *Example*

Weimin is angry at Peng for failing to repay a loan of £5,000. He asks his friend, Quon, if he can borrow his machete to 'finish Peng once and for all' and Quon agrees, intending that Weimin will kill Peng. Weimin attacks Peng and slashes him repeatedly with the machete, causing deep wounds to his stomach, from which Peng dies.

Weimin is the principal offender. He is guilty of murder as he caused Peng's death intending to kill. Quon is not a principal offender as he has not committed the actus reus of the offence of murder. He has, however, helped Weimin by supplying the weapon – the machete. He would be convicted as an accomplice to murder and, just like Weimin, will be subject to a mandatory sentence of life imprisonment. However, the actus reus and mens rea requirements that the prosecution need to prove for Quon will be different to those for Weimin.

11.4 Actus reus

According to the statute, an accomplice may satisfy the actus reus of accomplice liability in four different ways, namely by:

(a) aiding,

(b) abetting,

(c) counselling, or

(d) procuring

the commission of the principal offence.

In the case of Attorney General's Reference (No. 1 of 1975) *[1975] QB 773, the Court of Appeal stated that aiding, abetting, counselling and procuring should be given their ordinary meaning. Furthermore, Lord Widgery CJ confirmed that each meant something different as otherwise there would be no point in Parliament 'wasting time in using four words where two or three would do'.*

In reality, a criminal charge will usually allege that the defendant aided, abetted, counselled or procured the offence and no term is singled out.

11.4.1 Aiding

The first way in which an accomplice may be criminally liable is if they aid the principal offender in some manner.

- *What does the term mean?*

  The word 'aiding' suggests helping, assisting or supporting the principal in some way to enable them to commit the offence.

- *When?*

  Generally, aid will be given at the time of the offence, although it can also be earlier. It does not include those whose only involvement is after the offence, for example disposing of evidence or deleting incriminating emails (there are separate offences that cover scenarios such as these).

- *How?*

  Aiding before the offence would include providing the principal offender with the weapon or giving specific information to allow the crime to succeed, such as when a householder will be on holiday so a burglary may be committed, or teaching a person the technology skills to commit internet fraud. Aiding at the time of the offence could include acting as a look out, or holding the victim down while the principal assaults the victim.

11.4.2 Abetting

The second word listed in s 8 of the Accessories and Abettors Act 1861 is 'abet'.

- *What?*

  Abetting requires the accomplice to encourage the principal in some way to commit the offence.

- *When?*

  Abetting occurs at the time of the offence, so during its commission.

- *How?*

  An accomplice may be found to have abetted a crime by either words or actions. The accused may shout specific words of encouragement, for example 'Kick him!' while a victim is being assaulted, or use gestures, such as miming the action of a punch or even giving a thumbs up.

11.4.3 Counselling

An accomplice can also counsel the offence.

- *What?*

    Counselling involves instigating, soliciting or encouraging, or even threatening, the principal to commit the offence.

- *When?*

    Counselling occurs at some stage before the offence. This is how it differs from abetting, which requires the prosecution to prove that the defendant wilfully encouraged the offence at the scene, thus when the offence is in the process of being committed.

- *How?*

    Encouraging an assault by 'winding up' the principal offender, for example stating, in response to the principal's comment that he would 'punch his son's teacher', that the teacher deserved it and should show some respect to the child. Alternatively, a defendant who suggested it would be a 'brilliant idea' for the principal to scrawl graffiti on a local politician's house.

The amount of encouragement offered does not need to be particularly great for liability to arise.

In R v Gianetto [1997] 1 Cr App R 1, the principal offender stated, 'I am going to kill your wife' to which the accomplice responded, 'Oh goody'. This was found to be enough to convict the husband as an accomplice on the basis that he had counselled the offence of murder.

11.4.4 Procuring

Procuring is a different concept entirely to the other three types of behaviour.

- *What?*

    According to Lord Widgery in the *Attorney General's Reference (No.1 of 1975)* (see above) this means 'to produce by endeavour'. The accused sets out to achieve a particular state of affairs and takes appropriate steps to bring about that offence.

- *When?*

    Because procuring usually requires the accomplice to actually cause the crime, this will occur at an earlier time to the offence.

- *How?*

    An accused who secretly adds alcohol to their friend's drink, knowing that the friend would shortly be driving home, procures the offence of driving with excess alcohol contrary to s 5 of the RTA 1988. By 'spiking' the drink, the defendant puts the principal offender in a position whereby they commit an offence they would not otherwise have done.

11.4.5 Mere presence at the scene

Abetting requires proof, not only that the defendant was physically present at the scene of the crime, but also that they wilfully encouraged its commission. This will require evidence that some active steps were taken, whether it be words or action. Mere presence at the scene and a failure to intervene or prevent the offence is not sufficient even if that presence did, in fact, encourage the principal.

In R v Allan [1965] 1 QB 130, the defendant was present at the scene of a fight. He was entirely passive and did nothing to encourage either party, but he did admit to harbouring a secret desire to become involved if needed.

The Court of Appeal held that mere presence alone was insufficient because: 'To hold otherwise would be in effect ... to convict a man on his thoughts, unaccompanied by any physical act other than the fact of his mere presence.'

Contrast the outcome of this case to that of Wilcox v Jeffery [1951] 1 All ER 464, where the defendant was found guilty as an accomplice simply by being a spectator at a jazz concert. The musician (Hawkins) was allowed entry into the country provided he did not work; thus, his performance at the concert was illegal. Despite only being present, it was held that Wilcox had encouraged the commission of the offence by:

- meeting Hawkins at the airport;
- buying a ticket for the concert;
- attending the concert; and
- writing about it in his magazine.

The justification for this decision was that there would not have been a performance without the audience, so the presence of each spectator was an encouragement to the principal offender to perform.

Whether presence at the scene of a crime will be sufficient depends upon the particular facts.

Example

Enrico has just bought a new sports car and agrees to allow his friend, Raoul, to drive the vehicle to demonstrate its performance. Raoul drives at high speed, weaving in and out of the traffic and, consequently, is found guilty of dangerous driving. Enrico denies being an accomplice arguing that he just sat in the passenger seat of the car passively. The court may find:

(a) Enrico is not an accomplice as he was merely present at the scene of the crime and this is not sufficient for liability as an accomplice.

(b) Enrico is an accomplice because, by staying silent, he was implying that he consented to the style of driving particularly as it was his car.

11.4.5.1 Overview of presence at the scene

Whether a person is criminally liable for their presence will depend upon the facts of the particular case.

- Mere presence at the scene of a crime is not, in itself, usually sufficient to amount to the actus reus of being an accomplice.
- An accomplice may be liable for their presence if:
  - Attendance was by prior arrangement with the principal; effectively they are acting as a support in the situation.
  - Alternatively, if the accused actually encouraged or assisted the principal (by words and/or actions) at the scene of the crime.

11.4.6 Summary of actus reus components

Table 11.2 Actus reus of accomplice liability

	What must the accomplice do for the principal offender?	Before the offence?	During the offence?
Aid	Help or assist	✓	✓
Abet	Encourage	X	✓
Counsel	Instigate, solicit or encourage	✓	X
Procure	Produce by endeavour	✓	X

One way to remember the correct order for the different components of the actus reus of s 8 of the Accessories and Abettors Act 1861 is to note that they are actually the wrong way around. Aiding and abetting (the first two in the list) usually occur at the time of the offence whereas counselling and procuring (the second two) happen before the principal commits the offence.

11.5 Links between the principal and the accomplice

In most situations, the prosecution will have no difficulty in establishing that the parties met or liaised in some way to discuss the crime, but is it a requirement for there to be a link between them? In other words, does it matter whether the principal would have committed the offence without any help or encouragement from the accomplice?

11.5.1 Mental link

A mental link between the principal and the accomplice has been described as a 'meeting of minds'. However, this does not mean the parties have discussed the matter beforehand.

In the case of Attorney General's Reference (No. 1 of 1975) *(see section* **11.4**), *the issue of causation was considered by the Court of Appeal. Lord Widgery CJ commented that there would usually be a 'meeting of minds' between the principal and the accomplice where it was alleged that the accomplice aided, abetted or counselled the offence. He said that such cases would 'almost inevitably' involve contact between principal and accomplice.*

However, the judges confirmed that there was no need for a mental link, indeed any contact at all, where it was alleged the accomplice had procured the commission of the offence. The view of the Court of Appeal was there were 'plenty of instances in which a person may be said to procure the commission of a crime ... even though there is no attempt at agreement or discussion'.

In summary, in cases of procurement, it is clear from case law that the prosecution do not need to establish there was any contact between the principal and the accomplice. In contrast, in cases of aiding, abetting or counselling, there will usually be some form of contact between them.

Example

(a) Elaine is walking home from work one night when she sees Angus selling cannabis to a young woman. She also notices a police officer approaching but, because she believes cannabis should be legalised, Elaine distracts him. Angus spots what she has done and quickly walks away from the scene. Whilst Elaine may not be a typical accomplice, in law she aids Angus by enabling him to commit the offence of supplying illegal drugs.

In this instance, although there was no prior discussion, Angus became aware of Elaine's assistance. However, if the basis of the charge is that the accomplice aided the principal, it is possible for such assistance to be given even if the principal is entirely unaware of the help given.

(b) Elaine distracts the police officer from noticing the ongoing drug deal. Angus is oblivious to her action and, after having completed the transaction, he strolls down the street away from the scene. As before, Elaine is criminally liable as an accomplice to the drugs offence.

Although it is possible to countenance situations where the accomplice is guilty of aiding a crime without the principal knowing of it, these tend to relate to providing physical assistance. In contrast, it would be difficult to prove that the accomplice advised or encouraged the principal to commit an offence if the latter was not even aware of the advice or encouragement. Thus, in cases of counselling and abetting, there generally does need to be a meeting of minds at some stage between the principal and the accomplice.

Example

Sudesh posts on social media that he intends to smash the windows of the headquarters of an energy company as an environmental protest. Miriam reads this and posts the words: 'Go Green Action!' on her own private account. There is no meeting of minds here and she is not guilty as an accomplice to criminal damage.

11.5.2 Causal link

In cases where the prosecution allege procurement, there is a requirement for a causal link between what the procurer does and the commission of the offence by the principal. In other words, it must be established that there is a causal connection between the accomplice's behaviour and the commission of the offence. An accomplice who secretly adds alcohol to the principal's drink has caused the principal to break the law by driving when over the legal drink driving limit.

However, where the allegation is that the accomplice aided, abetted or counselled the offence, there is no requirement for a causal link. Whilst the principal will often be motivated, at least in part, by the assistance of the accomplice, situations will arise where the principal would have acted anyway.

Example

Tazleen is walking in the town centre one evening when she comes across two people having a fight. She shouts encouragement and both hear her words, but take no notice as they are too engrossed in trying to hit each other. Although the assault would have happened regardless of whether Tazleen was there or not, she still abets the affray and is liable as an accomplice.

The same approach is adopted when dealing with cases of counselling; it is irrelevant that the principal would have committed the offence whether the accomplice was involved or not.

> *In R v Calhaem [1985] 2 WLR 826, the defendant hired a hit man (the principal offender) to kill her love rival. The 'hit man' claimed he had no intention of carrying out the deed but went to the house to give this impression. When the intended victim saw him, she screamed, causing the principal to go berserk and kill her. The defendant argued that she was not an accomplice to the murder as her counselling had not caused the 'hit man' to commit the offence. Unsurprisingly, her submission was rejected and she was convicted.*

It is apparent from case law that the need for a causal link is restricted to cases where the accomplice procured the crime. For those of aiding, abetting and counselling there does not need to be any causal link between the assistance or encouragement and the commission of the offence. In other words, it does not matter that the crime would have happened anyway.

11.5.3 Summary of mental and causal link

Table 11.3 Requirement for mental and causal link

	Mental link required?	Causal link required?
Aid	X	X
Abet	✓	X
Counsel	✓	X
Procure	X	✓

- In cases of aiding, neither a mental nor a causal link between the principal offender and the accomplice is required; indeed, the principal may not even know of the assistance. Furthermore, there is no need to establish that this help impacted or influenced their decision to commit the crime.
- Where the accomplice is accused of abetting or counselling, a mental link is required so the principal must be aware of the encouragement or advice but there need not be a causal link.
- In cases where the accomplice procured the offence, there is no necessity for a mental link with the principal but there must be a causal link.

11.6 Practical application of actus reus of accomplice liability

Chrissie is married to Victor, her elderly and rich husband. Chrissie has a lover, Bjorn, who persuades her to arrange for Victor to be killed. She contacts Arnold, a killer for hire, and agrees to pay him £50,000 to murder her husband. Chrissie pays Arnold £25,000 in advance and tells him when Victor will be alone in the house. The second instalment will be paid after the job has been completed.

Duncan is aware of Arnold's plan and provides him with a gun. Ethan drives Arnold to Victor's home and then stays in the car to act as a lookout. As Arnold enters the property, he is seen by Finn, the gardener, who dislikes his employer intensely. He realises that Victor is going to be shot, but simply hides in some bushes, secretly hoping that Arnold will succeed.

Arnold is also spotted by Gwen, the cleaner. She is aware that Victor is about to dismiss her as her work is sloppy, so she unlocks the doors to enable Arnold to access the house and leave quickly. Gwen then shouts encouragement as Arnold raises the gun to fire at Victor, who dies instantly. Finally, Bjorn's brother, Heinz, assists Arnold by helping to dispose of Victor's body.

Table 11.4 Criminal liability of the parties

	Principal	Aid	Abet	Counsel	Procure
Arnold (killer)	Kills Victor.				
Bjorn (lover)				Encourages Chrissie to have Victor killed.	
Chrissie (wife)				Gives Arnold information on when Victor will be alone in the house.	Hires Arnold to kill Victor; gives him £25,000 and agrees to pay the remaining £25,000 when the job is complete.
Duncan (provides weapon)		Provides Arnold with the gun.			
Ethan (lookout)		Drives Arnold to the house and acts as a lookout.			
Finn (gardener)					
Gwen (cleaner)		Unlocks the doors.	Shouts encouragement		
Heinz (brother)					

Finn is not liable as a secondary party because mere presence at the scene and failure to intervene or prevent the principal from acting will not usually be sufficient. Here, although Finn may have been under a moral obligation to do something, he is not under a legal obligation and cannot be convicted only on the basis of his secret wish for Arnold to succeed.

Heinz cannot be an accomplice to the murder as his only involvement is after the crime has been committed (although he may be liable for other offences).

11.7 The relationship between the principal and the accomplice

It is well established that the actus reus of the principal offence must have occurred for an accomplice to be criminally liable and, in practice, the principal will usually also be prosecuted and convicted. However, there is no requirement for this to happen. On occasion, situations will arise where the principal may not be convicted but the accomplice is.

Two rather unusual cases illustrate this point.

11.7.1 Principal has a defence

On occasion, the principal offender will escape liability as they satisfy the court, they have a defence.

> In R v Cogan and Leak *[1976] 1 QB 217*, Leak's conviction as an accomplice to the rape of his wife was upheld by the Court of Appeal. Leak had encouraged Cogan to have sexual intercourse with his wife, knowing she would not consent. Cogan (the principal offender) was acquitted of rape, due to his belief in her consent, but despite this, Leak (the accomplice) was convicted. [Note the law has now changed so that a reasonable and not just an honest belief in consent is required to evade liability for rape.]

11.7.2 Principal cannot be found

The second situation where only the accomplice may be convicted is where the principal cannot be found.

> In R v Gnango *[2011] UKSC 59*, the defendant was engaged in a shootout with a second unidentified male (referred to in court as 'Bandana Man' as he was wearing a red bandana) in which both were trying to shoot and kill each other. Bandana Man accidentally killed a passer-by. Bandana Man was never arrested but Gnango was and he was charged as an accomplice to the murder of the passer-by. The Supreme Court upheld his conviction on the basis there was a common plan to shoot each other and therefore Gnango was guilty of aiding the principal in killing the victim.

Cases such as these are the exception rather than the norm. However, in both situations, the actus reus of the principal offence has been carried out and this must occur before an accomplice may attract liability.

11.8 Innocent agency

An innocent agent is someone who commits the actus reus of a crime but who is not guilty of the offence because they lack the mens rea.

Example

Melinda has just ended her relationship with her partner, Beatrice. She tells her sister, Sarina, that she wants some of her own clothing destroyed and asks her to collect the items from Beatrice's house and burn them. Sarina does so, believing Melinda's story, but in fact the items belong to Beatrice who reports the matter to the police.

In this instance, Melinda has procured the offence of criminal damage, by acting to bring it about. However, rather than being liable as an accomplice, Melinda would be charged as a principal offender. This is because she has used an innocent agent (Sarina) to commit the actus reus of the crime.

11.9 Summary of the actus reus of accomplice liability

- A person will satisfy the actus reus requirements of accomplice liability if they:
    - help to bring about the offence by acting, advising, assisting or encouraging before the crime occurs;
    - are present at the scene of the crime in order to assist or encourage; or
    - are present at the scene of the crime and do assist or encourage.
- The four different ways in which the accomplice may attract criminal liability are aiding, abetting, counselling and procuring.
- Aiding may occur either before or during the commission of the principal offence. Abetting takes place during the offence, whilst counselling and procuring happen beforehand.
- Abetting and counselling require a mental link but only procuring requires a causal link.
- Mere presence may provide evidence from which it can be inferred that the defendant encouraged the principal offender, but presence alone does not automatically equate to encouragement.

11.10 Mens rea

The mens rea of accomplice liability is a complex area of the law that has caused difficulties for even the most senior judges, so much so that the Supreme Court concluded unanimously, in the leading case of *R v Jogee* [2016] UKSC 8, that the law on accomplice liability had gone astray.

There are two elements to the mens rea of accomplice. The first concerns the mens rea in relation to the act or words that establish the actus reus of accomplice liability. The second part involves a consideration of the accomplice's knowledge or awareness of the circumstances of the principal offence.

11.10.1 Joint venture

There is a particular phrase that is associated with accomplice liability, namely 'joint enterprise' or 'joint venture'. Where there is more than one party committing an offence, it will be described as a joint venture if they commit the crime with a *common purpose* or *plan*. This may be because there are a number of principal offenders, such as four defendants who all work in a greenhouse producing and cultivating cannabis. However, in more recent times, the term has come to be associated with those defendants who are on the periphery of the offence, but who are nevertheless caught up by the criminal justice system. In particular, individuals who are involved in gangs and were at the scene but who did not fire the gun or stab the victim with a knife.

11.11 Intention to do the act or say the words

The first requirement to be established is that the defendant intentionally (or deliberately):

(a) did the act that assisted, encouraged or procured the offence; or

(b) spoke the words that advised, encouraged or procured the crime.

Selling the principal offender a gun or discussing how to carry out a burglary would be clear examples of where the accomplice's actions are deliberate. However, further assistance on exactly what the prosecution need to prove was given by the judges in the following case.

The test for accomplice liability was outlined in the case of National Coal Board v Gamble *[1959] 1 QB 11. A weighbridge operator, employed by the defendant, allowed a lorry overloaded with coal to leave the colliery. As a result, the lorry was driven on a road when nearly four tonnes overweight.*

The National Coal Board was charged with aiding and abetting the offence. In response to their submission that they had neither wanted nor intended the offence to happen, Devlin J stated this was irrelevant as an indifference to a crime being committed does not negative abetting. All that is required is 'a positive act of assistance voluntarily done'.

This first part of the test rarely presents any difficulties for the prosecution as all that must be proved is the accomplice intentionally (rather than accidentally) did an act or spoke words that amounted to assistance or encouragement. If the conduct is deliberate, it is difficult to imagine situations where this will not be established.

11.12 Knowledge of the circumstances

Moving on to the second part of the test, to be criminally liable the accomplice must have knowledge of the relevant circumstances.

In Johnson v Youden *[1950] 1 KB 544, Lord Goddard stated that for a person to be convicted of aiding and abetting a crime, it must be shown that they knew 'the essential matters which constitute that offence'. Specifically, the accused must know the circumstances that satisfy the elements of the actus reus of a crime, and have an awareness of the principal's state of mind (their mens rea) at the time they commit the offence.*

The effect of this ruling is the accomplice must know that certain things are going to happen, or at least they contemplate that those things might happen, which *in fact* constitute an offence.

Example

In the case of Derek Bentley, aged 19, it was argued that the accused did not intend to assist an offence. Bentley was hanged in 1953 for the murder of Police Constable Sidney Miles, committed in the course of an attempted burglary.

The murder of the police officer was actually carried out by a friend of Bentley's, Christopher Craig, who was only aged 16 at the time and therefore too young to receive the death penalty. Bentley was convicted as an accomplice to the murder on the basis that the killing amounted to a joint enterprise. The crucial evidence against Bentley was his alleged instruction to Craig to 'Let him have it!' Lord Chief Justice Goddard, who was the trial judge, sentenced Bentley to death describing him as 'mentally aiding the murder'. In fact, Bentley could equally have meant 'hand over the gun', in which case the mens rea for accomplice liability would not have been satisfied.

The outcome for Bentley was dire and the case led to a 45-year-long campaign to win him a posthumous pardon. This was granted in 1993 and his murder conviction was also subsequently quashed – unfortunately, far too late for Bentley himself.

11.12.1 Accomplice has full knowledge

The accomplice will satisfy this requirement if they intend the principal to commit the actus reus of the offence with the required mens rea. Obviously, if the accomplice is aware of the crime that the principal intends to commit, the second limb of the mens rea will be established quite easily.

Example

Donal accompanies Baptiste to act as a look out while Baptiste breaks into an office building to steal a number of computers.

Donal satisfies the actus reus of accomplice liability as he aids Baptiste at the time of the offence by acting as a lookout. With regard to the mens rea, not only does Donal act intentionally, he also has knowledge of the circumstances that make this a crime. He knows that Baptiste intends to enter the building as a trespasser and steal property from inside. Thus, Donal satisfies both the first and second elements of the mens rea of accomplice liability.

Figure 11.2 Liability of accomplice who knows the offence

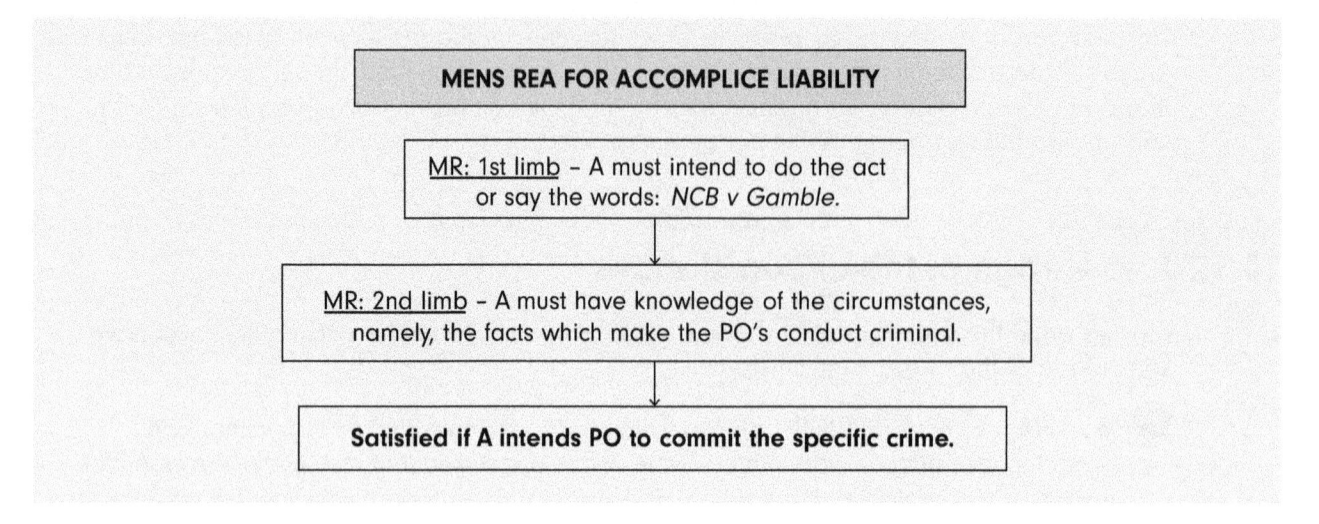

MENS REA FOR ACCOMPLICE LIABILITY

MR: 1st limb – A must intend to do the act or say the words: *NCB v Gamble*.

MR: 2nd limb – A must have knowledge of the circumstances, namely, the facts which make the PO's conduct criminal.

Satisfied if A intends PO to commit the specific crime.

11.12.2 Accomplice has knowledge of an offence

In most instances, the accomplice will be fully involved and entirely aware of the facts that lead to the commission of a crime. However, the circumstances may not be as clear cut and determining what level of knowledge the defendant has becomes key to establishing whether they are guilty as an accomplice. Does the accused merely need to suspect a particular type of crime may be committed, or must they have precise details of the offence? The question of how specific the accomplice's knowledge must be has been considered in two important cases, which provide some helpful guidance.

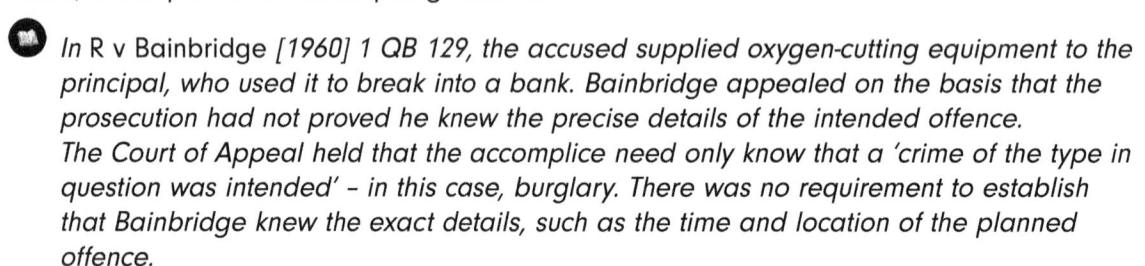

In R v Bainbridge [1960] 1 QB 129, the accused supplied oxygen-cutting equipment to the principal, who used it to break into a bank. Bainbridge appealed on the basis that the prosecution had not proved he knew the precise details of the intended offence. The Court of Appeal held that the accomplice need only know that a 'crime of the type in question was intended' – in this case, burglary. There was no requirement to establish that Bainbridge knew the exact details, such as the time and location of the planned offence.

However, the judges also confirmed that an awareness only that the principal was going to commit some form of illegal act was insufficient to satisfy the mens rea of accomplice liability.

This principle was then approved and extended by the House of Lords in a later case.

In Maxwell v DPP for Northern Ireland [1978] 1 WLR 1350, Maxwell drove a car that guided members of the Ulster Volunteer Force (an illegal organisation) to a public house. He knew that a terrorist attack was going to take place at the premises, whether by guns, bombs or otherwise. In fact, a pipe bomb was thrown into the pub and Maxwell was charged as an accomplice in this attack. It was held that an accomplice will be liable where he knows the commission of one or more of a range of offences by the principal will take place and he intentionally assists the principal who then commits one or more of these crimes. In this instance, the defendant's appeal was dismissed as he knew that a 'military' operation was to take place and bombing the pub was one of the possible offences.

Figure 11.3 Liability of accomplice who knows of an offence

MENS REA FOR ACCOMPLICE LIABILITY

MR: 1st limb – A must intend to do the act or say the words: *NCB v Gamble*.

↓

MR: 2nd limb – A must have knowledge of the circumstances, namely, the facts which make the PO's conduct criminal.

↓

A does not have knowledge of the specific offence PO intends to commit but...

↓

1. A knows type of crime but not the exact details: *Bainbridge*; or
2. A knows offence will be in a limited range: *Maxwell*.

↓

A is guilty as an accomplice to the offence committed.

11.13 Accomplice's liability for a different offence to the principal offender

As stated previously, there can be no liability as an accomplice unless the actus reus of the principal offence is committed.

⊛ Example

Farah suggests to her friend, Amy, that their disruptive neighbour should be killed. Amy ignores the comment and the neighbour remains alive and well. Clearly there can be no liability as an accomplice to murder as the actus reus of murder is not made out.

However, some offences share the same actus reus but have different mens rea, for example:

- murder and manslaughter (the unlawful killing of a human being); and
- ss 18 and 20 of the OAPA 1861 (wounding or causing grievous bodily harm).

The only difference between the two crimes is what is going on in the defendant's mind at the time they carry out the attack and this determines the offence for which they are criminally liable.

So how does this impact on accomplice liability? What if the accomplice's level of mens rea is different to that of the principal? As is apparent from the next two cases, the accomplice's liability will be based on their own level of mens rea, whether that be higher or lower than the principal's.

Remember that if the accomplice has the same plan in mind as the defendant, they have the mens rea for the offence committed. An alternative scenario is being considered here – where the parties do the agreed act but with a different mens rea. From the outside, it would appear that both defendants have a common goal but in fact their thought processes are not the same.

Criminal Law

> In R v Howe [1987] AC 417, the victim was driven to an isolated area where he was killed. To assist in determining the appropriate offence to which the accused was an accomplice, Lord Mackay gave the following example. Names have been added for clarity.

⭐ Example

The accomplice, Ben, hands a gun to Alex but reassures him that it is loaded with blank ammunition. He then tells Alex to go and scare the victim, Connor, by firing the gun at him. In fact, the gun is loaded with live ammunition. Alex shoots Connor and kills him.

Alex is the principal offender because he is the person who actually killed Connor. However, he had no idea the gun contained real ammunition, so he is only guilty of unlawful act manslaughter. The reason is that he intentionally committed an unlawful and dangerous act, specifically an assault because his aim was to scare the victim, and this caused Connor's death.

Figure 11.4 Parties with different mens rea: liability of principal offender

| Alex is the principal offender | ⇒ | Ben tells Alex the gun is loaded with blanks | ⇒ | Alex shoots and kills Connor (*I'm going to scare Connor*) | ⇒ | Guilty of unlawful act manslaughter |

In contrast, Ben is guilty as an accomplice to murder. This is because Ben knew the gun was loaded with real ammunition and intended to kill Connor. Effectively, Ben becomes liable as an accomplice to the crime that, if he himself had committed it, he would have been guilty of.

Figure 11.5 Parties with different mens rea: liability of accomplice

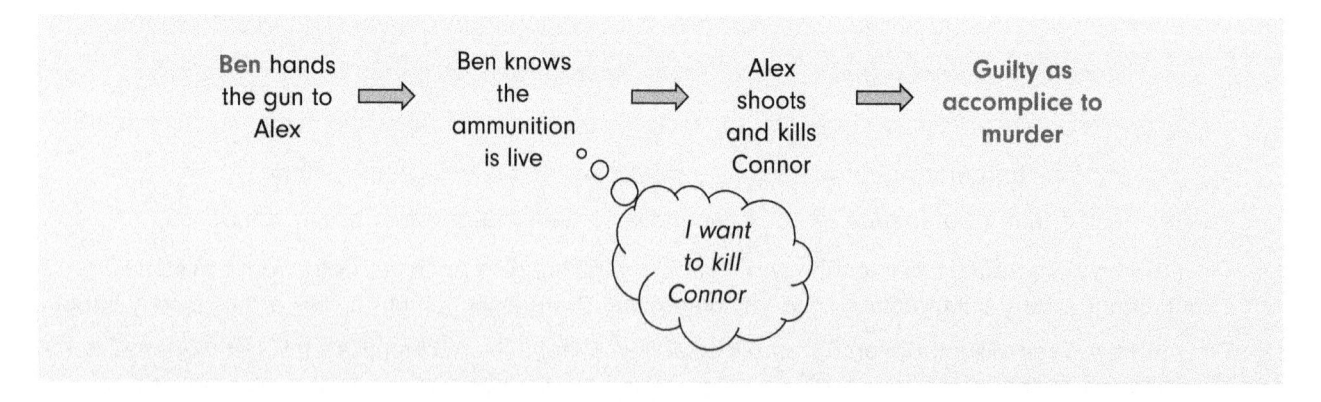

| Ben hands the gun to Alex | ⇒ | Ben knows the ammunition is live | ⇒ | Alex shoots and kills Connor (*I want to kill Connor*) | ⇒ | Guilty as accomplice to murder |

In this example, the accomplice had a higher mens rea than the principal, but the opposite may apply.

> In R v Gilmour [2000] 2 Cr App R 407, the defendant drove the two principals to a house, where they threw a petrol bomb. Sadly, three children died from the resulting house fire.

Gilmour remained in the car throughout. Whilst the principals intended to cause death or grievous bodily harm and so were guilty of murder, Gilmour only believed they were going to cause criminal damage. Because of this, his conviction as an accomplice to murder was overturned and replaced with one for manslaughter.

The law in this regard is summarised in the flowchart in **Figure 11.6**.

Figure 11.6 Liability of accomplice for a different offence

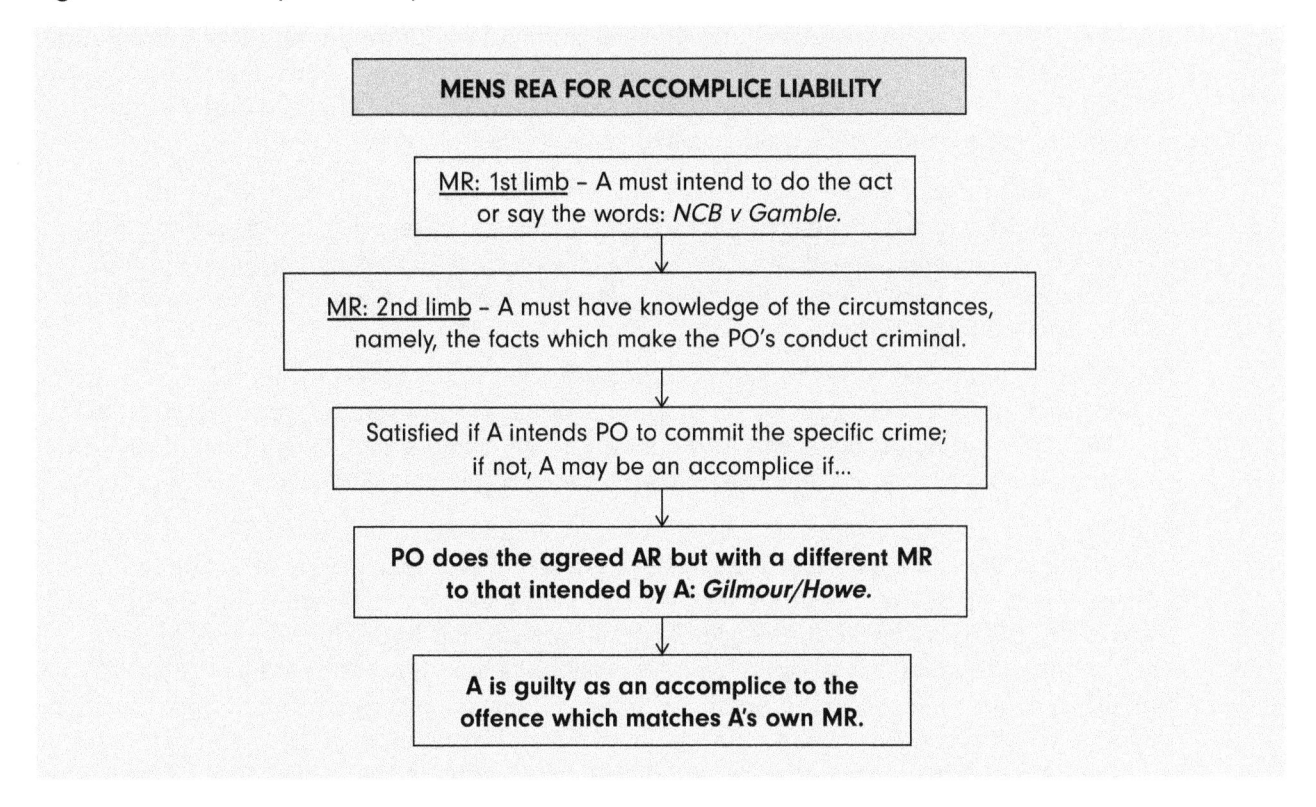

```
┌─────────────────────────────────────────┐
│    MENS REA FOR ACCOMPLICE LIABILITY    │
└─────────────────────────────────────────┘
                    │
                    ▼
┌─────────────────────────────────────────┐
│  MR: 1st limb – A must intend to do the │
│  act or say the words: NCB v Gamble.    │
└─────────────────────────────────────────┘
                    │
                    ▼
┌─────────────────────────────────────────┐
│  MR: 2nd limb – A must have knowledge   │
│  of the circumstances, namely, the facts│
│  which make the PO's conduct criminal.  │
└─────────────────────────────────────────┘
                    │
                    ▼
┌─────────────────────────────────────────┐
│  Satisfied if A intends PO to commit    │
│  the specific crime; if not, A may be   │
│  an accomplice if...                    │
└─────────────────────────────────────────┘
                    │
                    ▼
┌─────────────────────────────────────────┐
│  PO does the agreed AR but with a       │
│  different MR to that intended by A:    │
│  Gilmour/Howe.                          │
└─────────────────────────────────────────┘
                    │
                    ▼
┌─────────────────────────────────────────┐
│  A is guilty as an accomplice to the    │
│  offence which matches A's own MR.      │
└─────────────────────────────────────────┘
```

To conclude, the accomplice may be guilty of a more or less serious offence than the principal based on their own level of mens rea where different offences share the same actus reus. Such offences are relatively uncommon with murder/manslaughter and ss 18/20 assaults being the most likely.

11.14 Liability of the accomplice where the principal goes beyond the plan

Although many crimes will proceed as planned by the participants, the situation may develop, unexpectedly or otherwise, so there is a departure by the principal offender from the original plan or joint venture. In other words, two or more people set out to commit one offence and, in the course of that joint venture, the principal offender commits a different crime. Whether the accomplice remains liable for the principal's acts and what mens rea is required for them to be guilty as an accomplice to this new offence is considered below.

In the case of R v Jogee [2016] UKSC 8, the principal offender stabbed the victim to death in the house using a knife that he took from the kitchen. Jogee remained outside with a bottle but shouted to the principal to do something to the victim and came to the door and threatened to smash the bottle over the victim's head. The principal was convicted of murder and Jogee as an accomplice to the same offence. Jogee appealed and the Supreme Court took the opportunity to review previous authorities on this area of the law.

To determine liability, the court must evaluate what was going on in the accomplice's mind at the time and whether they intended that the 'new' offence would be committed. However:

- just because the accomplice foresees that the 'new' offence *might* occur, does not mean they intended it to; and
- such foresight is only evidence of intent but no more.

How does this work in practice? If the jury is satisfied there was an agreed common purpose to commit Crime A but also that the accomplice foresaw that, in the course of committing Crime A, the principal may well commit Crime B, it may be appropriate for them to conclude the accomplice had the necessary intent that Crime B be committed should the occasion arise. In other words, it was within the scope of the plan to which the accomplice consented and gave their support. The judges gave two examples to illustrate this:

(a) If the defendants attack a bank where one or more of them are armed, whilst the accused may hope it is unnecessary to use their weapons, the jury could properly infer they were intending to use the guns should they be met with resistance. Thus, if a bank employee is shot dead, the principal is guilty of murder and the accomplice is liable for the same offence.

(b) Similarly, if a group of young men face down a rival group, they may hope the other gang will slink away, but it is a perfectly proper inference to draw that all were prepared to inflict grievous bodily harm should a fight ensue. As a consequence, the gang members may all be liable as accomplices to assault causing grievous bodily harm if this occurs.

But what if the accomplice intends that an assault will take place but the violence escalates and results in the victim's death? In this instance, whether the defendant is liable as an accomplice to murder, or indeed to the death at all, will depend upon the circumstances. If the accomplice was aware the principal carried a knife and had a history of violence, including for wounding, this would provide evidence of intent from which the jury could infer that the accomplice intended the death. In contrast, if the secondary party had no knowledge of the principal's tendency to use violence, they may be acquitted entirely as an accomplice to the death. In summary, whether they are liable as an accomplice at all, and if so whether it be for murder or manslaughter, will depend upon their own mens rea.

⭐ Example

(a) *Akeju and Theo decide to steal Hugo's wallet. Theo distracts the victim while Akeju removes the wallet from the victim's pocket. Both defendants are guilty of theft as it was their common purpose to steal, one as principal and the other as accomplice.*

(b) *During the theft, Akeju departs from the scope of the plan by producing a knife and cutting the victim, Hugo. Akeju is clearly the principal to the offence of robbery but the issue is whether Theo is liable for the consequences of the 'new' act. Theo's evidence is that he knew Akeju carried a knife but believed this was only for the purposes of 'self-defence' as the estate on which they live is notoriously violent; further, that despite committing numerous similar thefts, Akeju had never previously used the knife. Nevertheless, in cross-examination, Theo accepts that carrying a knife makes it more likely such a weapon will be used. Despite this, the jury may conclude that Theo is not guilty as an accomplice to the robbery as his foresight of what Akeju may do is evidence of intent only and the overall weight of the evidence favours Theo.*

The law in relation to joint enterprise (or joint venture) is set out in **Figure 11.7**.

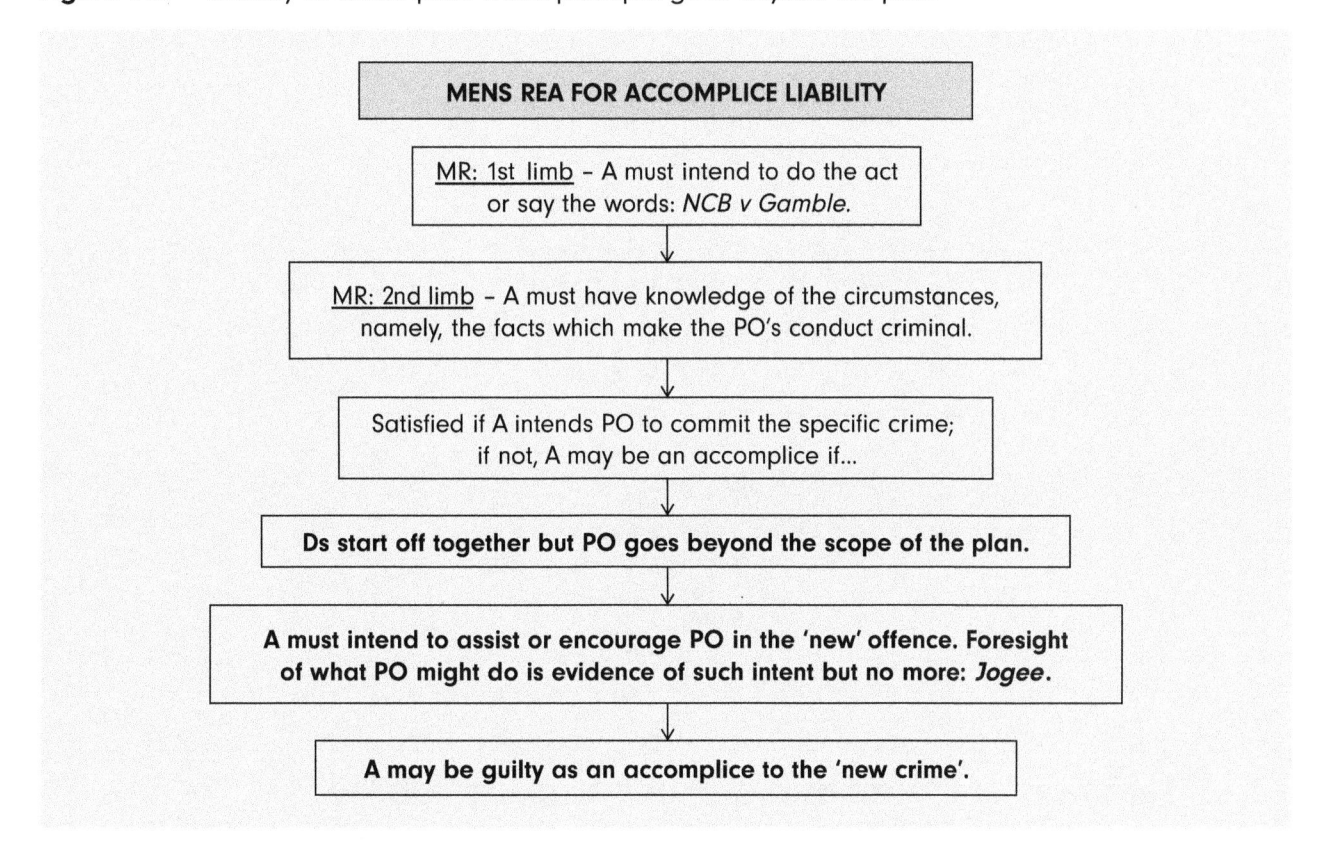

Figure 11.7 Liability of accomplice when principal goes beyond the plan

```
┌─────────────────────────────────────────┐
│     MENS REA FOR ACCOMPLICE LIABILITY   │
└─────────────────────────────────────────┘
                    ↓
┌─────────────────────────────────────────┐
│  MR: 1st limb – A must intend to do the act │
│  or say the words: NCB v Gamble.        │
└─────────────────────────────────────────┘
                    ↓
┌─────────────────────────────────────────┐
│ MR: 2nd limb – A must have knowledge of the circumstances, │
│ namely, the facts which make the PO's conduct criminal.    │
└─────────────────────────────────────────┘
                    ↓
┌─────────────────────────────────────────┐
│ Satisfied if A intends PO to commit the specific crime; │
│ if not, A may be an accomplice if...    │
└─────────────────────────────────────────┘
                    ↓
┌─────────────────────────────────────────┐
│ Ds start off together but PO goes beyond the scope of the plan. │
└─────────────────────────────────────────┘
                    ↓
┌─────────────────────────────────────────┐
│ A must intend to assist or encourage PO in the 'new' offence. Foresight │
│ of what PO might do is evidence of such intent but no more: Jogee.      │
└─────────────────────────────────────────┘
                    ↓
┌─────────────────────────────────────────┐
│ A may be guilty as an accomplice to the 'new crime'. │
└─────────────────────────────────────────┘
```

11.15 Practical application of accomplice liability mens rea

In this example, the defendants start off together but the situation changes. Otis and Polly go to buy illegal drugs together but, during the transaction, there is a dispute over payment. Otis suddenly produces a gun and shoots the drug dealer dead. Otis has gone beyond the scope of the plan, which was to purchase drugs (Crime A – possession of a controlled drug), and committed an entirely different offence (Crime B – murder).

Whether the accomplice, Polly, is liable for this development will depend upon the particular facts. To be criminally liable, the accomplice must *intend* to assist or encourage the principal in the commission of the 'new' offence. The court will consider the evidence to determine exactly how much the accomplice knew.

If the jury is satisfied that Polly knew Otis was an aggressive man who carried a weapon and was likely to use it, her foresight of what he might do is *evidence* that she herself intended Otis to act in this way. In law, she may be liable as an accomplice for murder. Effectively, by accompanying a man such as Otis, she is going with a loaded weapon, albeit in human form.

What if Polly genuinely did not have this foresight? If the jury believes her, she will not be guilty as an accomplice to the death at all, as she would not have intended Otis to act in that way.

The jury is required to make an assessment of the level of Polly's knowledge and what is going through her mind in the lead up to and during the commission of the offence to determine her criminal culpability. This is summarised in **Figure 11.8**.

Figure 11.8 Practical application of accomplice liability mens rea

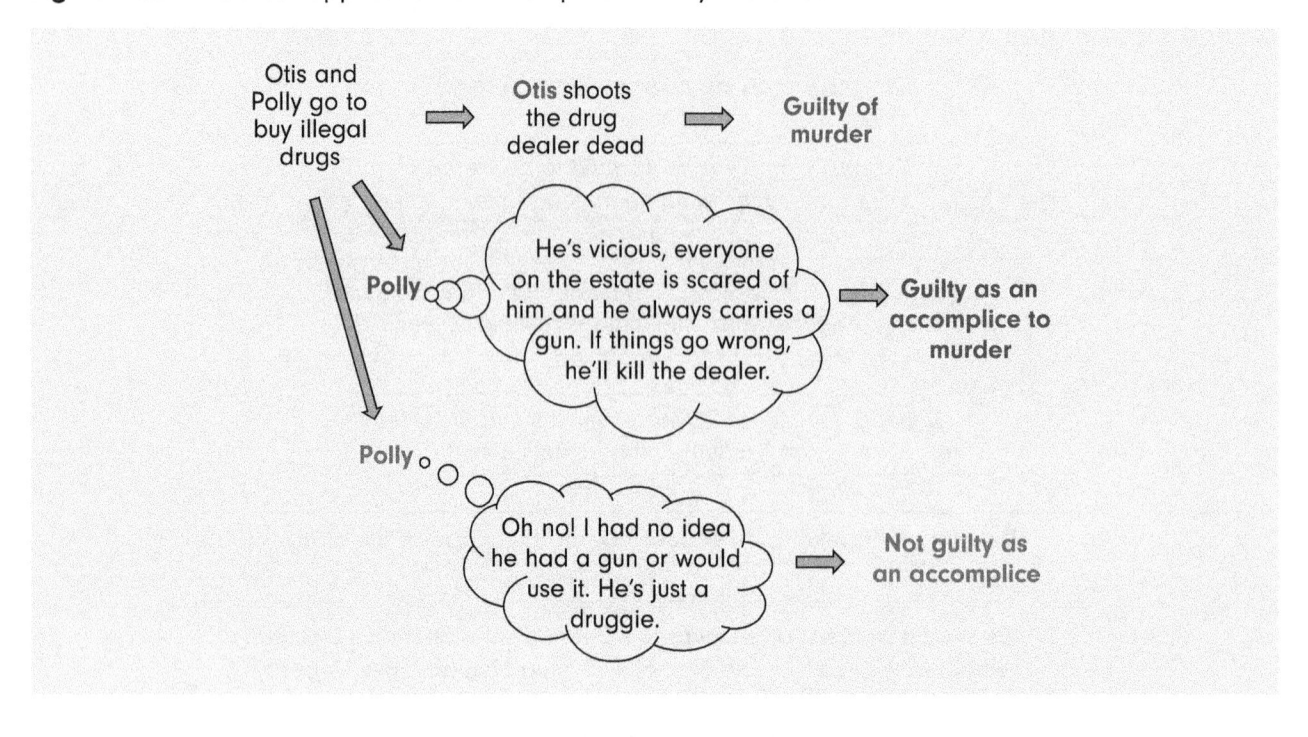

```
Otis and Polly go to buy illegal drugs → Otis shoots the drug dealer dead → Guilty of murder

Polly: "He's vicious, everyone on the estate is scared of him and he always carries a gun. If things go wrong, he'll kill the dealer." → Guilty as an accomplice to murder

Polly: "Oh no! I had no idea he had a gun or would use it. He's just a druggie." → Not guilty as an accomplice
```

11.16 Summary of the mens rea of accomplice liability

This is a complex area of the law but the flowchart in **Figure 11.9** should assist your understanding.

Figure 11.9 Mens rea of accomplice liability

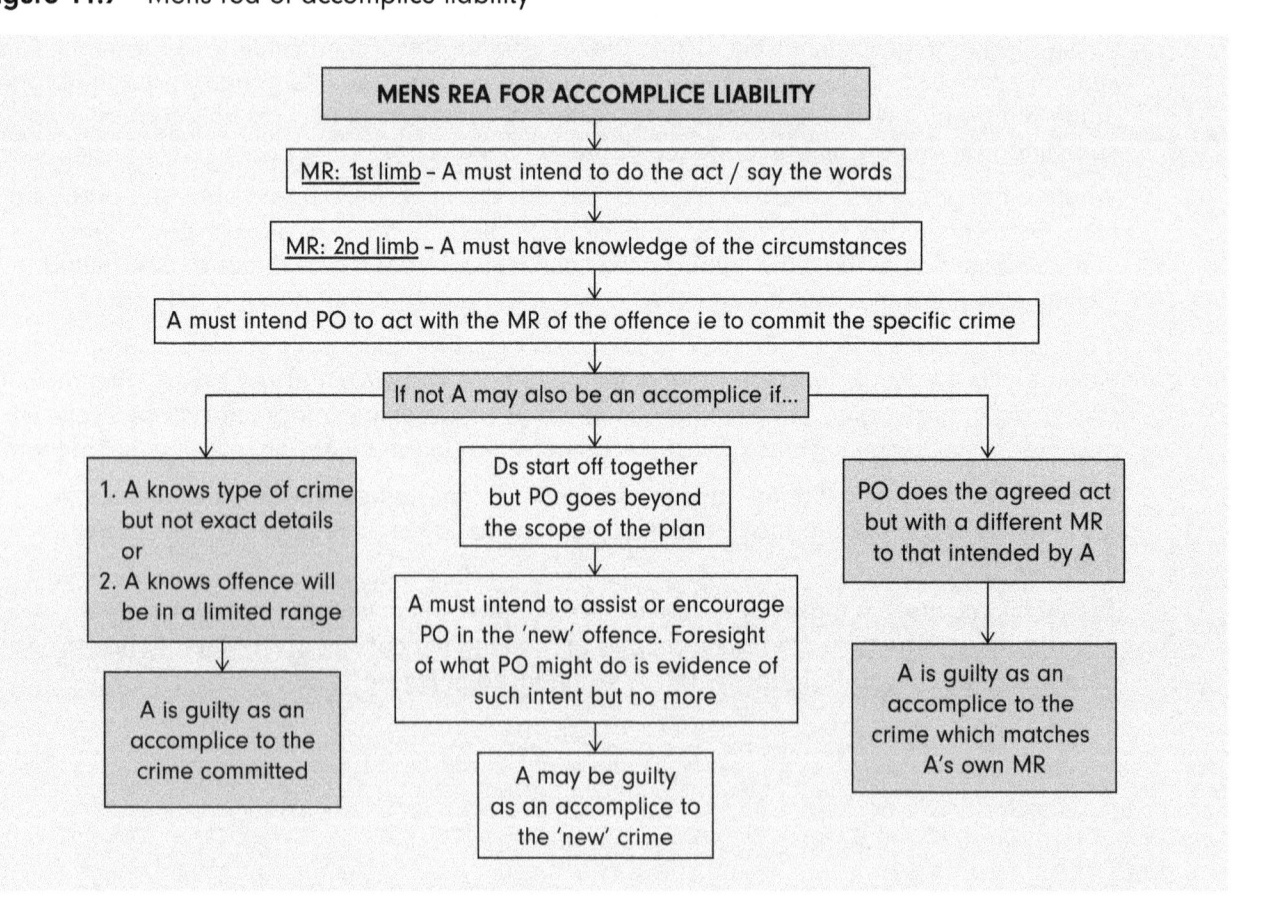

MENS REA FOR ACCOMPLICE LIABILITY

MR: 1st limb – A must intend to do the act / say the words

MR: 2nd limb – A must have knowledge of the circumstances

A must intend PO to act with the MR of the offence ie to commit the specific crime

If not A may also be an accomplice if...

1. A knows type of crime but not exact details or
2. A knows offence will be in a limited range

↓

A is guilty as an accomplice to the crime committed

Ds start off together but PO goes beyond the scope of the plan

↓

A must intend to assist or encourage PO in the 'new' offence. Foresight of what PO might do is evidence of such intent but no more

↓

A may be guilty as an accomplice to the 'new' crime

PO does the agreed act but with a different MR to that intended by A

↓

A is guilty as an accomplice to the crime which matches A's own MR

11.17 Withdrawing participation

A defendant may initially be happy to be involved in the common plan but, thereafter, change their mind. Can such a defendant rely upon their withdrawal to escape liability for what the principal goes on to do? The brief answer is yes, but only provided the withdrawal is an effective one. This will depend upon the stage at which the defendant attempts to withdraw and the method by which they do so. Ultimately this will be a question of fact for a jury to decide, although case law suggests the accomplice will need to try and negate whatever they originally did to assist the principal.

11.17.1 Withdrawal before the offence

Where the defendant has a change of heart before the offence takes place, they may do so by communicating that withdrawal. However, this must be timely and unequivocal.

> In R v Grundy [1977] Crim LR 543, Grundy gave information to burglars about a premises and the habits of the occupants six weeks beforehand. Two weeks before the burglary took place he tried to persuade the men not to commit the burglary. The Court of Appeal held that this was evidence of an effective withdrawal and the matter should then have been left to the jury to decide.

Communication is vital and failing to turn up at the scene of the planned crime at the agreed time does not amount to unequivocal communication of the withdrawal.

Example

> Bella is a manager at a local supermarket. She agrees with her friend, Quentin, to carry out a robbery of the premises after hours. She provides Quentin with details of when the cash will be collected and her key to give him access to the yard at the rear where the security van will be parked. She also agrees to act as look out. Bella subsequently changes her mind and tries to persuade Quentin not to go ahead, but he commits the robbery anyway. Has Bella done enough to withdraw from their joint venture?
>
> Bella is clearly an accomplice to Quentin's robbery as she aided the offence by providing him with information and giving him a key; she would also have abetted at the time of the crime if she had acted as a lookout.
>
> Whether Bella can argue she has successfully withdrawn is a question of fact for the jury but it would need to know exactly what she did once she changed her mind. To be an effective withdrawal, Bella would at least have to try and persuade Quentin not to commit the robbery, which she did. Although this may have been enough had Bella only agreed to act as a lookout, as she gave Quentin a key and 'inside' information, it is likely she would have to do more in this situation such as:
>
> (a) trying to persuade Quentin not to go ahead
>
> (b) getting the key back from him
>
> (c) warning her employers (particularly as she is a manager at the supermarket)?
>
> (d) informing the police?

11.17.2 Withdrawal during the offence

Where the defendant decides to withdraw after the offence has begun, they must do more than simply communicate their intention to do so.

> In R v Becerra (1976) 62 Cr App R 212, the defendants agreed to burgle a house. Becerra gave his co-accused a knife, telling him to use it if necessary. When they were disturbed by a tenant, Becerra shouted: 'There's a bloke coming. Let's go', before jumping out of the

window and running away. The principal offender remained behind and stabbed the victim to death. In upholding Becerra's conviction as an accomplice to murder, the Court of Appeal decided his actions did not constitute an effective withdrawal.

Although the court was of the view that more was needed, precisely what was not articulated. The judges did suggest that physical intervention may have been required at this late stage such as:

(a) *grabbing the knife off the principal offender; or*

(b) *standing in front of the victim to protect them.*

11.17.3 Summary of withdrawal

The law in relation to withdrawal from the joint venture may be summarised as follows:

- Whether there has been an effective withdrawal will depend upon the circumstances of each case.
- Words alone may suffice where the withdrawal takes place before the offence, unless physical assistance has also been given.
- Where the withdrawal takes place during the commission of the crime, simply urging the principal to leave and departing from the scene are not sufficient to be effective; some form of physical intervention may be required.
- In all cases, it is a question of fact for the jury to determine if the accused has withdrawn from the common plan.

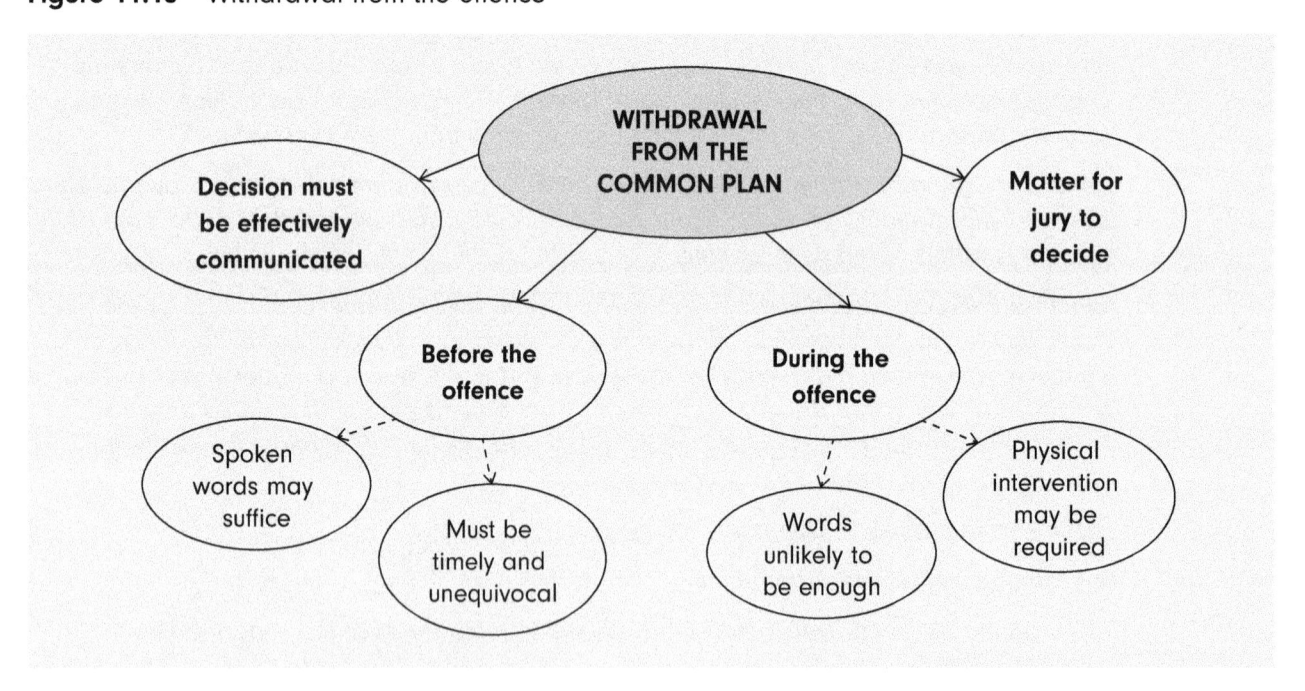

Figure 11.10 Withdrawal from the offence

In simple terms, the more the accused has done to set up the crime, the more they are expected to do to withdraw from it.

Summary

- When assessing criminal liability, the starting point is to identify the principal offender(s), namely those who commit the substantive offence with the appropriate mens rea.
- The actus reus of accomplice liability is established by proof that the defendant aided, abetted, counselled or procured the commission of the offence.
  - This usually involves physical or verbal advice or assistance before or at the time of the offence.
  - Any situation where an individual becomes involved only after the principal offence has been committed will not attract accomplice liability.
- To convict someone as an accomplice, mens rea must also be proved, specifically that the defendant:
  - intended to do the act or say the words that assisted or encouraged; and
  - had knowledge of all the circumstances of the principal offence within their contemplation.
- The accomplice does not need to know (or intend) the specific crime that the principal commits or the exact details. However, they must be aware of the type of offence or that it is within a limited range of possible offences.
- If the principal goes beyond the scope of the plan, the accomplice must intend to assist or encourage the principal in the commission of the 'new' offence. Foresight of what the principal might do is evidence of such intent but no more.
- Depending upon the level of mens rea of the parties, the principal may be convicted of a different offence to that of the accomplice.
- A person can be convicted as an accomplice notwithstanding the fact that the principal is acquitted (or is not charged).
- A person may avoid accomplice liability if they have withdrawn from the joint venture but only if it is 'effective'; and this will depend upon the participation of the defendant and the stage at which they seek to withdraw.

Sample questions

Question 1

The principal offender is told by his girlfriend that a man slapped her at a nightclub one evening. She says: 'If you find him, I hope you teach him a lesson!' Later that night, the principal comes across the man and knocks him to the ground, where he repeatedly kicks and stamps on him. The man dies of his injuries.

Which of the following best describes whether the girlfriend satisfies the actus reus of secondary liability for the man's death?

A   The girlfriend is a joint principal to the man's death.

B   The girlfriend does not satisfy the actus reus of accomplice liability for the man's death.

C   The girlfriend abets the principal in the man's death.

D   The girlfriend counsels the principal in the man's death.

E   The girlfriend procures the principal in the man's death.

Criminal Law

Answer

Option D is correct. The girlfriend counsels the principal by encouraging him before the death of the man takes place and, thus, she satisfies the actus reus of secondary liability.

Option A is wrong because the girlfriend is not a principal offender; her involvement is a lesser one to the principal who actually carries out the attack. Option B is also wrong as the girlfriend does satisfy the actus reus of accomplice liability. Option C is wrong as the girlfriend's words of encouragement take place before the offence and abetting must be during it. Option E is wrong because more is required to establish that the girlfriend procured the killing. She only suggests the man be taught a lesson, whereas procurement requires her to take a more active role and to produce his death by endeavour.

Question 2

A man asks a woman if he can borrow her car. He tells her the car will be used as the getaway vehicle for a burglary of Number 23, Sycamore Drive that evening. The woman asks whether the man can find an alternative vehicle and only agrees reluctantly when he says not. However, on approaching the house, it becomes apparent that the property is occupied. The man drives away and then uses the car in a burglary of Number 15, Aspen Close the following day.

Is the woman liable as an accomplice to burglary?

A   No, because she only lent the car reluctantly and wanted the man to find an alternative vehicle.

B   No, because she was unaware of the burglary at Number 15 and believed the car would be used in the burglary of Number 23.

C   No, because although the woman satisfied the actus reus, she did not know the exact details of the crime that was to be committed.

D   Yes, because the woman abetted the offence and had knowledge of the circumstances as she was aware that a burglary was to be committed.

E   Yes, because the woman aided the offence, intended to do the act that assisted the offence and had knowledge that a burglary would be committed.

Answer

The correct answer is option E. The woman aided the crime as she assisted by providing a car before the offence took place. She intended to do the act (it was deliberate) and had knowledge of the circumstances as she was aware of sufficient of the facts to know a crime would be committed. Even though the woman does not have the mens rea for the actual crime of burgling Number 15, Aspen Close on the following day, she is criminally liable as this is the same type of offence as burgling a different house (Number 23, Sycamore Drive) that same day, of which she did have knowledge.

Option A is wrong because it does not matter whether the woman lent the car reluctantly provided the act was intentional, which it was. Option B is wrong as accomplice liability only requires the defendant to know enough of the circumstances that make the conduct criminal, not necessarily the exact address of the burglary. Option C is wrong as it is irrelevant the woman did not know the exact details of the crime as long as the crime was of the same type as that committed and here, it was. Option D is wrong as abetting requires encouragement at the time of the offence and the woman assisted the crime before it took place.

Question 3

A girl and a boy have fallen out with the victim in their class because she reported them to the school authorities for bullying her online. They decide to punish her in the next games lesson by hitting her with a cricket bat. The girl acts as a lookout while the boy beats the victim repeatedly with his cricket bat, causing a fractured jaw and a broken arm. He confirms in his police interview that he intended to cause the victim serious bodily harm. In contrast, the girl only thought that the boy would cause the victim some injury such as bruising, just to 'teach her a lesson that we don't like snitches' (those who inform on others).

The boy is convicted of causing grievous bodily harm with intent. Which one of the following correctly identifies the liability of the girl?

A   Accomplice to assault occasioning actual bodily harm.

B   Accomplice to inflicting grievous bodily harm.

C   Accomplice to causing grievous bodily harm with intent.

D   Principal to causing grievous bodily harm with intent.

E   No liability for the victim's injuries.

Answer

The correct answer is option B. The girl commits the actus reus of accomplice liability as she aids the offence. She also satisfies the first limb of the mens rea as she acted deliberately or intentionally in being the lookout. She is an accomplice to a s 20 assault as she contemplated the victim receiving 'some injury such as bruising' but not a really serious one. She aids the agreed act (the assault) but with a different mens rea from that of the principal and so she will be judged on the basis of her own level of mens rea.

Options A and C are wrong for the reasons set out in the discussion of option B. The girl does not intend to assist or encourage the boy in causing the victim grievous bodily harm with intent, or with intention or recklessness as to an assault only. The evidence is that the girl thought the boy would cause the victim 'some injury'.

Option D is wrong as the girl has a lesser involvement in the assault and is merely an accomplice. The person who actually commits the assault is the principal offender – the boy. However, because the boy has not completely departed from the plan, the girl does not escape liability altogether, so E is wrong. This is because there was an agreement to assault the victim, albeit not as severely as occurred.

Index

A

abandoned property 115–16
abetting 206
    definition 200–1, 203, 208
    links between principal and
        accomplice 203–5
    mens rea 208–9
    presence at the scene 201–2
    sample questions 219–20
    withdrawal before offence 217
abnormality of mental functioning 75–8, 90–1
abuse of position (fraud) 145–6, 147–8, 150
accessories *see* parties to a crime
accomplices *see* parties to a crime
Acts of God 16
actual bodily harm 52–4
actus reus 1–19
    causation 8–16
    and coincidence of mens rea 37–40
    general principles of 3
    omissions 5–8
    sample questions 17–19
    summary of 40
    transferred malice 34–6
    types of crimes 3–5
adultery 83–4, 89–90
aggravated arson 160, 161, 162
aggravated burglary 133–4
aggravated criminal damage 158–60, 161, 162, 191
aiding (accomplices) 206
    definition 200, 203, 208, 219
    disappearance of principal 207
    links between principal and
        accomplice 203–5
    mens rea 208–11
    sample questions 220–1
    withdrawal before offence 217
anger trigger 82–4, 89–90
appropriation (theft) 110–12, 116
arson 158, 159, 191
    aggravated 160, 161, 162
    intoxication defence 173–4
    sample questions 162
assault *see* simple assault
assault occasioning actual bodily harm
    (s 47 OAPA 1861) 47, 52–4, 61–2, 64
    actus reus 52–3, 54, 61
    consent as a defence 62
    mens rea 53–4, 61
    sample questions 66–7
assaults 45–67
    assault occasioning actual bodily harm
        (s 47 OAPA 1861) 47, 52–4, 61–2, 64
    battery 46, 47, 50–2, 61–2
    common law assaults 47–52
    consent as a defence 62–4
    hierarchy of 46–7
    intoxication defence 169, 173, 174
    overview of 60–2
    sample questions 64–7
    simple assault 46, 47–50, 51–2, 61–2
    statutory assaults 52–62
    summary of 64
    wounding or causing grievous bodily harm
        with intent (s 18 OAPA 1861) 46, 47,
        58–60, 61–4
    wounding or inflicting grievous bodily
        harm (s 20 OAPA 1861) 47, 47, 55–7,
        61–2, 64
attempted crimes *see* inchoate offences

B

basic intent 39, 40
    and intoxication 167, 168, 170
battery 46, 47, 50–2, 61–2
    actus reus 51, 61
    consent as a defence 62
    mens rea 51, 61
    sample questions 66–7
beyond reasonable doubt 2–3
borrowing (and theft) 120–1
building definition (burglary) 126–9, 130, 131–2
    part of a building 128–9, 130, 132
burden of proof 2–3, 17
burglary 125–32
    actus reus 126–30, 131–2
    aggravated burglary 133–4
    concept of "entry" 126–7
    definition of 125–6
    definition of building 126–9, 130, 131–2
    mens rea 130–2
    sample questions 135–6
    summary of 132
    trespass 129–30

Index

C

careless driving 30
causation 8–16
    chain of causation 13–17
    and diminished responsibility 77–8
    factual causation 9–10
    intervening acts or events 13–17
    legal causation 10–16
    sample questions 18–19
chain of causation 13–17
chose in action 112
circumstances crimes 4, 5
classification of offences (intent) 39–40
coincidence of actus reus and mens rea 37–9
common law assaults *see* battery;
    simple assault
conduct crimes 4
consent
    belief in consent (lawful excuse) 155–6, 161, 173
    as defence to assaults 62–4
    sample questions 65–6
    valid consent 63–4
constructive manslaughter 95–9, 103
    actus reus 95–7
    causes death 97
    dangerous act 96–7
    distinguished from gross negligence manslaughter 100
    mens rea 97–8
    sample questions 105–7
    summary of 99, 104
    unlawful act 95–6
continuing act principle 37–8, 39
contracts
    duty to act 6
    and fraud 144
co-principals definition 198, 199
counselling (accomplices) 206
    definition 200, 201–3, 208
    links between principal and accomplice 203–5
    mens rea 208–9
    relationship between principal and accomplice 207
    sample questions 219–20
crimes, types of 3–5
criminal damage 151–64
    aggravated arson 160, 161, 162
    aggravated criminal damage 158–60, 162, 191
    arson 158, 159, 160, 161, 162, 173–4, 191
    belief in consent 155, 161
    destruction or damage 152–3, 159
    endangerment of life 158–60
    intoxication defence 173–4
    lawful excuse 155–8, 159
    property definition 153–4
    property in need of protection 156–7
    property ownership 153–4, 155–6, 159
    recklessness 154–5, 159–60
    sample questions 162–4
    simple criminal damage 152–8
    summary of 161
criminal liability, components of 2

D

dangerous situations, creation of 7–8
defences 165–86
    and burden of proof 2–3
    diminished responsibility 74–8, 90–1, 105
    intoxication 166–74
    loss of control 78–87
    prevention of a crime 174–82
    sample questions 184–6
    self-defence 174–82
    summary of 182–4
diminished responsibility 74–8, 90–1, 105
direct intention 22–6, 72
dishonesty 110, 116–19, 135
    fraud 138, 142, 143, 144, 145, 147, 149
    theft 116–19
domestic violence
    loss of control 80–1, 82
    manslaughter 73
drink driving 5, 32–3, 41–2
Dutch courage 172
duty to act/care 6, 7

E

eggshell skull rule 12
either way offences, definition 46
entry (burglary) 126–7
evidential burden of proof 2–3, 17, 175

F

factual causation 9–10
failing to disclose information (fraud) 138, 143–4, 147–8, 150
false representation (fraud) 138–43, 147–8, 149–50
fear trigger 82, 84, 85

force
- and robbery 122-5
- sample questions 185-6
- and self-defence 174-84
- *see also* assaults

fraud 137-50
- by abuse of position 145-6, 147-8, 150
- definition of 138
- dishonesty 138, 142, 143, 144, 145, 147, 149
- by failing to disclose information 138, 143-4, 147-8, 150
- by false representation 138-43, 147-8, 149-50
- gain and/or loss 142-3, 144, 145, 147, 148
- overlap between offences 146-7
- sample questions 148-50
- summary of 147-8

fright and flight cases 13

G

gain and/or loss (fraud) 142-3, 144, 145, 147, 148

grievous bodily harm
- assaults 45, 47, 55-62, 65-7
- and burglary 126, 130-2
- mens rea for murder 71-2, 89, 94, 98
- sample questions 65-7

gross negligence manslaughter 29-30, 99-104
- breach of duty 101
- causes death 101
- distinguished from constructive manslaughter 100
- duty of care 100
- establishing gross negligence 101-3
- sample questions 105-7

H

heat of the moment (self-defence) 181-2
homicide definition 70-1, 94
- *see also* involuntary manslaughter; murder; voluntary manslaughter
honour killings 83
horseplay 63
householder cases (self-defence) 179-81, 183, 185-6

I

impairment of the defendant's ability 76-7, 78, 88, 90-1
impossibility (attempted crimes) 191-2

inchoate offences 187-96
- actus reus 188-90, 192, 193
- definition of 188
- and impossibility 191-2
- mens rea 190-1, 192, 193
- sample questions 194-6
- summary of 193

indictable only offences, definition 46
indirect intention 23-6, 41, 72, 89, 190
infidelity 83-4, 89-90
innocent agency (accomplices) 207
intention 22-6
- basic intent 39, 40, 167, 168, 170
- classification of offences 39-40
- direct intention 22-6, 72
- indirect intention 23-6, 41, 72, 89, 190
- sample questions 41-3
- specific intent 39, 40, 167, 168-9
- transferred malice 34-6
- ulterior intent 39-40, 191

intention to permanently deprive (theft) 119-21
intervening acts or events 12-16, 18-19
intoxication defence 166-74
- and diminished responsibility 76
- Dutch courage 172
- and intent 39
- involuntary intoxication 170-2, 183, 185
- and lawful excuse 173-4
- and mistaken belief 156, 172-4, 176-7
- sample questions 184-5
- and self-defence 176-7
- summary of 182-3
- and type of offence 166-7
- voluntary intoxication 167, 168-70, 176-7, 182-3, 184

involuntary intoxication 170-2, 183, 185
involuntary manslaughter 93-107
- constructive manslaughter 95-9
- gross negligence manslaughter 99-104
- sample questions 105-7
- summary of 104-7
- *see also* murder

Ivey test 118-19, 142

J

Jehovah's Witnesses 12
joint principals definition 198, 199
joint venture/enterprise concept 208
- *see also* parties to a crime
justification of risk (recklessness) 27, 28

Index

L

land
    criminal damage to 153
    theft of 112-13
lawful excuse
    criminal damage 155-8, 159
    intoxication defence 173-4
legal burden of proof 2-3, 17, 75
legal causation 10-16
loss of control 78-87
    establishing loss 79-81
    qualifying triggers 82-4
    sample questions 89-91
    similar reaction of a person of the same age and sex 85-6
    sufficiency of evidence 87

M

manslaughter 73
    constructive manslaughter 95-9, 100
    gross negligence manslaughter 29-30, 99-104
    involuntary manslaughter 93-107
    voluntary manslaughter 73-4, 88, 90, 104
    see also murder
medical conditions, and diminished responsibility 75-8, 90-1
medical negligence 14-15, 19
mens rea 21-43
    classification of offences 39-40
    and coincidence of actus reus 37-9
    intention 22-6, 39-40
    negligence 29-31
    recklessness 26-8, 29, 36
    sample questions 41-3
    strict liability offences 31-4
    summary of 40
    transferred malice 34-6
mental harm 53
mistaken belief
    and intoxication 156, 172-4, 176-7
    and self-defence 176-7, 183, 184
murder 71-2
    actus reus 71, 72
    causation 8-16
    definition of 71
    diminished responsibility defence 74-8, 90-1, 104
    distinguished from voluntary manslaughter 74
    intoxication defence 168-9, 172, 184
    loss of control defence 73, 78-87, 88, 89-91
    mens rea 22-5, 71-2
    sample questions 89-91
    self-defence 73, 178, 179
    summary of 72, 88, 104
    see also involuntary manslaughter; voluntary manslaughter

N

negligence 29-31
    gross negligence manslaughter 99-104
    medical negligence 14-15, 19
    and statutory offences 30
novus actus interveniens 12-16

O

oblique intention *see* indirect intention
offences, classification of 39-40
offences, types of 3-5
omissions 5-8, 16
    creation of dangerous situation 7-8
    criminal liability 5-6, 16, 18
    gross negligence manslaughter 100-1
    sample question 18
    special relationships 7

P

parties to a crime 197-221
    abetting 200-6, 208-9, 217, 219-20
    accomplice actus reus 200-3, 205-7, 208
    accomplice liability definition 199
    accomplice mens rea 208-16
    aiding 200, 203-10, 217, 220-1
    causal link 203-4, 205
    counselling 200, 201-9, 219-20
    different offence to principal 211-13
    innocent agency 207
    joint principals definition 198, 199
    joint venture/enterprise concept 208
    knowledge of the circumstances 209-11
    links between principal and accomplice 203-5
    mental link 203-4, 205
    mere presence at the scene 201-2
    principal goes beyond plan 213-15
    principal not convicted 207
    principals definition 198, 199
    procuring 200, 201, 203-8, 219-20
    sample questions 219-21
    summary of 219
    terminology 198-9
    withdrawing participation 217-19

physical assault *see* battery
pre-emptive strikes 182
presence at scene of crime (accomplices) 201-2
prevention of a crime, defence of
see self-defence
principals definition 198, 199
procuring (accomplices) 206
    definition 200, 201, 203, 208
    and innocent agency 207
    links between principal and
        accomplice 203-5
    mens rea 208
    sample questions 219-20
proof 2-3, 17
property definitions
    abandoned property 115-16
    criminal damage 153-4
    ownership 113-14, 153-4, 159
    theft 112-13

R

reasonable doubt 2-3
recklessness 26-9, 36, 39-41
representation definition (fraud) 139-40
resisting arrest 58, 59, 60, 61
result crimes 4-5
    and causation 8-16
revenge 80
robbery 122-5
    compared to theft 123
    definition of 122
    flowchart 125
    force used or threatened 122-5
    sample questions 135-6
    summary of 124
    timing of the force 124

S

secondary parties *see* parties to a crime
section 18 assault *see* wounding or causing
    grievous bodily harm with intent
    (s 18 OAPA 1861)
section 20 assault *see* wounding or inflicting
    grievous bodily harm (s 20 OAPA 1861)
section 47 assault *see* assault occasioning
    actual bodily harm (s 47 OAPA 1861)
self-control *see* loss of control
self-defence 174-82
    duty to retreat 181
    evidential burden of proof 175
    heat of the moment 181-2

    householder cases 179-81, 183, 185-6
    mistaken belief 176-7, 183, 184
    necessary use of force 175-7, 183
    pre-emptive strikes 182
    reasonable force 177-9, 183
    sample questions 185-6
    summary of 183-4
    voluntary intoxication 146-7
sexual infidelity 83-4, 89-90
silence, as assault 48-9
simple assault 46, 47-50, 51-2, 61-2
    actus reus 48-9, 50, 61
    consent as a defence 62, 64
    mens rea 49-50, 61
    sample questions 64-5
simple criminal damage 152-8
    actus reus 152-4
    definition of 152
    intoxication defence 173-4
    mens rea 154-5
    sample question 164
single transaction principle 38-9, 43
social utility 27
special relationships, and omissions 7
specific intent 39, 40
    and intoxication 167, 168-9
standard of proof 2-3, 17
state of affairs crimes 4, 5
statutory assaults 52-62
    consent as a defence 62-4
statutory offences
    and negligence 30
    and omissions 6
strict liability offences 31-4
subjective recklessness 27-8
suicide, as intervening act 13-14
summary offences definition 46

T

technical assault *see* simple assault
theft 110-22
    actus reus 110-16
    appropriation 110-11
    belonging to another 113-16
    compared to robbery 123
    definition of 110
    dishonesty 116-19
    intention to permanently deprive 119-21
    mens rea 116-21
    property definition 112-13
    sample questions 134-5
third party intervention 14, 16

transferred malice 34–6, 42–3
trespass 126, 129–32, 136

U

ulterior intent 39–40, 191
unlawful and dangerous act manslaughter
 see constructive manslaughter

V

valid consent 63–4
voluntary euthanasia 14
voluntary intoxication 167, 168–70, 182–3, 184
 self-defence 176–7
voluntary manslaughter 73–4, 88, 90, 104
 see also murder

W

weapons definition (aggravated burglary) 133
words, as assault 48–9
wounding, definition 55–6
wounding or causing grievous bodily harm
 with intent (s 18 OAPA 1861) 46, 47,
 58–60, 61–4
 actus reus 58, 60, 61
 four ways of committing 59
 mens rea 58–60, 61
 sample questions 66–7
wounding or inflicting grievous bodily harm
 (s 20 OAPA 1861) 46, 47, 55–7, 61–2, 64
 actus reus 55–6, 57, 61
 mens rea 56–7, 61
 sample questions 65–7